The Iceblade Sorcerer Shall Rule the World

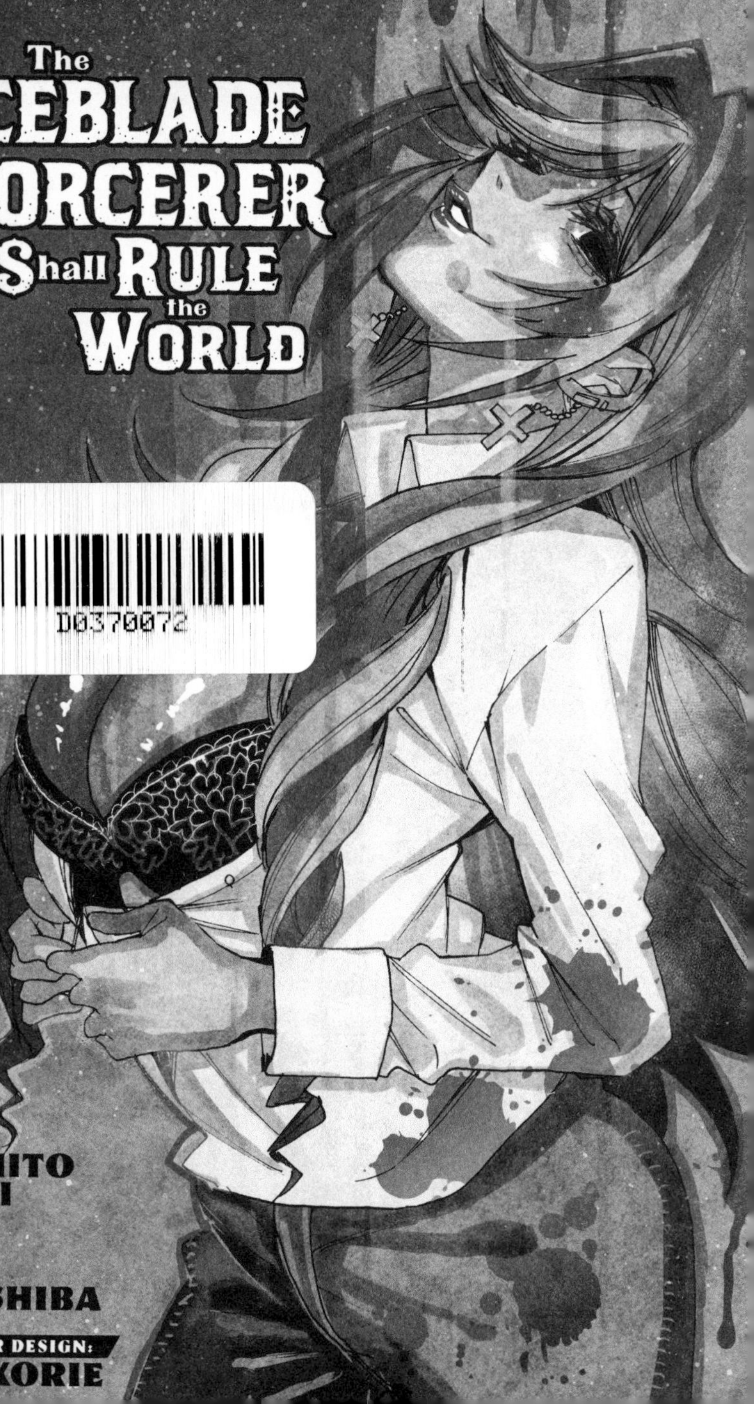

4

ART:
NORIHITO SASAKI

STORY:
NANA MIKOSHIBA

CHARACTER DESIGN:
RIKO KORIE

CONTENTS

Content Warning: Sexual Violence
This title contains depictions of sexual violence and addiction. If you are experiencing or have experienced sexual violence or addiction, know that you are not alone, and there is help. Please visit findahelpline.com to find support.

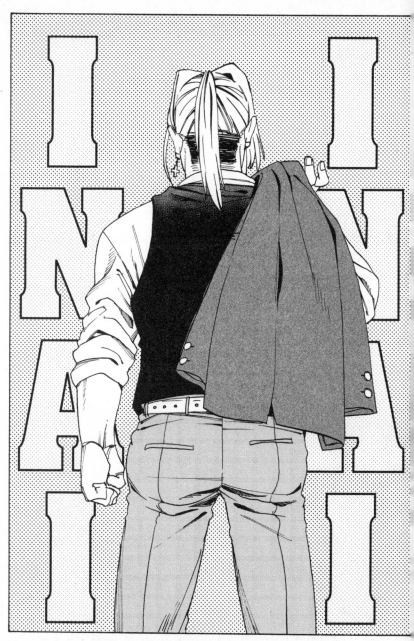

Chapter 25 The New Teacher

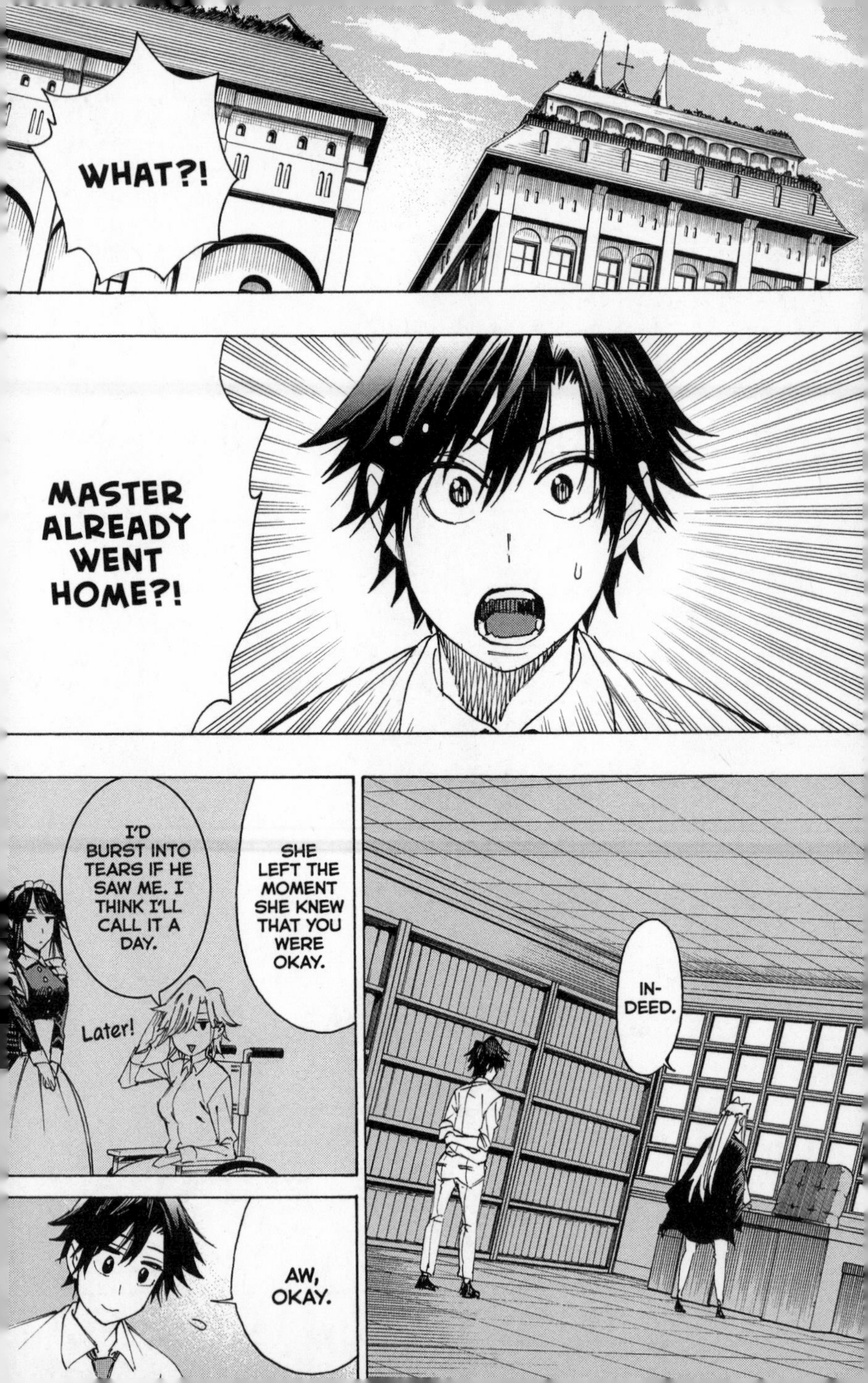
WHAT?!
MASTER ALREADY WENT HOME?!
IN-DEED.
SHE LEFT THE MOMENT SHE KNEW THAT YOU WERE OKAY.
I'D BURST INTO TEARS IF HE SAW ME. I THINK I'LL CALL IT A DAY.
Later!
AW, OKAY.

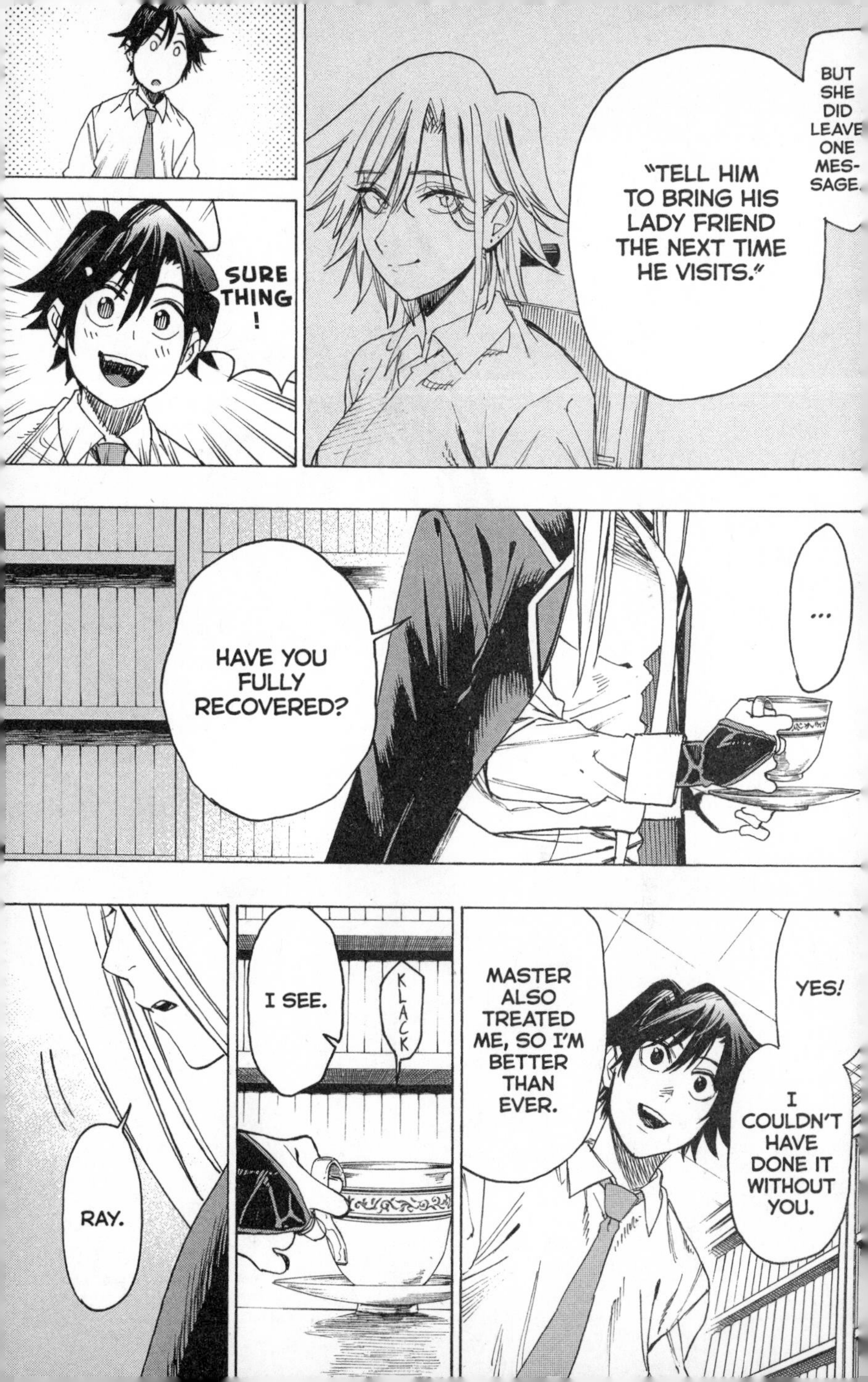
BUT SHE DID LEAVE ONE MES-SAGE.
"TELL HIM TO BRING HIS LADY FRIEND THE NEXT TIME HE VISITS."
SURE THING!
...
HAVE YOU FULLY RECOVERED?
YES!
MASTER ALSO TREATED ME, SO I'M BETTER THAN EVER.
I COULDN'T HAVE DONE IT WITHOUT YOU.
KLACK
I SEE.
RAY.

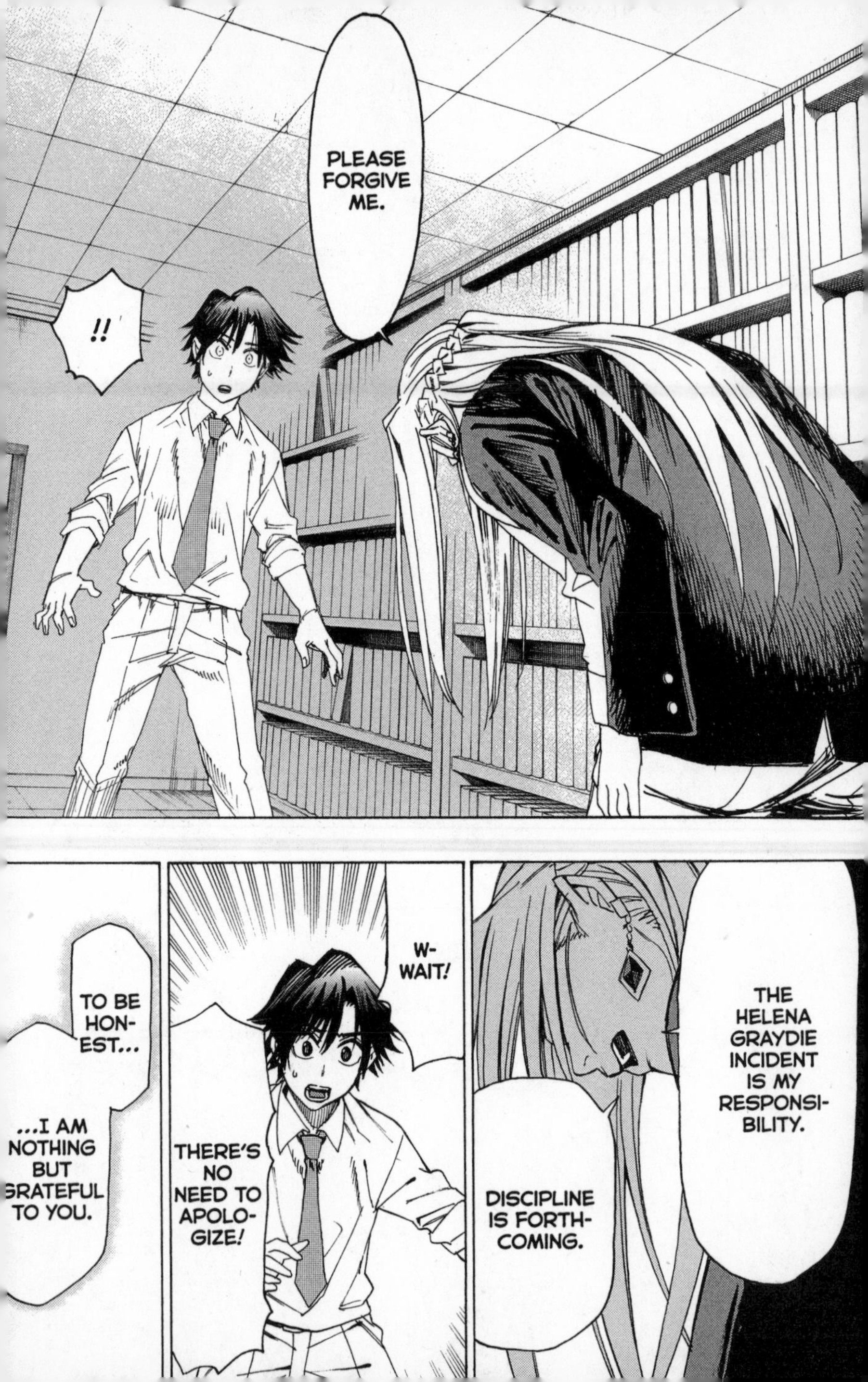
PLEASE FORGIVE ME.
!!
THE HELENA GRAYDIE INCIDENT IS MY RESPONSI-BILITY.
DISCIPLINE IS FORTH-COMING.
W-WAIT!
THERE'S NO NEED TO APOLO-GIZE!
TO BE HON-EST...
...I AM NOTHING BUT GRATEFUL TO YOU.

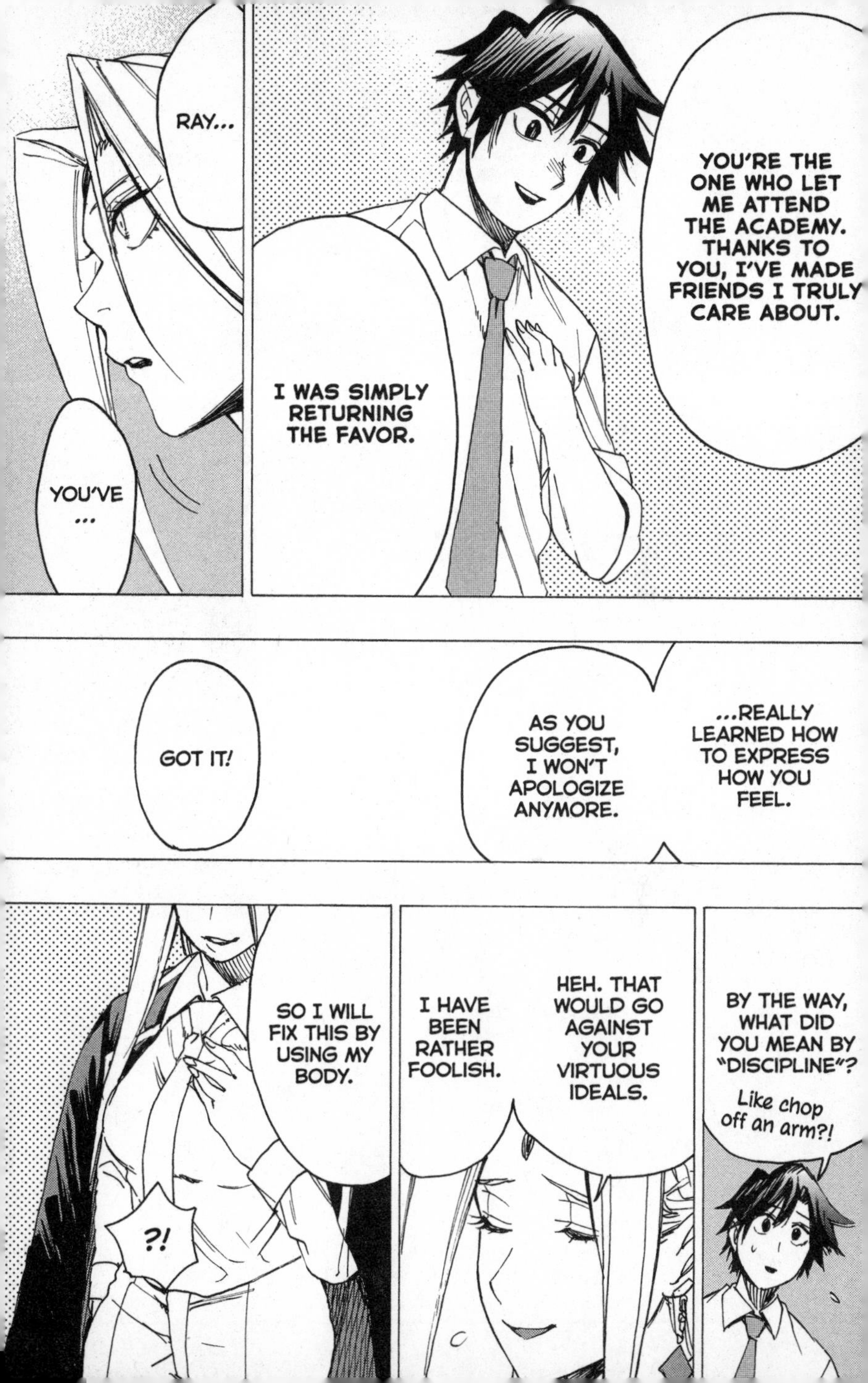
YOU'RE THE ONE WHO LET ME ATTEND THE ACADEMY. THANKS TO YOU, I'VE MADE FRIENDS I TRULY CARE ABOUT.
I WAS SIMPLY RETURNING THE FAVOR.
RAY...
YOU'VE ...
...REALLY LEARNED HOW TO EXPRESS HOW YOU FEEL.
AS YOU SUGGEST, I WON'T APOLOGIZE ANYMORE.
GOT IT!
BY THE WAY, WHAT DID YOU MEAN BY "DISCIPLINE"?
Like chop off an arm?!
HEH. THAT WOULD GO AGAINST YOUR VIRTUOUS IDEALS.
I HAVE BEEN RATHER FOOLISH.
SO I WILL FIX THIS BY USING MY BODY.
?!

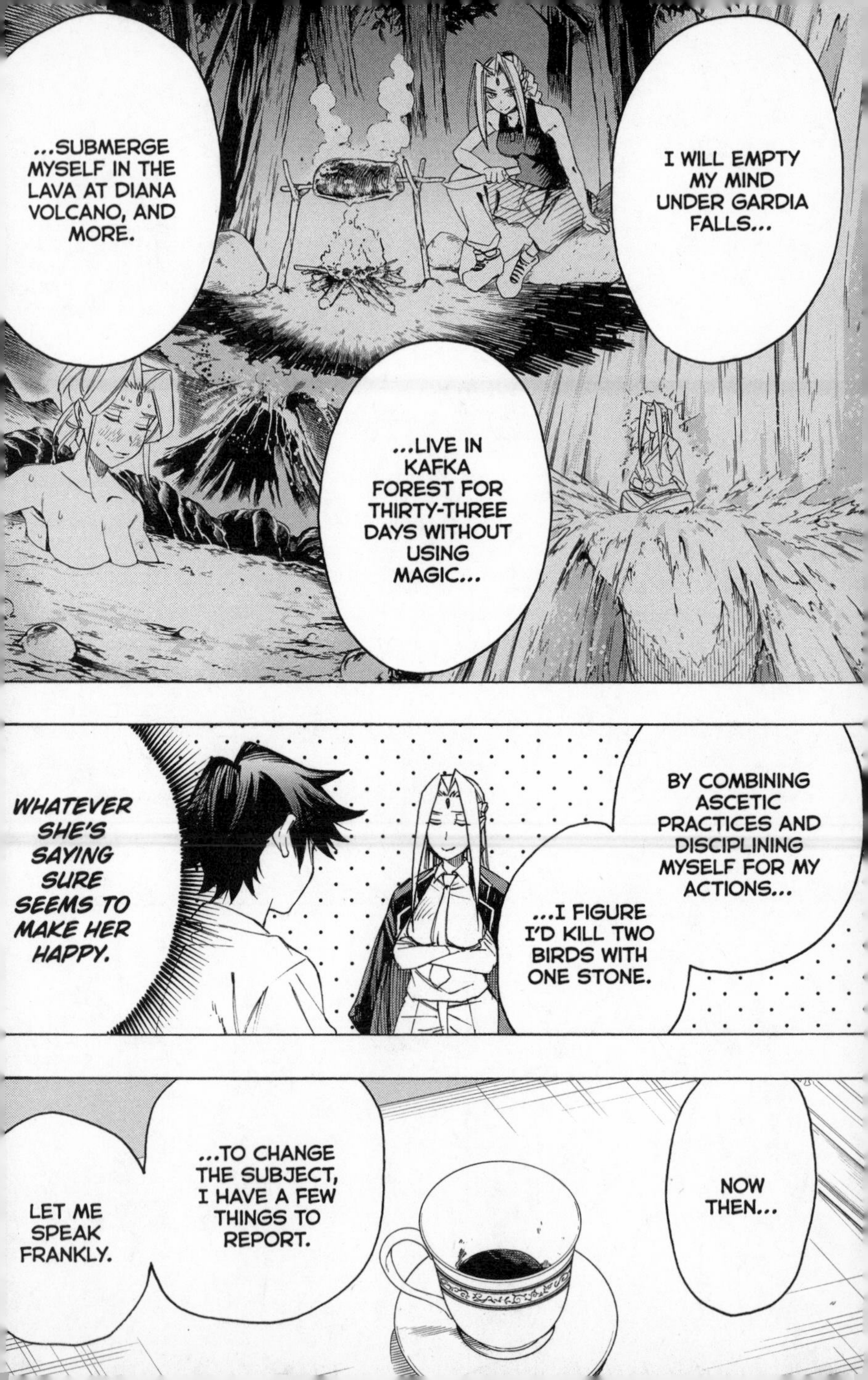
I WILL EMPTY MY MIND UNDER GARDIA FALLS...
...LIVE IN KAFKA FOREST FOR THIRTY-THREE DAYS WITHOUT USING MAGIC...
...SUBMERGE MYSELF IN THE LAVA AT DIANA VOLCANO, AND MORE.
BY COMBINING ASCETIC PRACTICES AND DISCIPLINING MYSELF FOR MY ACTIONS...
...I FIGURE I'D KILL TWO BIRDS WITH ONE STONE.
WHATEVER SHE'S SAYING SURE SEEMS TO MAKE HER HAPPY.
NOW THEN...
...TO CHANGE THE SUBJECT, I HAVE A FEW THINGS TO REPORT.
LET ME SPEAK FRANKLY.

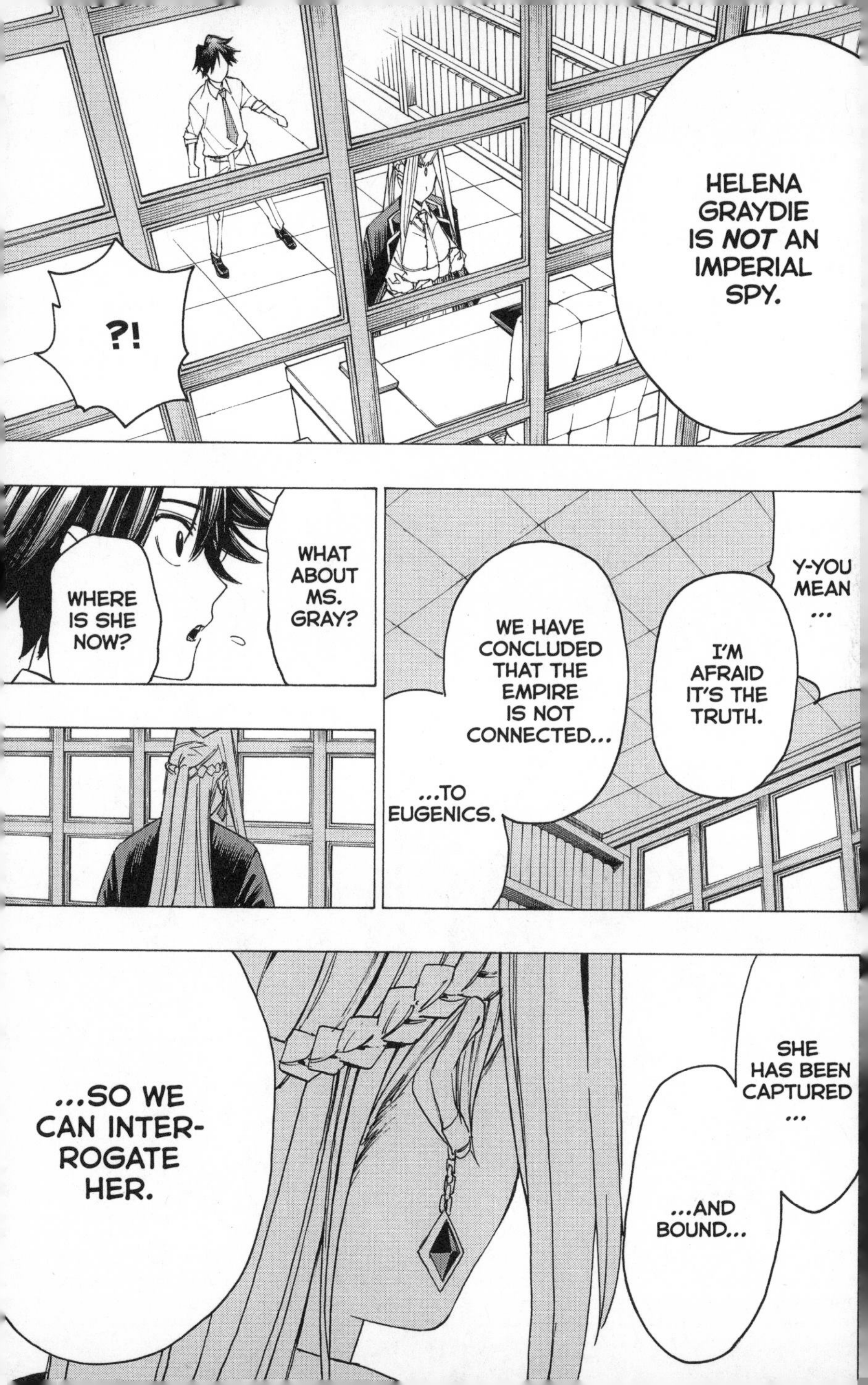
HELENA GRAYDIE IS *NOT* AN IMPERIAL SPY.
?!
Y-YOU MEAN...
I'M AFRAID IT'S THE TRUTH.
WE HAVE CONCLUDED THAT THE EMPIRE IS NOT CONNECTED...
...TO EUGENICS.
WHAT ABOUT MS. GRAY?
WHERE IS SHE NOW?
SHE HAS BEEN CAPTURED...
...AND BOUND...
...SO WE CAN INTER-ROGATE HER.

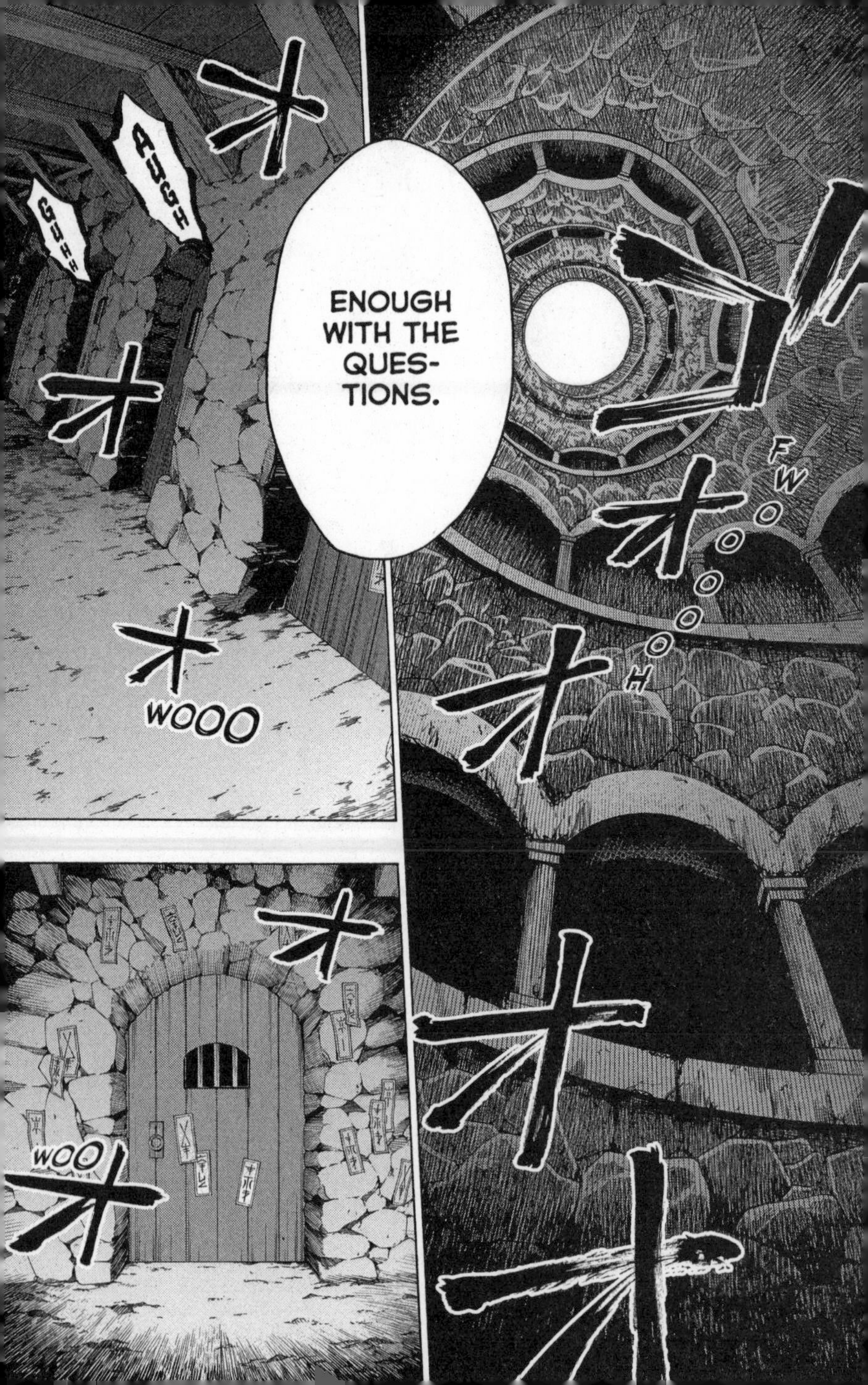
ENOUGH WITH THE QUES-TIONS.
FWOOOOOH
AUGH
GUHH
WOOO
WOO

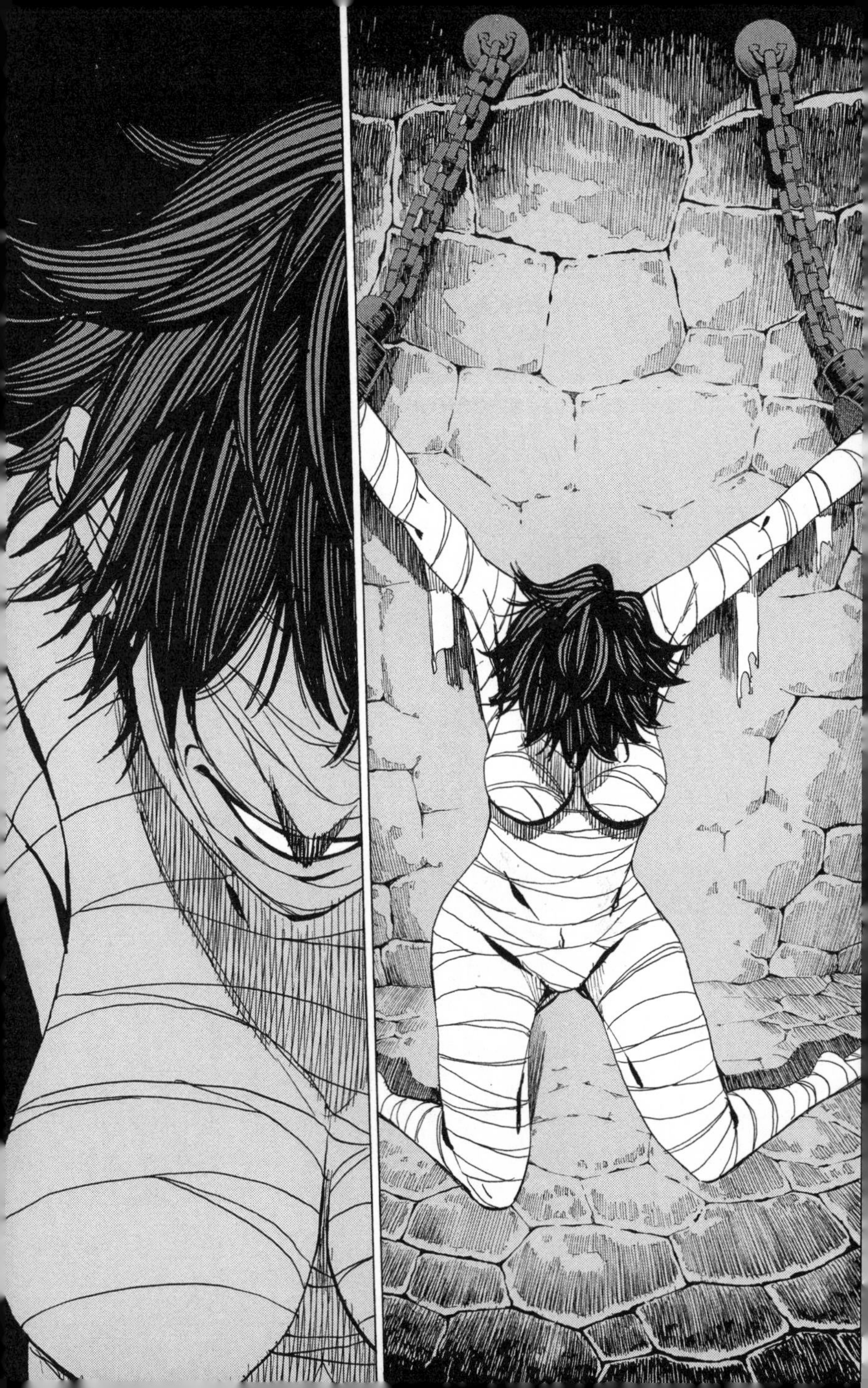

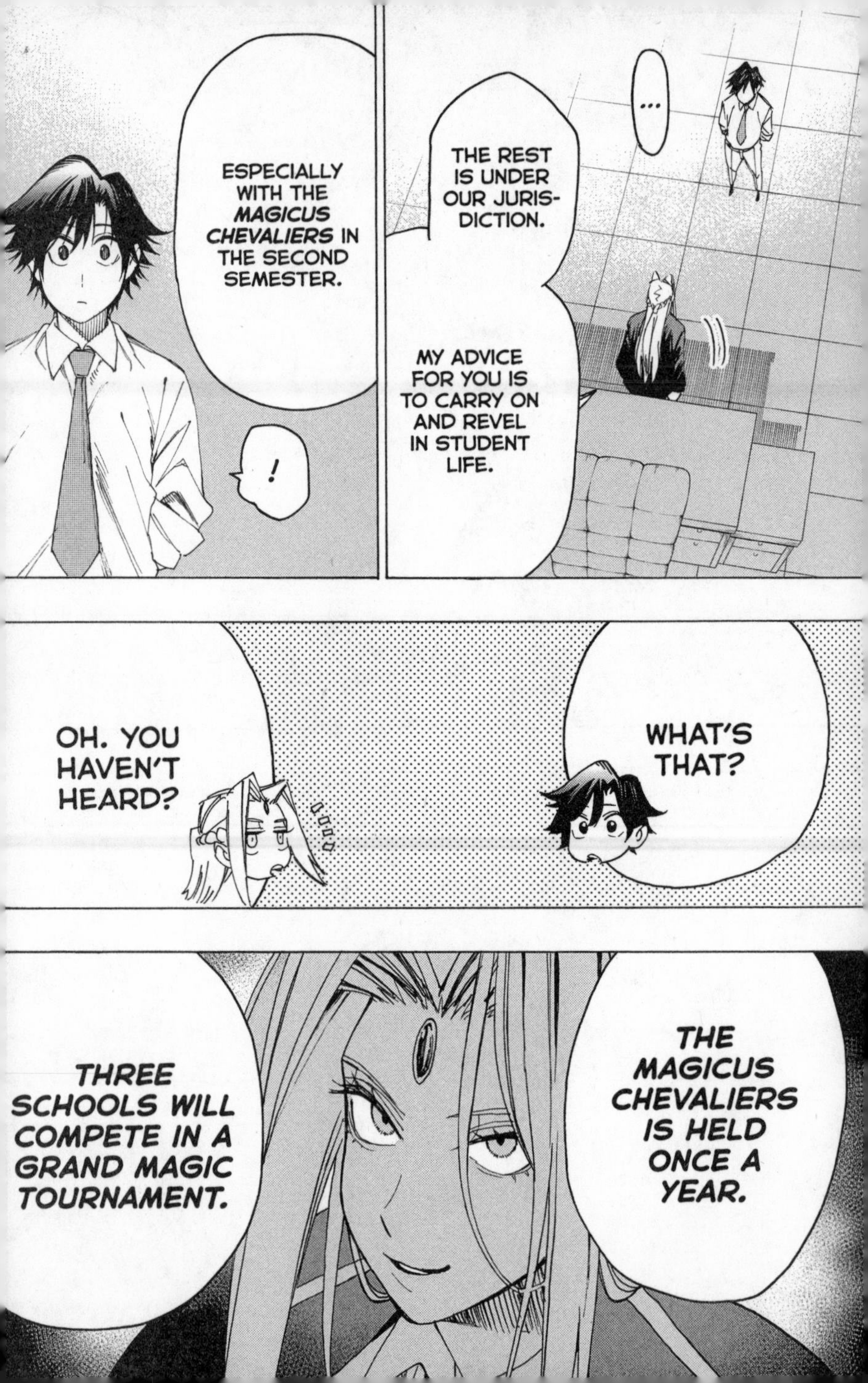
...
THE REST IS UNDER OUR JURISDICTION.
MY ADVICE FOR YOU IS TO CARRY ON AND REVEL IN STUDENT LIFE.
ESPECIALLY WITH THE *MAGICUS CHEVALIERS* IN THE SECOND SEMESTER.
!
WHAT'S THAT?
OH. YOU HAVEN'T HEARD?
THE MAGICUS CHEVALIERS IS HELD ONCE A YEAR.
THREE SCHOOLS WILL COMPETE IN A GRAND MAGIC TOURNAMENT.

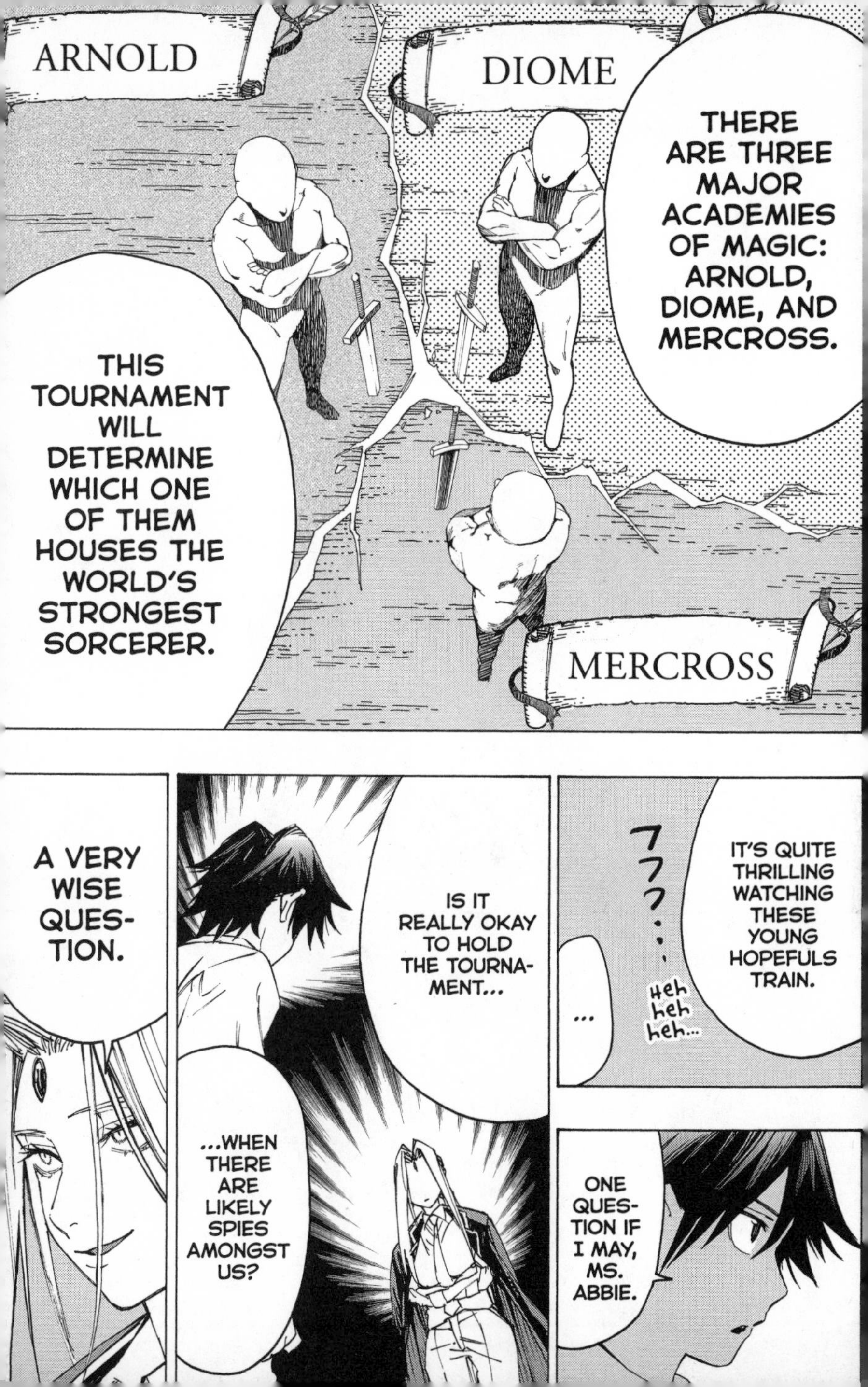
THERE ARE THREE MAJOR ACADEMIES OF MAGIC: ARNOLD, DIOME, AND MERCROSS.
DIOME
ARNOLD
MERCROSS
THIS TOURNAMENT WILL DETERMINE WHICH ONE OF THEM HOUSES THE WORLD'S STRONGEST SORCERER.
IT'S QUITE THRILLING WATCHING THESE YOUNG HOPEFULS TRAIN.
フフフ…
heh heh heh...
...
ONE QUESTION IF I MAY, MS. ABBIE.
IS IT REALLY OKAY TO HOLD THE TOURNAMENT...
...WHEN THERE ARE LIKELY SPIES AMONGST US?
A VERY WISE QUESTION.

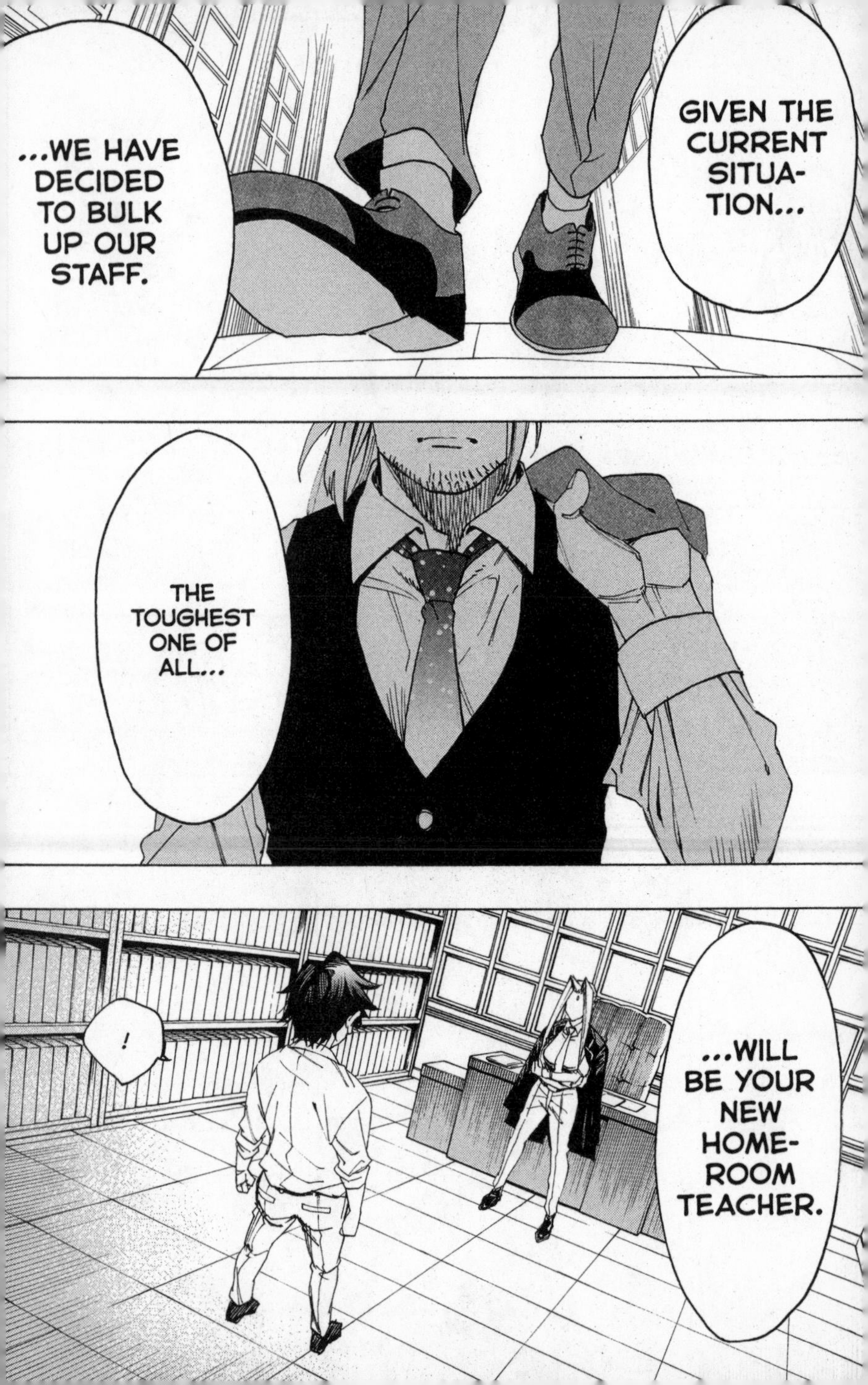
GIVEN THE CURRENT SITUA-TION...
...WE HAVE DECIDED TO BULK UP OUR STAFF.
THE TOUGHEST ONE OF ALL...
...WILL BE YOUR NEW HOME-ROOM TEACHER.
!

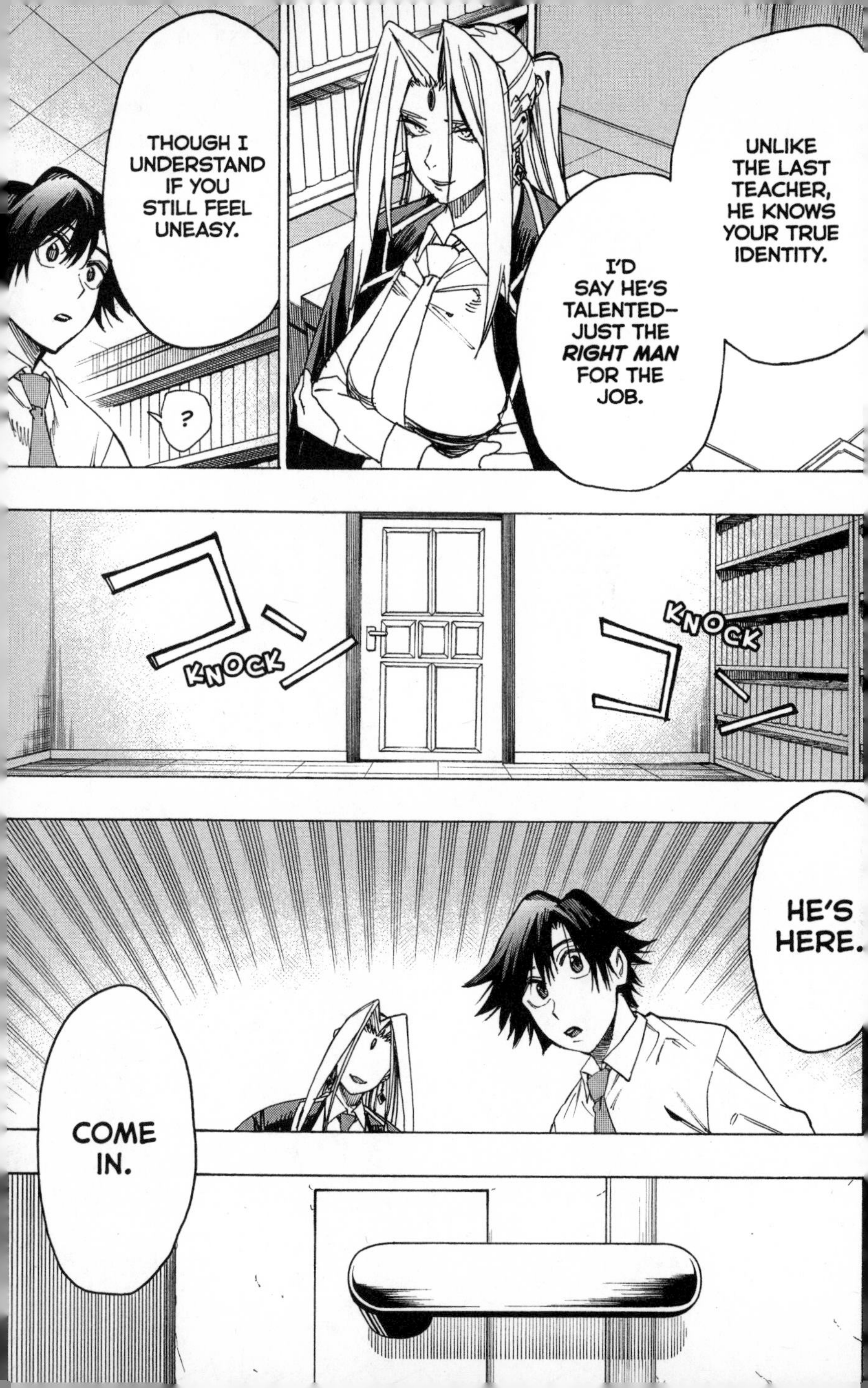
UNLIKE THE LAST TEACHER, HE KNOWS YOUR TRUE IDENTITY.
I'D SAY HE'S TALENTED— JUST THE *RIGHT MAN* FOR THE JOB.
THOUGH I UNDERSTAND IF YOU STILL FEEL UNEASY.
?
KNOCK
KNOCK
HE'S HERE.
COME IN.

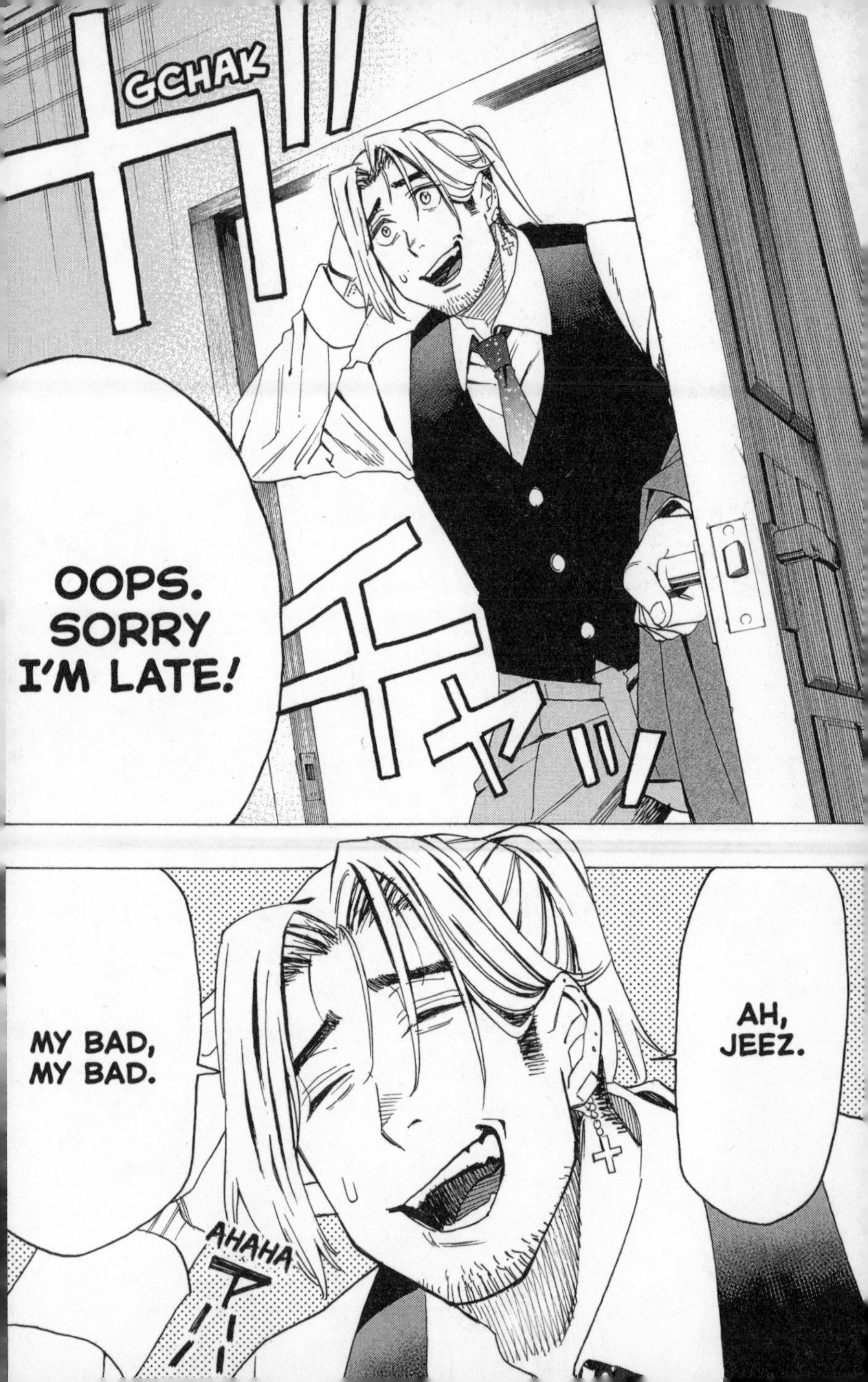
GCHAK
OOPS. SORRY I'M LATE!
AH, JEEZ.
MY BAD, MY BAD.
AHAHA

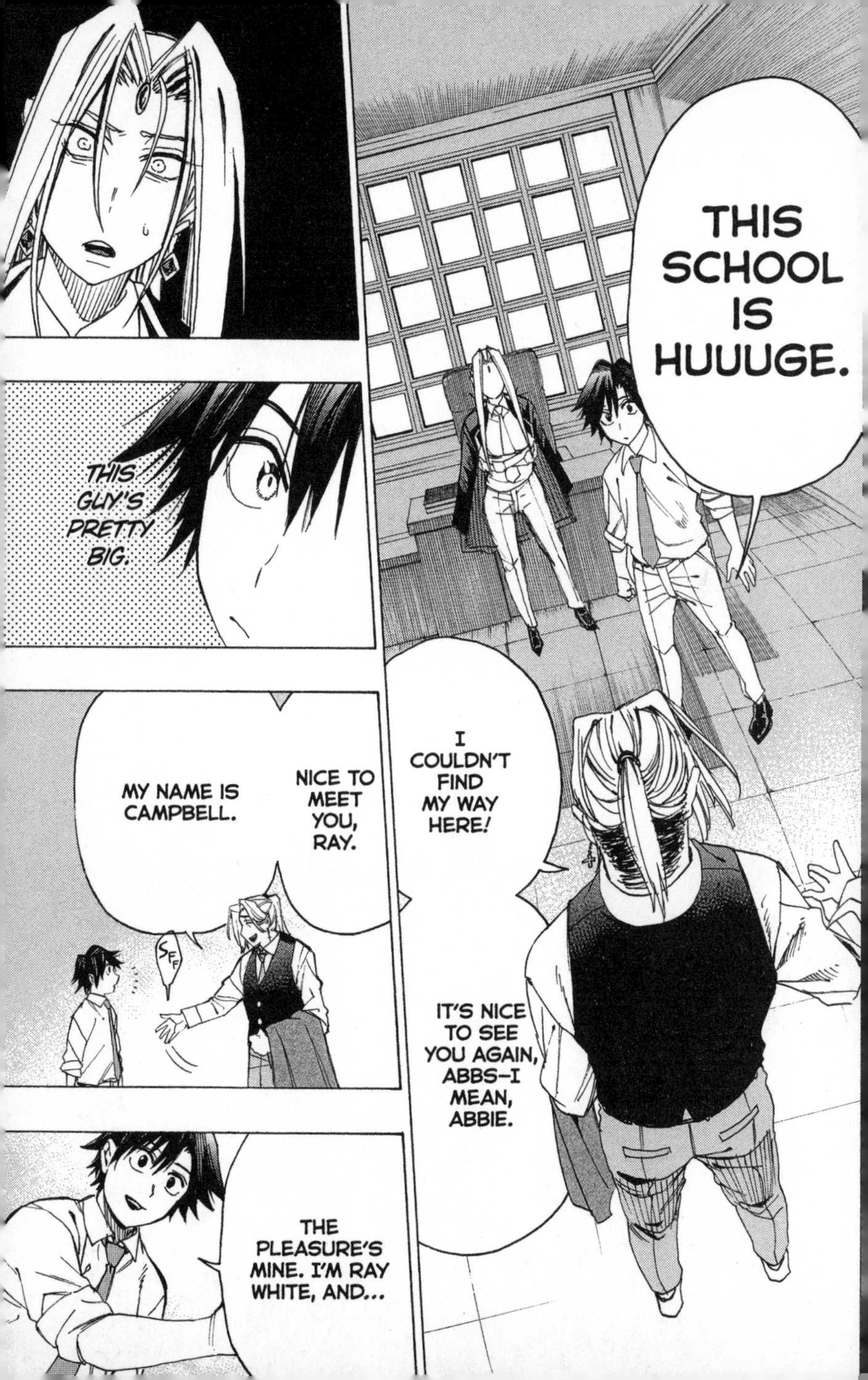
THIS SCHOOL IS HUUUGE.
I COULDN'T FIND MY WAY HERE!
IT'S NICE TO SEE YOU AGAIN, ABBS—I MEAN, ABBIE.
THIS GUY'S PRETTY BIG.
NICE TO MEET YOU, RAY.
MY NAME IS CAMPBELL.
SFF
THE PLEASURE'S MINE. I'M RAY WHITE, AND...

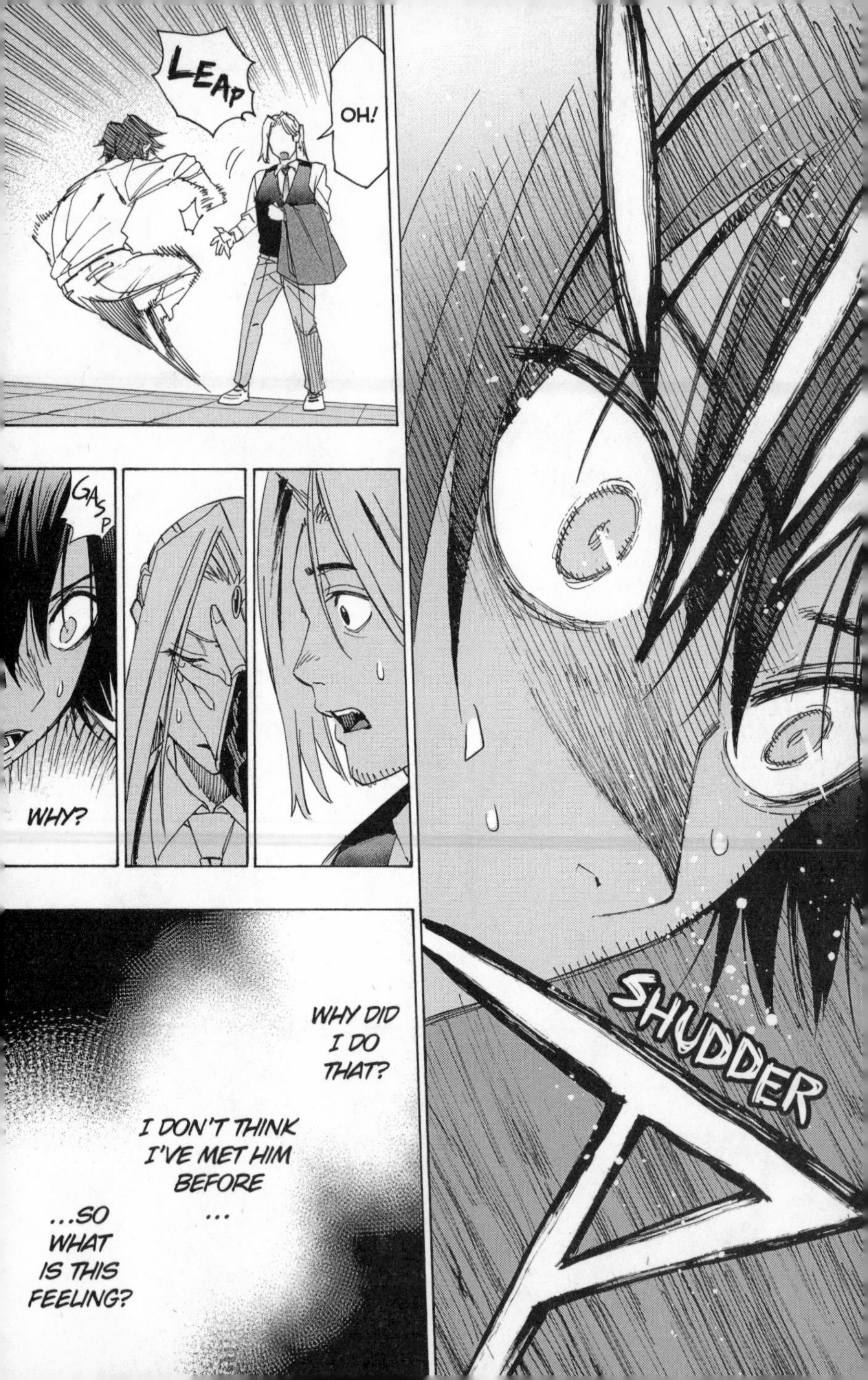
SHUDDER
LEAP
OH!
GASP
WHY?
WHY DID I DO THAT?
I DON'T THINK I'VE MET HIM BEFORE ...
...SO WHAT IS THIS FEELING?

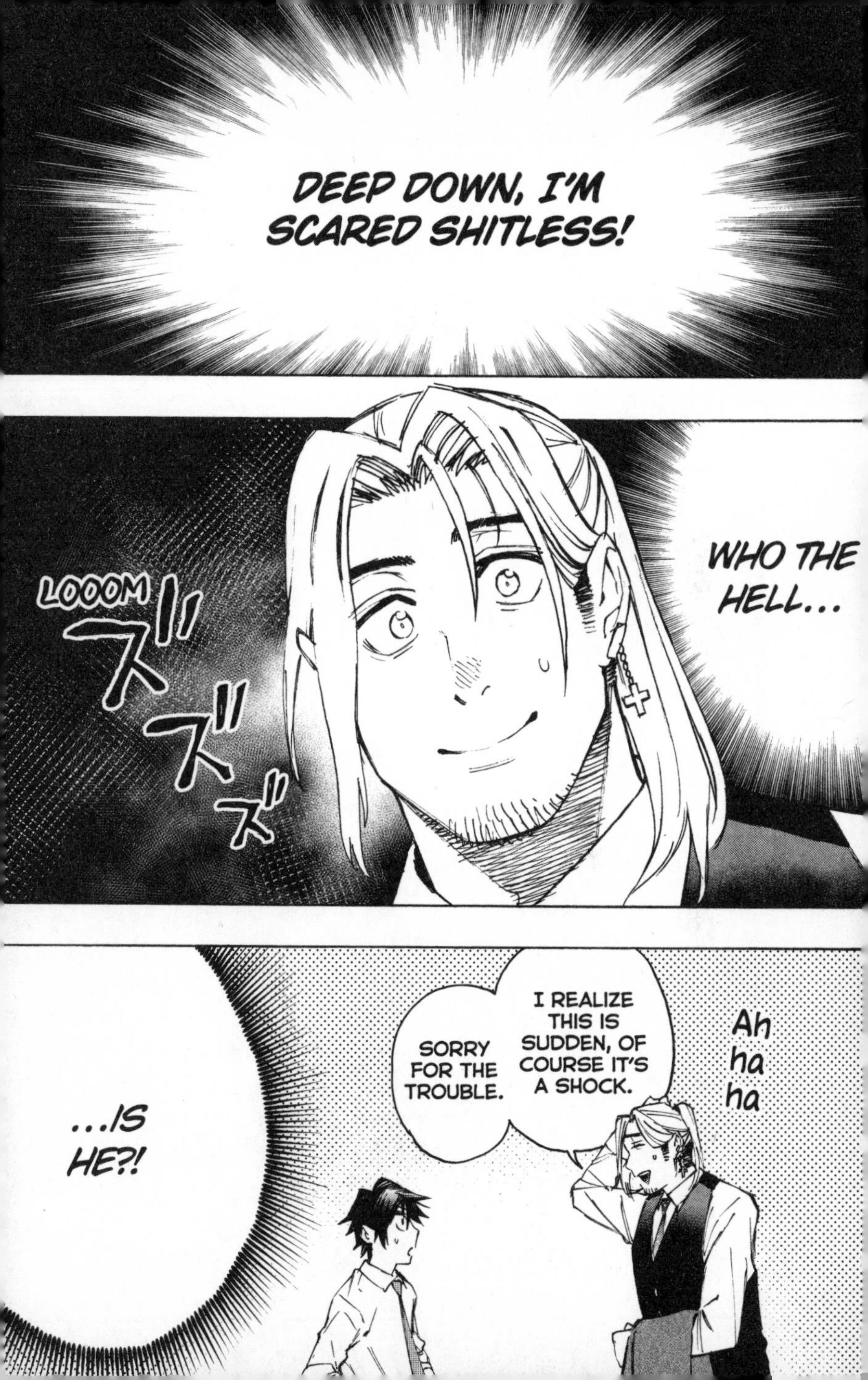
DEEP DOWN, I'M SCARED SHITLESS!
WHO THE HELL...
LOOOM
ズズズズ
Ah ha ha
I REALIZE THIS IS SUDDEN, OF COURSE IT'S A SHOCK.
SORRY FOR THE TROUBLE.
...IS HE?!

The **ICEBLADE**
SORCERER Shall **RULE**
the **WORLD**

Chapter 26 Nightclub

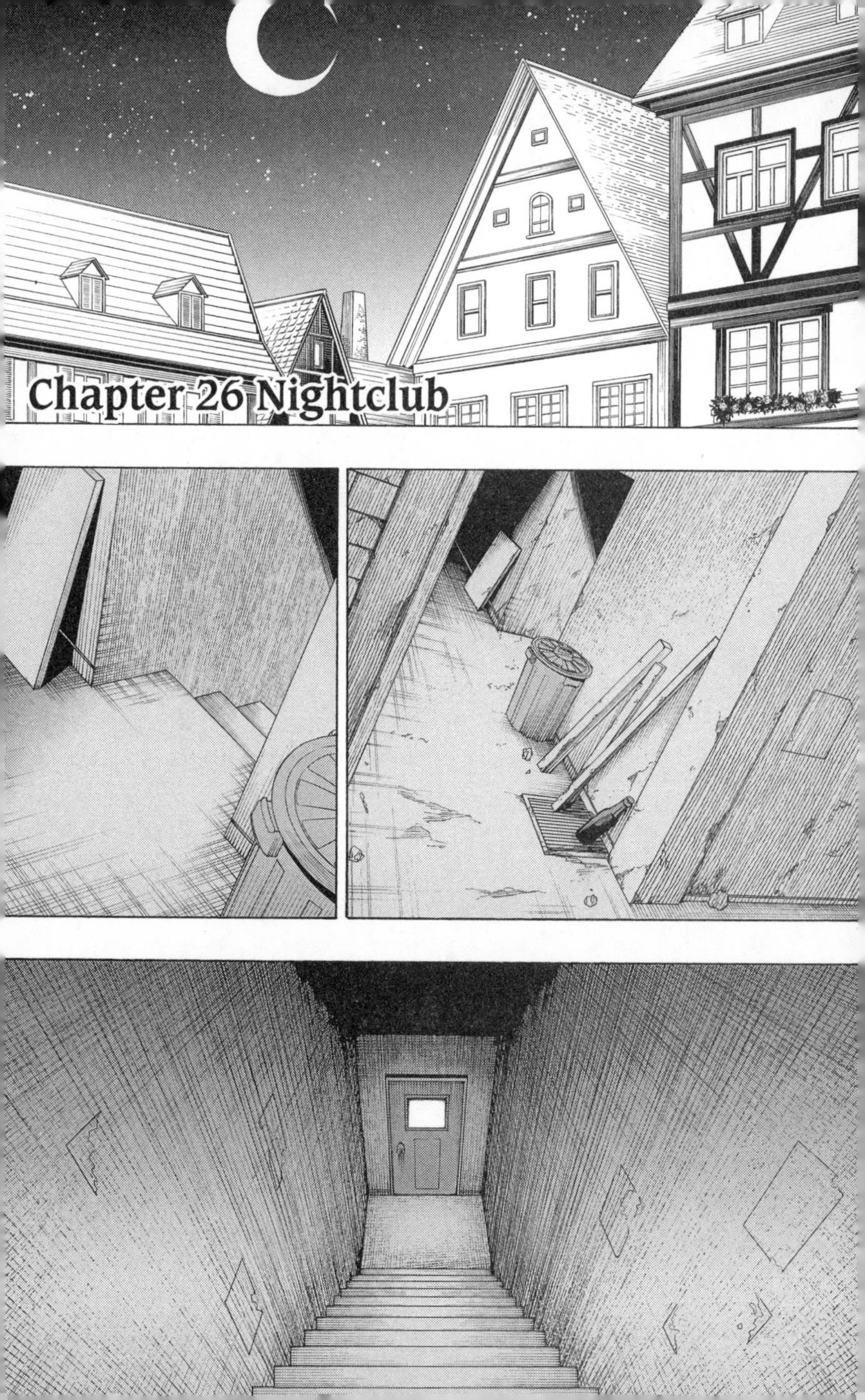

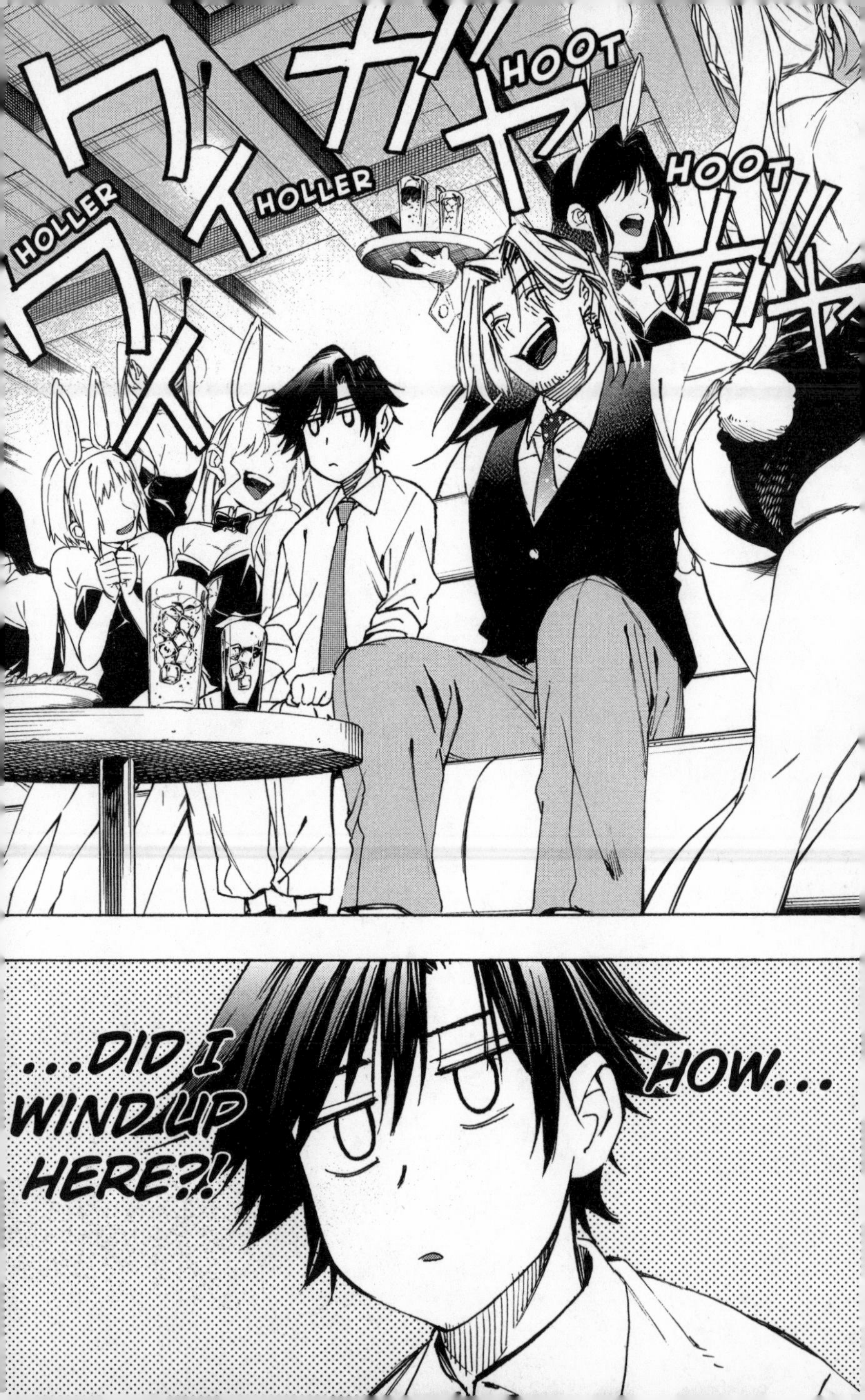
HOOT
HOOT
HOLLER
HOLLER
HOW...
...DID I WIND UP HERE?!

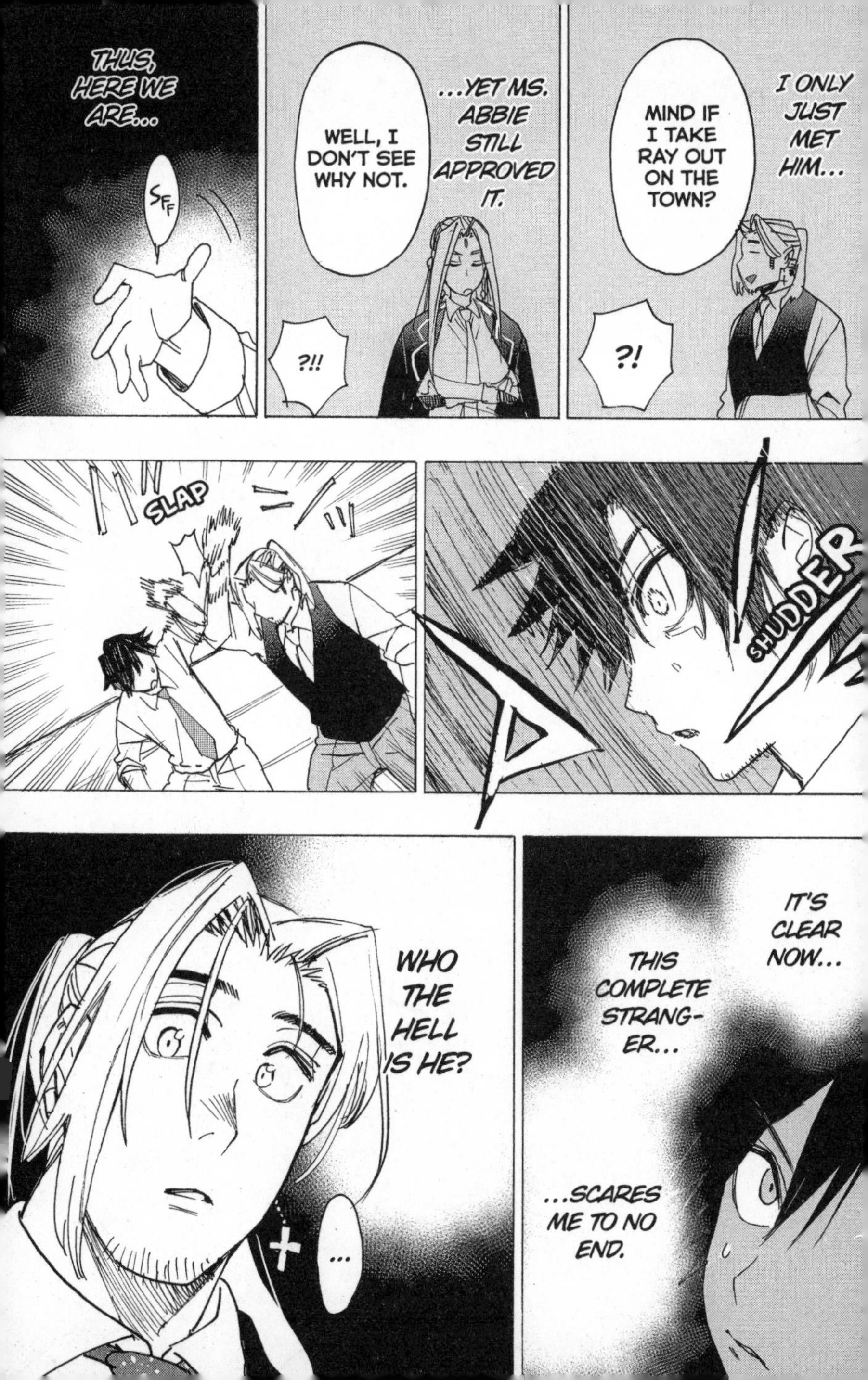
I ONLY JUST MET HIM...
MIND IF I TAKE RAY OUT ON THE TOWN?
?!
...YET MS. ABBIE STILL APPROVED IT.
WELL, I DON'T SEE WHY NOT.
?!!
THUS, HERE WE ARE...
SFF
SHUDDER
SLAP
IT'S CLEAR NOW...
THIS COMPLETE STRANG-ER...
...SCARES ME TO NO END.
WHO THE HELL IS HE?
...

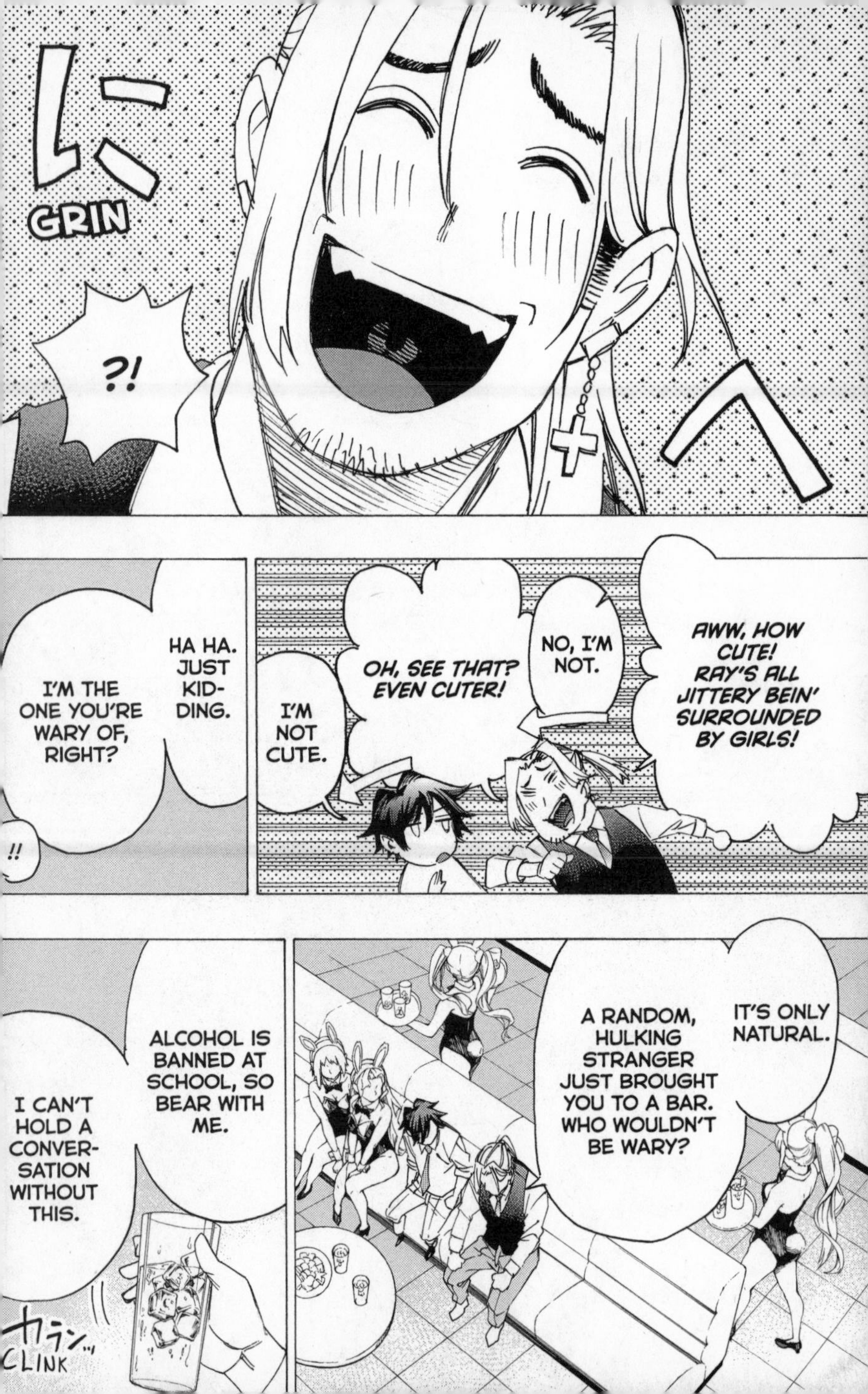
GRIN
?!
AWW, HOW CUTE! RAY'S ALL JITTERY BEIN' SURROUNDED BY GIRLS!
NO, I'M NOT.
OH, SEE THAT? EVEN CUTER!
I'M NOT CUTE.
HA HA. JUST KID-DING.
I'M THE ONE YOU'RE WARY OF, RIGHT?
!!
IT'S ONLY NATURAL.
A RANDOM, HULKING STRANGER JUST BROUGHT YOU TO A BAR. WHO WOULDN'T BE WARY?
ALCOHOL IS BANNED AT SCHOOL, SO BEAR WITH ME.
I CAN'T HOLD A CONVER-SATION WITHOUT THIS.
CLINK

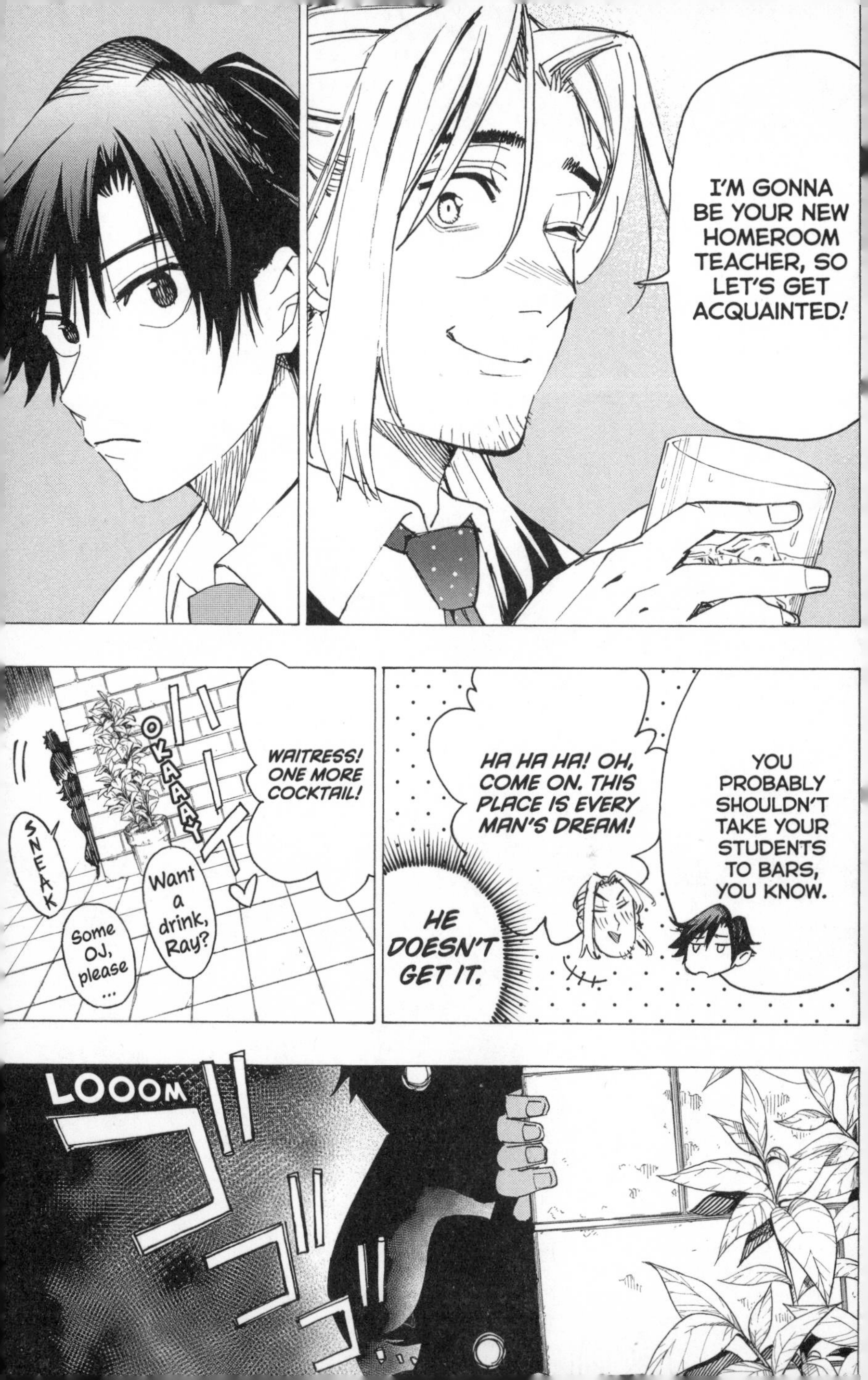
I'M GONNA BE YOUR NEW HOMEROOM TEACHER, SO LET'S GET ACQUAINTED!
YOU PROBABLY SHOULDN'T TAKE YOUR STUDENTS TO BARS, YOU KNOW.
HA HA HA! OH, COME ON. THIS PLACE IS EVERY MAN'S DREAM!
HE DOESN'T GET IT.
WAITRESS! ONE MORE COCKTAIL!
OKAAAAY
Want a drink, Ray?
Some OJ, please ...
SNEAK
LOOOM

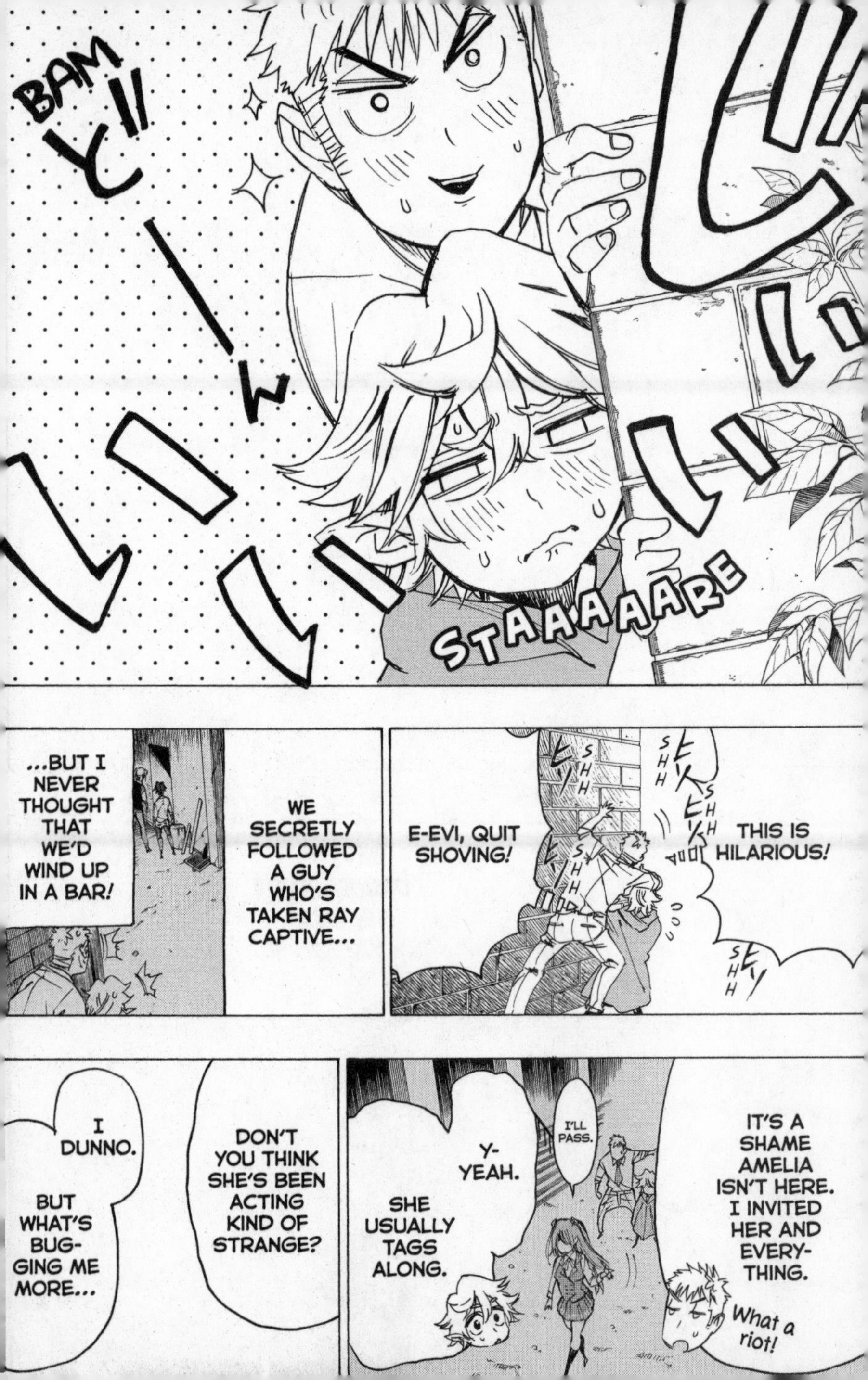
BAM
Y!!
STAAAAAARE
THIS IS HILARIOUS!
SHH
SHH
E-EVI, QUIT SHOVING!
SHH
SHH
WE SECRETLY FOLLOWED A GUY WHO'S TAKEN RAY CAPTIVE...
...BUT I NEVER THOUGHT THAT WE'D WIND UP IN A BAR!
IT'S A SHAME AMELIA ISN'T HERE. I INVITED HER AND EVERYTHING.
What a riot!
I'LL PASS.
Y-YEAH.
SHE USUALLY TAGS ALONG.
DON'T YOU THINK SHE'S BEEN ACTING KIND OF STRANGE?
I DUNNO.
BUT WHAT'S BUG-GING ME MORE...

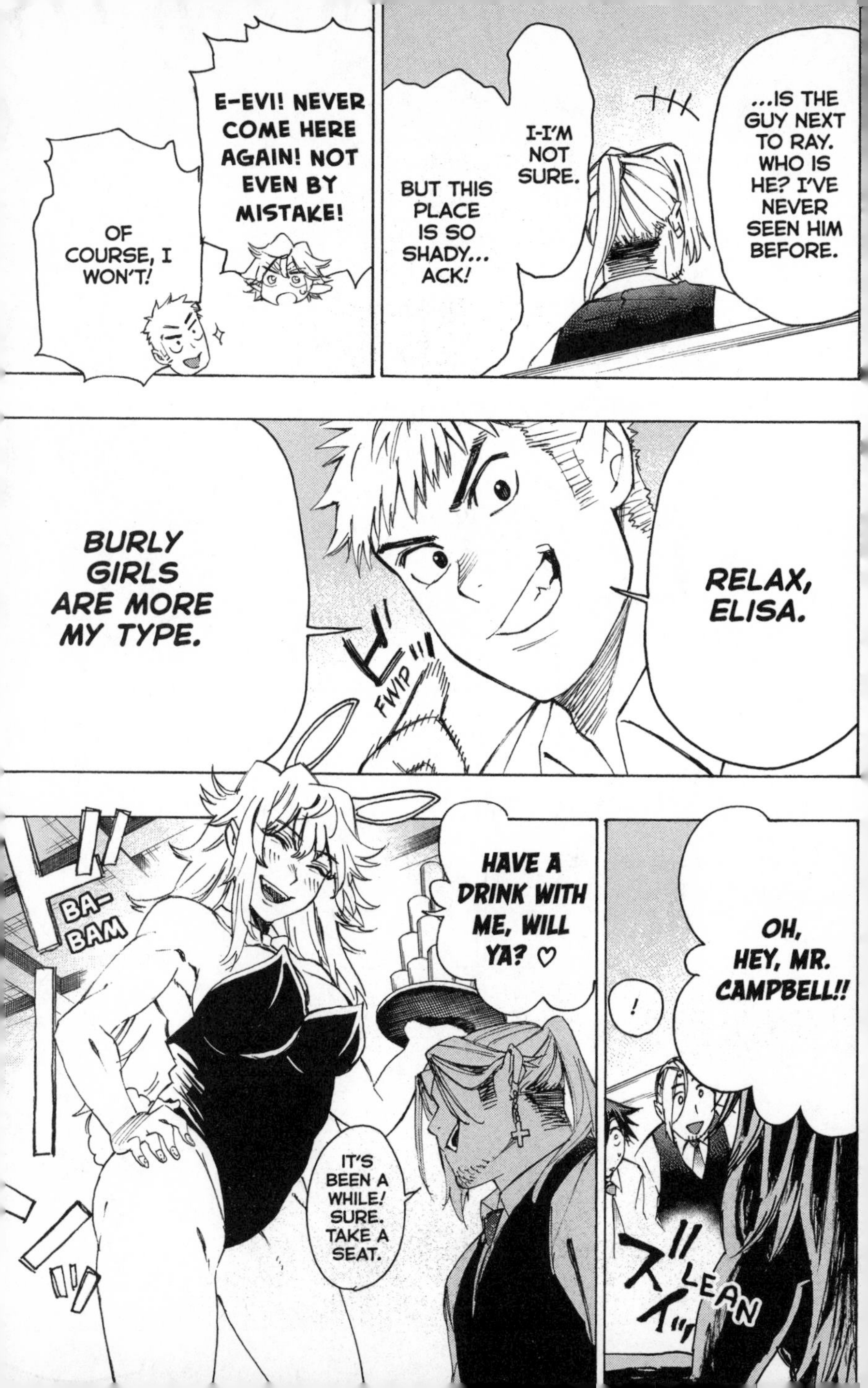
...IS THE GUY NEXT TO RAY. WHO IS HE? I'VE NEVER SEEN HIM BEFORE.
I-I'M NOT SURE.
BUT THIS PLACE IS SO SHADY... ACK!
E-EVI! NEVER COME HERE AGAIN! NOT EVEN BY MISTAKE!
OF COURSE, I WON'T!
RELAX, ELISA.
BURLY GIRLS ARE MORE MY TYPE.
FWIP
OH, HEY, MR. CAMPBELL!!
!
LEAN
HAVE A DRINK WITH ME, WILL YA? ♡
IT'S BEEN A WHILE! SURE. TAKE A SEAT.
BA-BAM

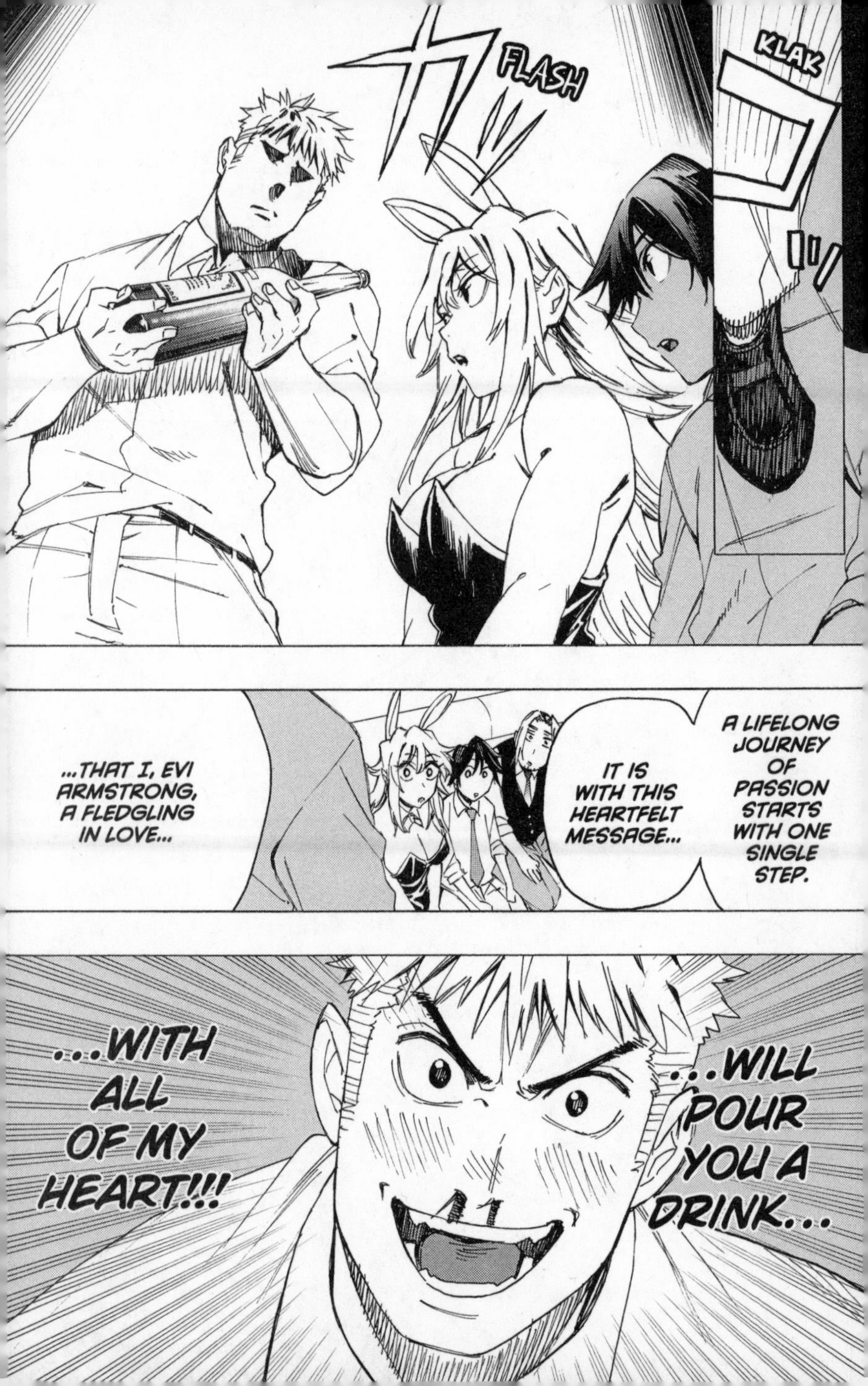
KLAK
FLASH
A LIFELONG JOURNEY OF PASSION STARTS WITH ONE SINGLE STEP.
IT IS WITH THIS HEARTFELT MESSAGE...
...THAT I, EVI ARMSTRONG, A FLEDGLING IN LOVE...
...WILL POUR YOU A DRINK...
...WITH ALL OF MY HEART!!!

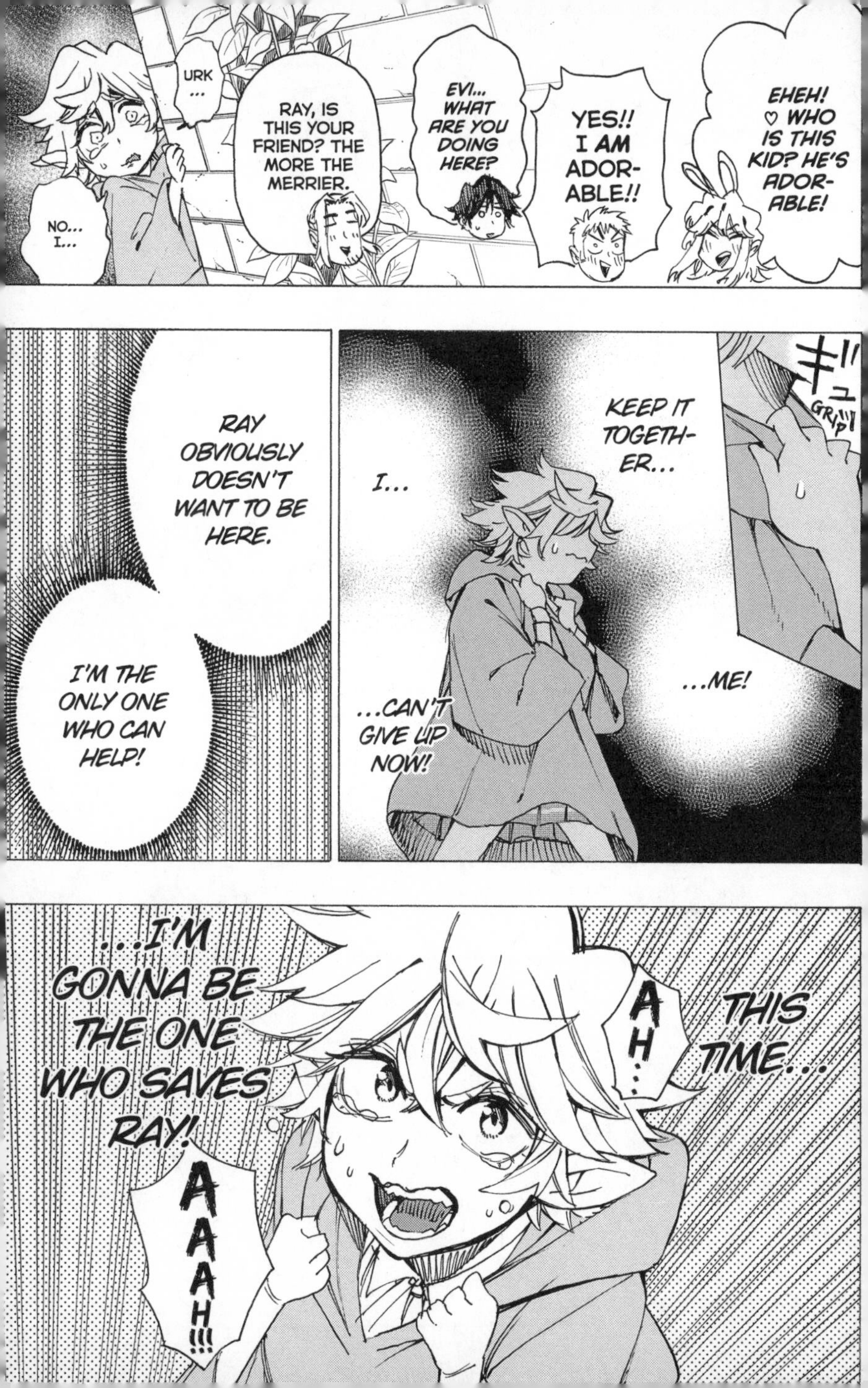
EHEH! ♡ WHO IS THIS KID? HE'S ADORABLE!
YES!! I AM ADORABLE!!
EVI... WHAT ARE YOU DOING HERE?
RAY, IS THIS YOUR FRIEND? THE MORE THE MERRIER.
URK ...
NO... I...
GRIP
KEEP IT TOGETHER...
I...
...ME!
...CAN'T GIVE UP NOW!
RAY OBVIOUSLY DOESN'T WANT TO BE HERE.
I'M THE ONLY ONE WHO CAN HELP!
THIS TIME...
AH...
...I'M GONNA BE THE ONE WHO SAVES RAY!
AAAAH!!!

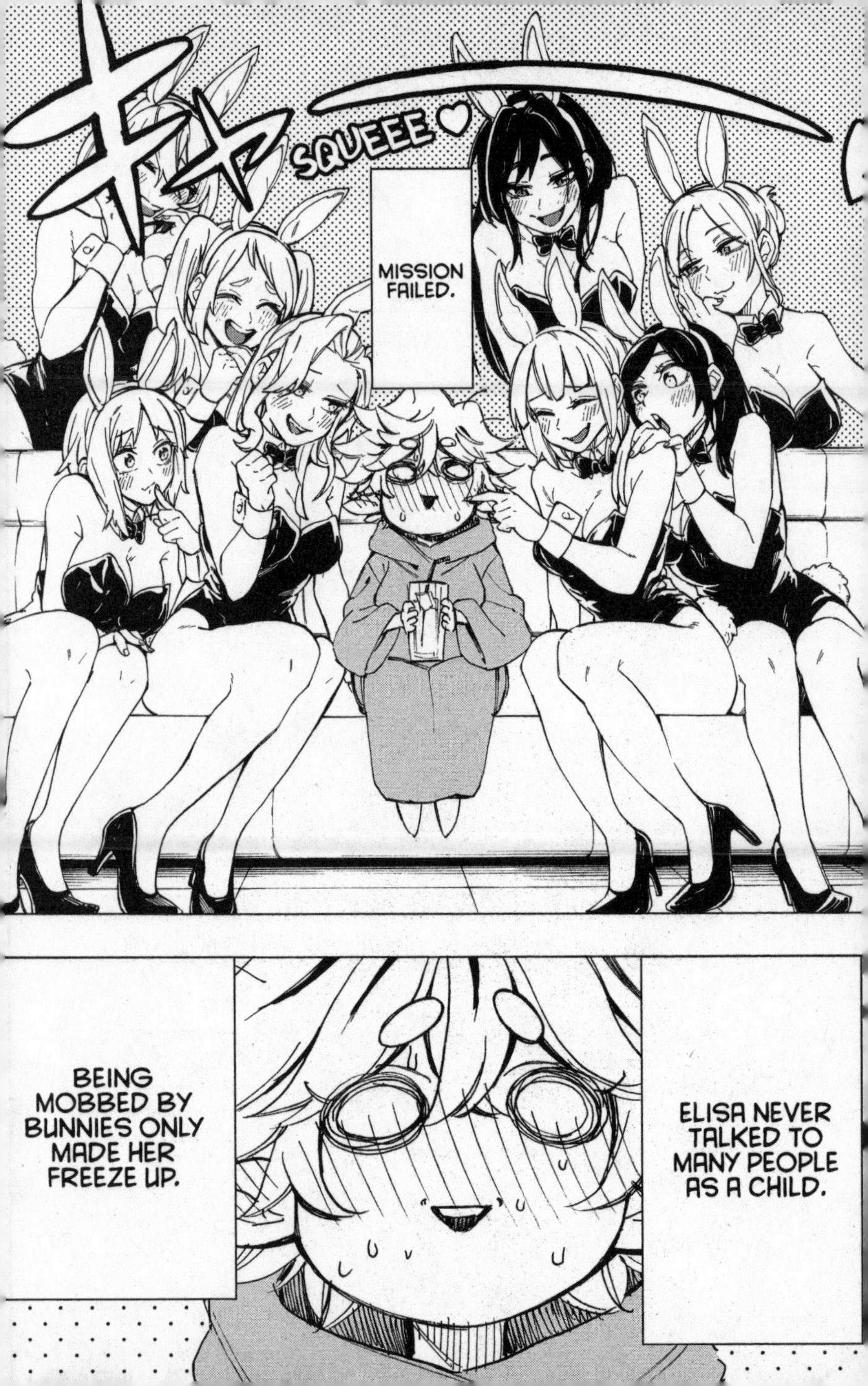
SQUEEE ♡
MISSION FAILED.
ELISA NEVER TALKED TO MANY PEOPLE AS A CHILD.
BEING MOBBED BY BUNNIES ONLY MADE HER FREEZE UP.

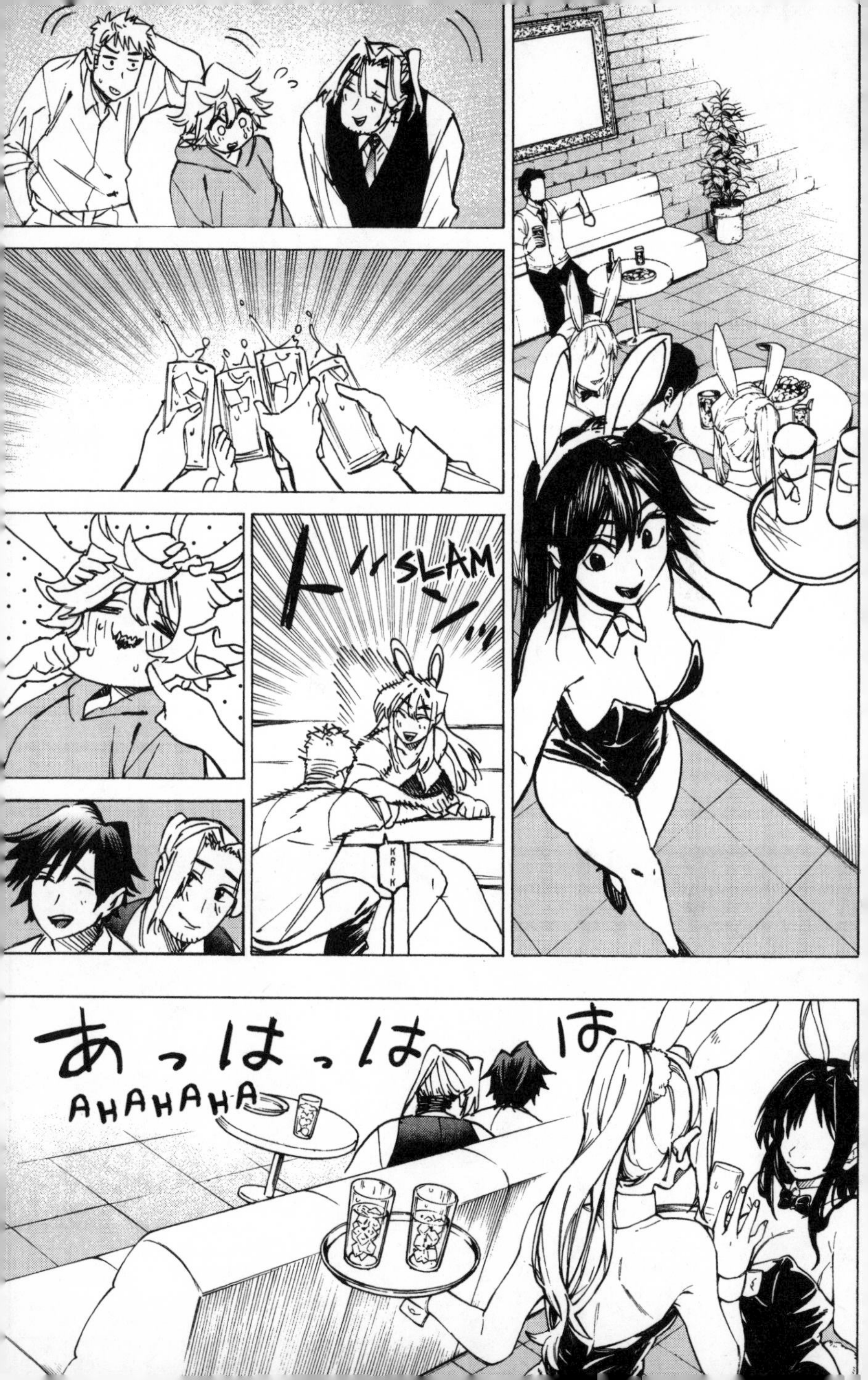
トン
SLAM
KRIK
あっはっはっは
AHAHAHA

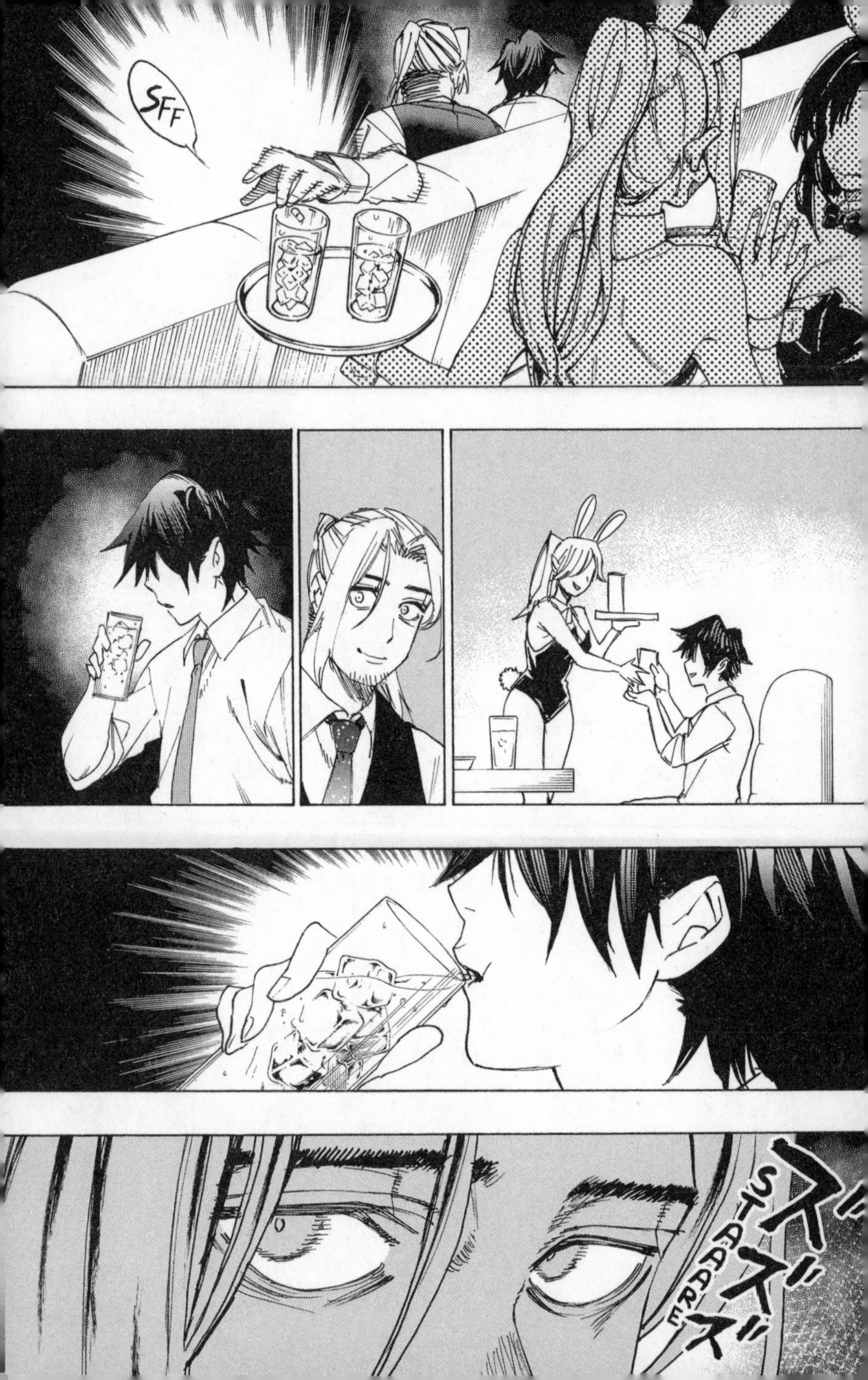
SFF
STAAARE

Ahaha! Cute!

Fwh

Deaaad

HEY, RAY. YOU ALL RIGHT?

LOOKS LIKE THE PARTY GOT HIM DRUNK. I'LL TAKE HIM TO THE LOO.

Let him throw up.

GCHAK

SLAM

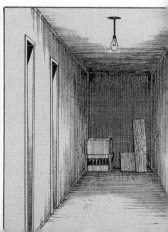

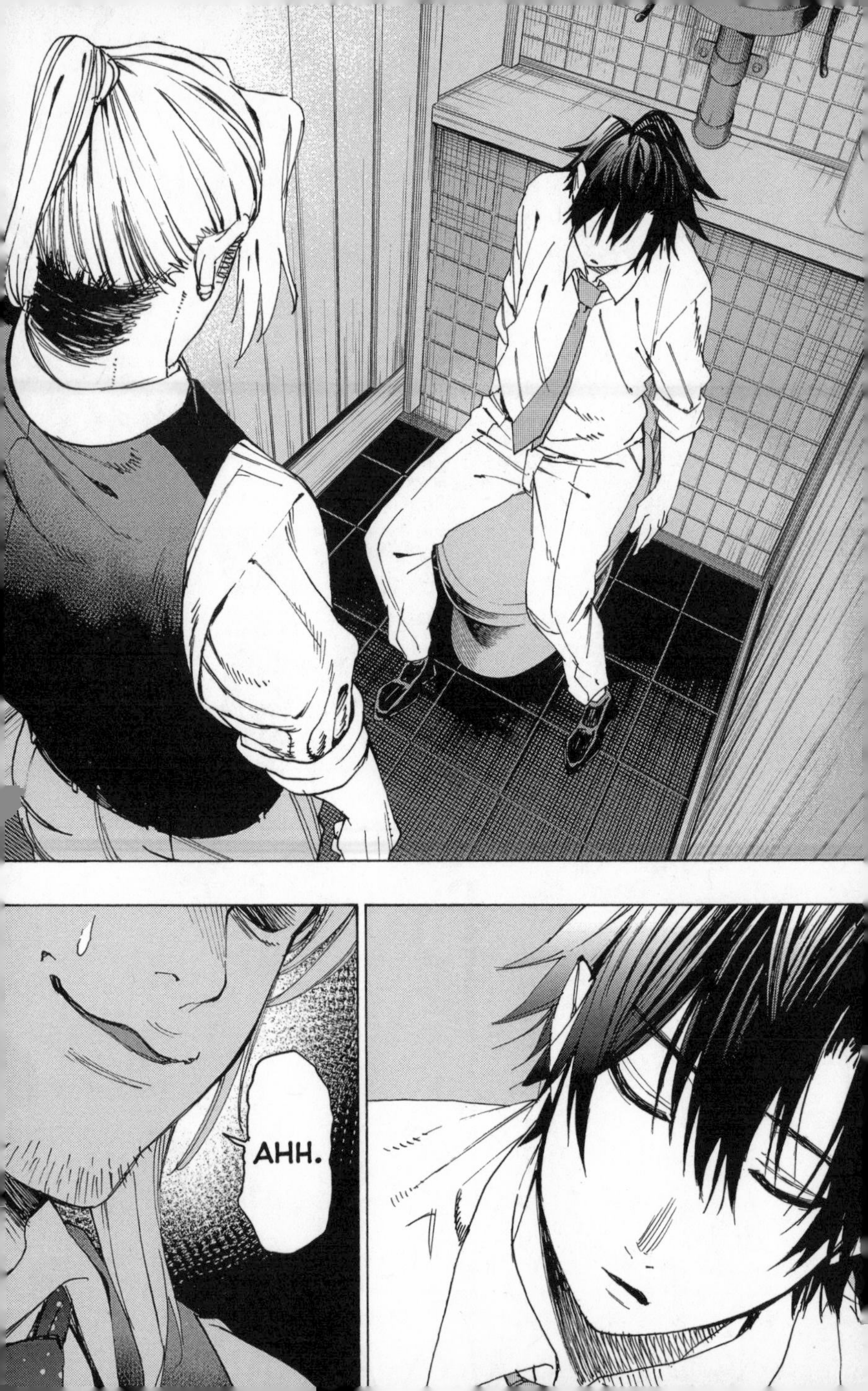
AHH.

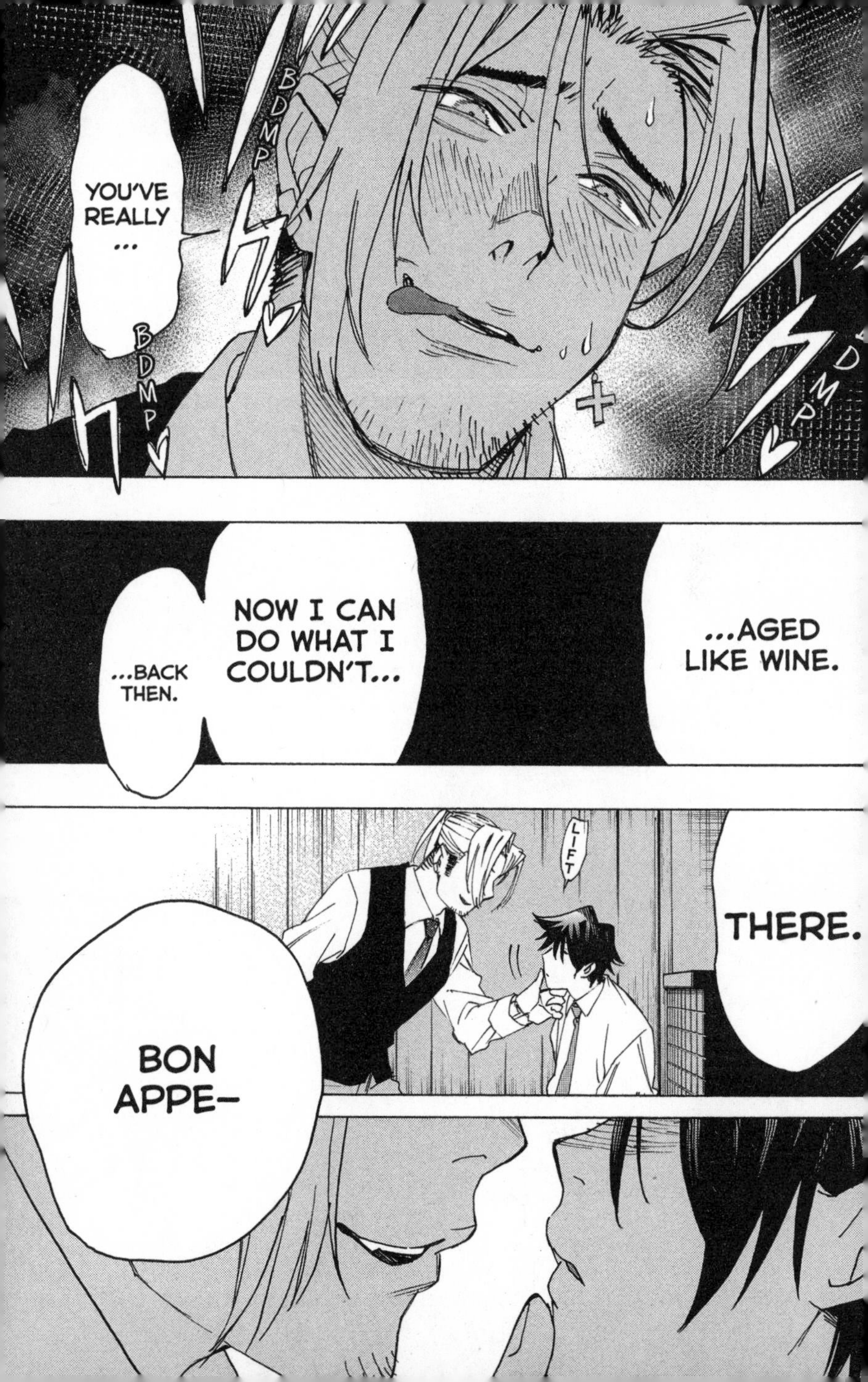
BDMP
YOU'VE REALLY ...
BDMP
...AGED LIKE WINE.
NOW I CAN DO WHAT I COULDN'T...
...BACK THEN.
THERE.
LIFT
BON APPE–

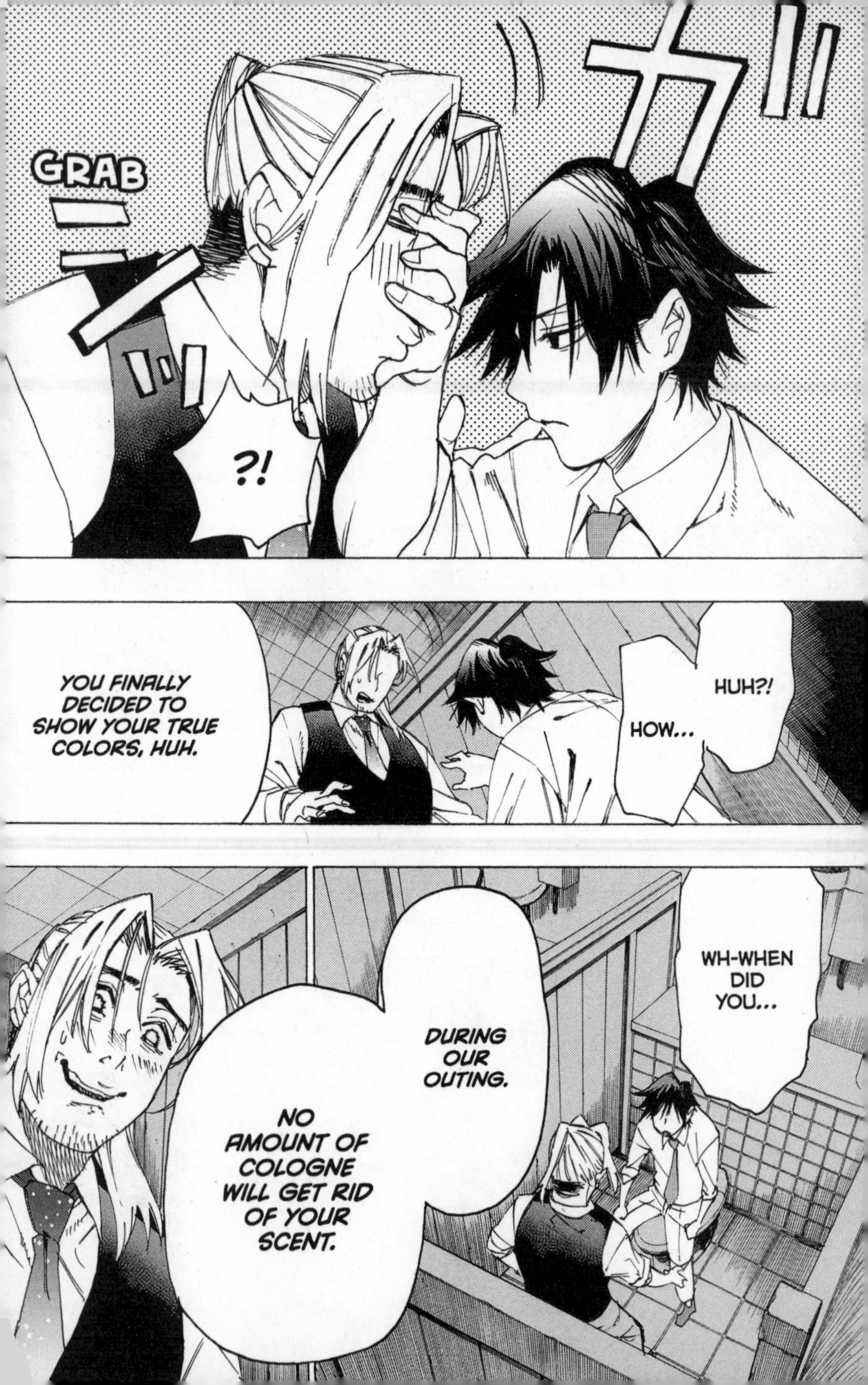
ガ
GRAB
?!
HUH?!
HOW...
YOU FINALLY DECIDED TO SHOW YOUR TRUE COLORS, HUH.
WH-WHEN DID YOU...
DURING OUR OUTING.
NO AMOUNT OF COLOGNE WILL GET RID OF YOUR SCENT.

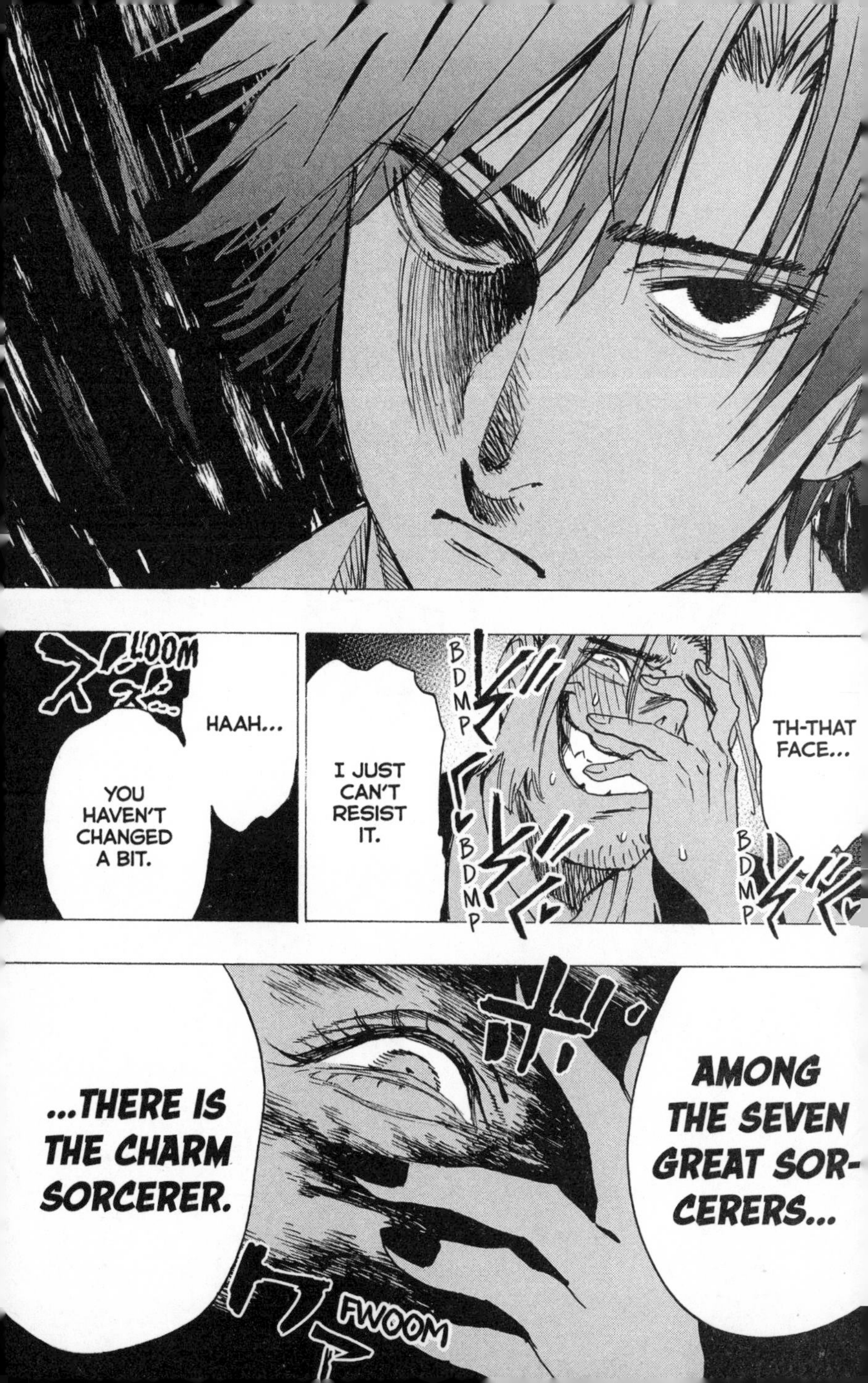
TH-THAT FACE...
BDMP
BDMP
BDMP
I JUST CAN'T RESIST IT.
LOOM
HAAH...
YOU HAVEN'T CHANGED A BIT.
AMONG THE SEVEN GREAT SOR-CERERS...
...THERE IS THE CHARM SORCERER.
FWOOM

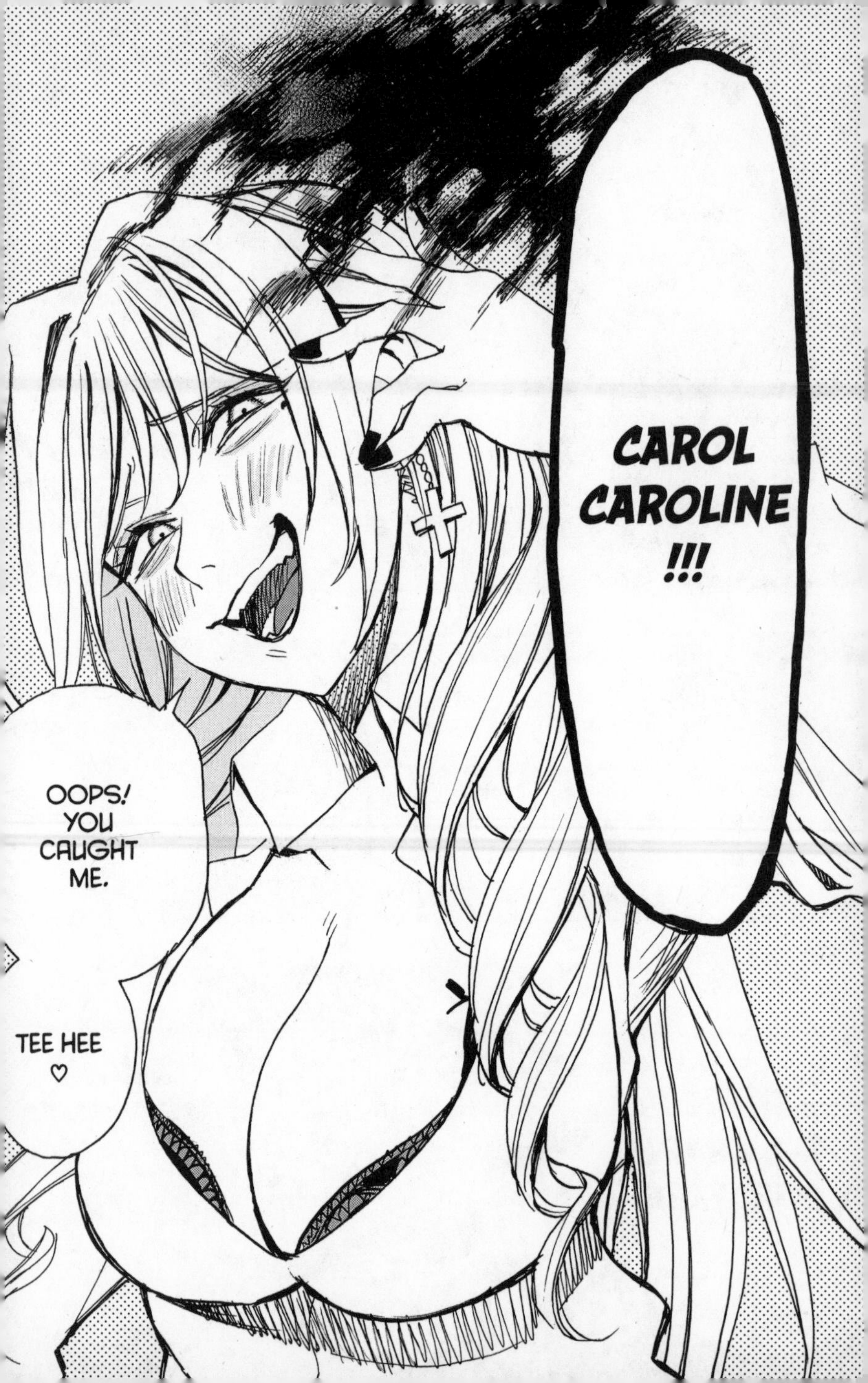
CAROL CAROLINE !!!
OOPS! YOU CAUGHT ME.
TEE HEE ♡

Chapter 27 The Charm-Sorcerer

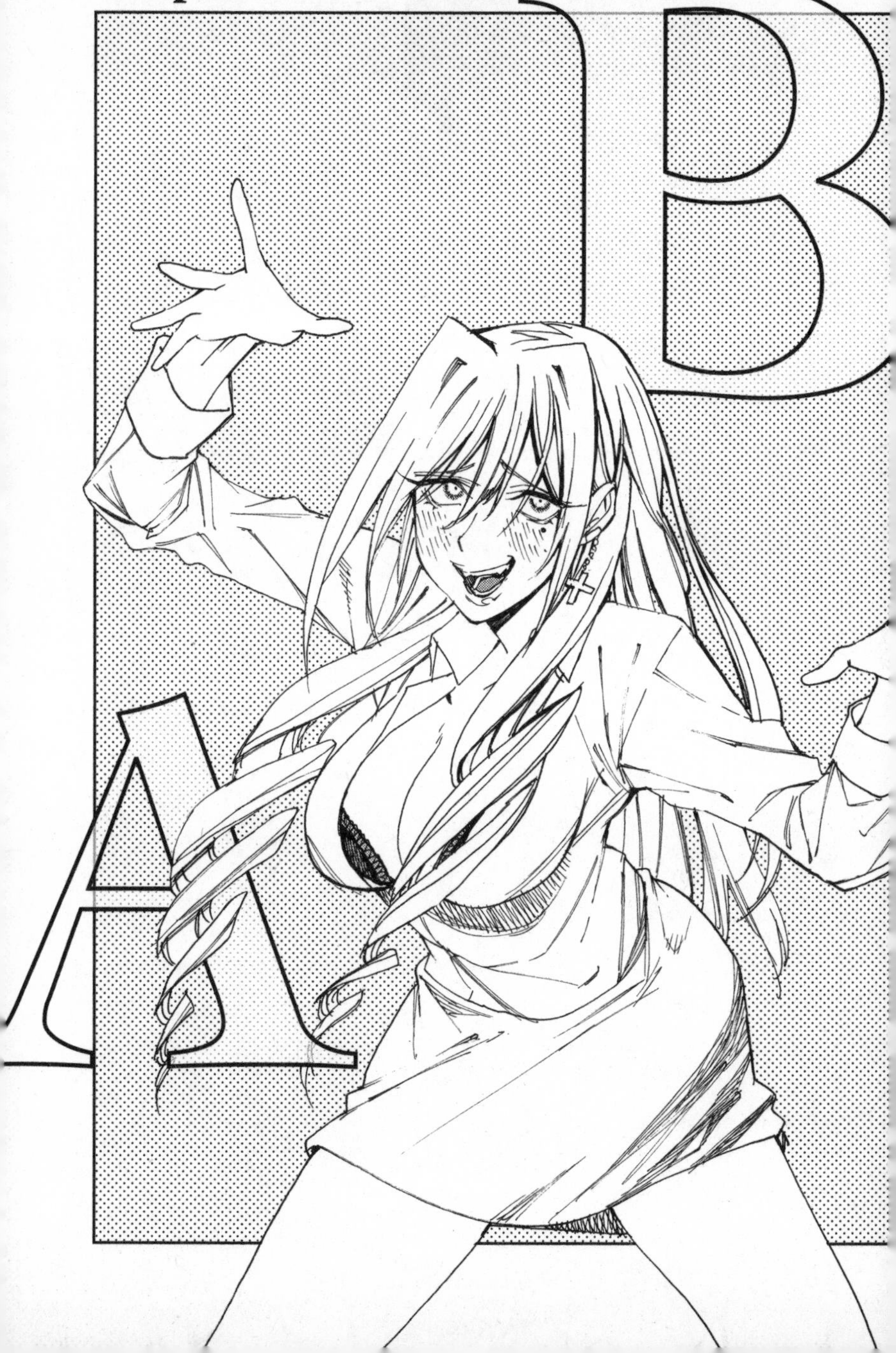

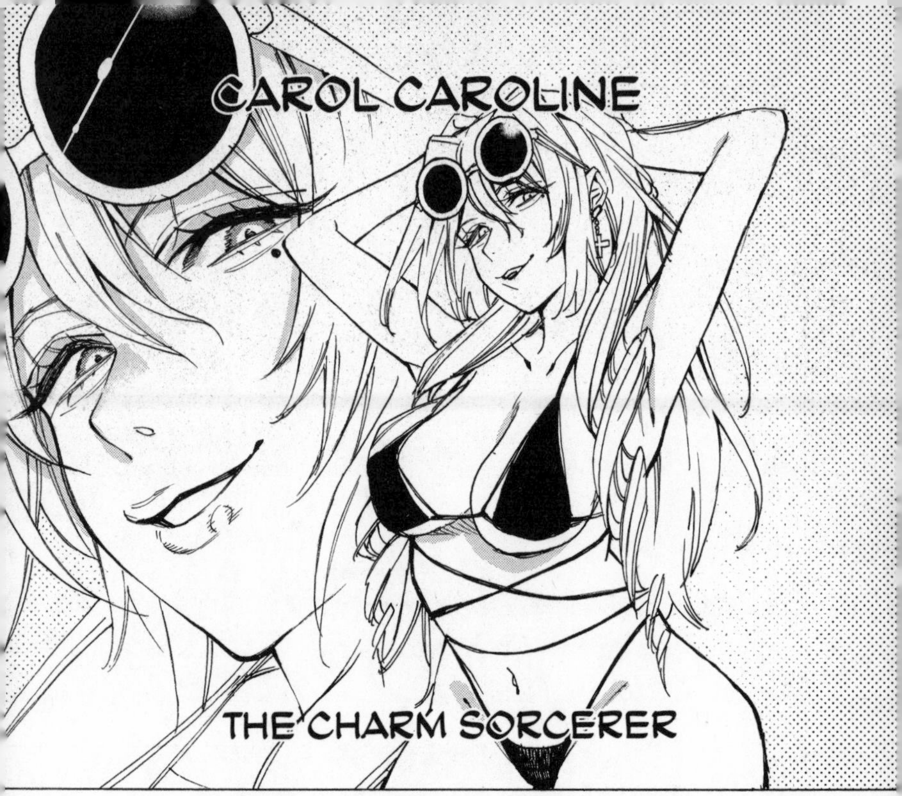
CAROL CAROLINE
THE CHARM SORCERER

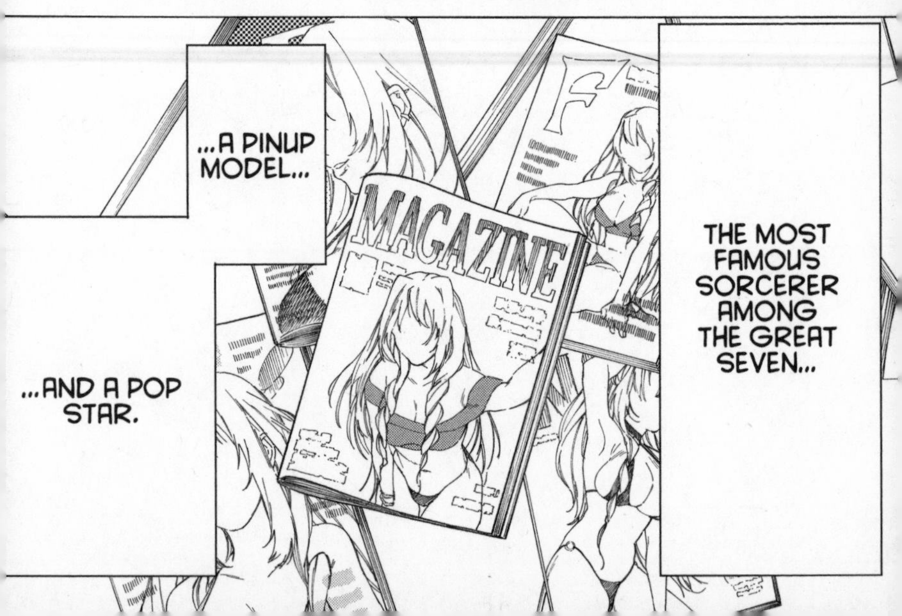
THE MOST FAMOUS SORCERER AMONG THE GREAT SEVEN...
...A PINUP MODEL...
MAGAZINE
...AND A POP STAR.

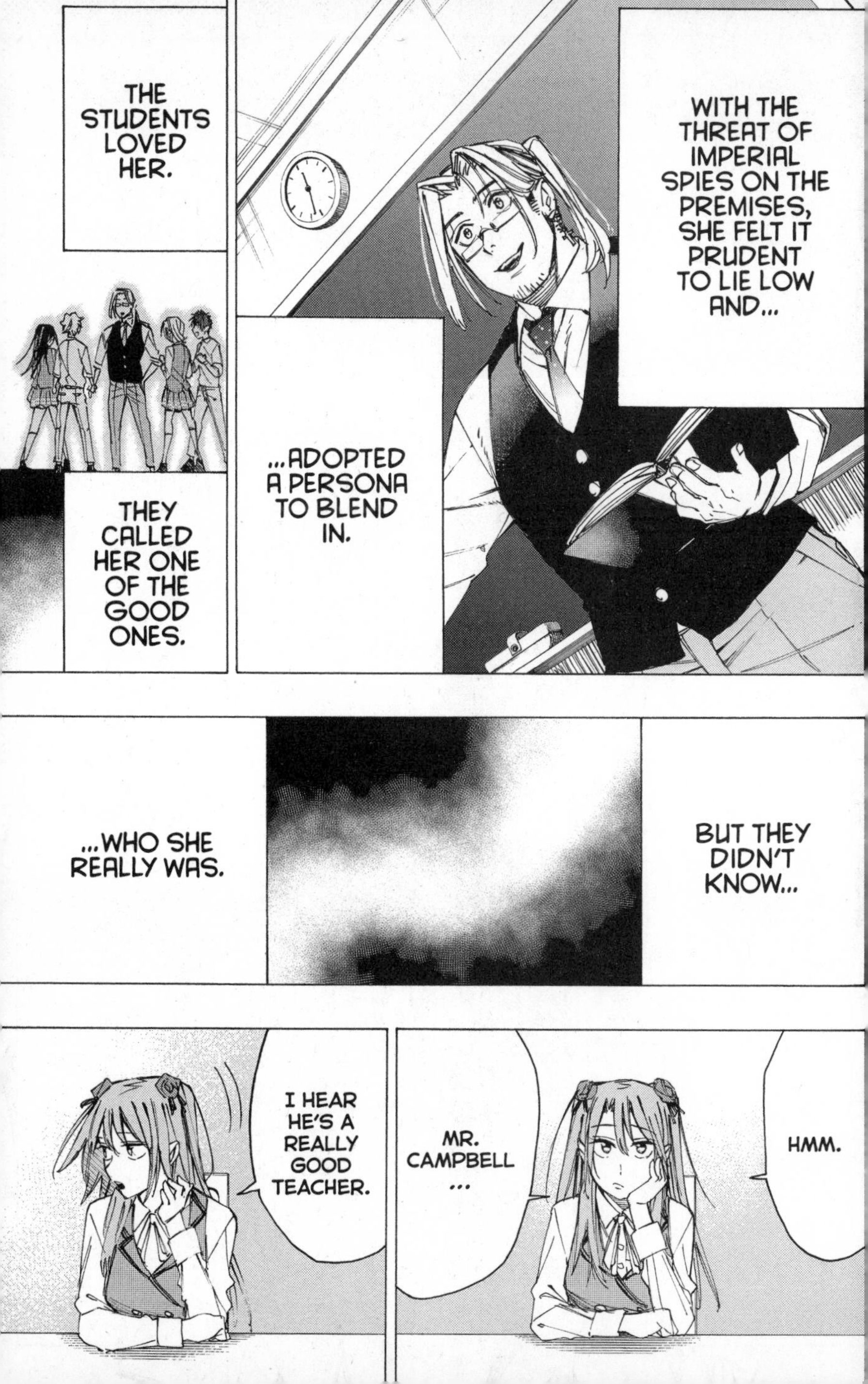
WITH THE THREAT OF IMPERIAL SPIES ON THE PREMISES, SHE FELT IT PRUDENT TO LIE LOW AND...
...ADOPTED A PERSONA TO BLEND IN.
THE STUDENTS LOVED HER.
THEY CALLED HER ONE OF THE GOOD ONES.
BUT THEY DIDN'T KNOW...
...WHO SHE REALLY WAS.
HMM.
MR. CAMPBELL ...
I HEAR HE'S A REALLY GOOD TEACHER.

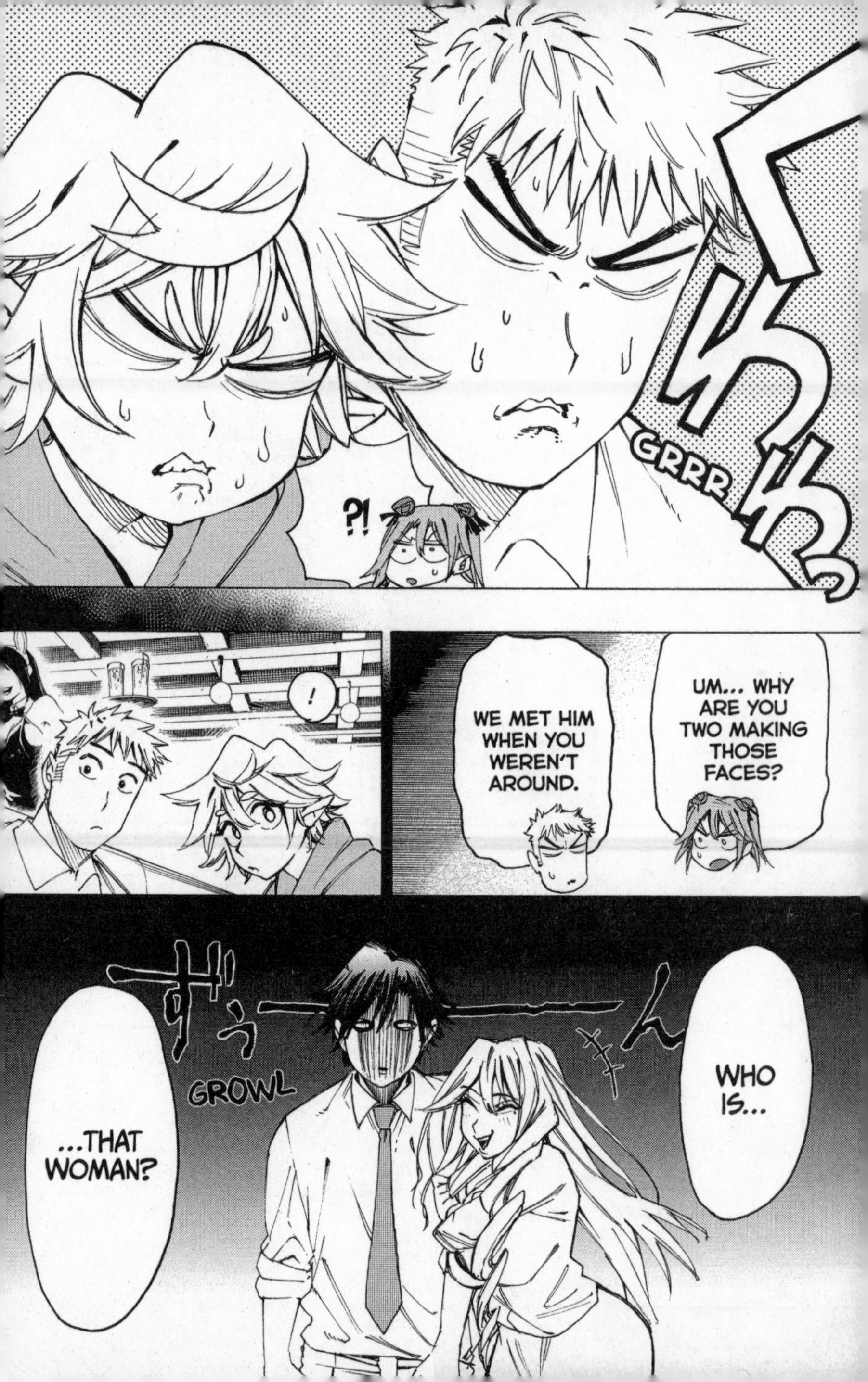
GRRR
?!
UM... WHY ARE YOU TWO MAKING THOSE FACES?
WE MET HIM WHEN YOU WEREN'T AROUND.
!
WHO IS...
GROWL
...THAT WOMAN?

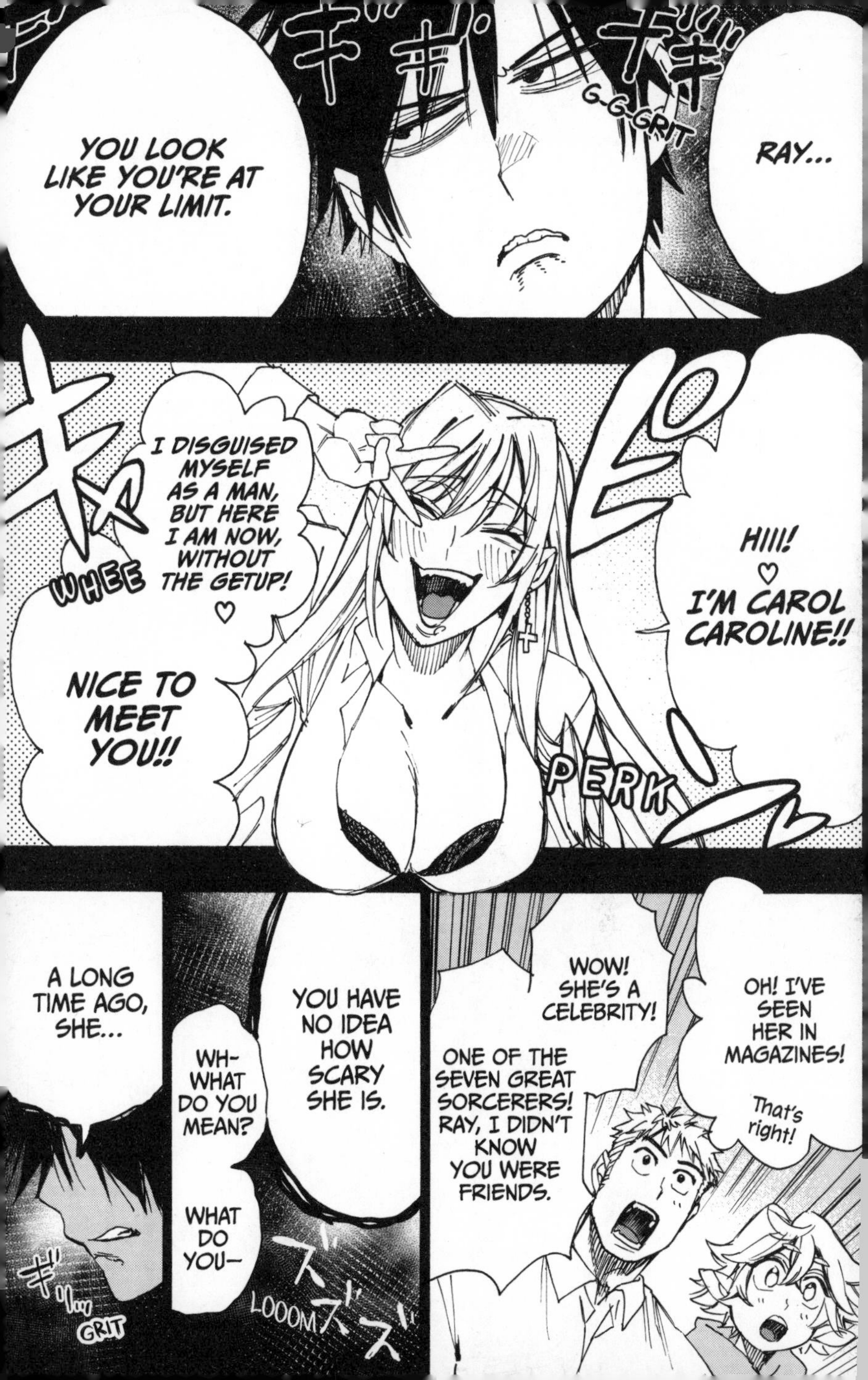
RAY...
G-G-GRIT
YOU LOOK LIKE YOU'RE AT YOUR LIMIT.
HIII! ♡ I'M CAROL CAROLINE!!
PERK
I DISGUISED MYSELF AS A MAN, BUT HERE I AM NOW, WITHOUT THE GETUP! ♡
WHEE
NICE TO MEET YOU!!
OH! I'VE SEEN HER IN MAGAZINES!
That's right!
WOW! SHE'S A CELEBRITY!
ONE OF THE SEVEN GREAT SORCERERS! RAY, I DIDN'T KNOW YOU WERE FRIENDS.
YOU HAVE NO IDEA HOW SCARY SHE IS.
WH- WHAT DO YOU MEAN?
WHAT DO YOU–
LOOOM
A LONG TIME AGO, SHE...
GRIT

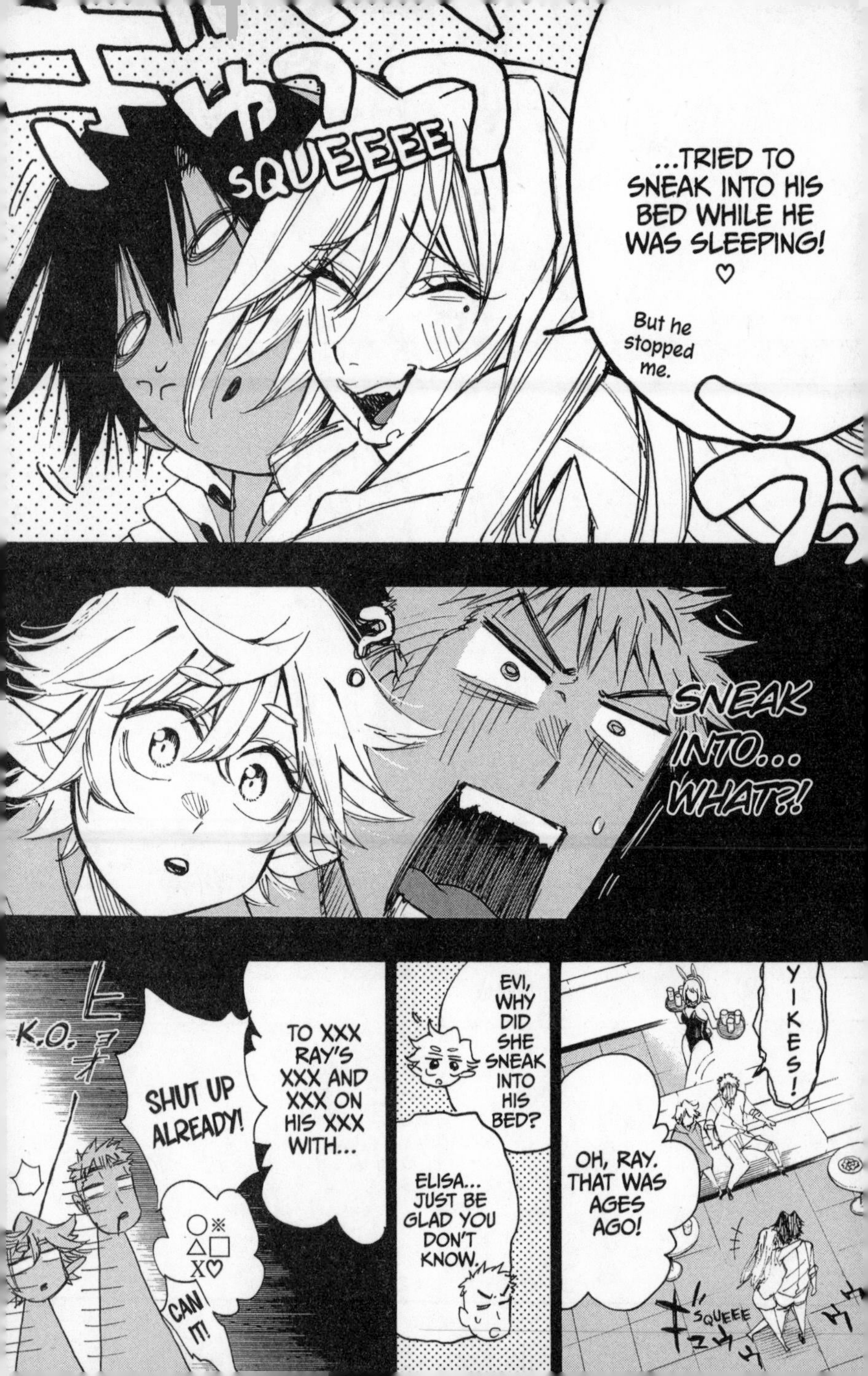
SQUEEEE
...TRIED TO SNEAK INTO HIS BED WHILE HE WAS SLEEPING! ♡
But he stopped me.
SNEAK INTO... WHAT?!
YIKES!
OH, RAY. THAT WAS AGES AGO!
SQUEEE
EVI, WHY DID SHE SNEAK INTO HIS BED?
ELISA... JUST BE GLAD YOU DON'T KNOW.
TO XXX RAY'S XXX AND XXX ON HIS XXX WITH...
SHUT UP ALREADY!
○※△□X♡
CAN IT!
K.O.

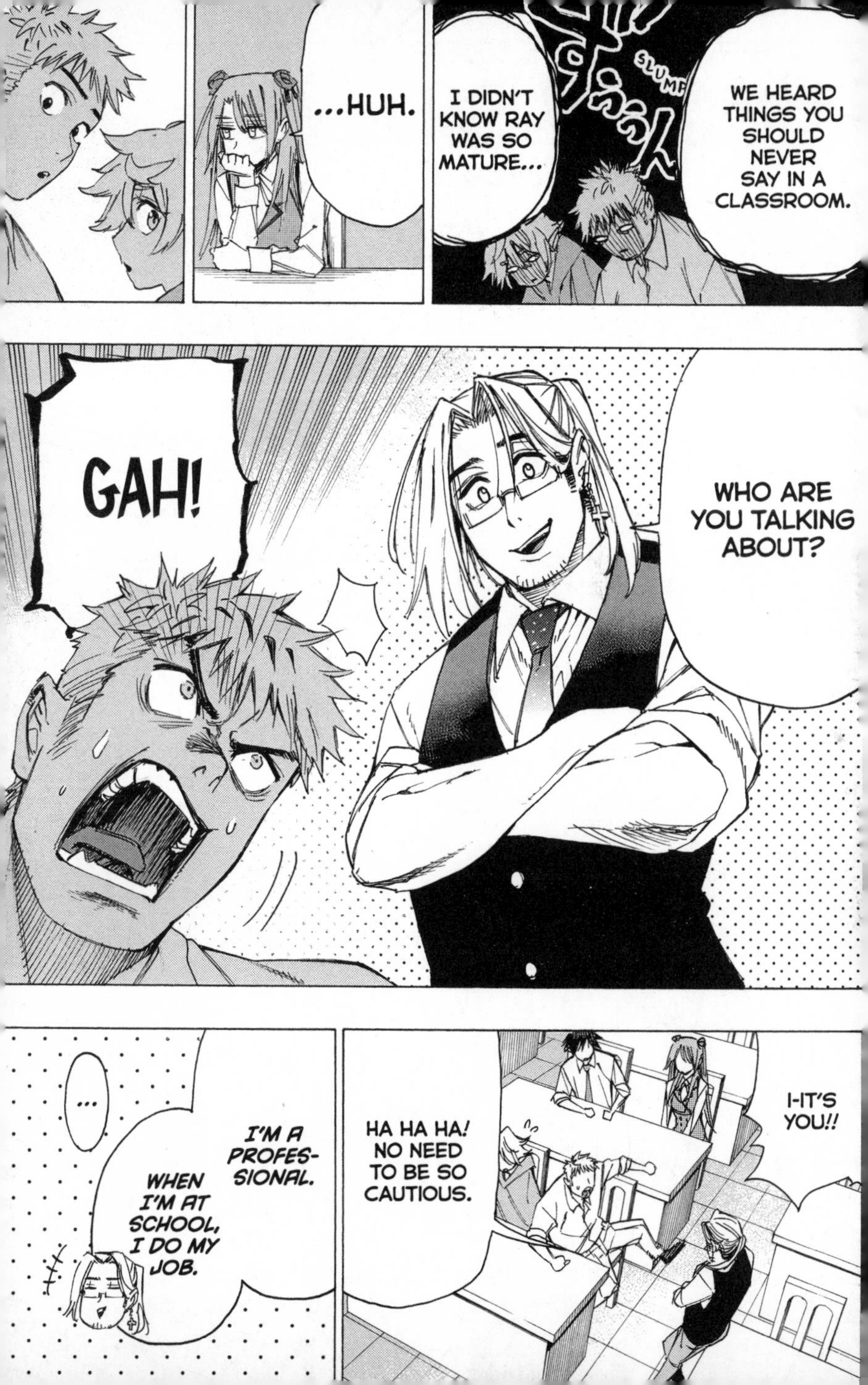
WE HEARD THINGS YOU SHOULD NEVER SAY IN A CLASSROOM.
SLUMP
I DIDN'T KNOW RAY WAS SO MATURE...
...HUH.
WHO ARE YOU TALKING ABOUT?
GAH!
I-IT'S YOU!!
HA HA HA! NO NEED TO BE SO CAUTIOUS.
I'M A PROFES-SIONAL.
WHEN I'M AT SCHOOL, I DO MY JOB.
...

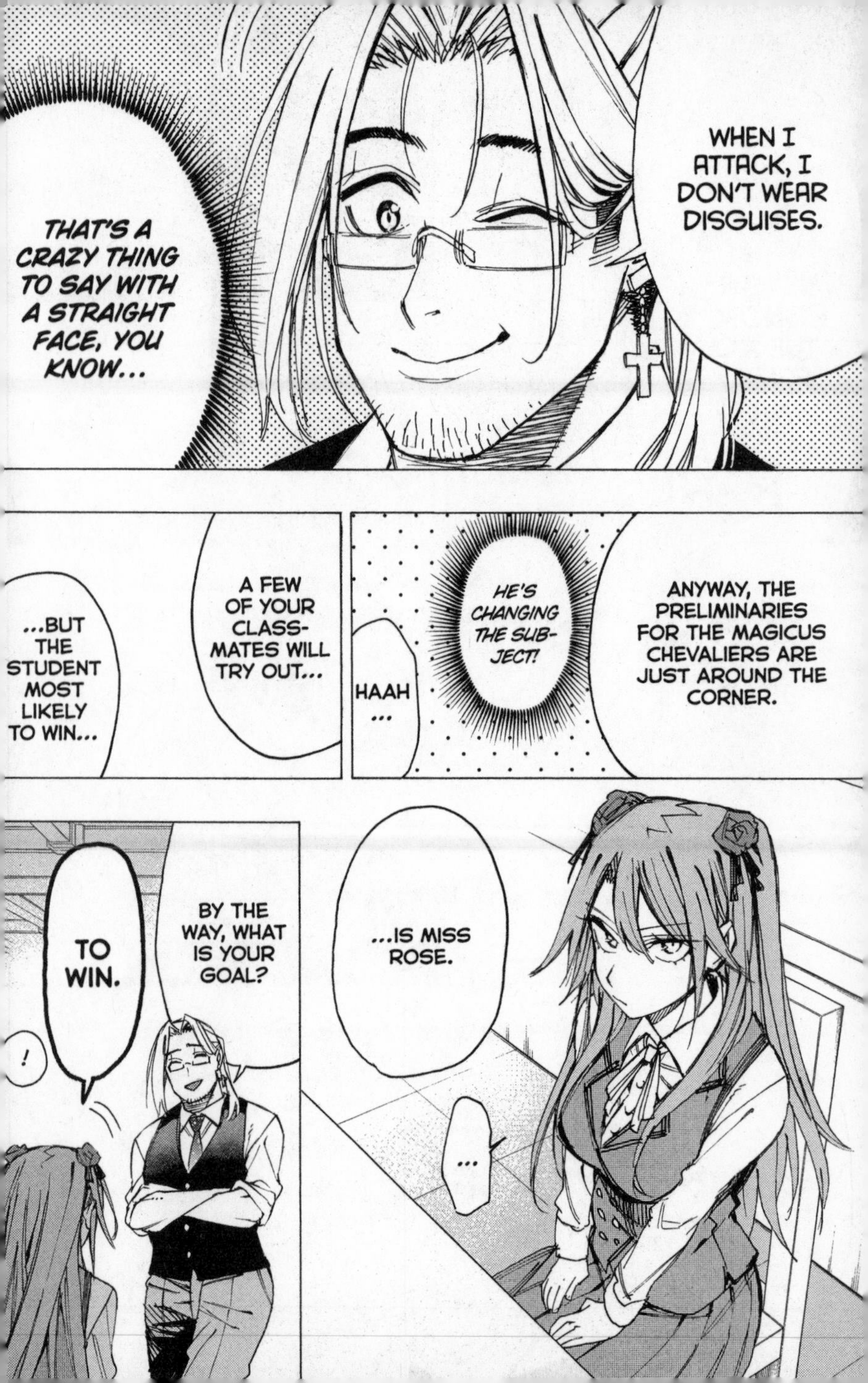
WHEN I ATTACK, I DON'T WEAR DISGUISES.
THAT'S A CRAZY THING TO SAY WITH A STRAIGHT FACE, YOU KNOW...
ANYWAY, THE PRELIMINARIES FOR THE MAGICUS CHEVALIERS ARE JUST AROUND THE CORNER.
HE'S CHANGING THE SUB-JECT!
HAAH...
A FEW OF YOUR CLASS-MATES WILL TRY OUT...
...BUT THE STUDENT MOST LIKELY TO WIN...
...IS MISS ROSE.
...
BY THE WAY, WHAT IS YOUR GOAL?
TO WIN.
!

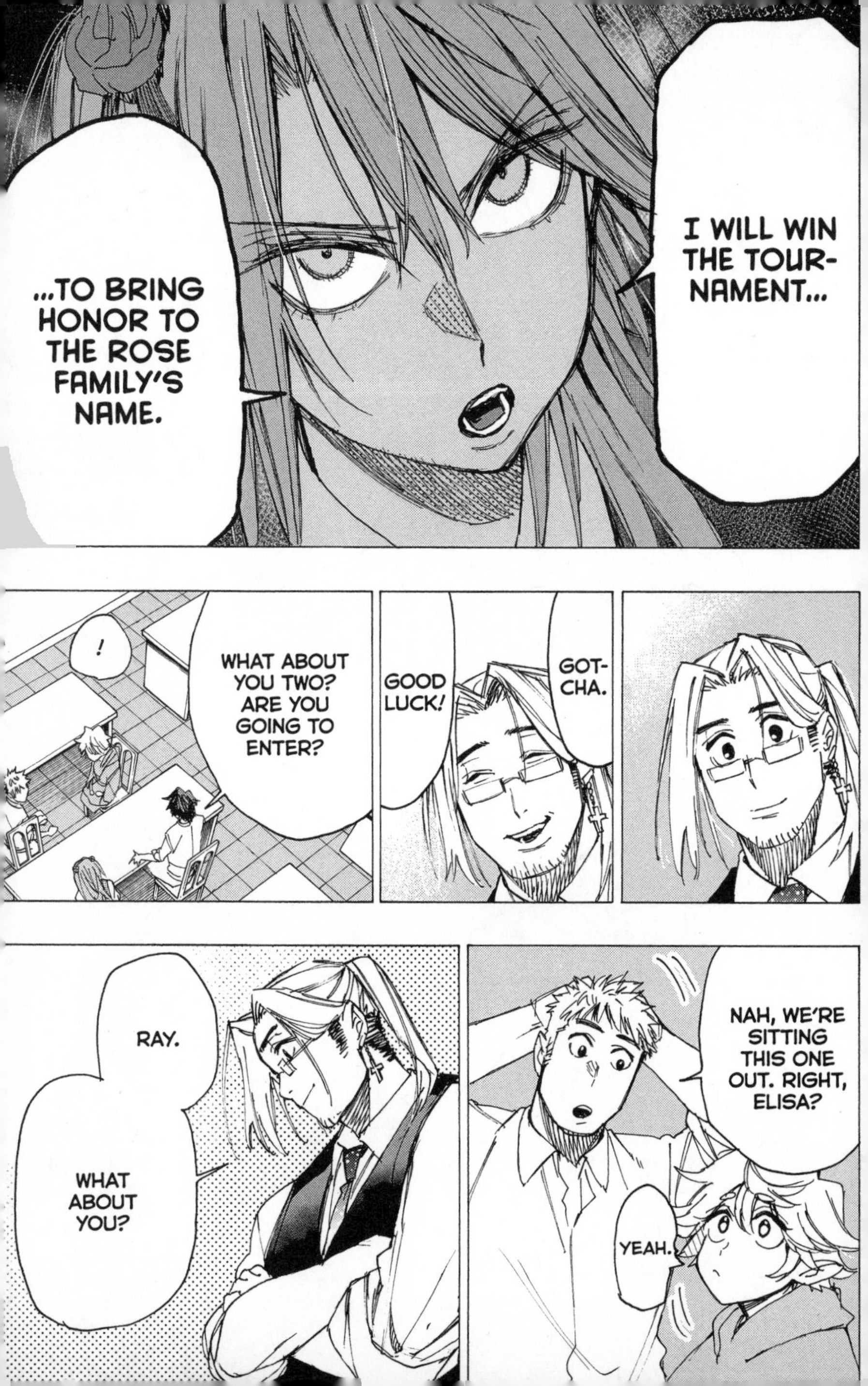
I WILL WIN THE TOUR-NAMENT...
...TO BRING HONOR TO THE ROSE FAMILY'S NAME.
GOT-CHA.
GOOD LUCK!
WHAT ABOUT YOU TWO? ARE YOU GOING TO ENTER?
!
NAH, WE'RE SITTING THIS ONE OUT. RIGHT, ELISA?
YEAH.
RAY.
WHAT ABOUT YOU?

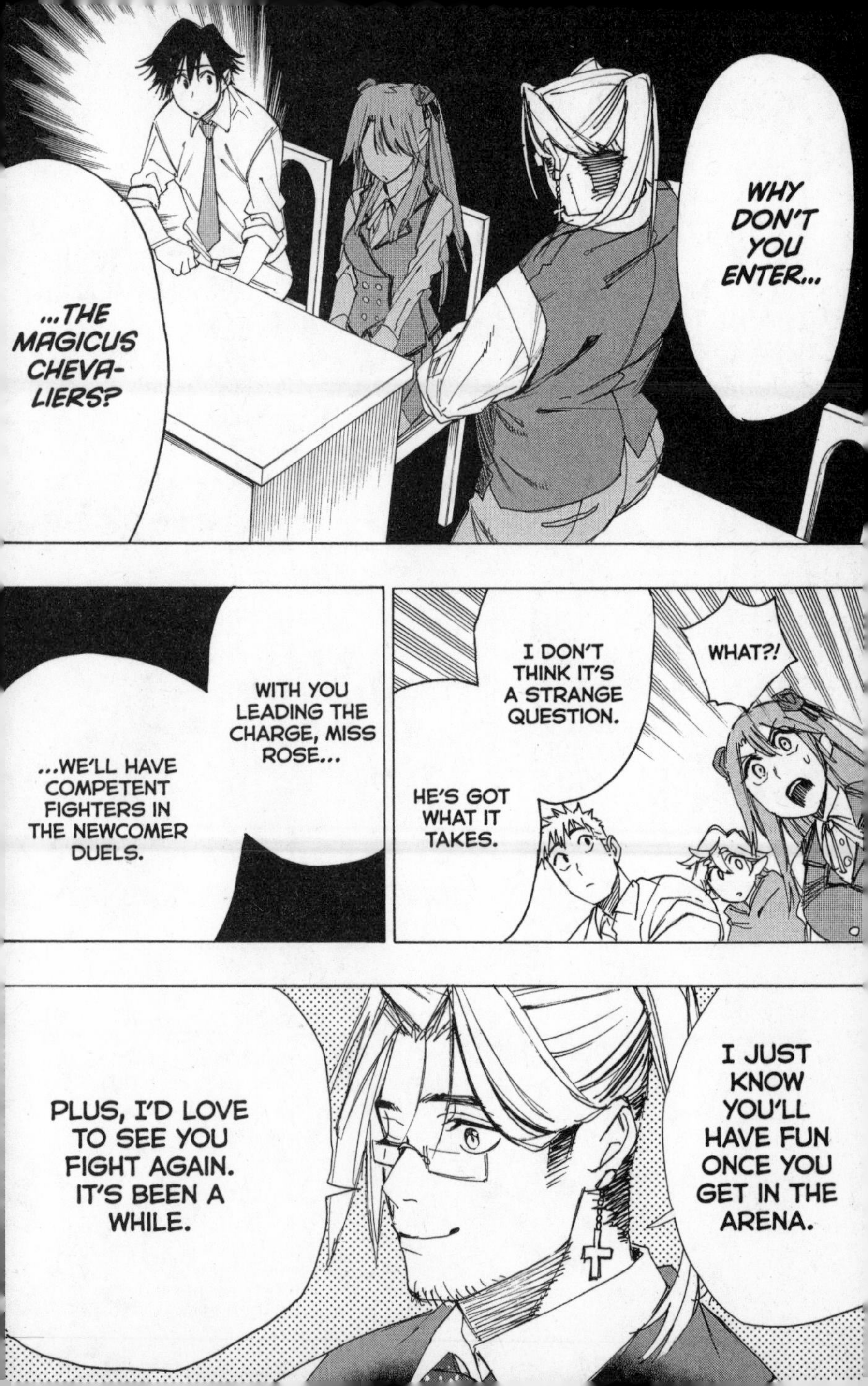
WHY DON'T YOU ENTER...
...THE MAGICUS CHEVALIERS?
WHAT?!
I DON'T THINK IT'S A STRANGE QUESTION.
HE'S GOT WHAT IT TAKES.
WITH YOU LEADING THE CHARGE, MISS ROSE...
...WE'LL HAVE COMPETENT FIGHTERS IN THE NEWCOMER DUELS.
I JUST KNOW YOU'LL HAVE FUN ONCE YOU GET IN THE ARENA.
PLUS, I'D LOVE TO SEE YOU FIGHT AGAIN. IT'S BEEN A WHILE.

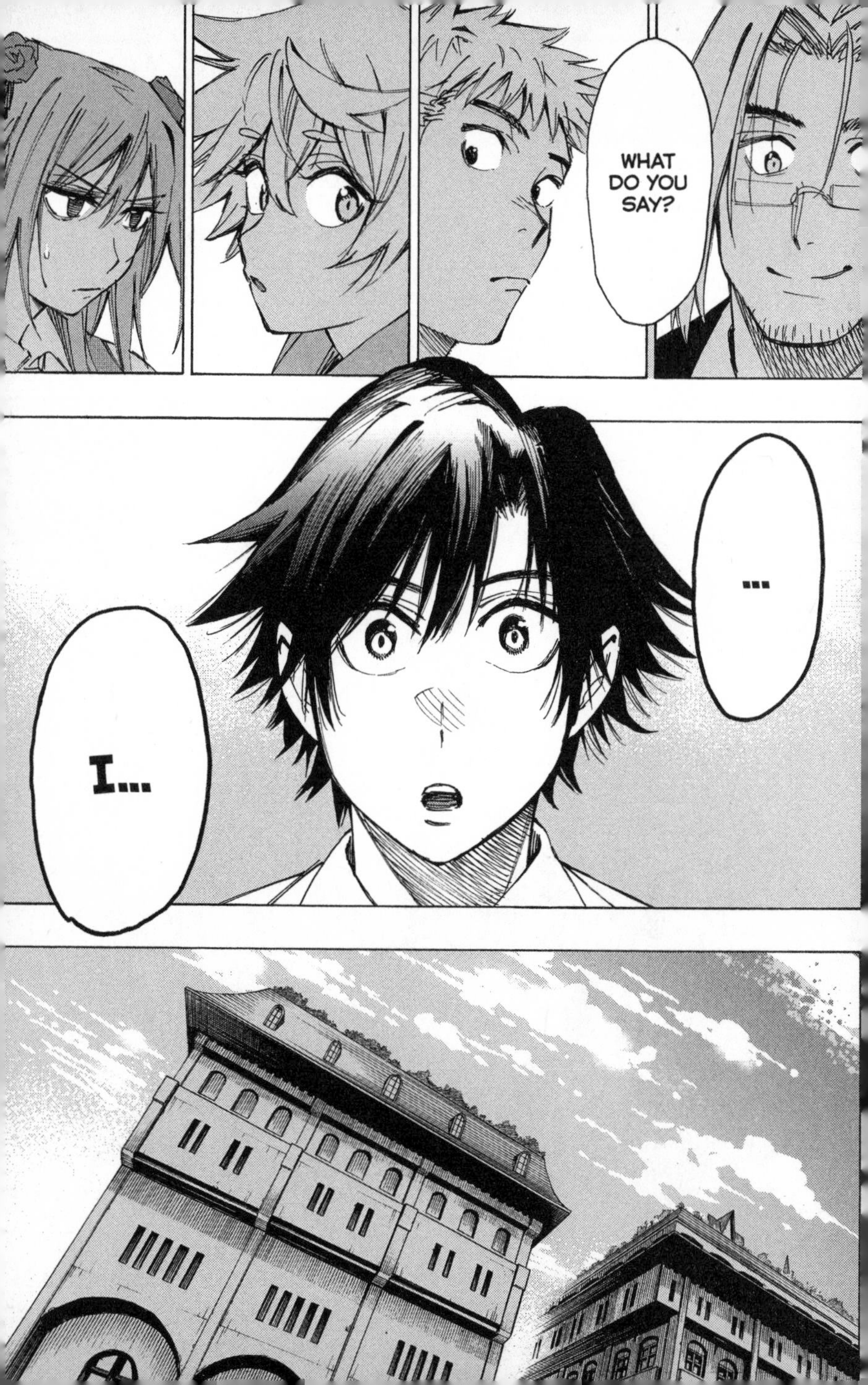
WHAT DO YOU SAY?
...
I...

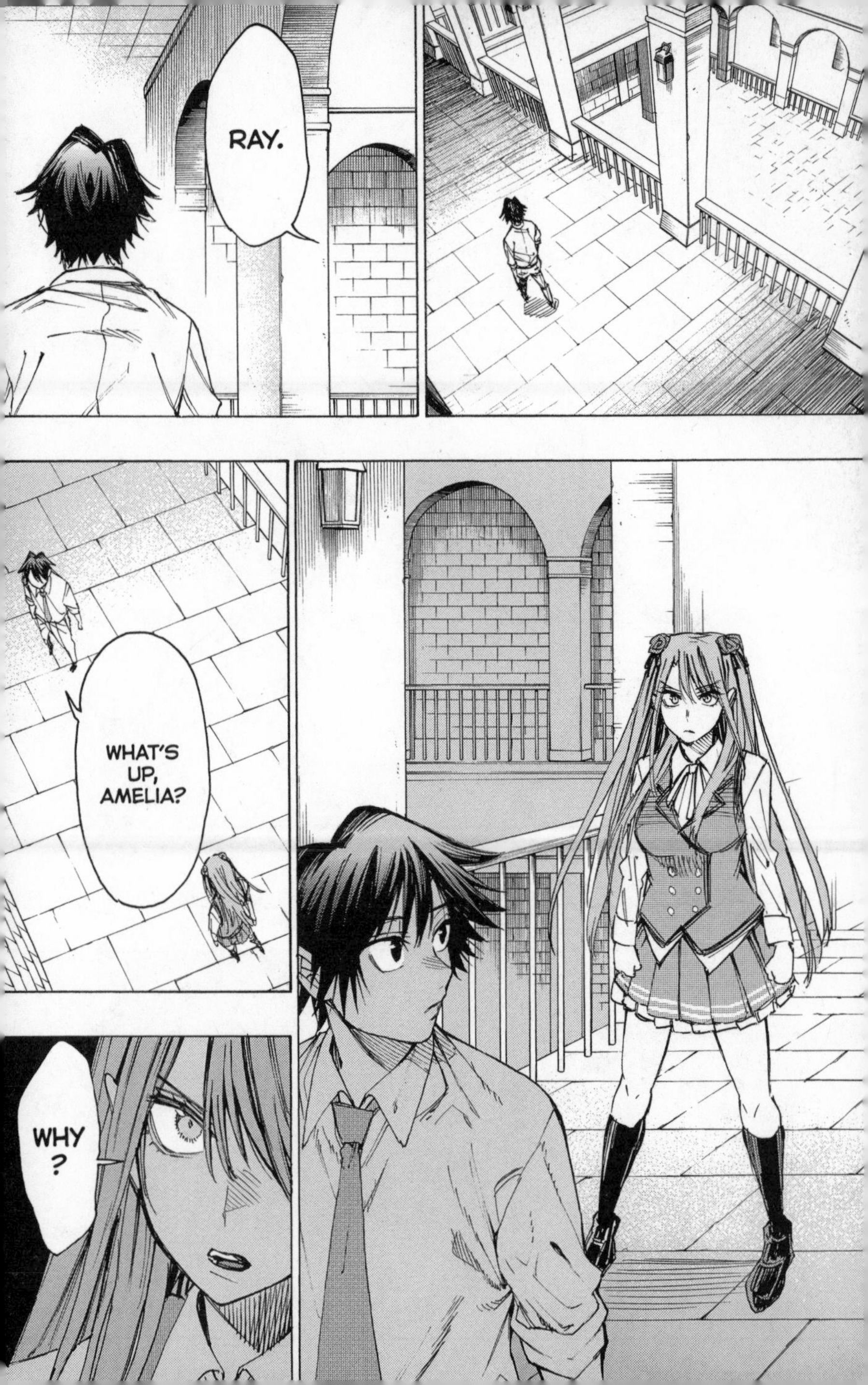
RAY.
WHAT'S UP, AMELIA?
WHY?

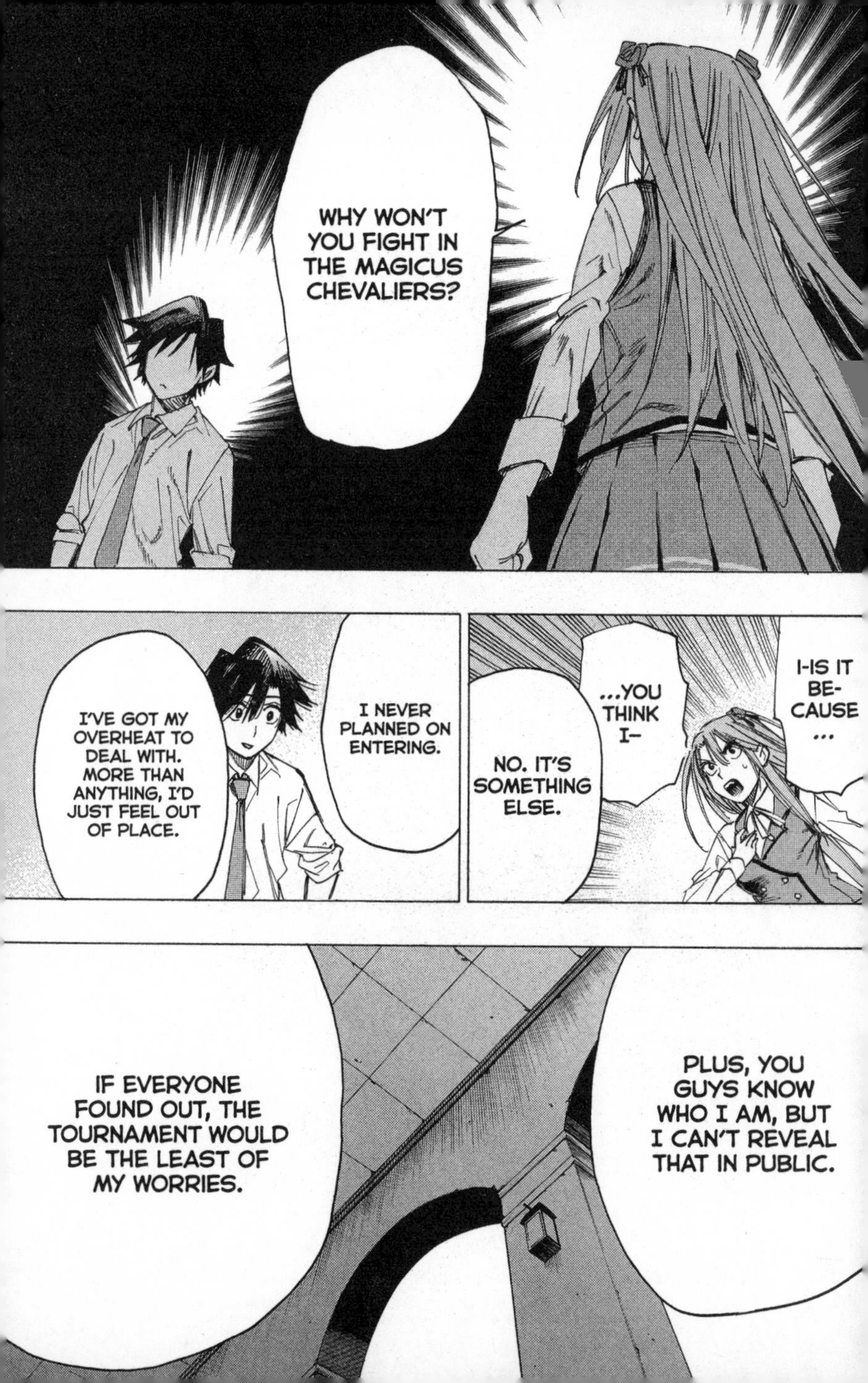
WHY WON'T YOU FIGHT IN THE MAGICUS CHEVALIERS?
I-IS IT BE-CAUSE ...
...YOU THINK I–
NO. IT'S SOMETHING ELSE.
I NEVER PLANNED ON ENTERING.
I'VE GOT MY OVERHEAT TO DEAL WITH. MORE THAN ANYTHING, I'D JUST FEEL OUT OF PLACE.
PLUS, YOU GUYS KNOW WHO I AM, BUT I CAN'T REVEAL THAT IN PUBLIC.
IF EVERYONE FOUND OUT, THE TOURNAMENT WOULD BE THE LEAST OF MY WORRIES.

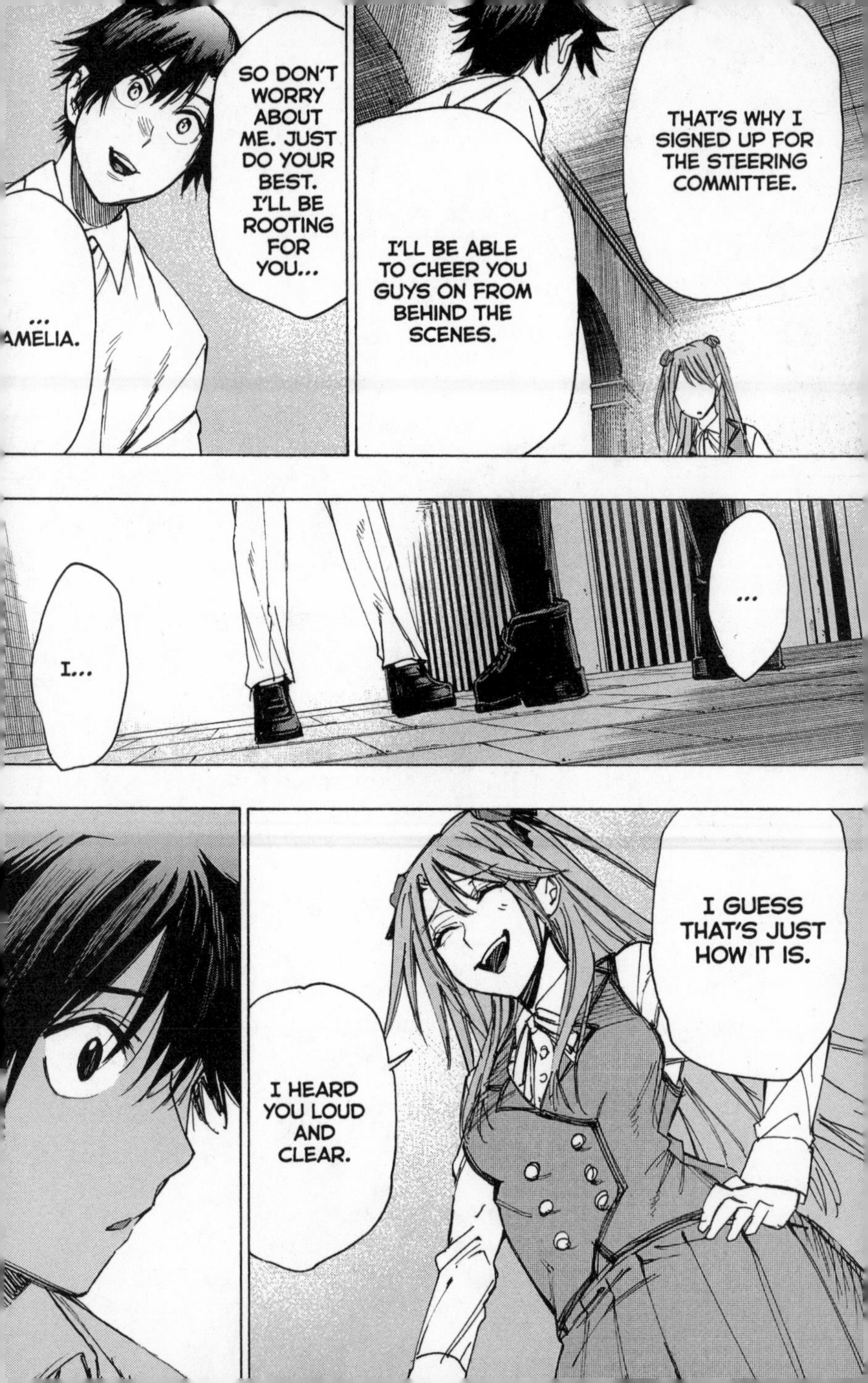
THAT'S WHY I SIGNED UP FOR THE STEERING COMMITTEE.
I'LL BE ABLE TO CHEER YOU GUYS ON FROM BEHIND THE SCENES.
SO DON'T WORRY ABOUT ME. JUST DO YOUR BEST. I'LL BE ROOTING FOR YOU...
... AMELIA.
...
I...
I GUESS THAT'S JUST HOW IT IS.
I HEARD YOU LOUD AND CLEAR.

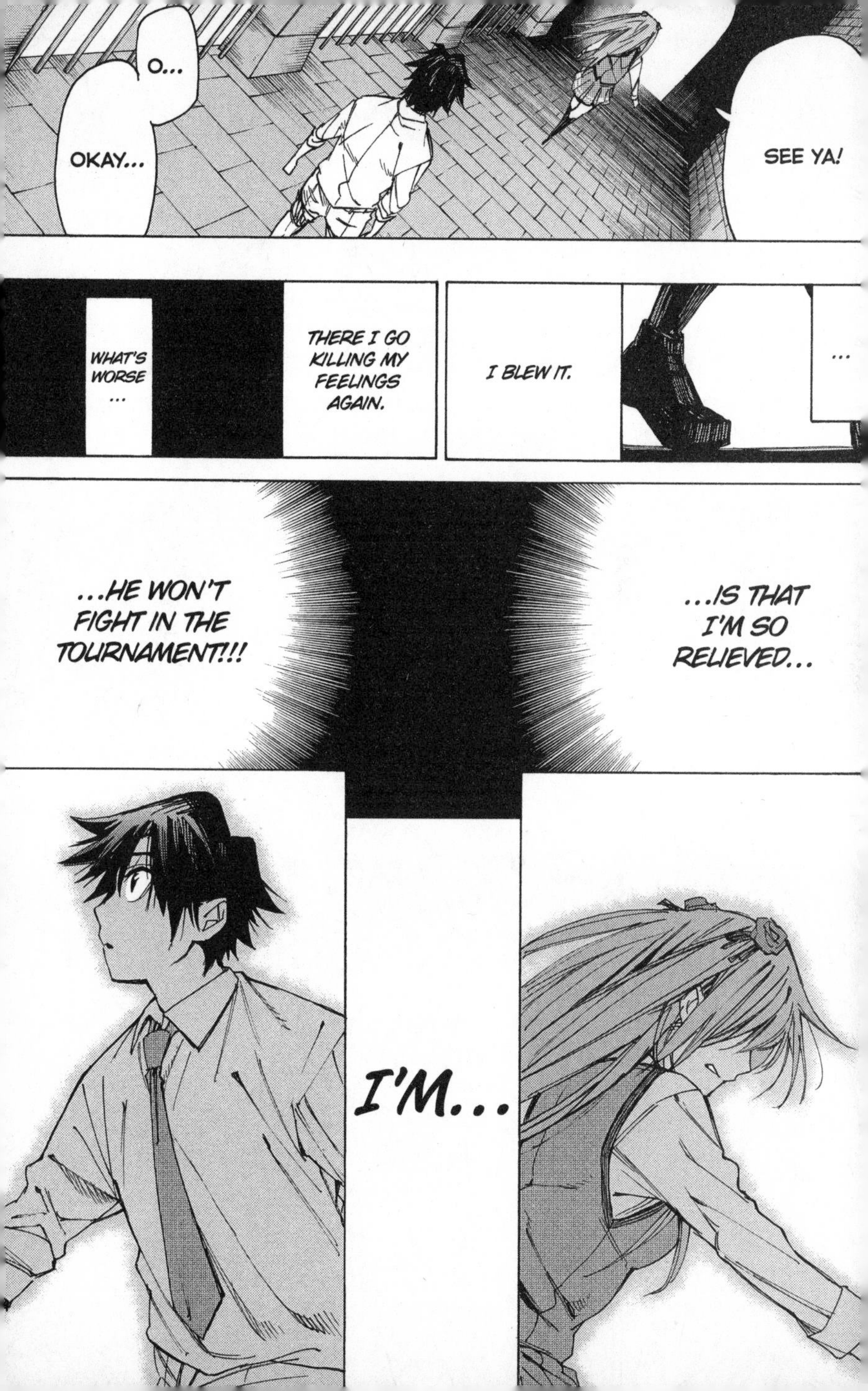
SEE YA!
O... OKAY...
...
I BLEW IT.
THERE I GO KILLING MY FEELINGS AGAIN.
WHAT'S WORSE ...
...IS THAT I'M SO RELIEVED...
...HE WON'T FIGHT IN THE TOURNAMENT!!!
I'M...

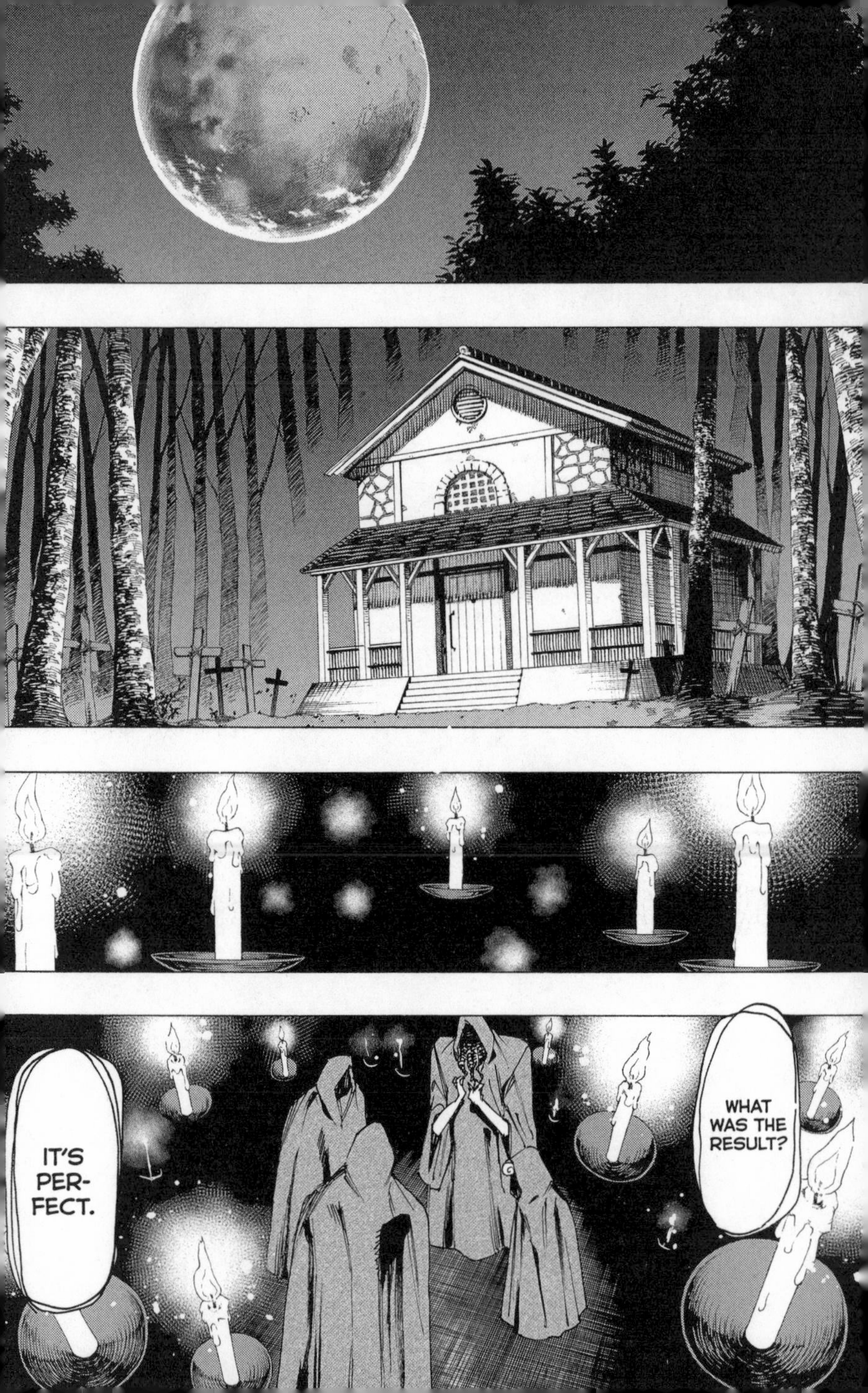
WHAT WAS THE RESULT?
IT'S PER- FECT.

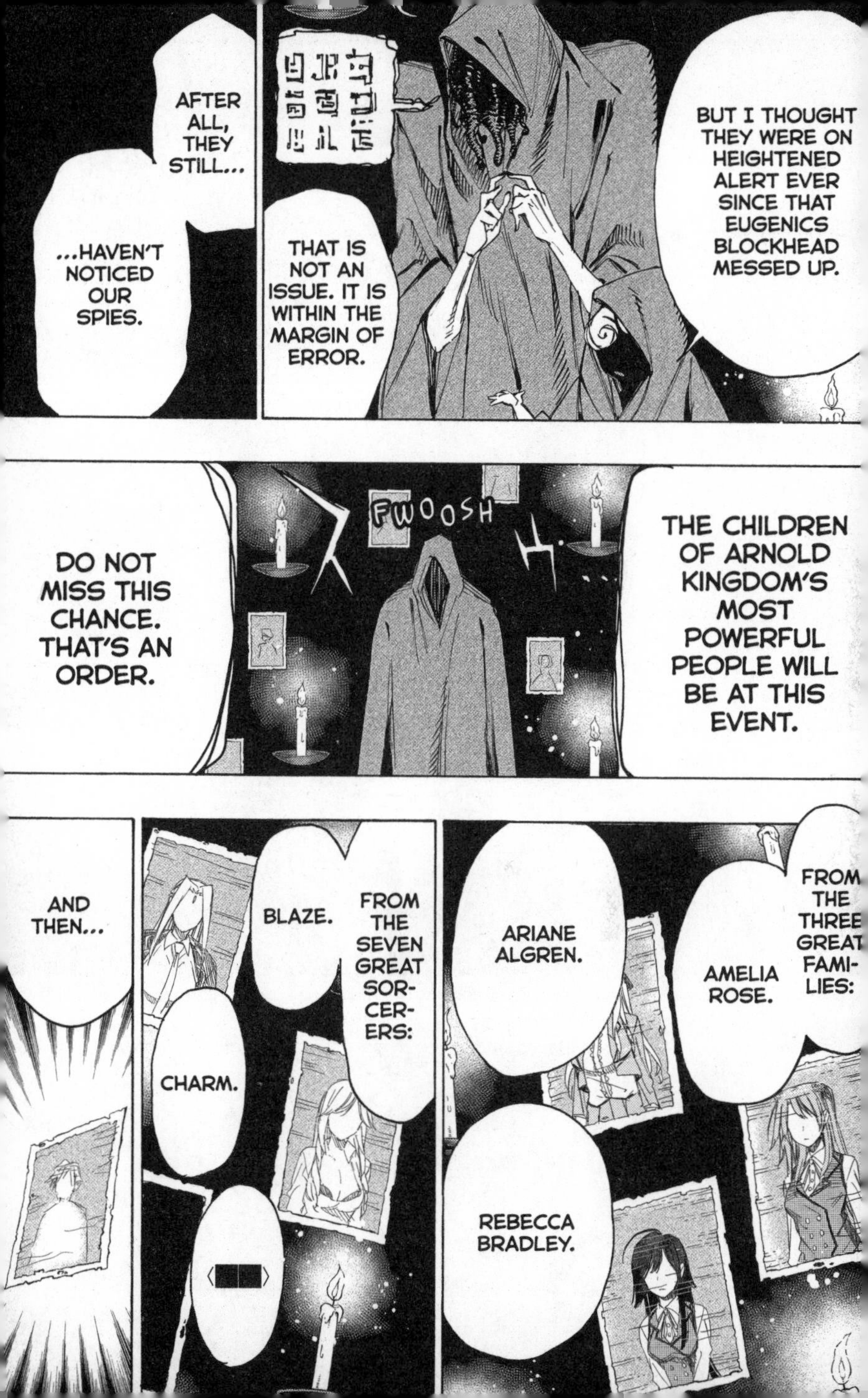
BUT I THOUGHT THEY WERE ON HEIGHTENED ALERT EVER SINCE THAT EUGENICS BLOCKHEAD MESSED UP.
THAT IS NOT AN ISSUE. IT IS WITHIN THE MARGIN OF ERROR.
AFTER ALL, THEY STILL...
...HAVEN'T NOTICED OUR SPIES.
THE CHILDREN OF ARNOLD KINGDOM'S MOST POWERFUL PEOPLE WILL BE AT THIS EVENT.
FWOOSH
DO NOT MISS THIS CHANCE. THAT'S AN ORDER.
FROM THE THREE GREAT FAMILIES:
AMELIA ROSE.
ARIANE ALGREN.
REBECCA BRADLEY.
FROM THE SEVEN GREAT SORCERERS:
BLAZE.
CHARM.
〈[redacted]〉
AND THEN...

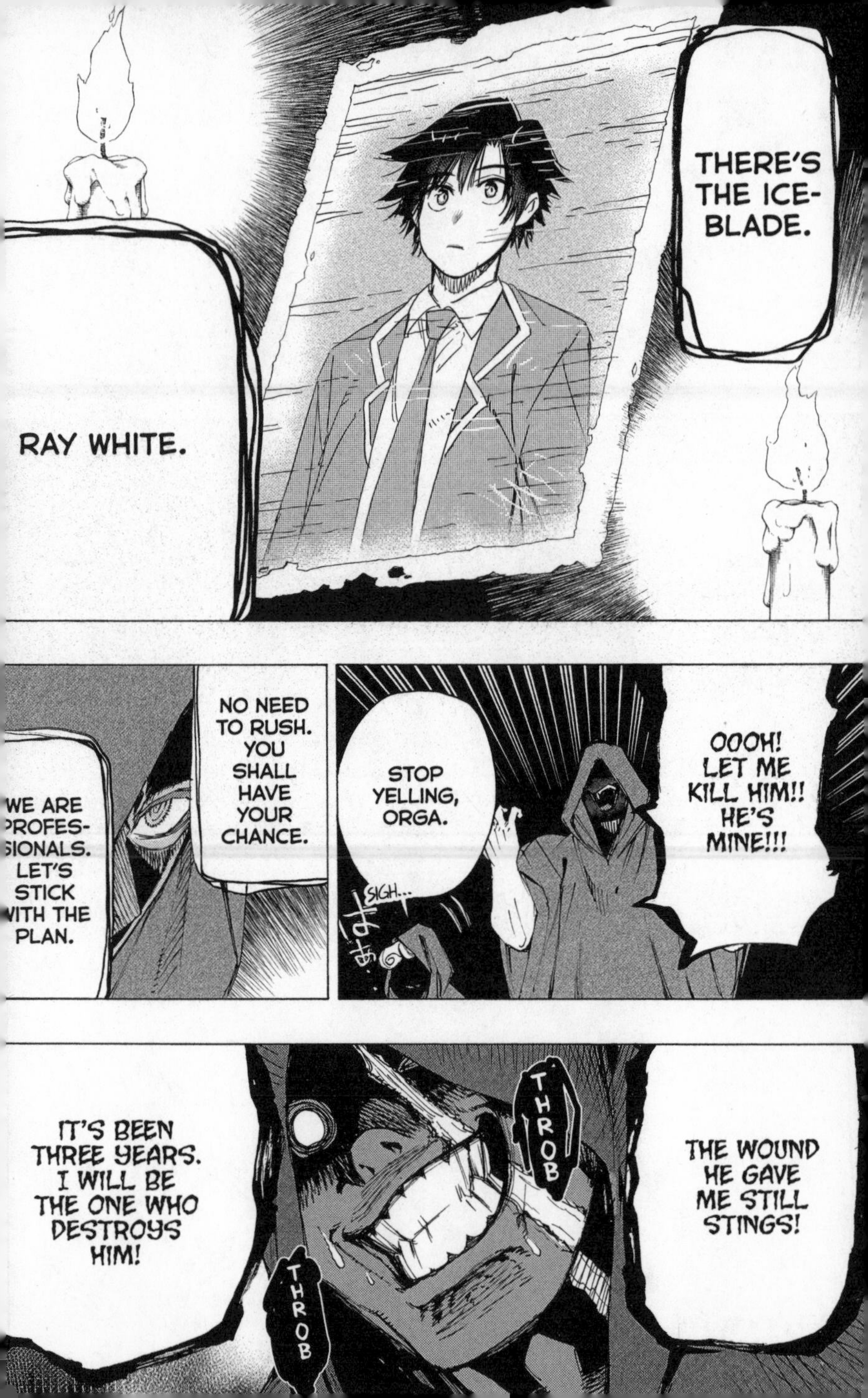
THERE'S THE ICE-BLADE.
RAY WHITE.
OOOH! LET ME KILL HIM!! HE'S MINE!!!
STOP YELLING, ORGA.
SIGH...
NO NEED TO RUSH. YOU SHALL HAVE YOUR CHANCE.
WE ARE PROFES-SIONALS. LET'S STICK WITH THE PLAN.
THE WOUND HE GAVE ME STILL STINGS!
THROB
IT'S BEEN THREE YEARS. I WILL BE THE ONE WHO DESTROYS HIM!
THROB

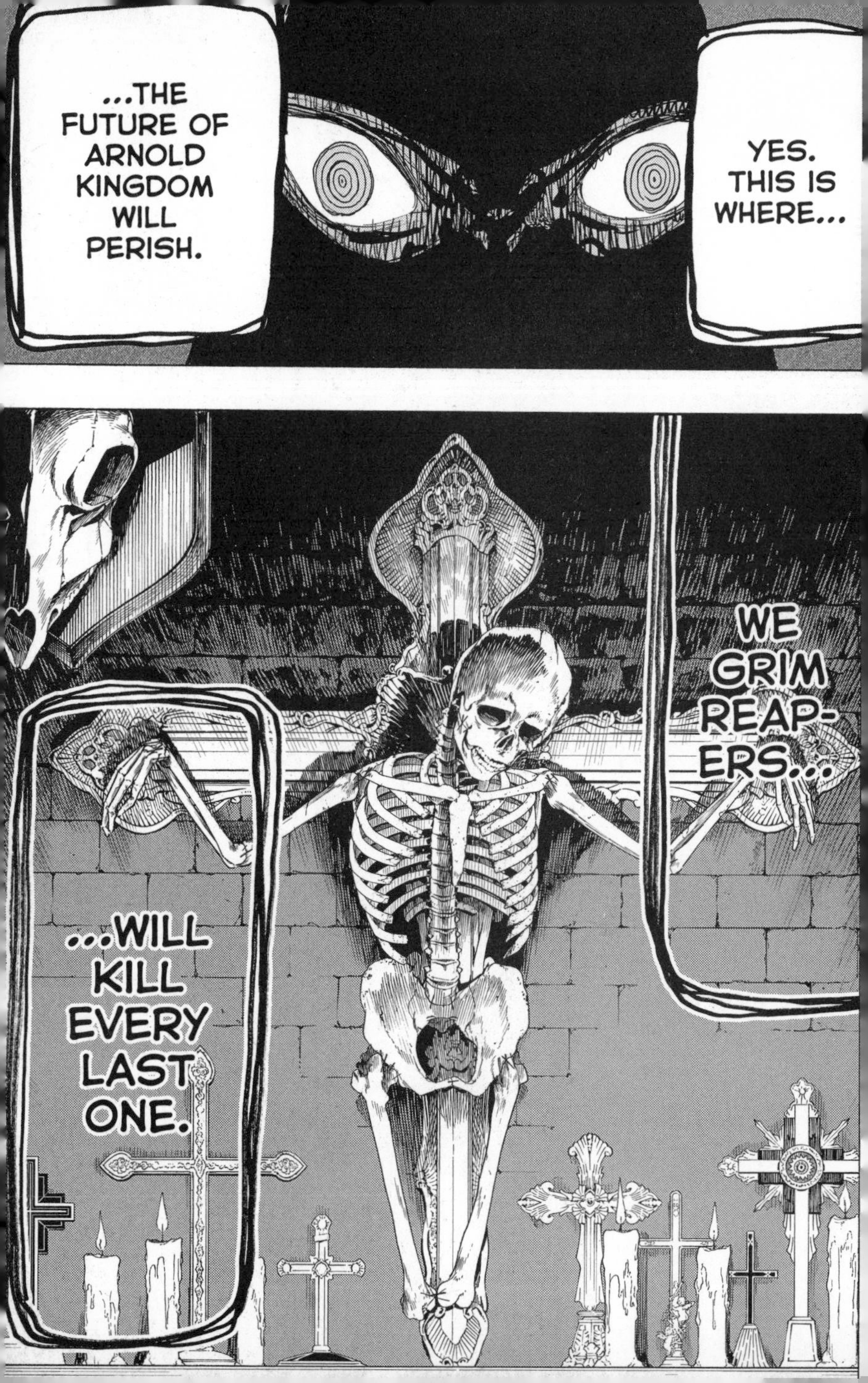
YES. THIS IS WHERE...
...THE FUTURE OF ARNOLD KINGDOM WILL PERISH.
WE GRIM REAPERS...
...WILL KILL EVERY LAST ONE.

The
ICEBLADE
SORCERER
Shall RULE
the
WORLD

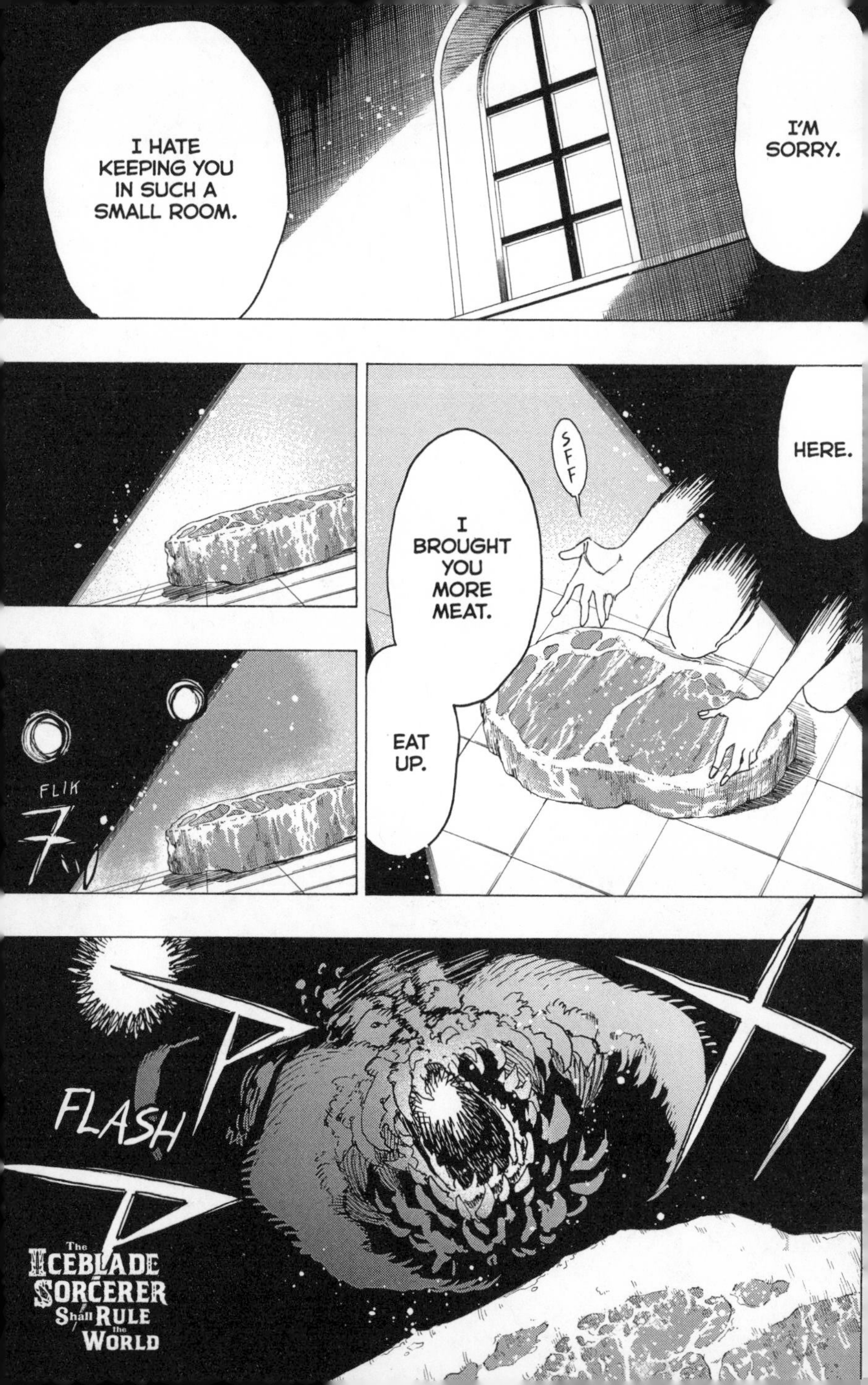
I'M SORRY.
I HATE KEEPING YOU IN SUCH A SMALL ROOM.
HERE.
SFF
I BROUGHT YOU MORE MEAT.
EAT UP.
FLIK
FLASH
The ICEBLADE SORCERER Shall RULE the WORLD

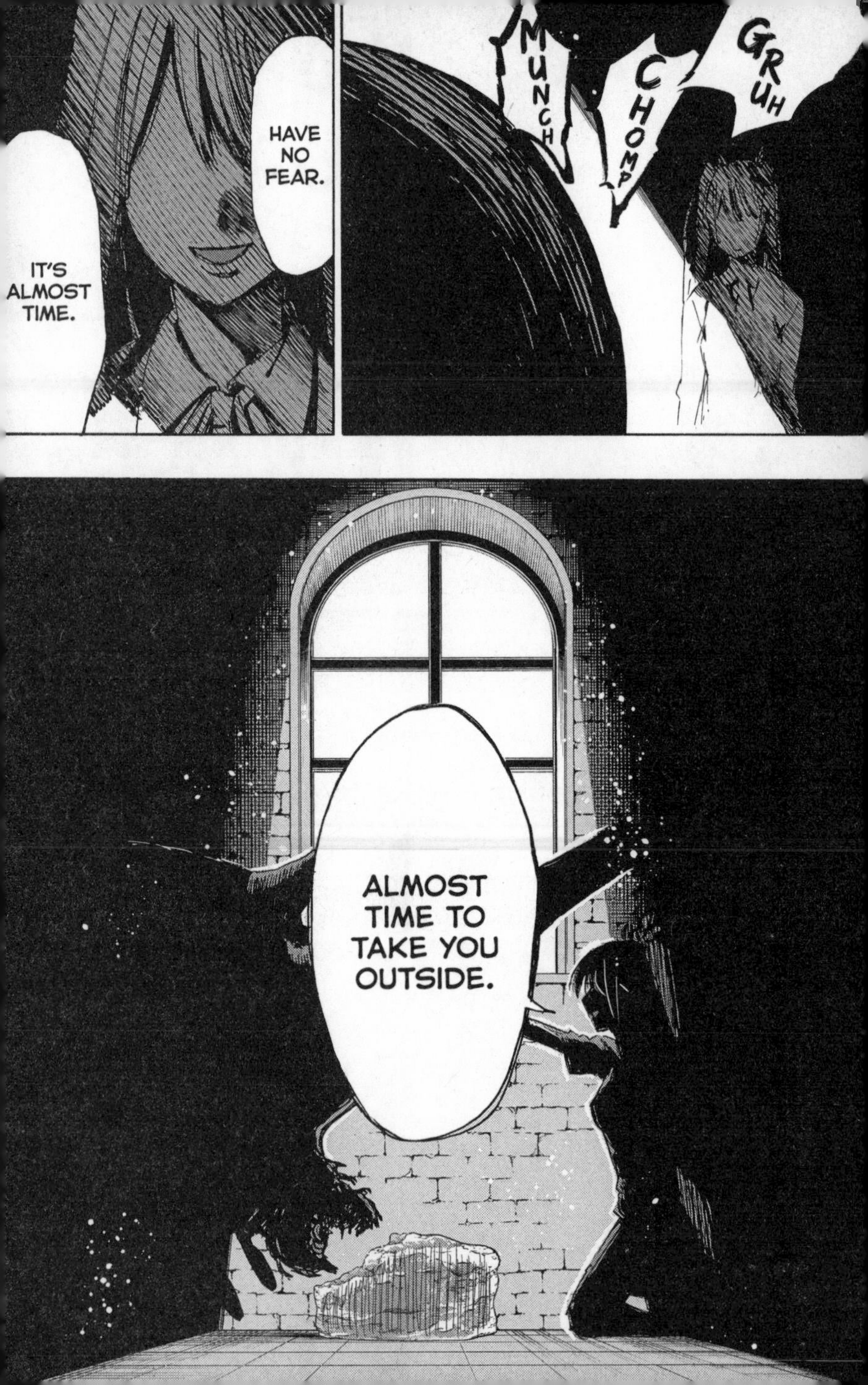
GRUH
CHOMP
MUNCH
HAVE NO FEAR.
IT'S ALMOST TIME.
ALMOST TIME TO TAKE YOU OUTSIDE.

SIGN: ICEBLADE

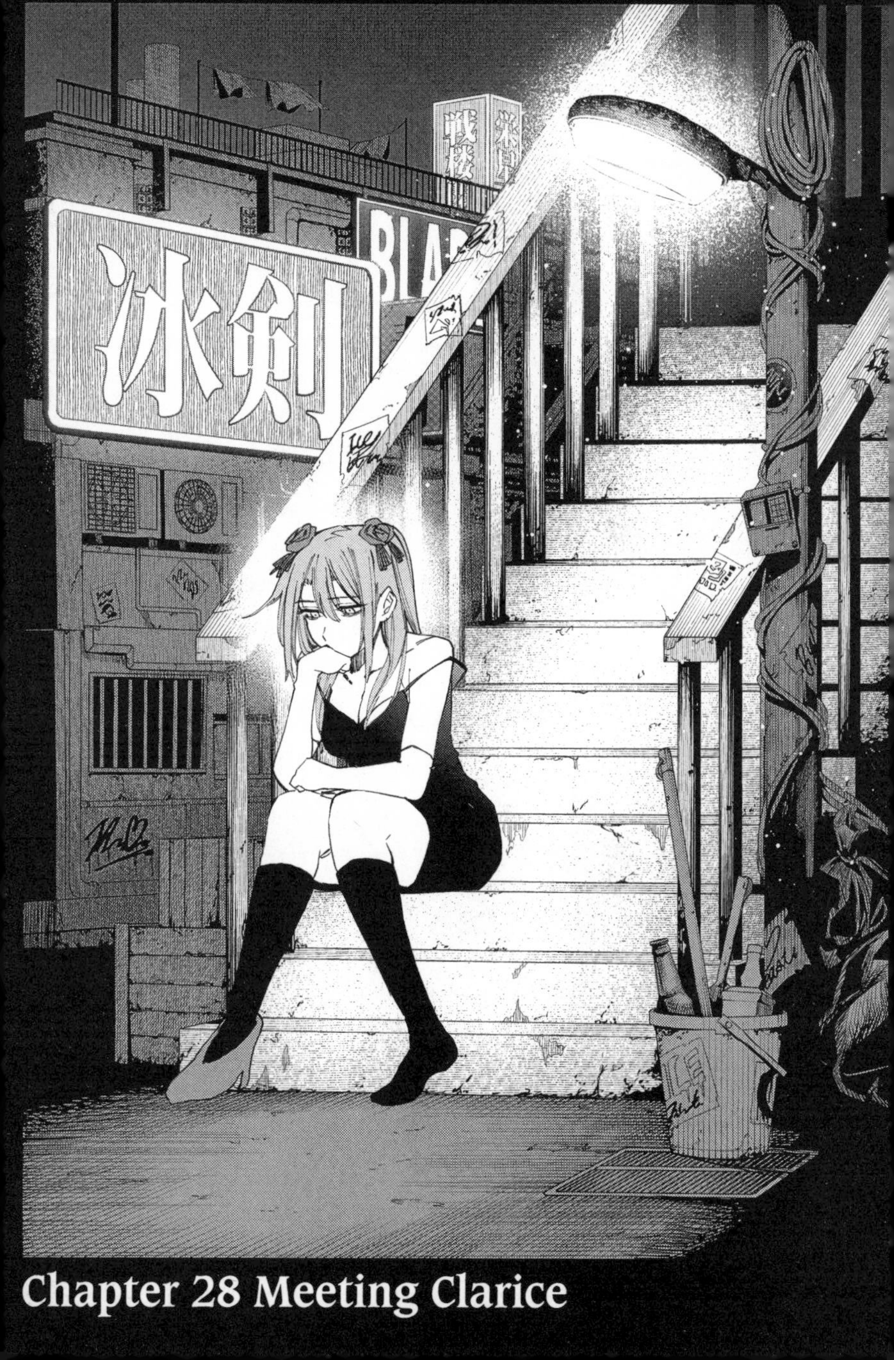
冰剣

Chapter 28 Meeting Clarice

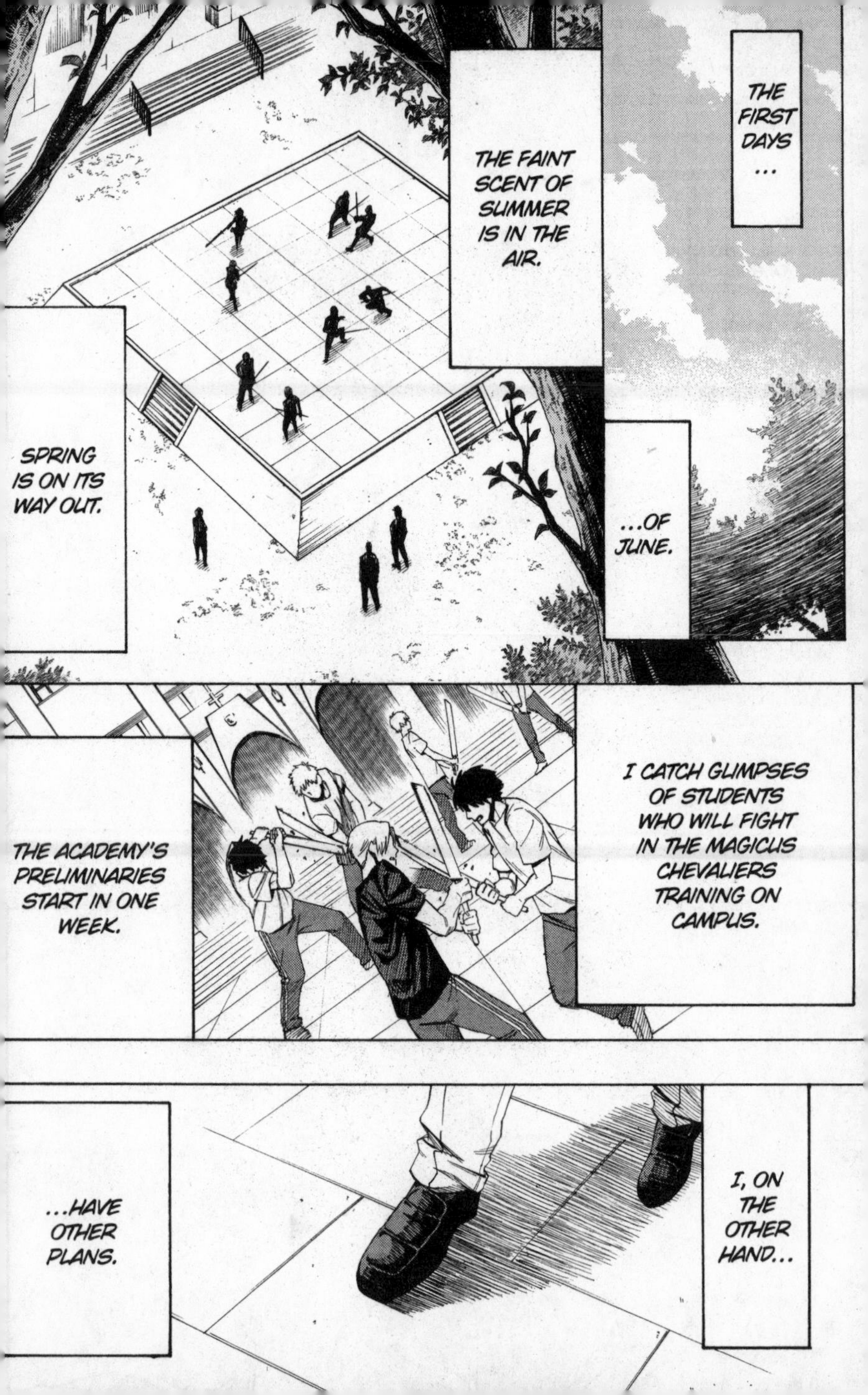

THE FIRST DAYS...
...OF JUNE.
THE FAINT SCENT OF SUMMER IS IN THE AIR.
SPRING IS ON ITS WAY OUT.
I CATCH GLIMPSES OF STUDENTS WHO WILL FIGHT IN THE MAGICUS CHEVALIERS TRAINING ON CAMPUS.
THE ACADEMY'S PRELIMINARIES START IN ONE WEEK.
I, ON THE OTHER HAND...
...HAVE OTHER PLANS.

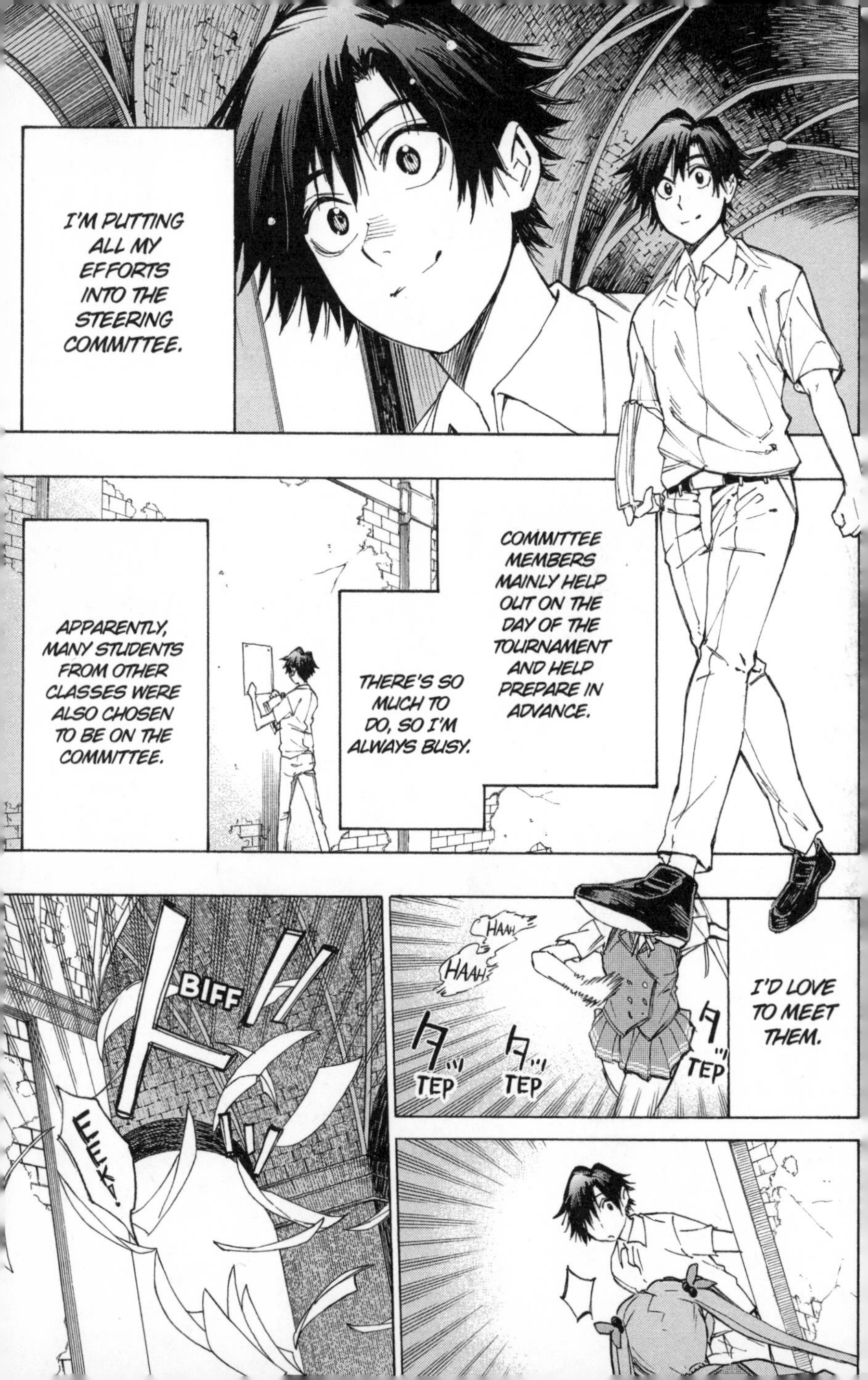

I'M PUTTING ALL MY EFFORTS INTO THE STEERING COMMITTEE.
COMMITTEE MEMBERS MAINLY HELP OUT ON THE DAY OF THE TOURNAMENT AND HELP PREPARE IN ADVANCE.
THERE'S SO MUCH TO DO, SO I'M ALWAYS BUSY.
APPARENTLY, MANY STUDENTS FROM OTHER CLASSES WERE ALSO CHOSEN TO BE ON THE COMMITTEE.
I'D LOVE TO MEET THEM.
TEP
HAAH
HAAH
TEP
TEP
BIFF
EEEK!

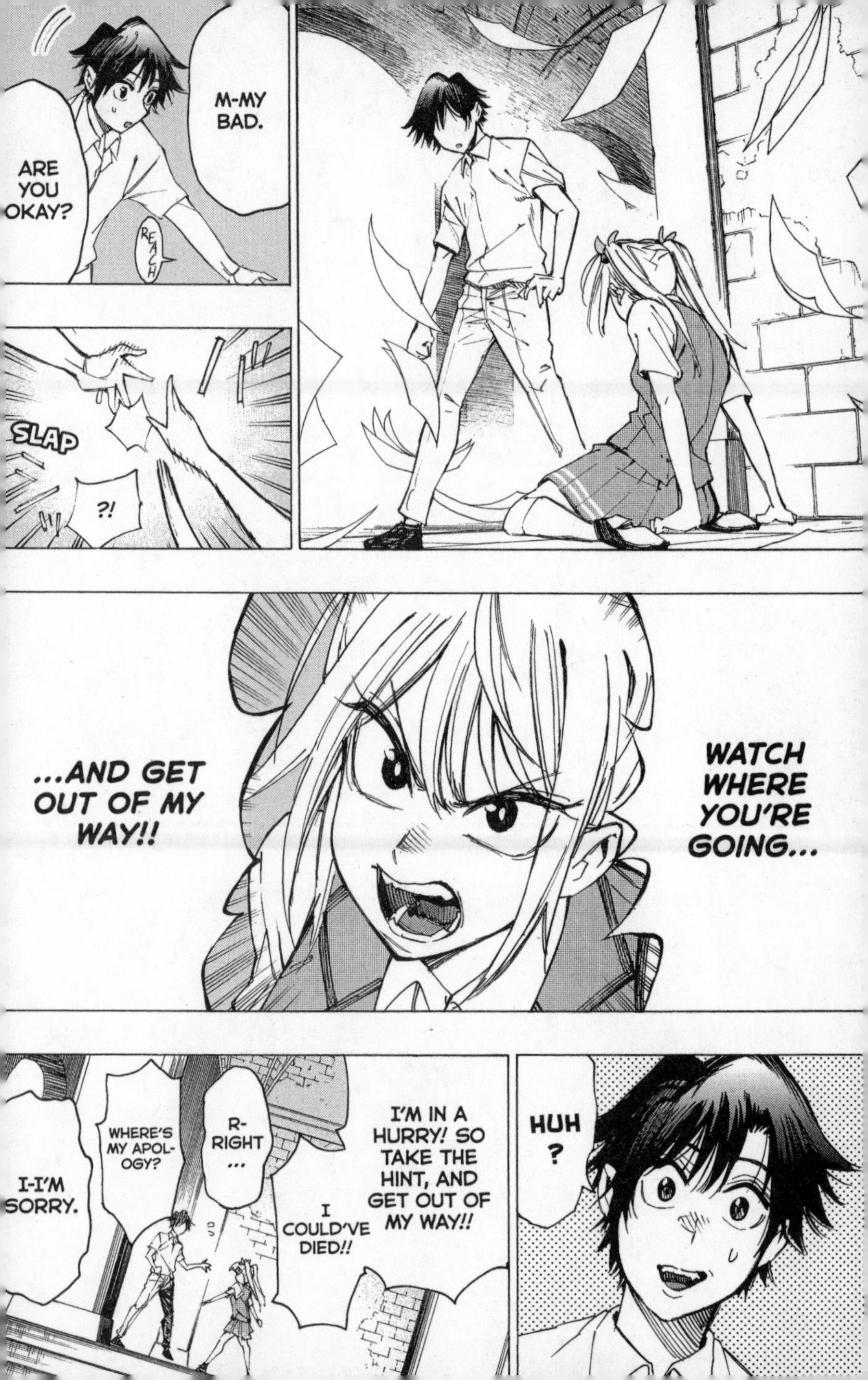
M-MY BAD.
ARE YOU OKAY?
REACH
SLAP
?!
WATCH WHERE YOU'RE GOING...
...AND GET OUT OF MY WAY!!
HUH ?
I'M IN A HURRY! SO TAKE THE HINT, AND GET OUT OF MY WAY!!
I COULD'VE DIED!!
R-RIGHT ...
WHERE'S MY APOLOGY?
I-I'M SORRY.

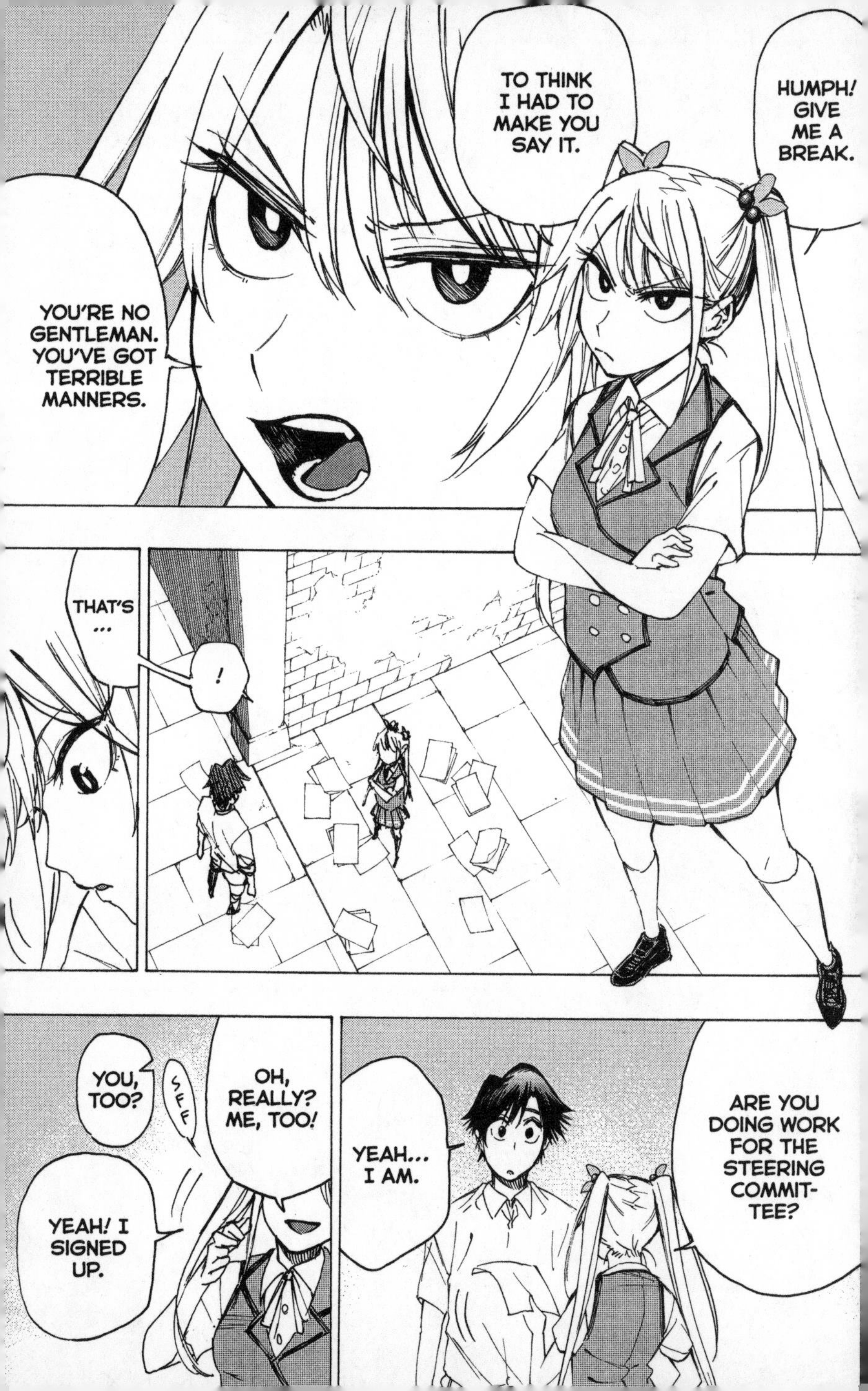
HUMPH! GIVE ME A BREAK.
TO THINK I HAD TO MAKE YOU SAY IT.
YOU'RE NO GENTLEMAN. YOU'VE GOT TERRIBLE MANNERS.
!
THAT'S ...
ARE YOU DOING WORK FOR THE STEERING COMMIT-TEE?
YEAH... I AM.
OH, REALLY? ME, TOO!
SFF
YOU, TOO?
YEAH! I SIGNED UP.

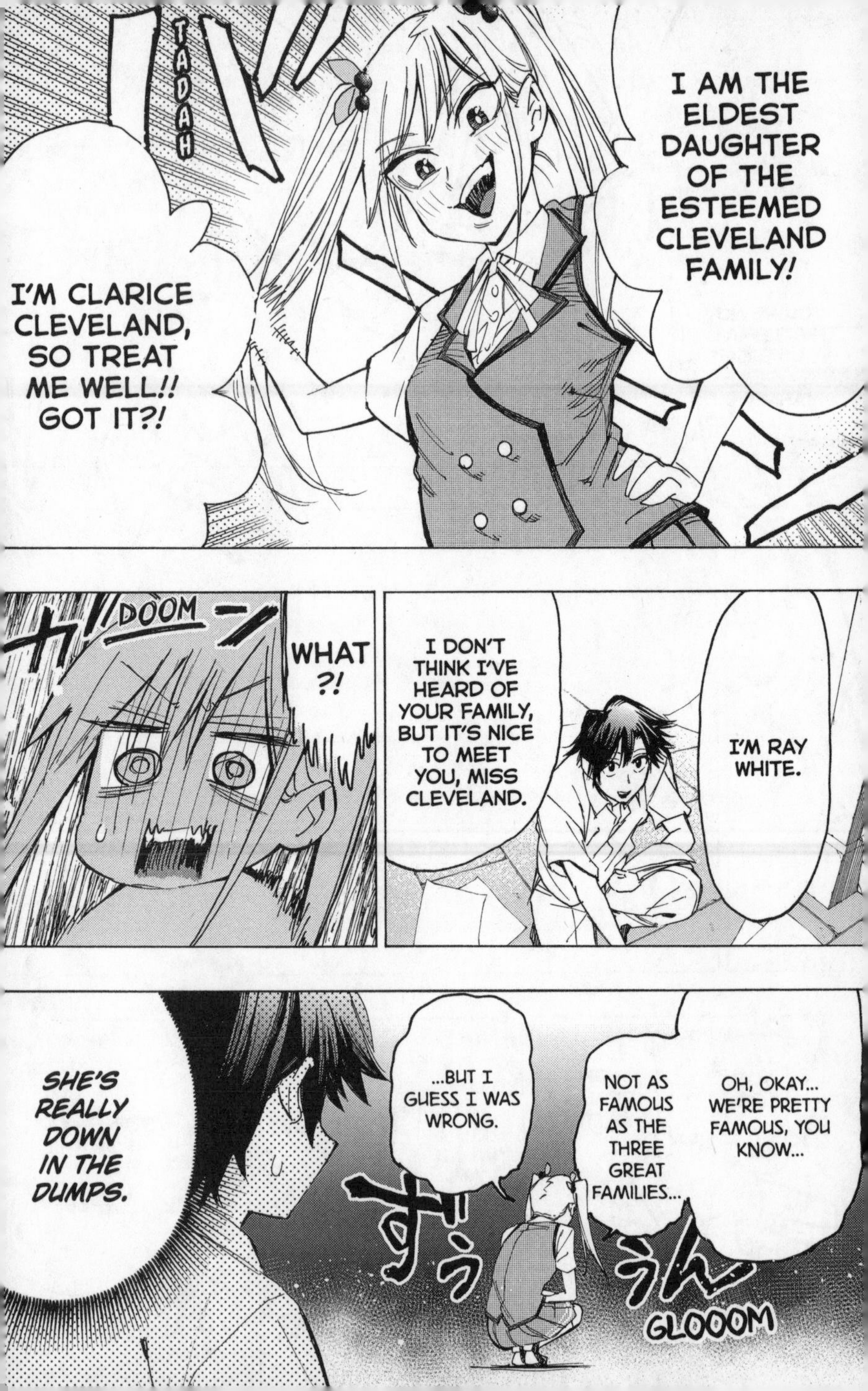
I AM THE ELDEST DAUGHTER OF THE ESTEEMED CLEVELAND FAMILY!
TADAH
I'M CLARICE CLEVELAND, SO TREAT ME WELL!! GOT IT?!
I'M RAY WHITE.
I DON'T THINK I'VE HEARD OF YOUR FAMILY, BUT IT'S NICE TO MEET YOU, MISS CLEVELAND.
DOOM
WHAT?!
OH, OKAY... WE'RE PRETTY FAMOUS, YOU KNOW...
NOT AS FAMOUS AS THE THREE GREAT FAMILIES...
...BUT I GUESS I WAS WRONG.
GLOOOM
SHE'S REALLY DOWN IN THE DUMPS.

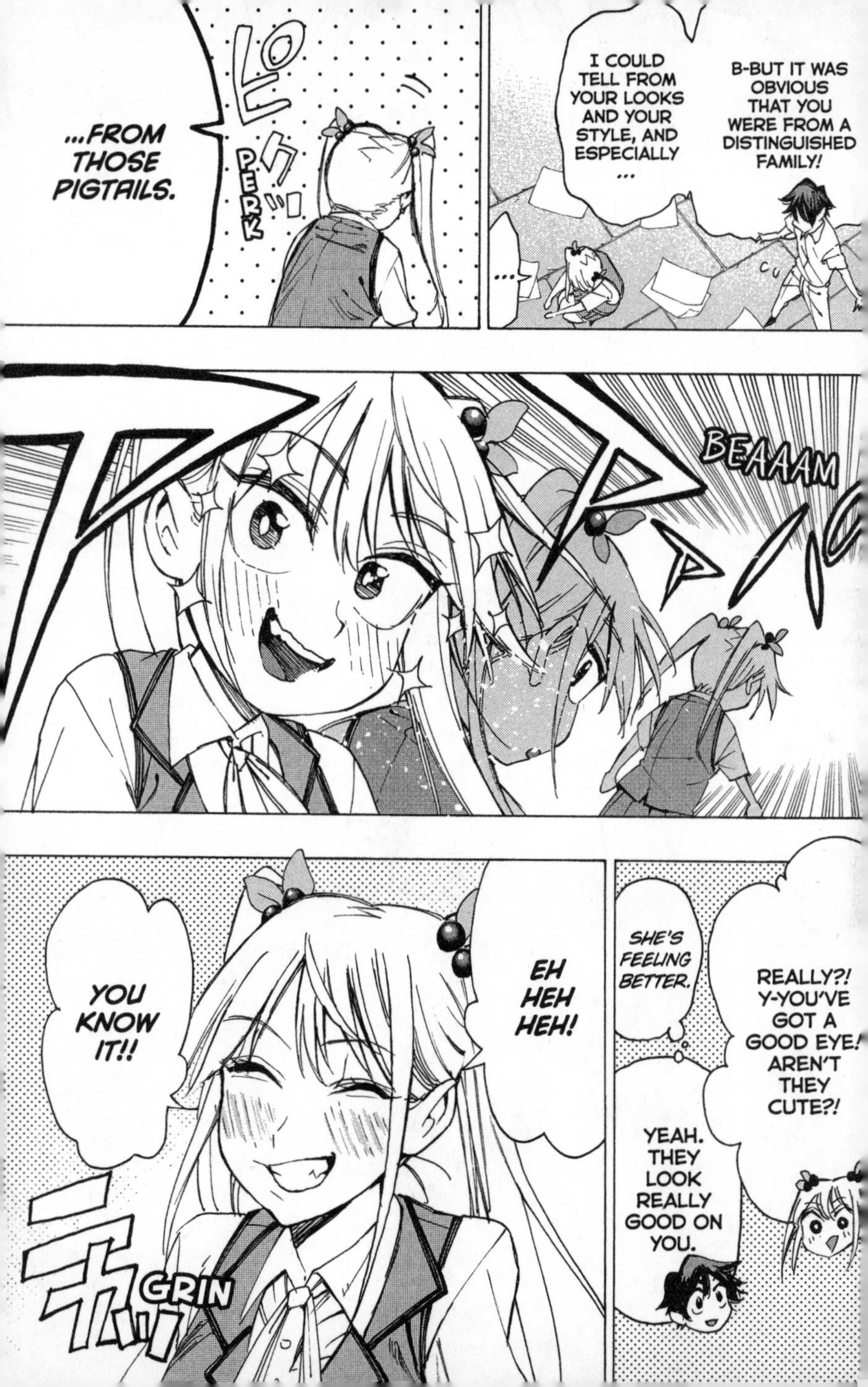
B-BUT IT WAS OBVIOUS THAT YOU WERE FROM A DISTINGUISHED FAMILY!
I COULD TELL FROM YOUR LOOKS AND YOUR STYLE, AND ESPECIALLY ...
...
...FROM THOSE PIGTAILS.
PERK
BEAAAM
REALLY?! Y-YOU'VE GOT A GOOD EYE! AREN'T THEY CUTE?!
SHE'S FEELING BETTER.
YEAH. THEY LOOK REALLY GOOD ON YOU.
EH HEH HEH!
YOU KNOW IT!!
GRIN

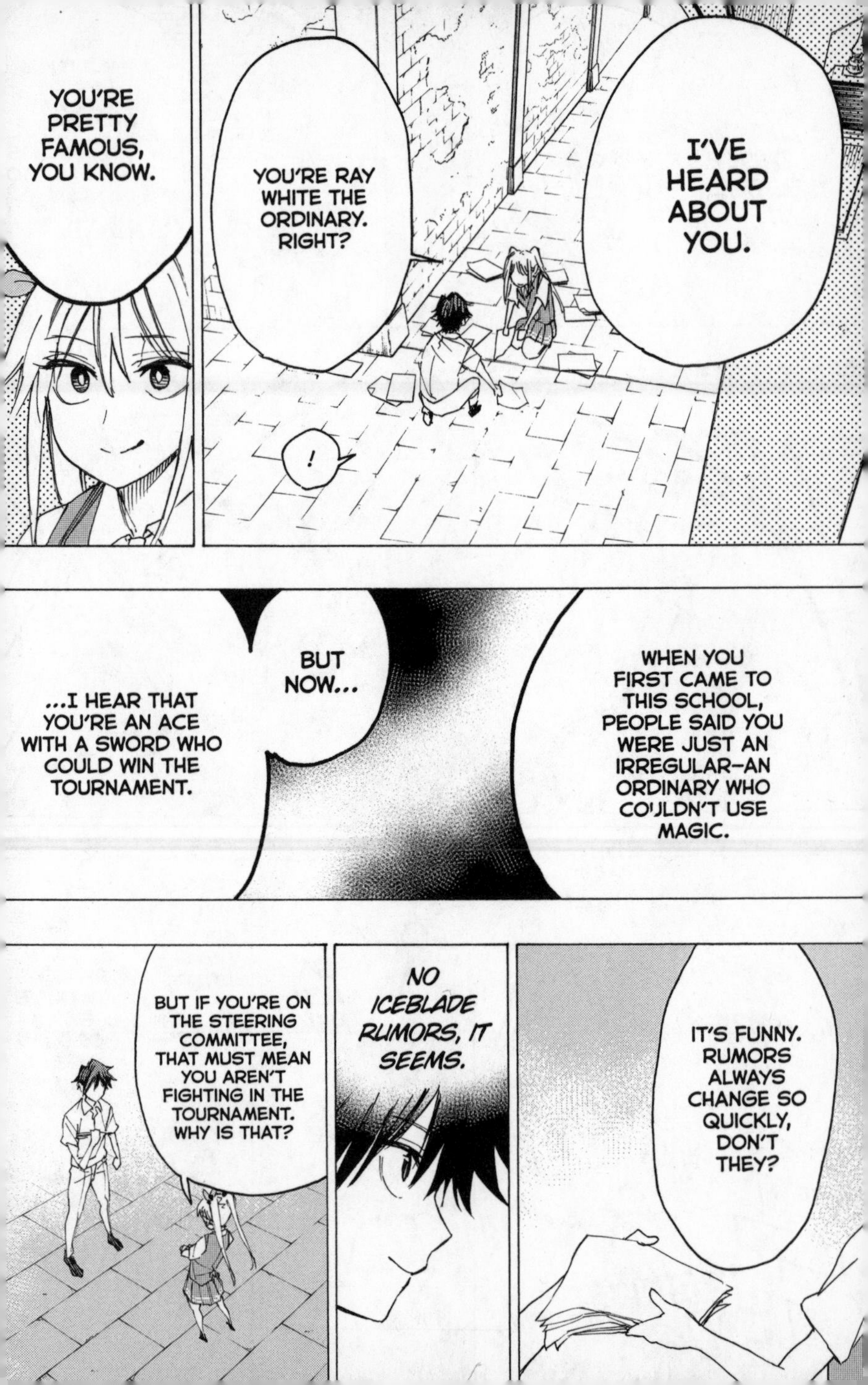
I'VE HEARD ABOUT YOU.
YOU'RE RAY WHITE THE ORDINARY. RIGHT?
!
YOU'RE PRETTY FAMOUS, YOU KNOW.
WHEN YOU FIRST CAME TO THIS SCHOOL, PEOPLE SAID YOU WERE JUST AN IRREGULAR—AN ORDINARY WHO COULDN'T USE MAGIC.
BUT NOW...
...I HEAR THAT YOU'RE AN ACE WITH A SWORD WHO COULD WIN THE TOURNAMENT.
IT'S FUNNY. RUMORS ALWAYS CHANGE SO QUICKLY, DON'T THEY?
NO ICEBLADE RUMORS, IT SEEMS.
BUT IF YOU'RE ON THE STEERING COMMITTEE, THAT MUST MEAN YOU AREN'T FIGHTING IN THE TOURNAMENT. WHY IS THAT?

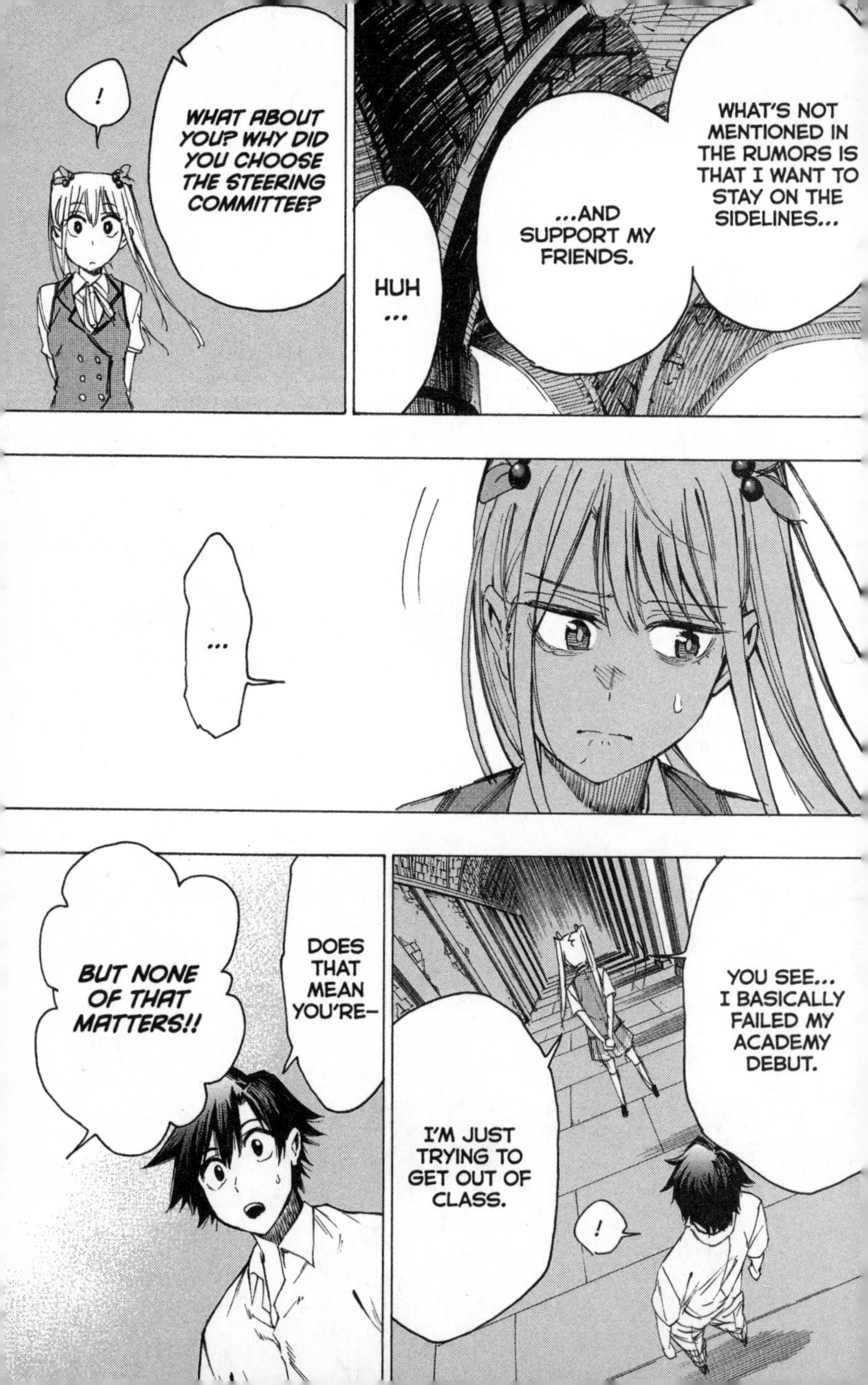
WHAT'S NOT MENTIONED IN THE RUMORS IS THAT I WANT TO STAY ON THE SIDELINES...
...AND SUPPORT MY FRIENDS.
HUH...
WHAT ABOUT YOU? WHY DID YOU CHOOSE THE STEERING COMMITTEE?
!
...
YOU SEE... I BASICALLY FAILED MY ACADEMY DEBUT.
I'M JUST TRYING TO GET OUT OF CLASS.
!
DOES THAT MEAN YOU'RE–
BUT NONE OF THAT MATTERS!!

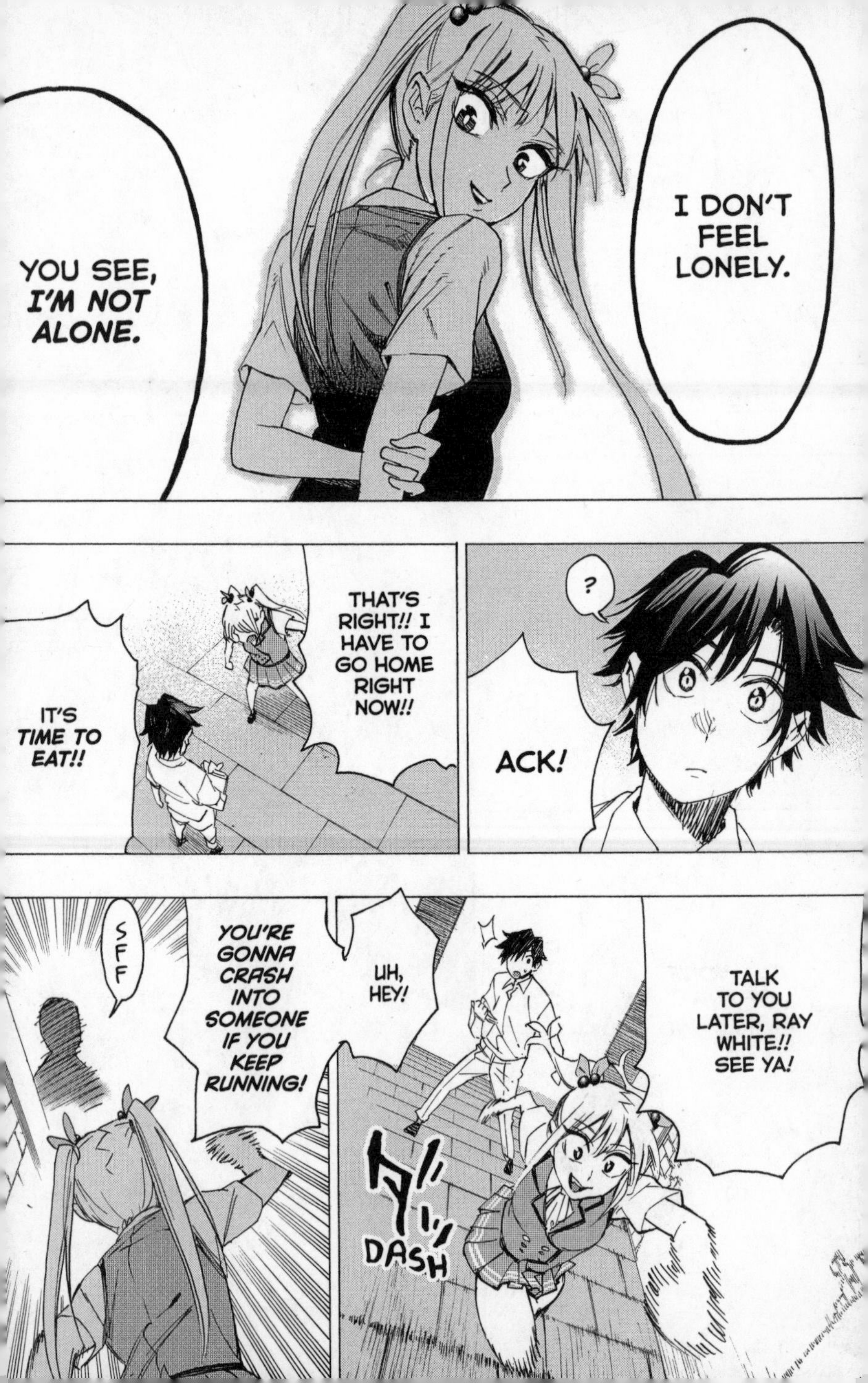
I DON'T FEEL LONELY.
YOU SEE, *I'M NOT* ALONE.
?
ACK!
THAT'S RIGHT!! I HAVE TO GO HOME RIGHT NOW!!
IT'S *TIME TO* EAT!!
TALK TO YOU LATER, RAY WHITE!! SEE YA!
UH, HEY!
DASH
YOU'RE GONNA CRASH INTO SOMEONE IF YOU KEEP RUNNING!
SFF

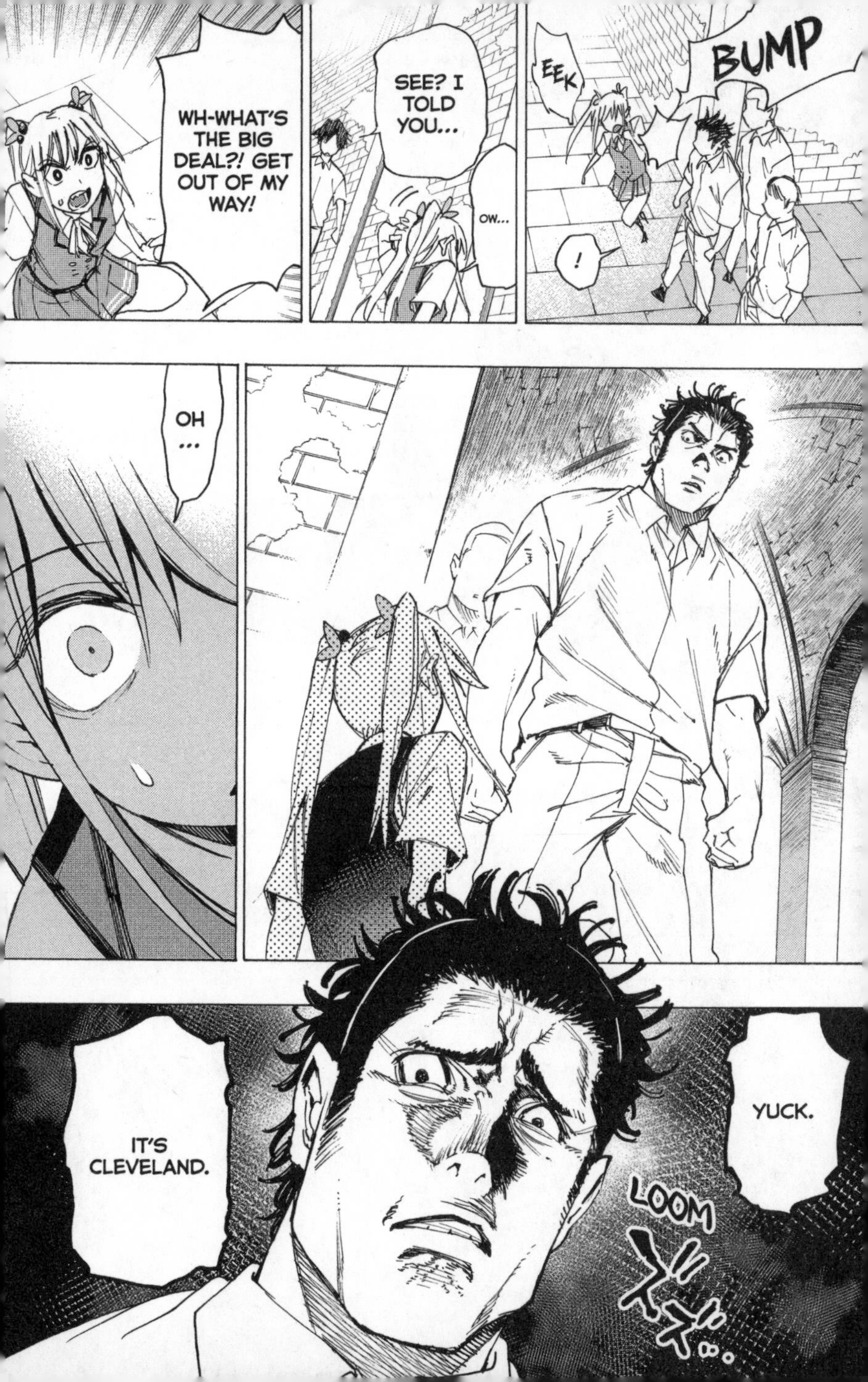
BUMP
EEK
!
SEE? I TOLD YOU...
OW...
WH-WHAT'S THE BIG DEAL?! GET OUT OF MY WAY!
OH ...
YUCK.
LOOM
IT'S CLEVELAND.

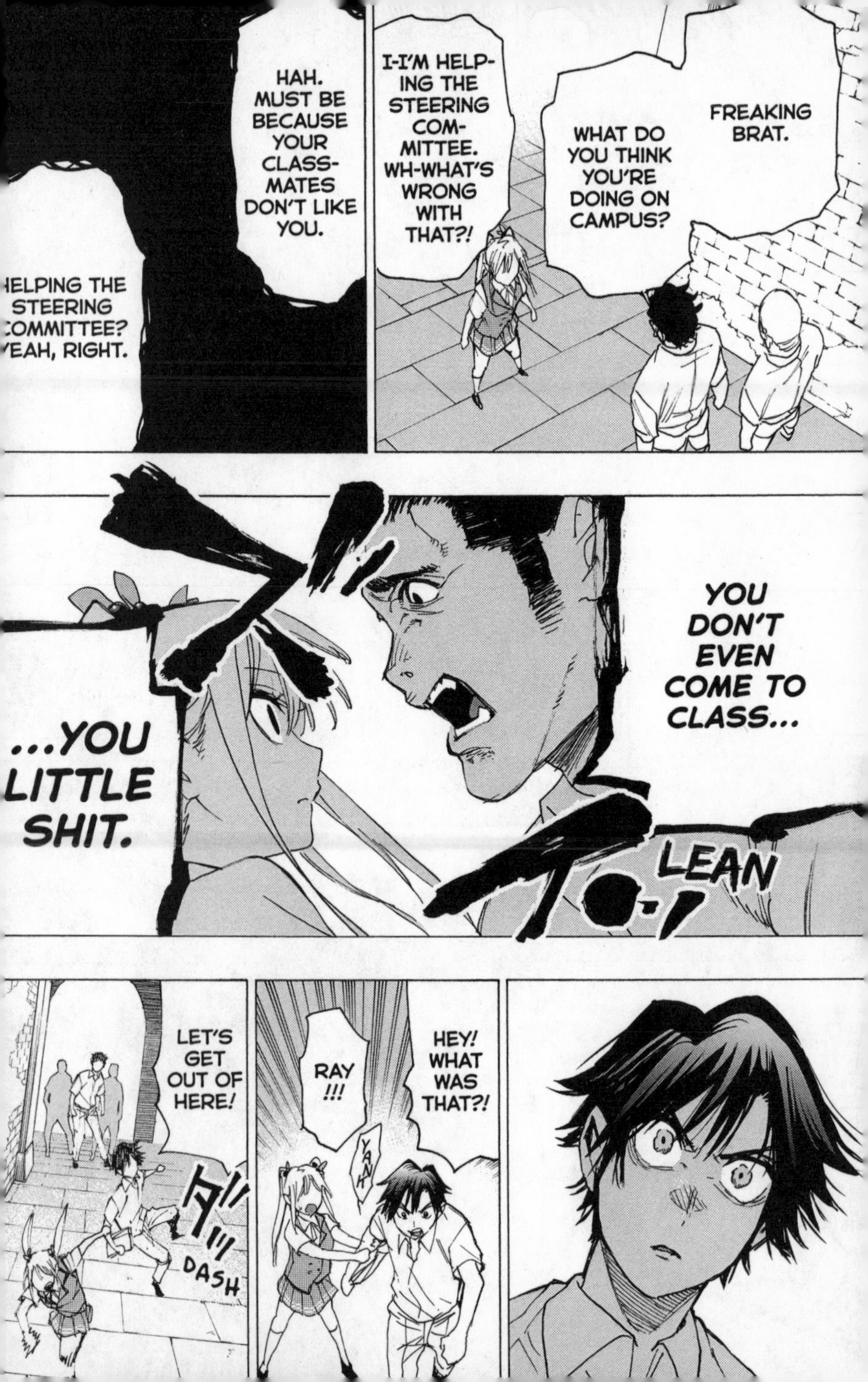
FREAKING BRAT.
WHAT DO YOU THINK YOU'RE DOING ON CAMPUS?
I-I'M HELPING THE STEERING COMMITTEE. WH-WHAT'S WRONG WITH THAT?!
HAH. MUST BE BECAUSE YOUR CLASSMATES DON'T LIKE YOU.
HELPING THE STEERING COMMITTEE? YEAH, RIGHT.
YOU DON'T EVEN COME TO CLASS...
...YOU LITTLE SHIT.
LEAN
HEY! WHAT WAS THAT?!
RAY !!!
YANK
LET'S GET OUT OF HERE!
DASH

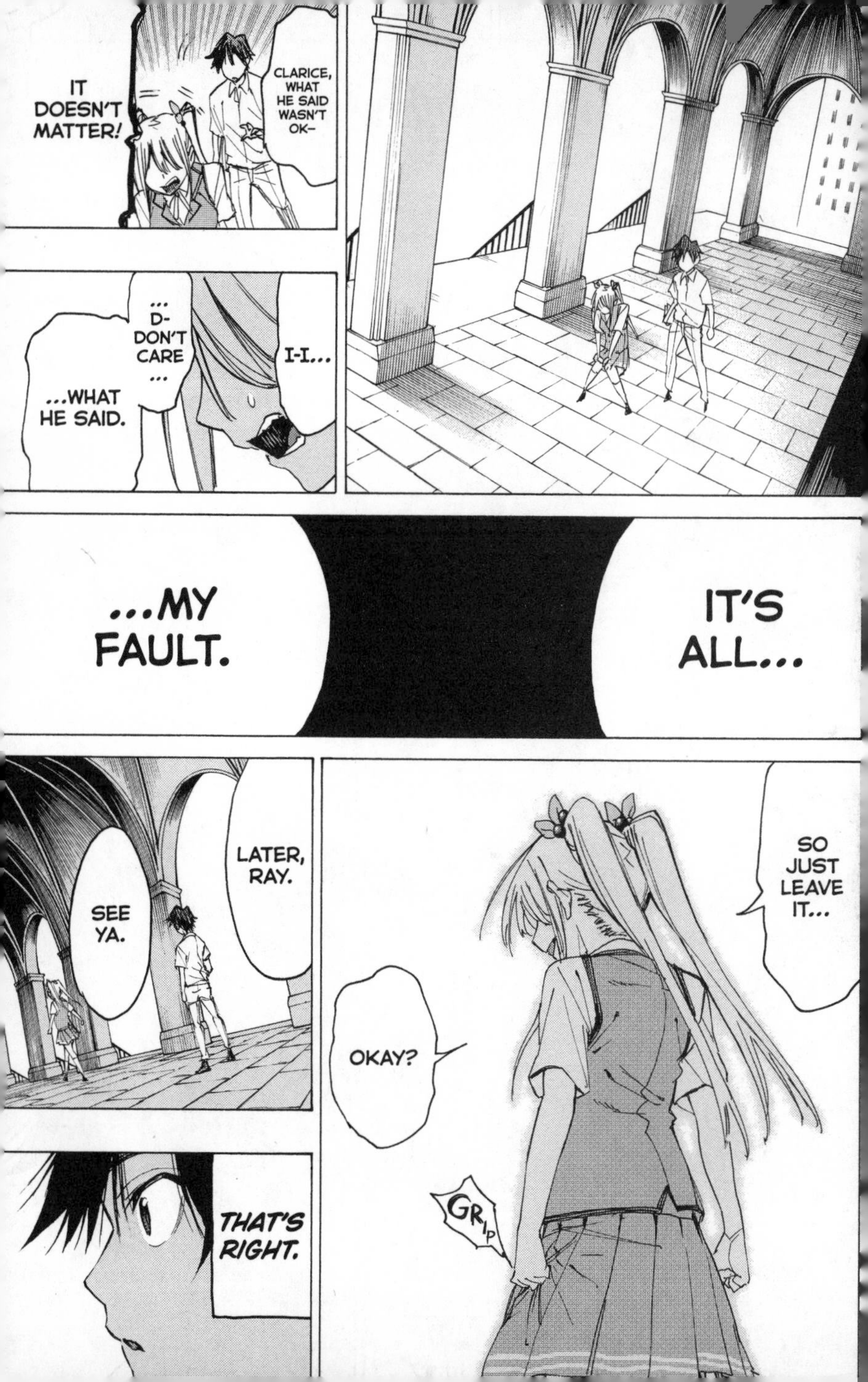
CLARICE, WHAT HE SAID WASN'T OK–
IT DOESN'T MATTER!
I-I...
...D-DON'T CARE...
...WHAT HE SAID.
IT'S ALL...
...MY FAULT.
SO JUST LEAVE IT...
OKAY?
GRIP
LATER, RAY.
SEE YA.
THAT'S RIGHT.

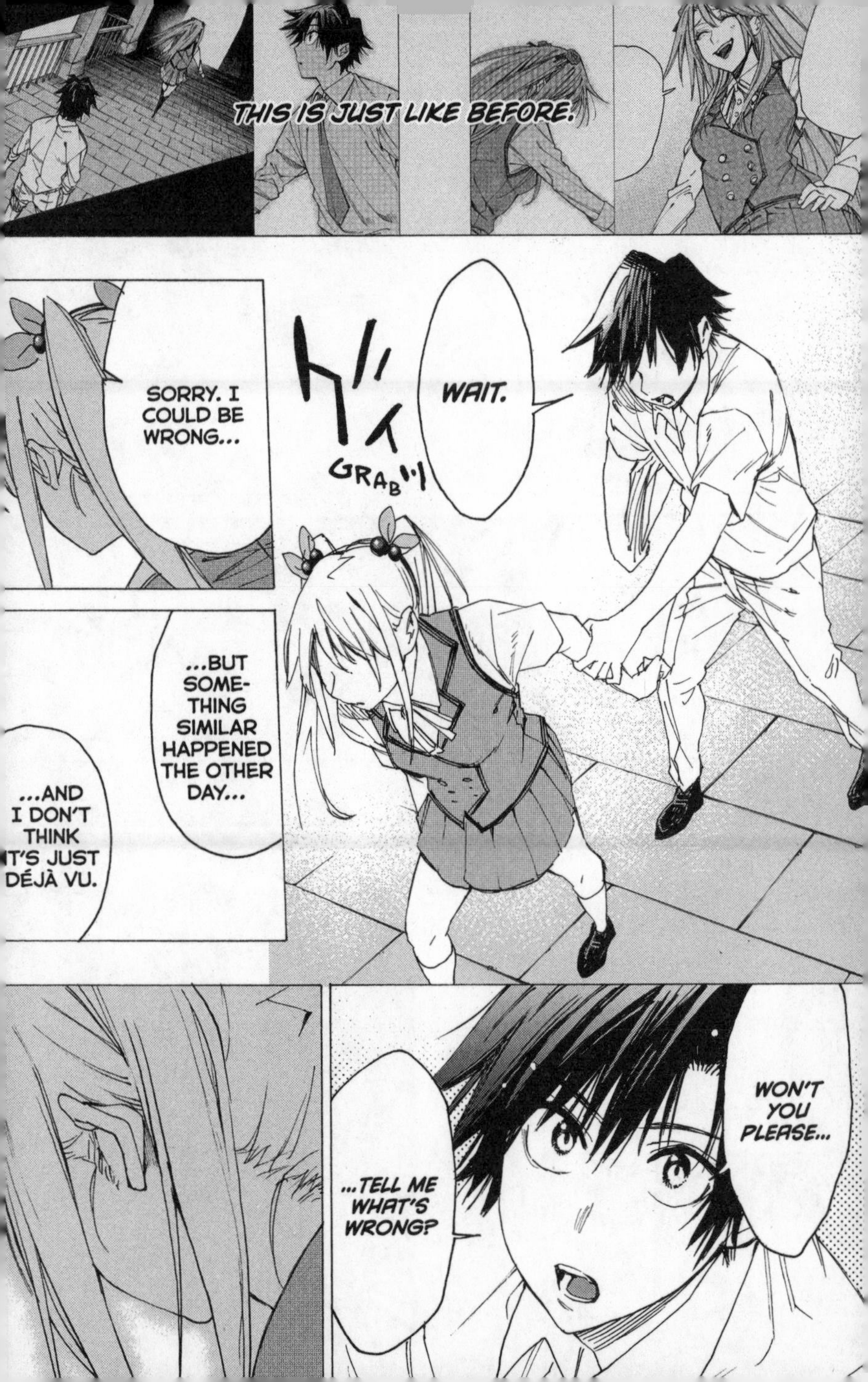
THIS IS JUST LIKE BEFORE.
WAIT.
GRAB
SORRY. I COULD BE WRONG...
...BUT SOME-THING SIMILAR HAPPENED THE OTHER DAY...
...AND I DON'T THINK IT'S JUST DÉJÀ VU.
WON'T YOU PLEASE...
...TELL ME WHAT'S WRONG?

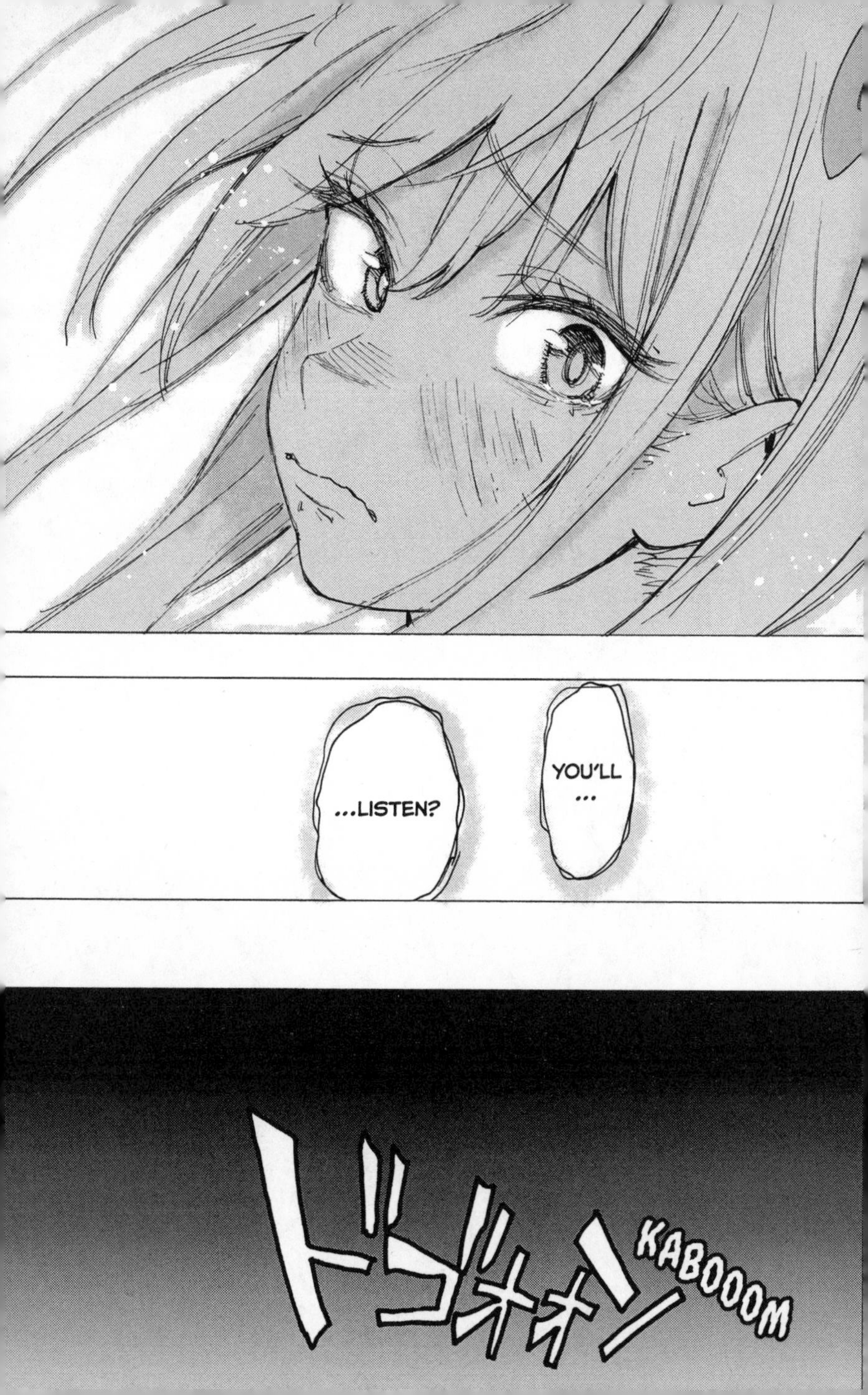
YOU'LL ...
...LISTEN?
ドゴオオン
KABOOOM

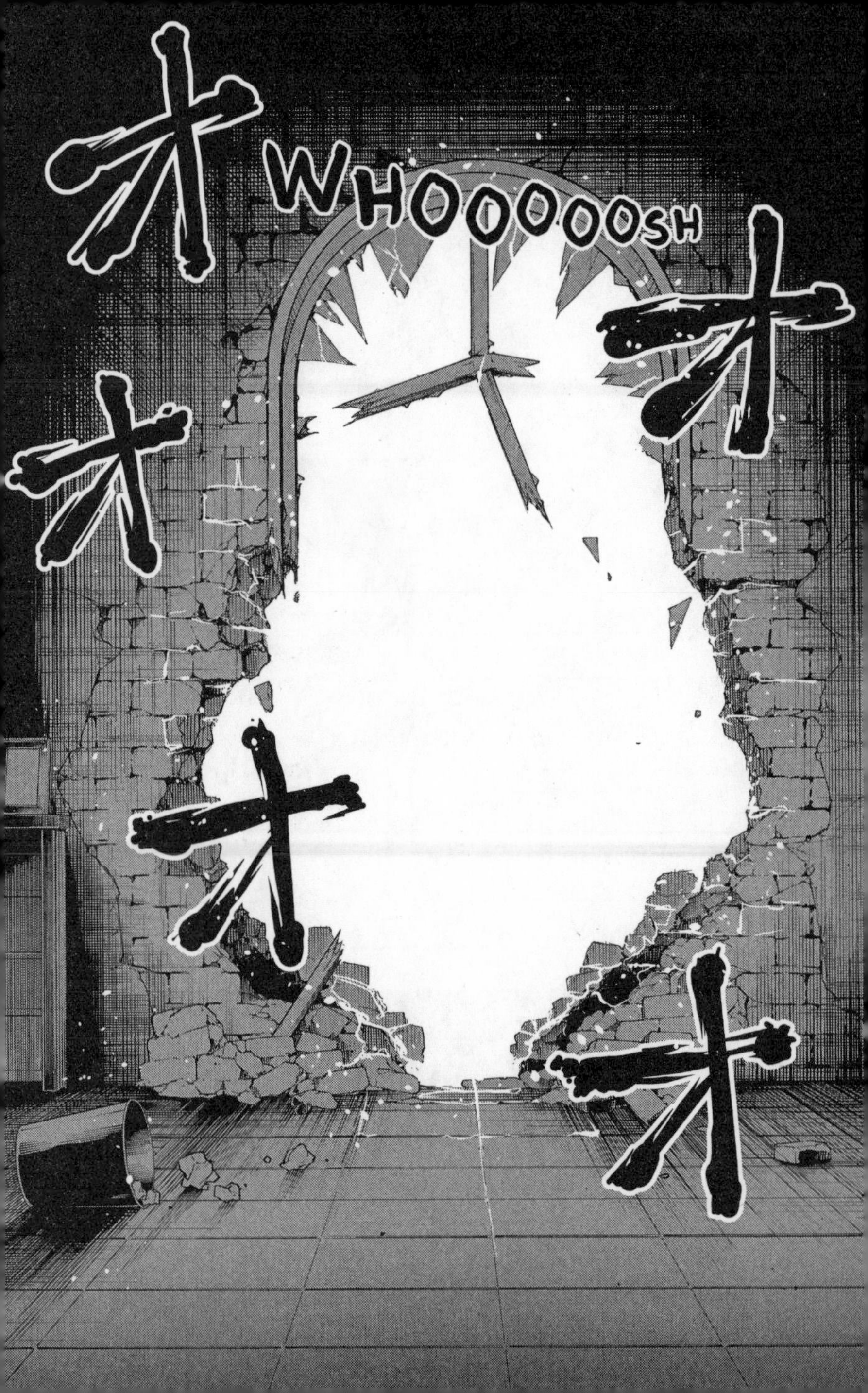
オオオオオ
WHOOOOOSH

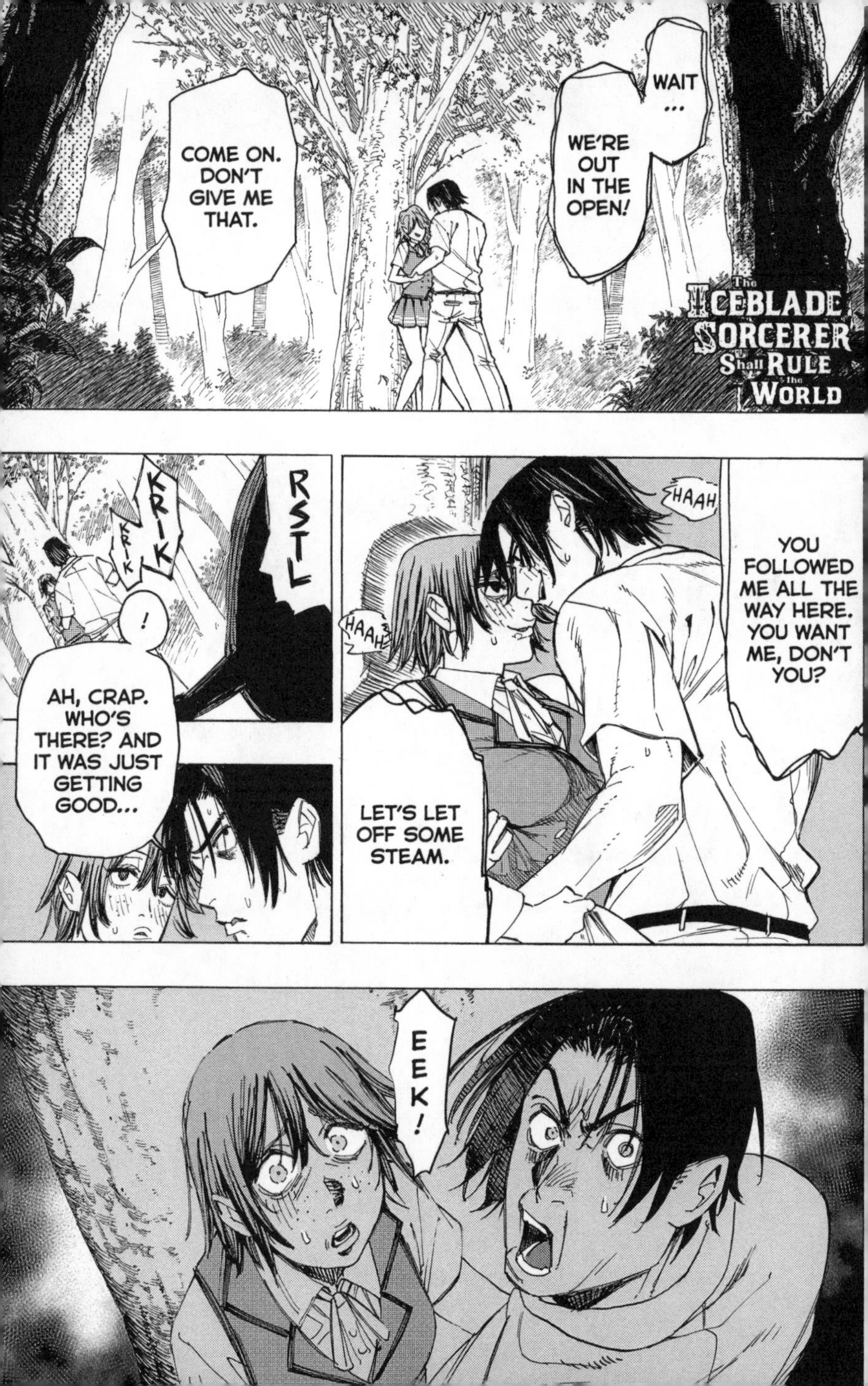
WAIT...
WE'RE OUT IN THE OPEN!
COME ON. DON'T GIVE ME THAT.
The ICEBLADE SORCERER Shall RULE the WORLD
HAAH
YOU FOLLOWED ME ALL THE WAY HERE. YOU WANT ME, DON'T YOU?
HAAH
LET'S LET OFF SOME STEAM.
RSTL
KRIK KRIK
!
AH, CRAP. WHO'S THERE? AND IT WAS JUST GETTING GOOD...
EEK!

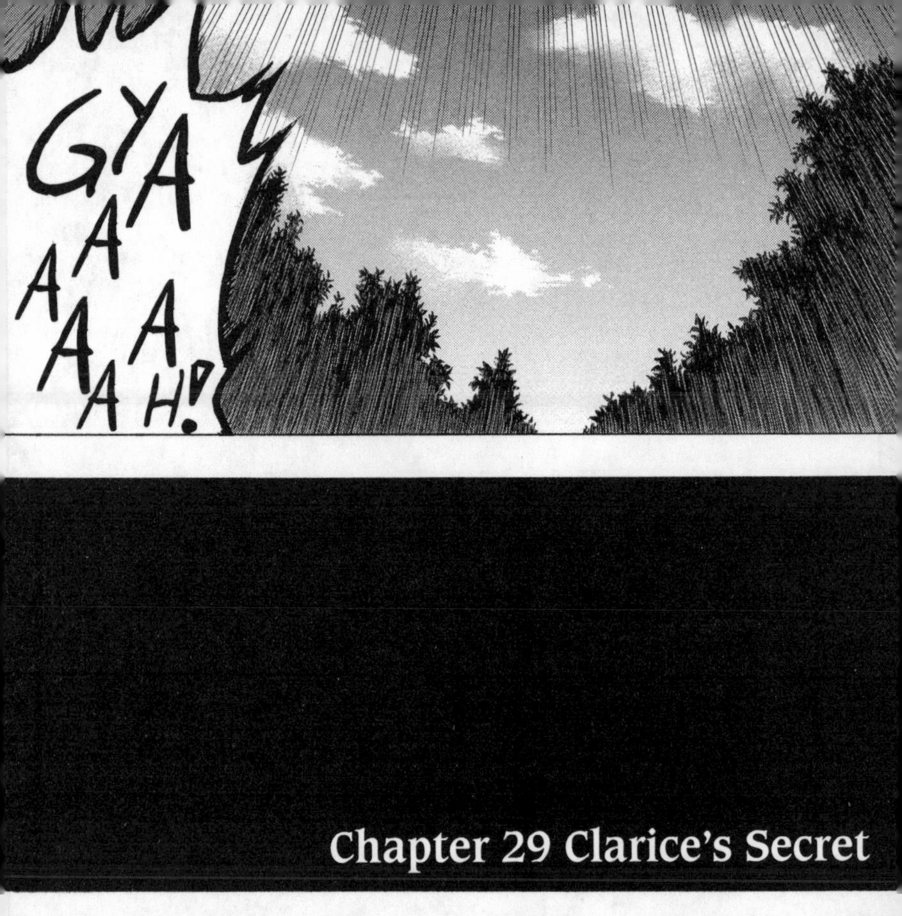
GYAAAAAAAH!?

Chapter 29 Clarice's Secret

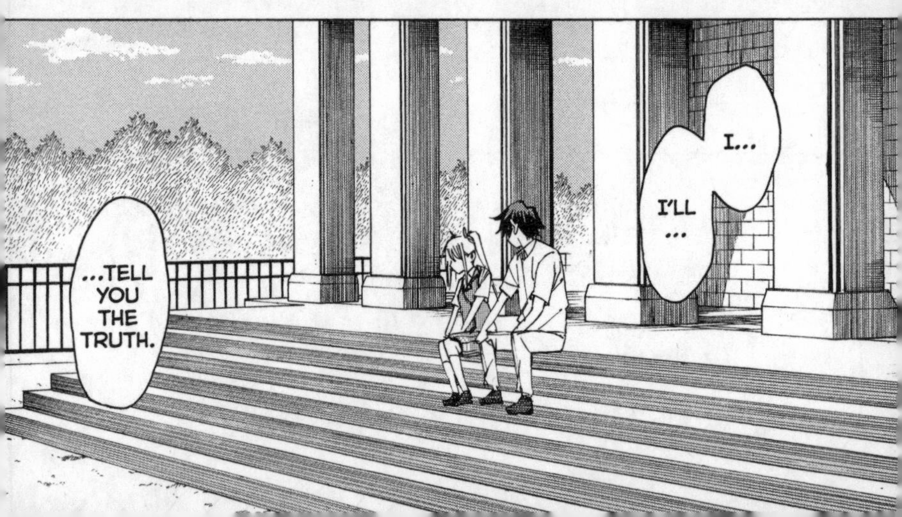
I... I'LL ...
...TELL YOU THE TRUTH.

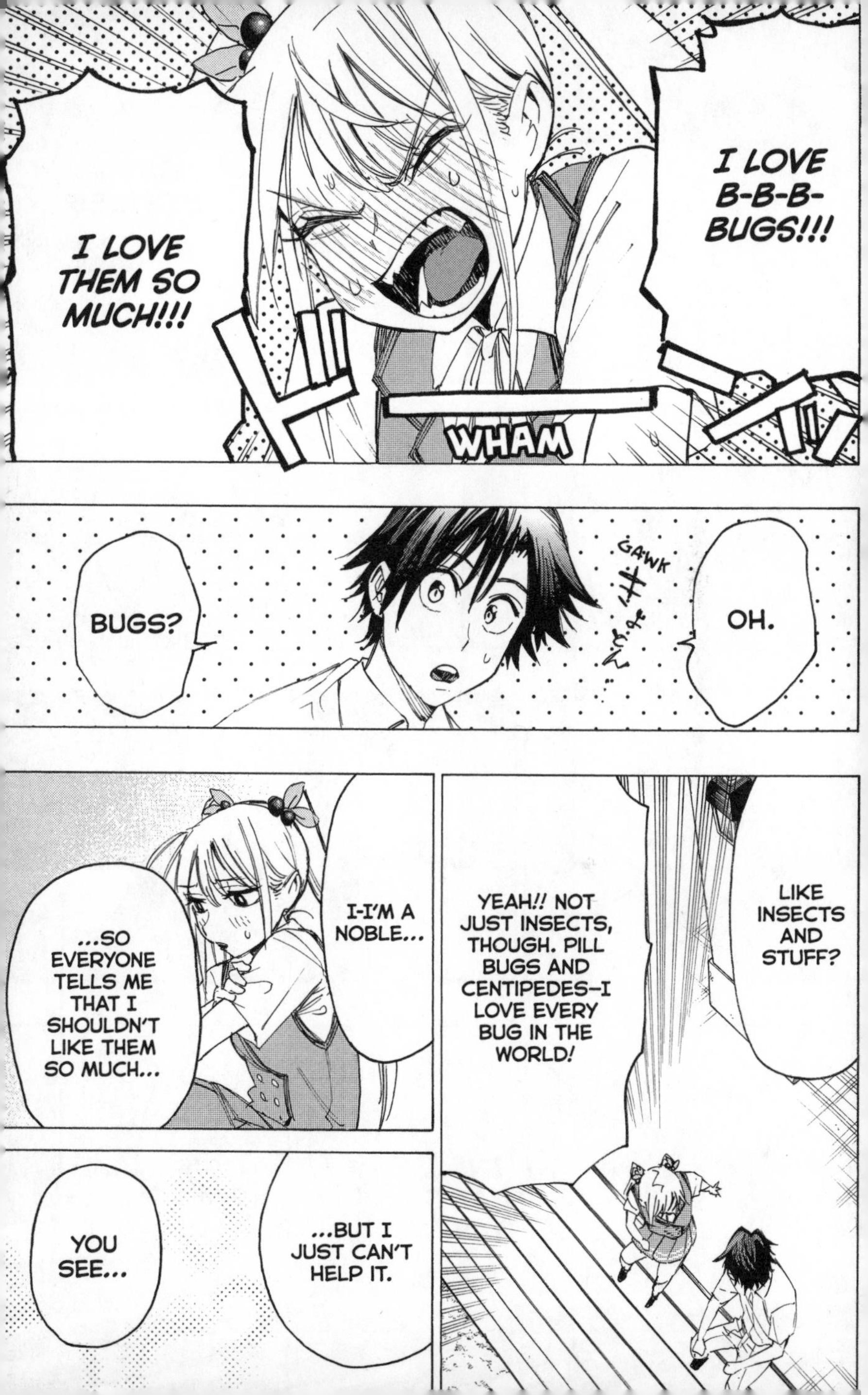
I LOVE B-B-B-BUGS!!!
I LOVE THEM SO MUCH!!!
WHAM
OH.
GAWK
BUGS?
LIKE INSECTS AND STUFF?
YEAH!! NOT JUST INSECTS, THOUGH. PILL BUGS AND CENTIPEDES—I LOVE EVERY BUG IN THE WORLD!
I-I'M A NOBLE...
...SO EVERYONE TELLS ME THAT I SHOULDN'T LIKE THEM SO MUCH...
...BUT I JUST CAN'T HELP IT.
YOU SEE...

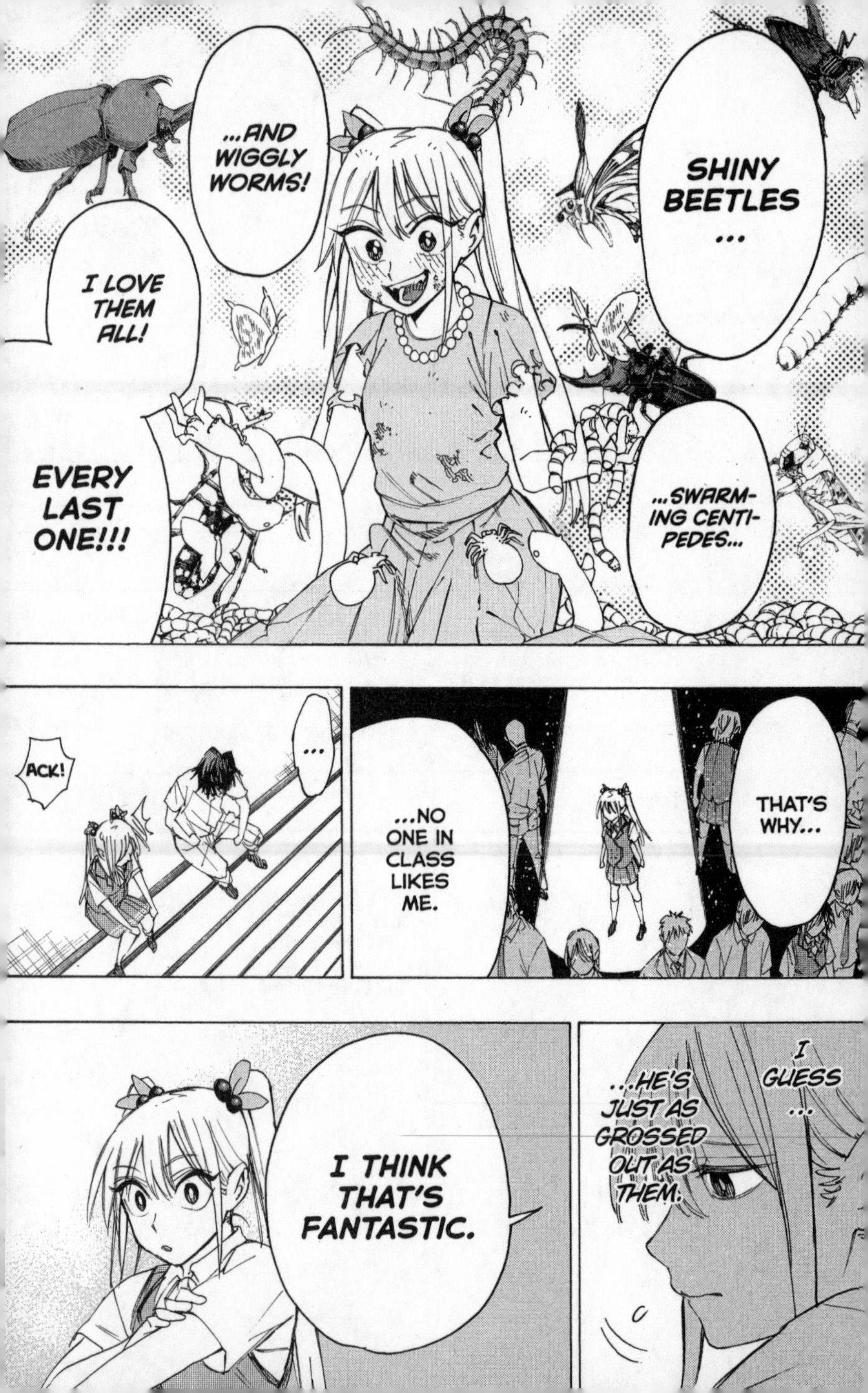
SHINY BEETLES ...
...AND WIGGLY WORMS!
...SWARMING CENTIPEDES...
I LOVE THEM ALL!
EVERY LAST ONE!!!
THAT'S WHY...
...NO ONE IN CLASS LIKES ME.
...
ACK!
I GUESS ...
...HE'S JUST AS GROSSED OUT AS THEM.
I THINK THAT'S FANTASTIC.

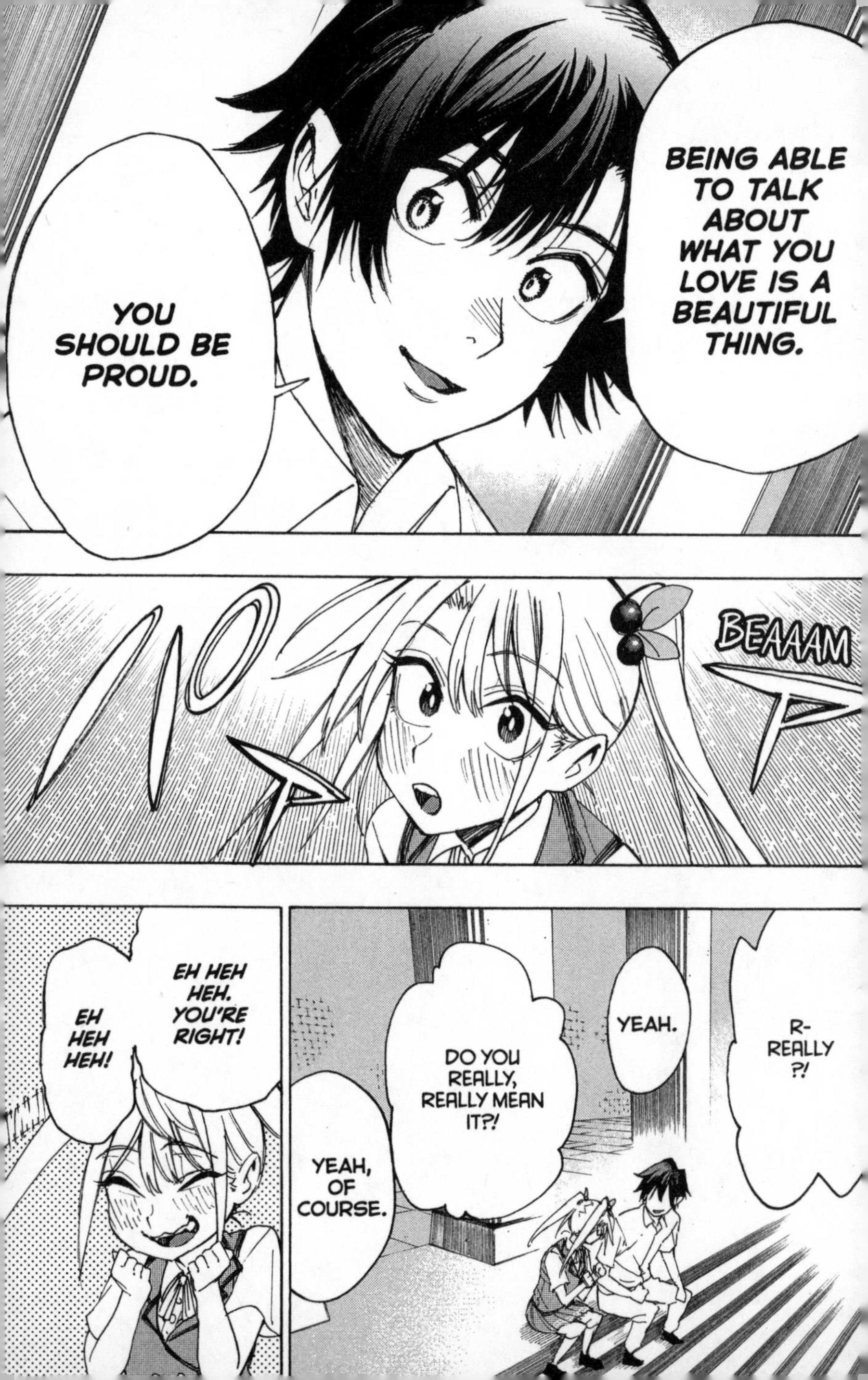
BEING ABLE TO TALK ABOUT WHAT YOU LOVE IS A BEAUTIFUL THING.
YOU SHOULD BE PROUD.
BEAAAM
R-REALLY?!
YEAH.
DO YOU REALLY, REALLY MEAN IT?!
YEAH, OF COURSE.
EH HEH HEH. YOU'RE RIGHT!
EH HEH HEH!

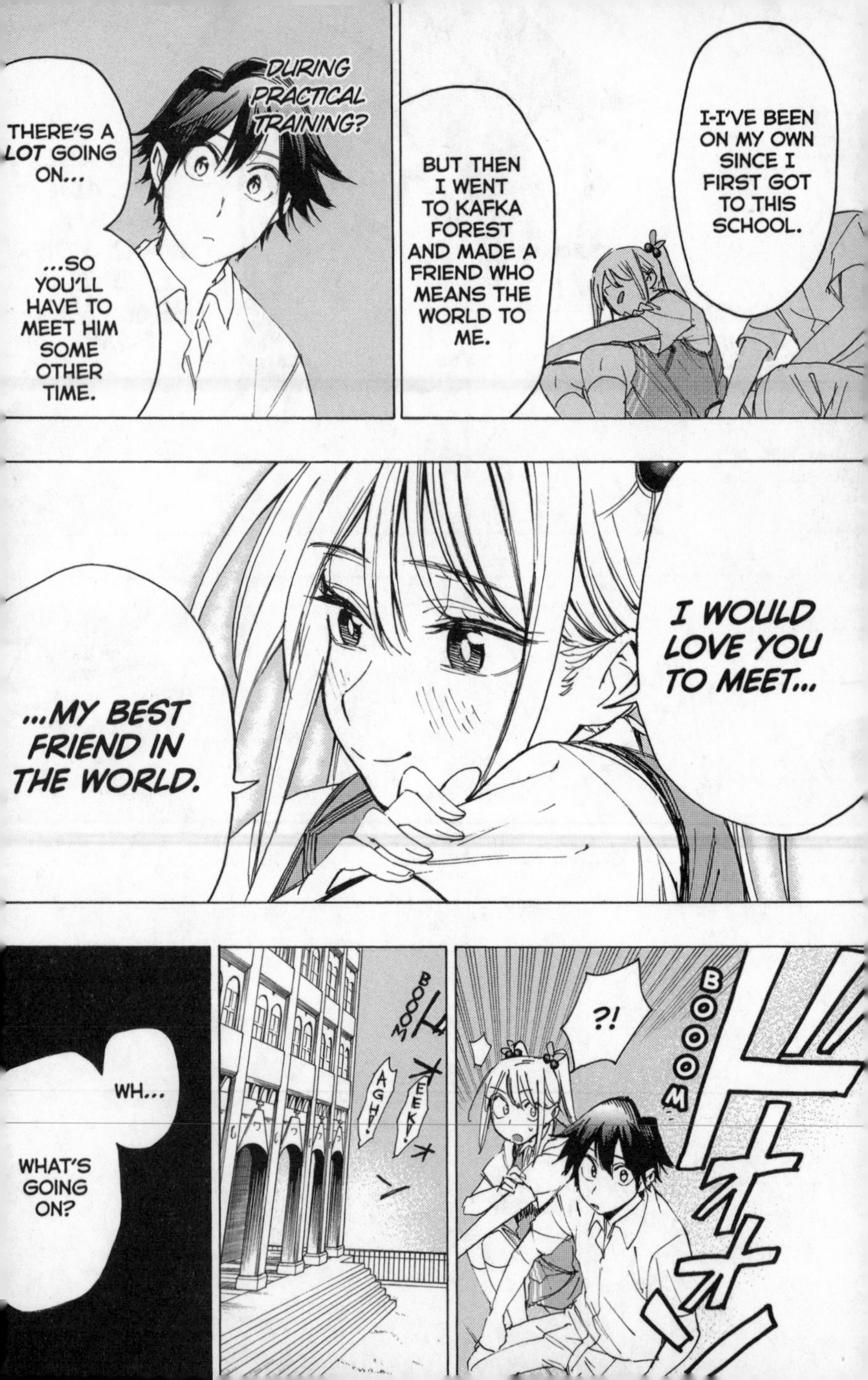
I-I'VE BEEN ON MY OWN SINCE I FIRST GOT TO THIS SCHOOL.
BUT THEN I WENT TO KAFKA FOREST AND MADE A FRIEND WHO MEANS THE WORLD TO ME.
DURING PRACTICAL TRAINING?
THERE'S A LOT GOING ON...
...SO YOU'LL HAVE TO MEET HIM SOME OTHER TIME.
I WOULD LOVE YOU TO MEET...
...MY BEST FRIEND IN THE WORLD.
BOOOOM
?!
BOOOM
EEK!
AGH!
WH...
WHAT'S GOING ON?

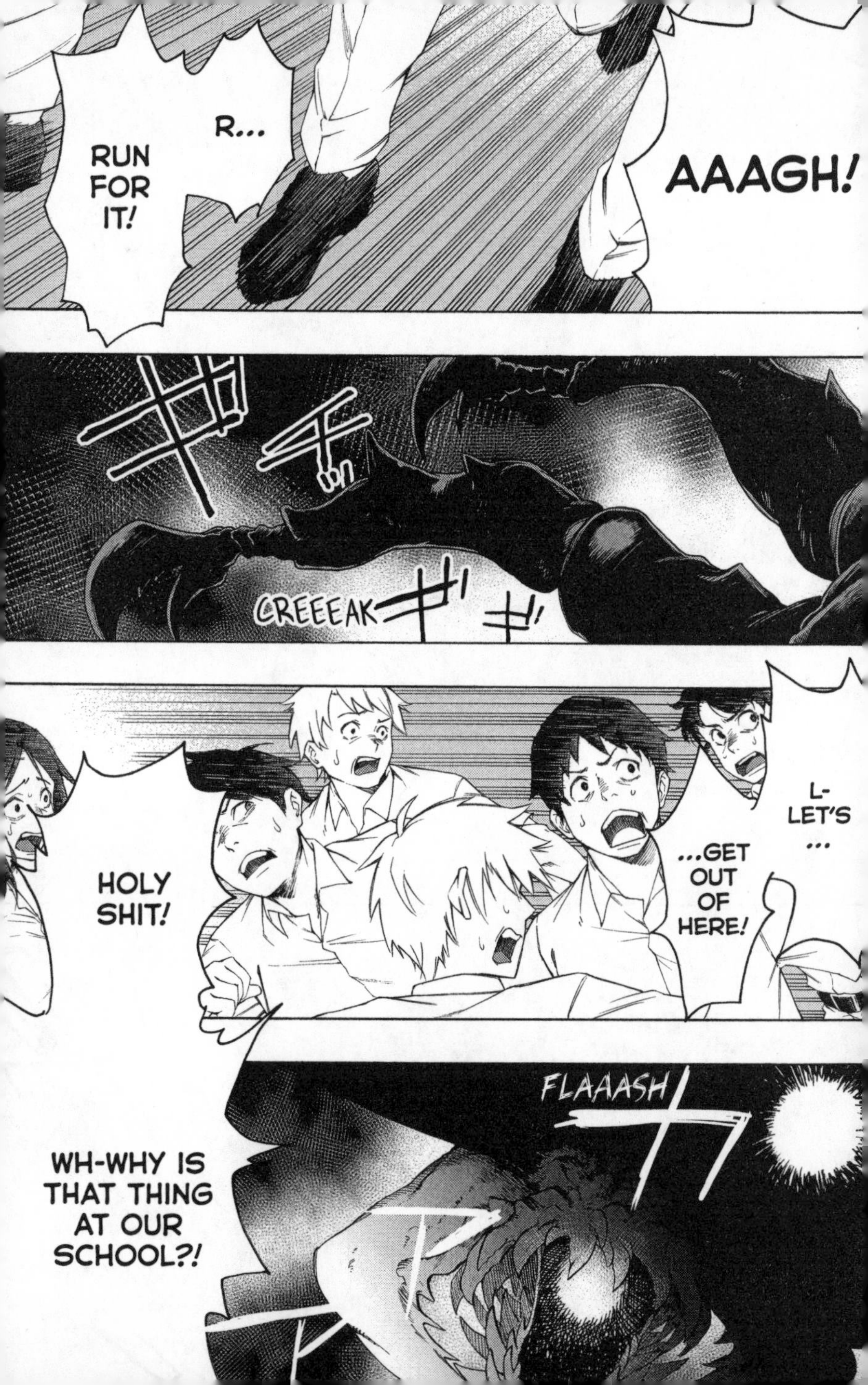
AAAGH!
R... RUN FOR IT!
CREEEAK
L-LET'S...
...GET OUT OF HERE!
HOLY SHIT!
FLAAASH
WH-WHY IS THAT THING AT OUR SCHOOL?!

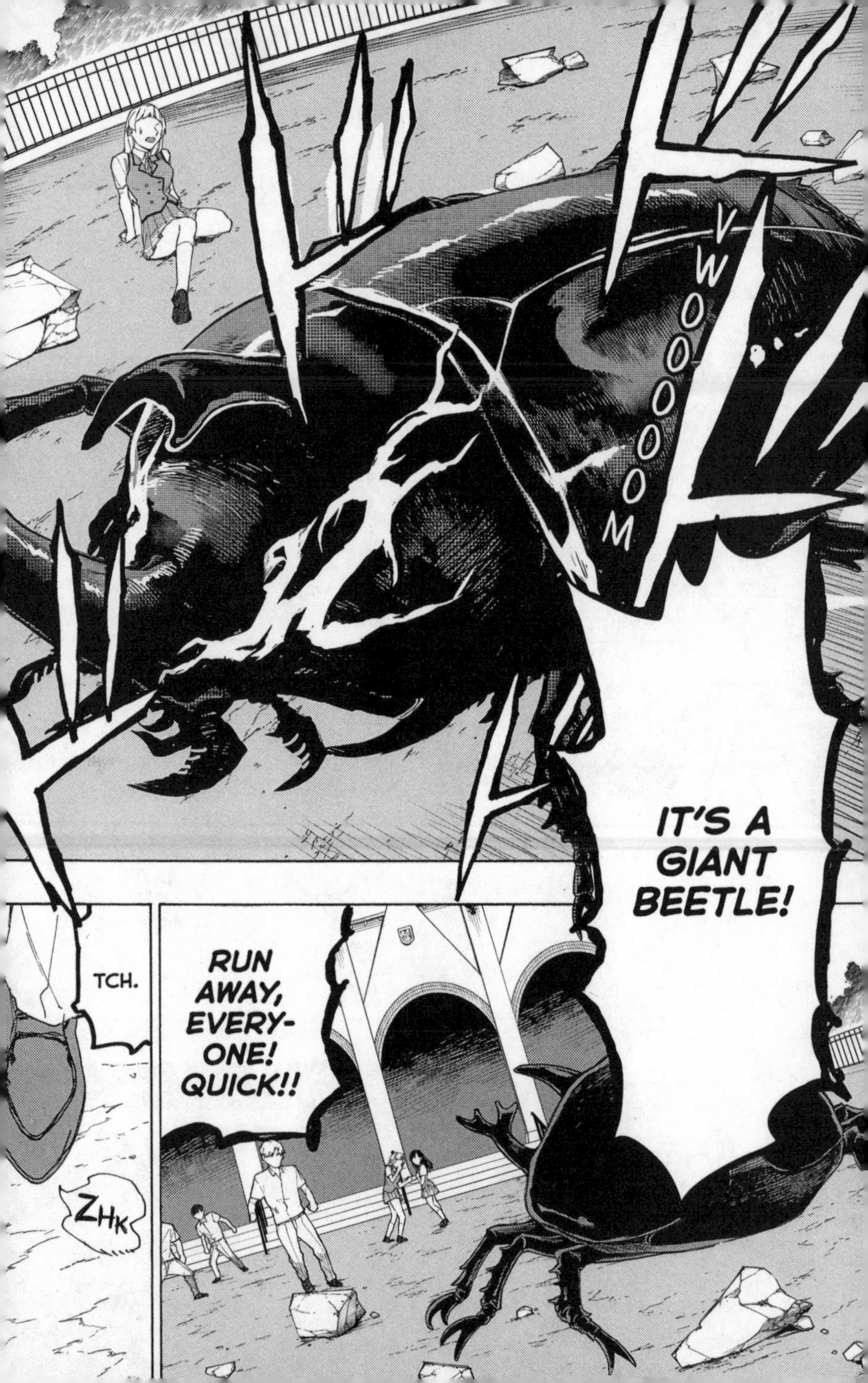
VWOOOOOM
IT'S A GIANT BEETLE!
RUN AWAY, EVERY-ONE! QUICK!!
TCH.
ZHK

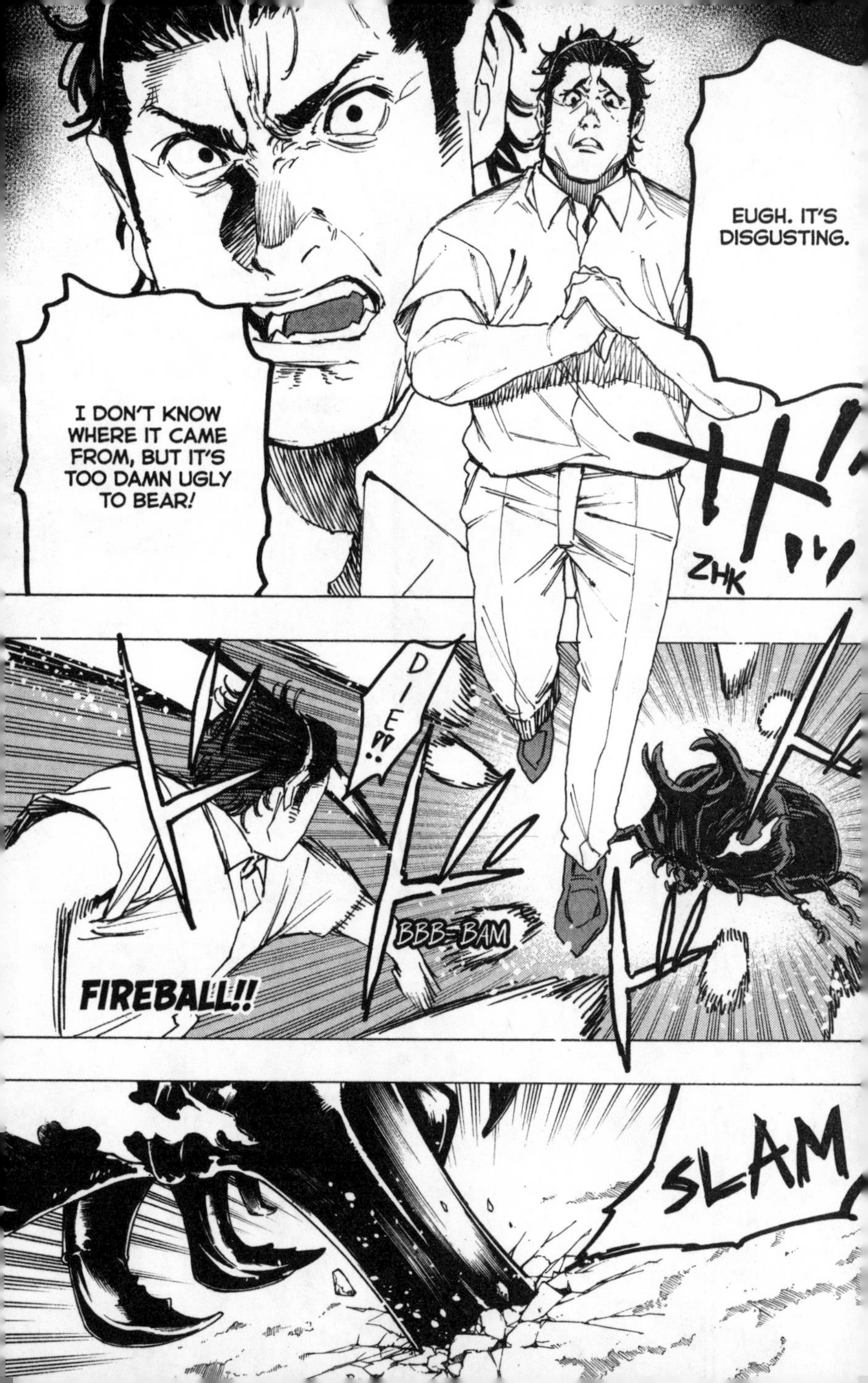
EUGH. IT'S DISGUSTING.
I DON'T KNOW WHERE IT CAME FROM, BUT IT'S TOO DAMN UGLY TO BEAR!
ZHK
DIE!!
BBB-BAM
FIREBALL!!
SLAM

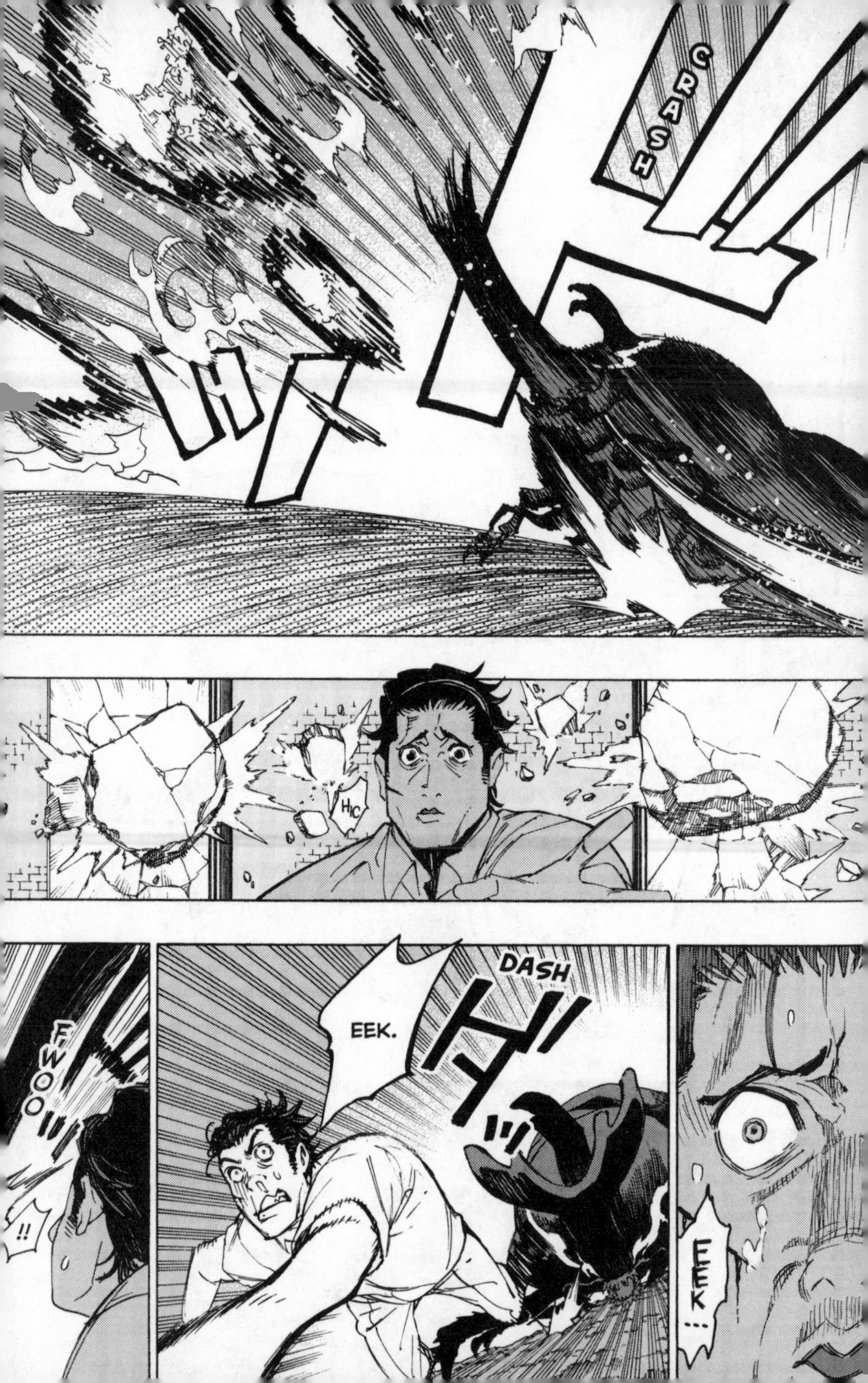
CRASH
HIC
EEK...
DASH
EEK.
FWOOO
!!

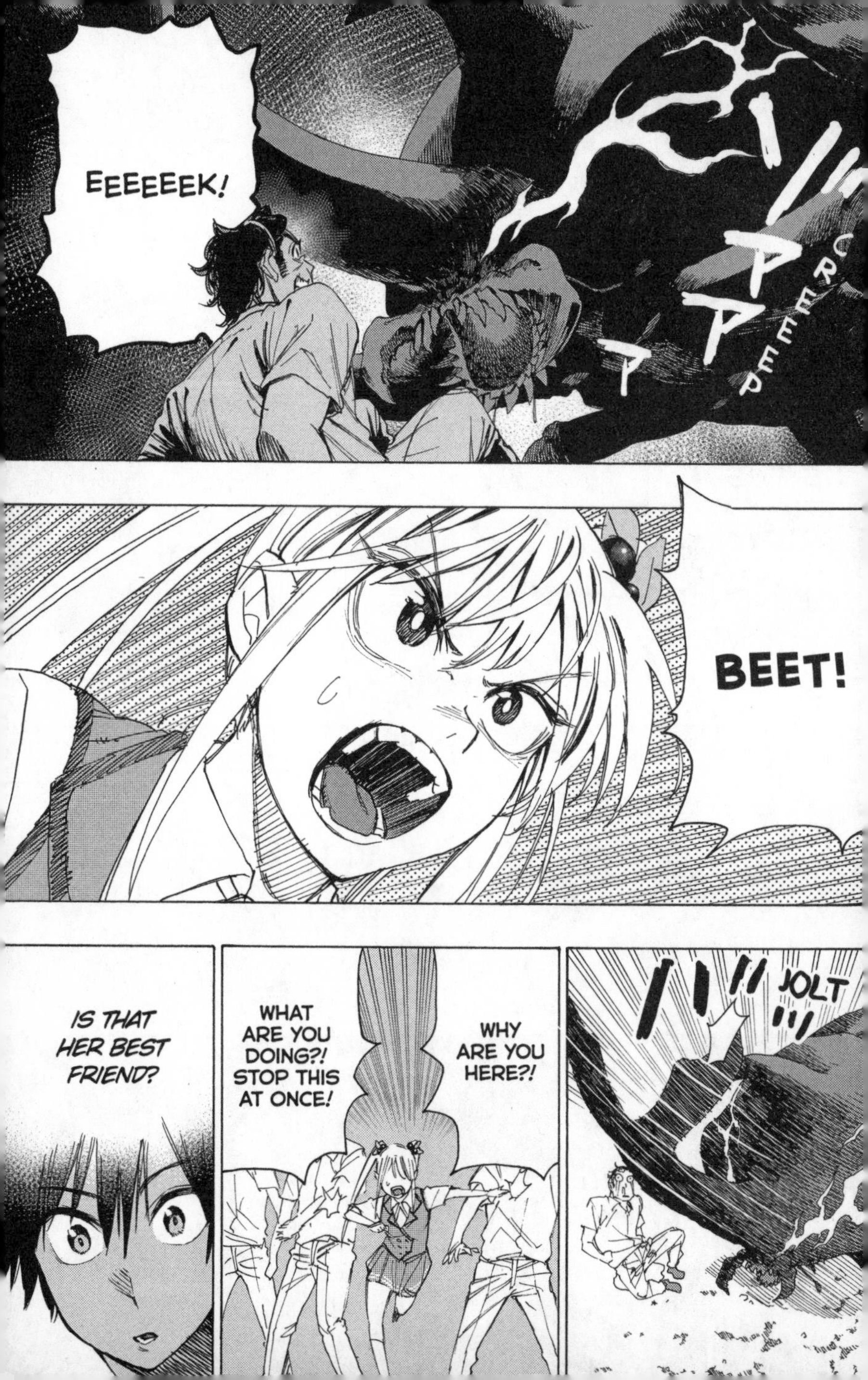
CREEEP
EEEEEEK!
BEET!
JOLT
WHY ARE YOU HERE?!
WHAT ARE YOU DOING?! STOP THIS AT ONCE!
IS THAT HER BEST FRIEND?

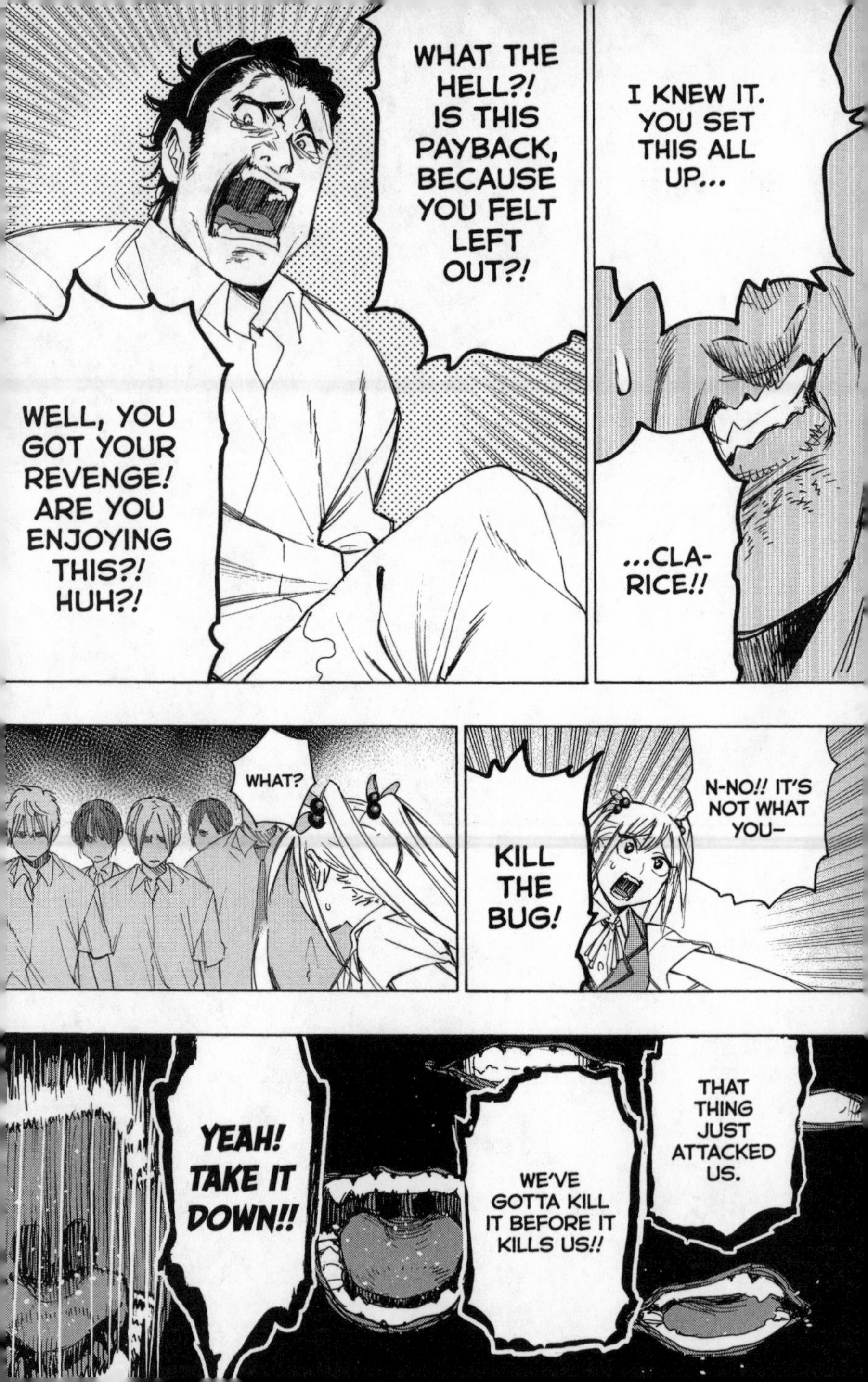
I KNEW IT. YOU SET THIS ALL UP...
...CLA-RICE!!
WHAT THE HELL?! IS THIS PAYBACK, BECAUSE YOU FELT LEFT OUT?!
WELL, YOU GOT YOUR REVENGE! ARE YOU ENJOYING THIS?! HUH?!
N-NO!! IT'S NOT WHAT YOU–
KILL THE BUG!
WHAT?
THAT THING JUST ATTACKED US.
WE'VE GOTTA KILL IT BEFORE IT KILLS US!!
YEAH! TAKE IT DOWN!!

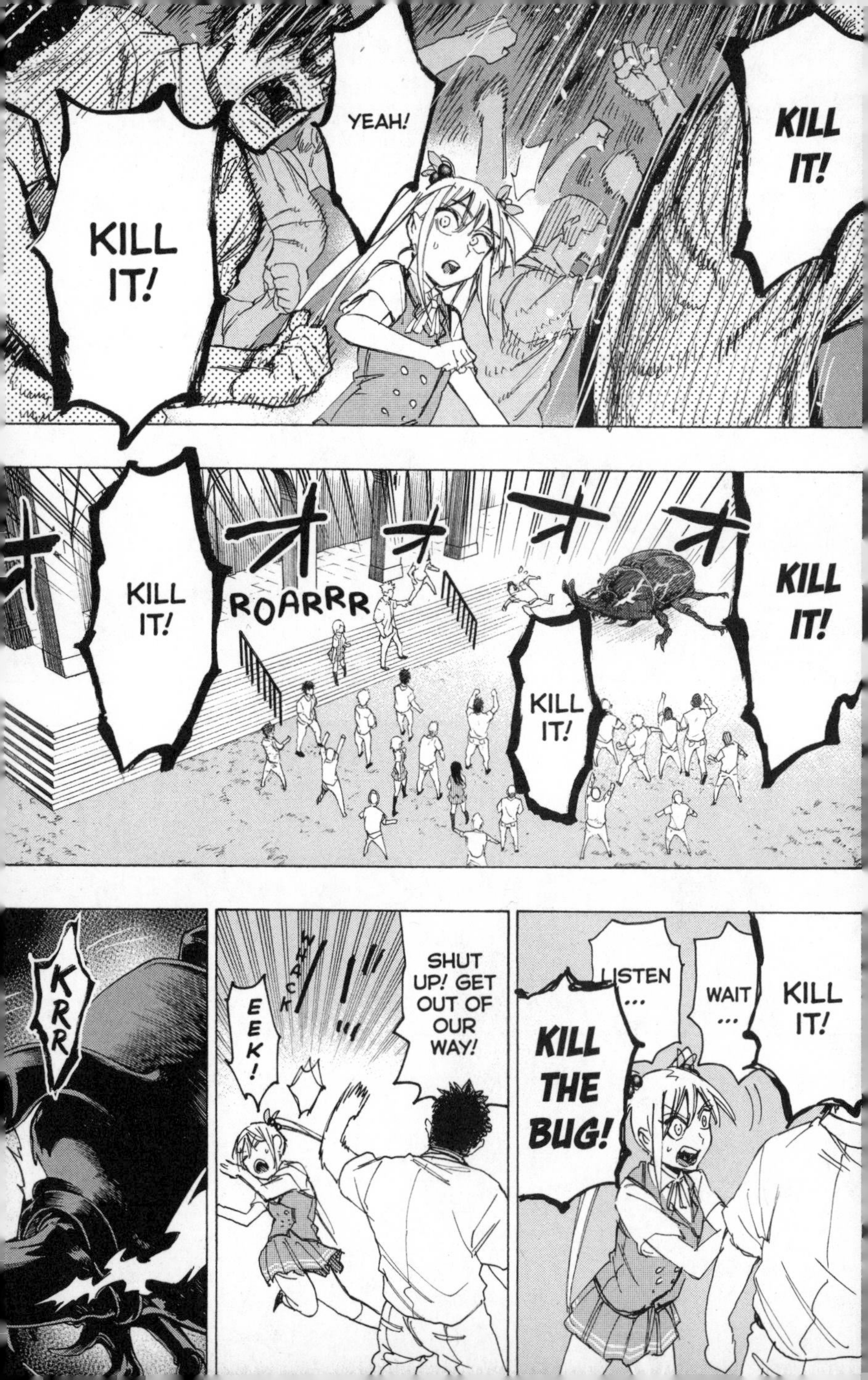

KILL IT!
YEAH!
KILL IT!
KILL IT!
KILL IT!
ROARRR
KILL IT!
KILL IT!
WAIT...
LISTEN...
KILL THE BUG!
SHUT UP! GET OUT OF OUR WAY!
WHACK
EEK!
KRR

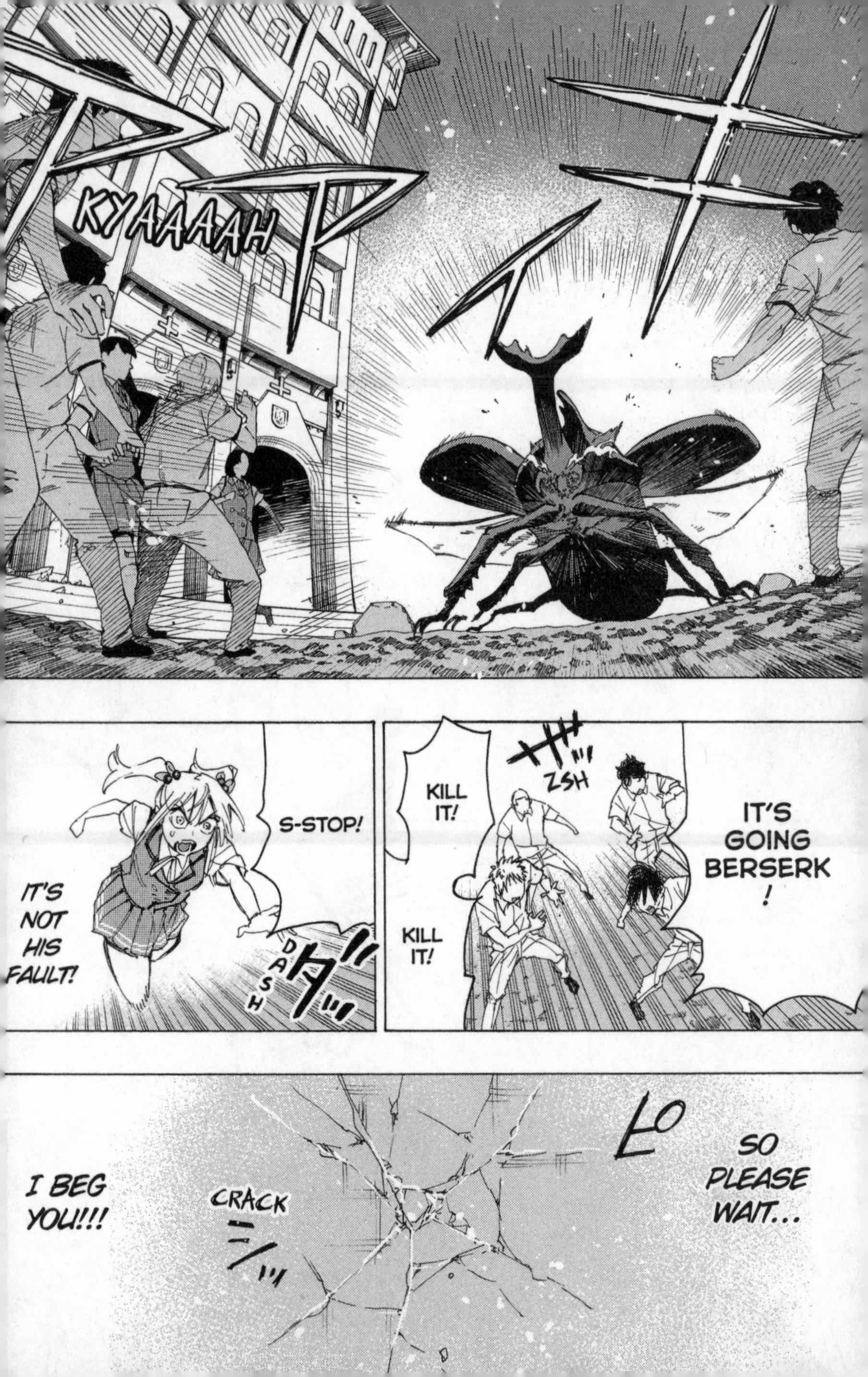
KYAAAAH
IT'S GOING BERSERK!
ZSH
KILL IT!
KILL IT!
S-STOP!
IT'S NOT HIS FAULT!
DASH
SO PLEASE WAIT...
CRACK
I BEG YOU!!!

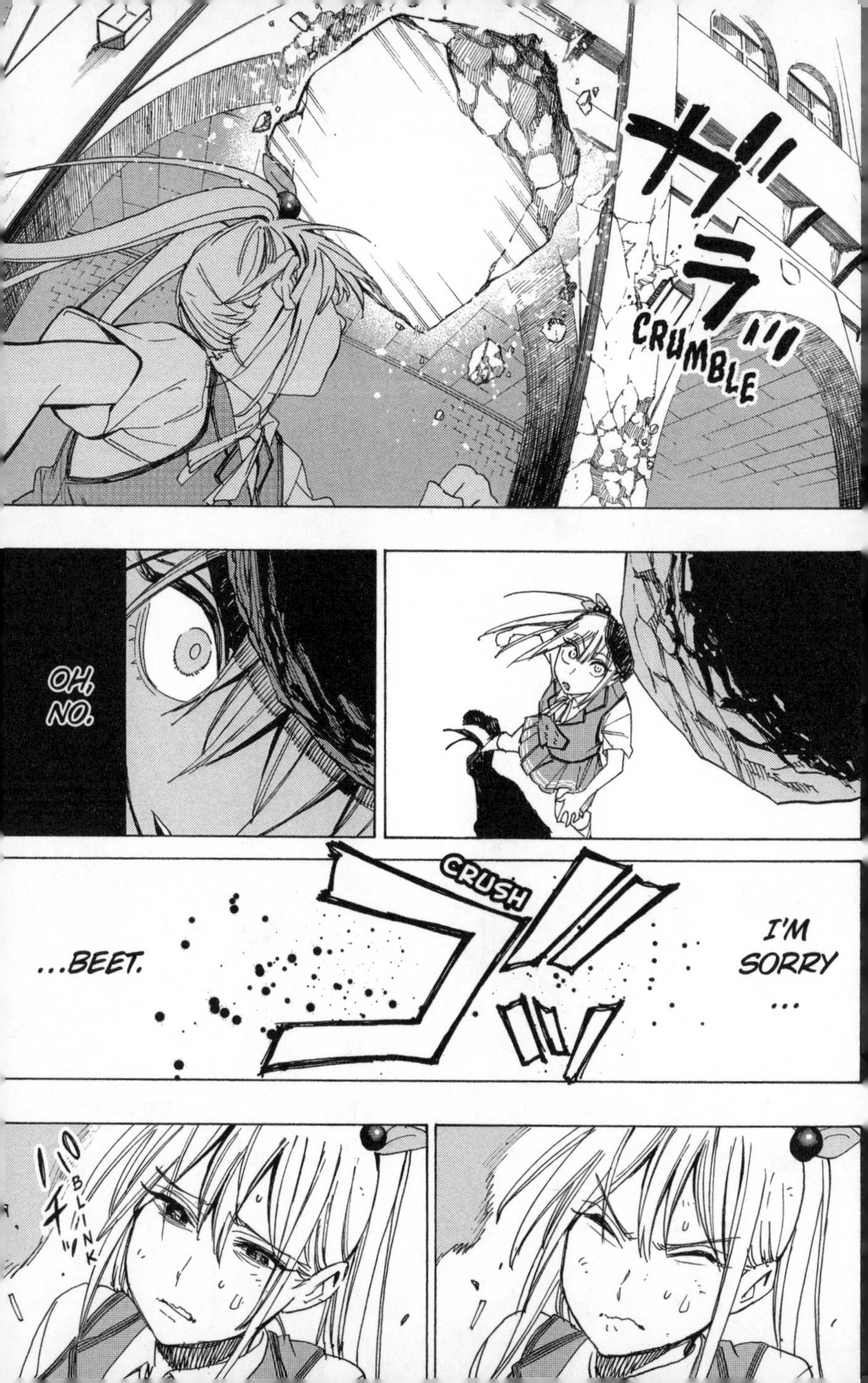
ガラ
CRUMBLE
OH, NO.
I'M SORRY ...
ゴッ
CRUSH
...BEET.
チ
BLINK

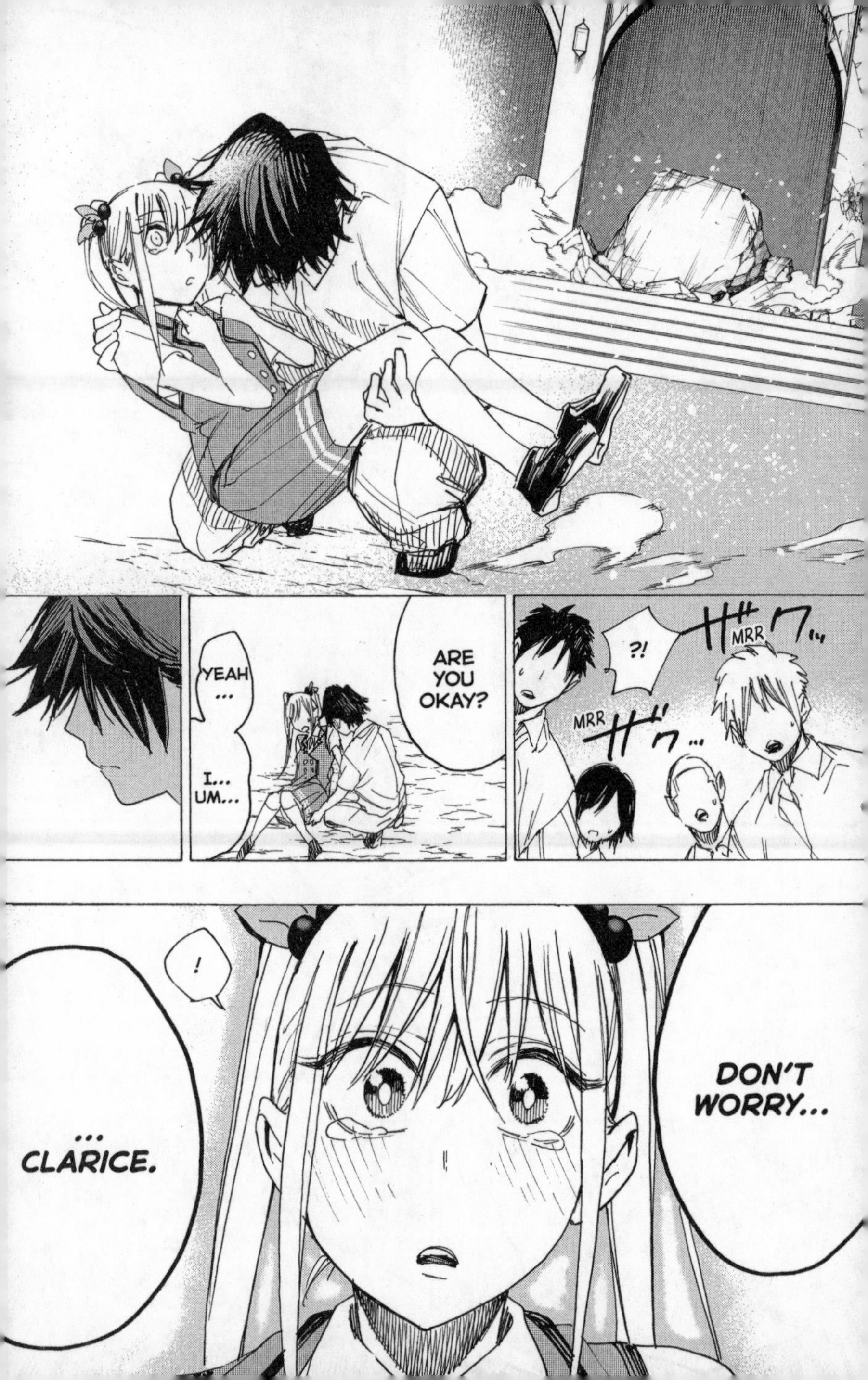
ザワッ
MRR
?!
MRR
ザワ…
ARE YOU OKAY?
YEAH ...
I... UM...
DON'T WORRY...
!
... CLARICE.

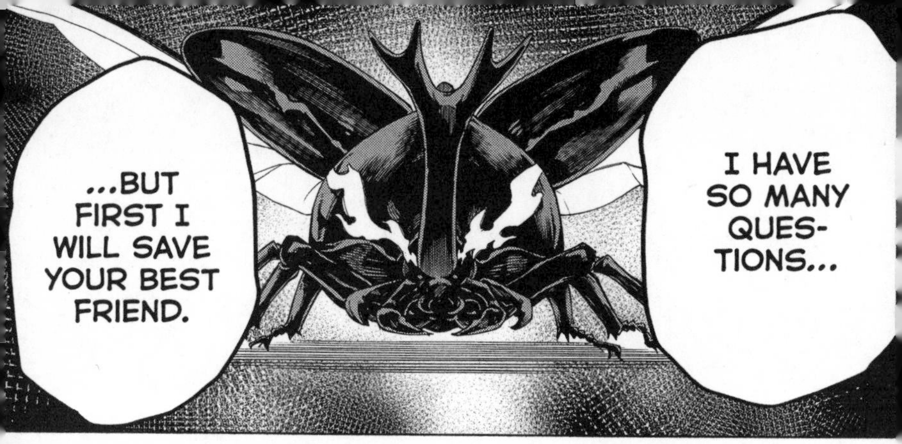
I HAVE SO MANY QUES-TIONS...
...BUT FIRST I WILL SAVE YOUR BEST FRIEND.
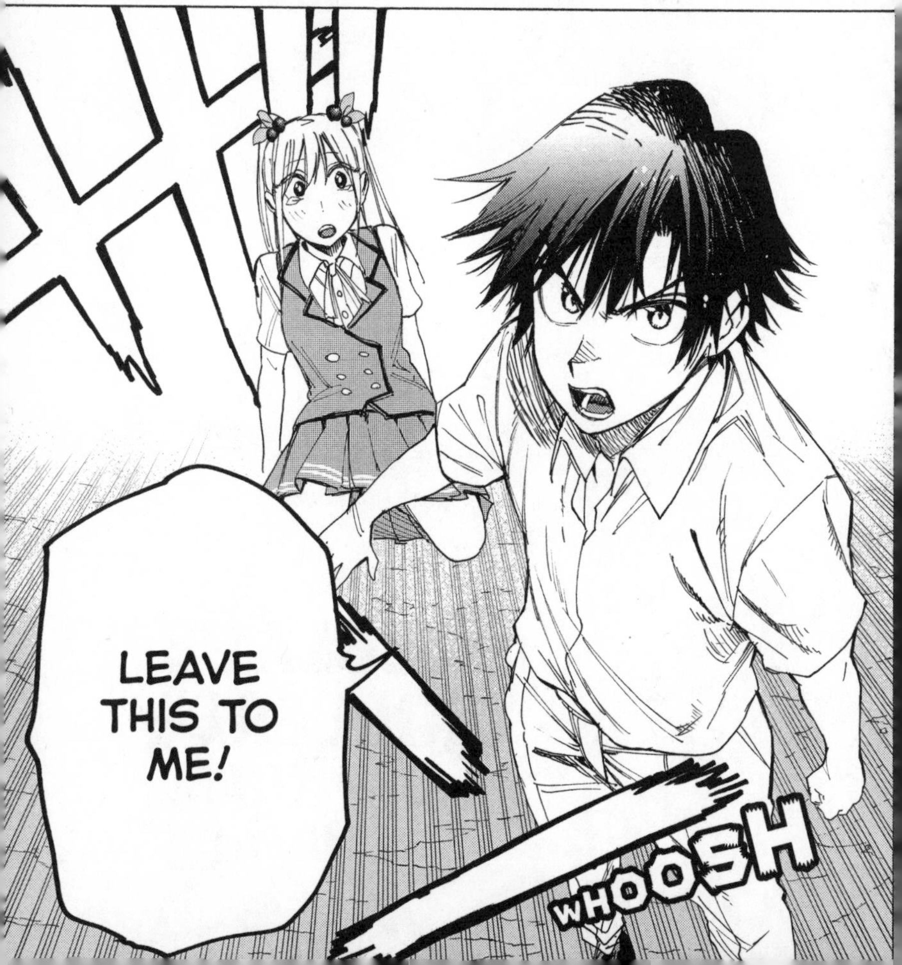
LEAVE THIS TO ME!
WHOOSH

The
ICEBLADE
SORCERER
Shall RULE
the
WORLD

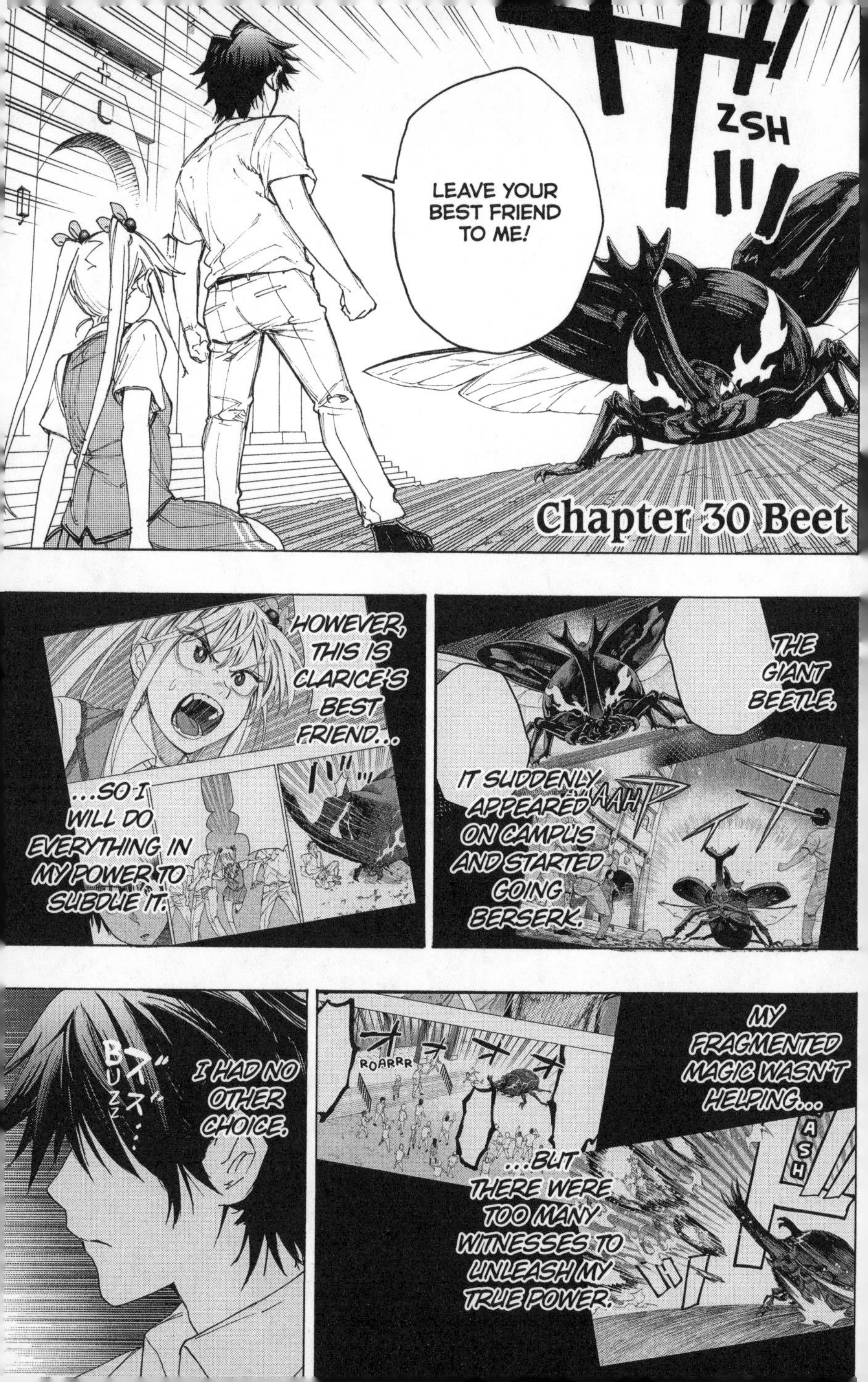
ZSH
LEAVE YOUR BEST FRIEND TO ME!
Chapter 30 Beet
THE GIANT BEETLE.
IT SUDDENLY APPEARED ON CAMPUS AND STARTED GOING BERSERK.
AAH
HOWEVER, THIS IS CLARICE'S BEST FRIEND...
...SO I WILL DO EVERYTHING IN MY POWER TO SUBDUE IT.
MY FRAGMENTED MAGIC WASN'T HELPING...
ROARRR
...BUT THERE WERE TOO MANY WITNESSES TO UNLEASH MY TRUE POWER.
ASH
BUZZ
I HAD NO OTHER CHOICE.

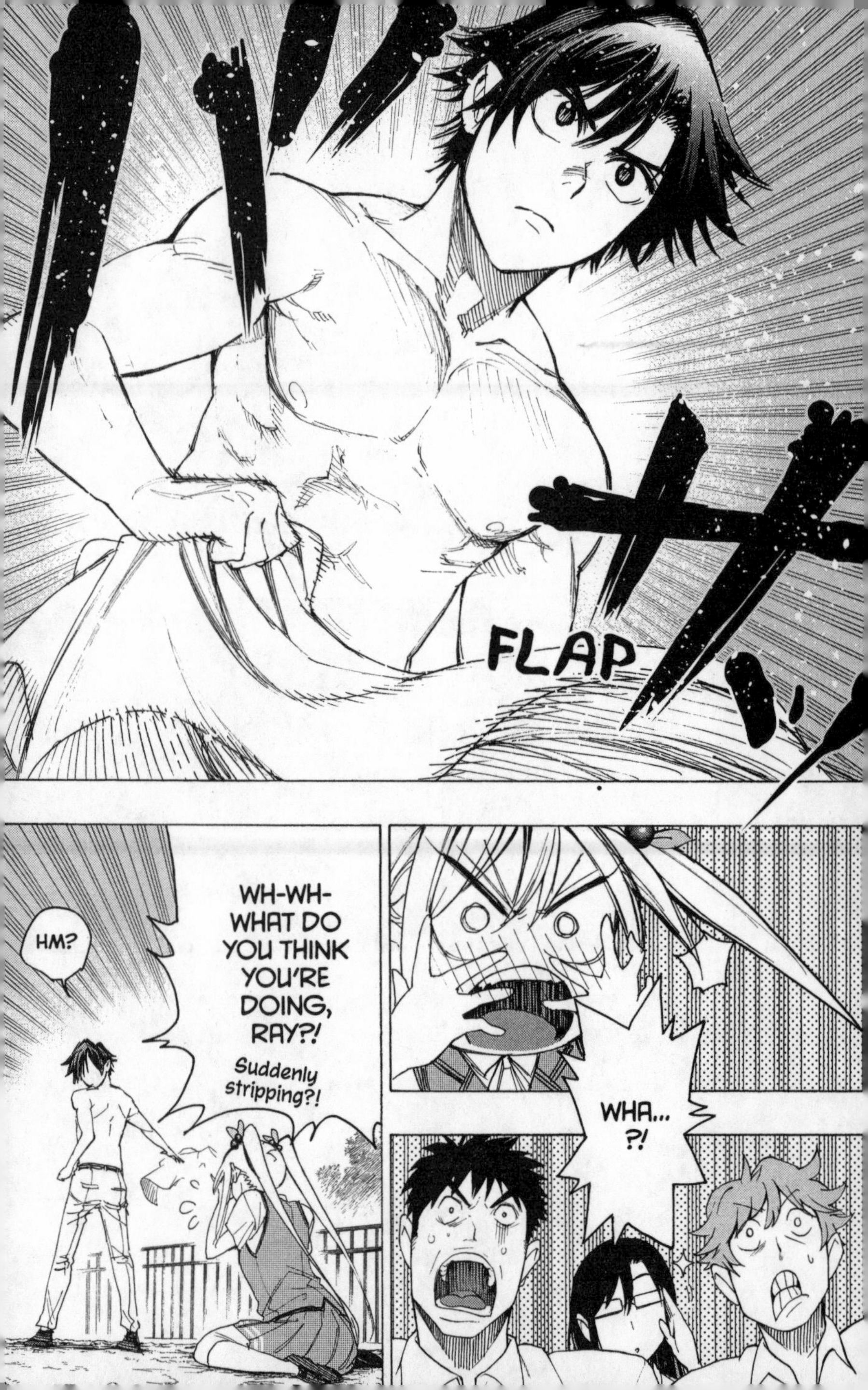
FLAP
WHA... ?!
WH-WH- WHAT DO YOU THINK YOU'RE DOING, RAY?!
HM?
Suddenly stripping?!

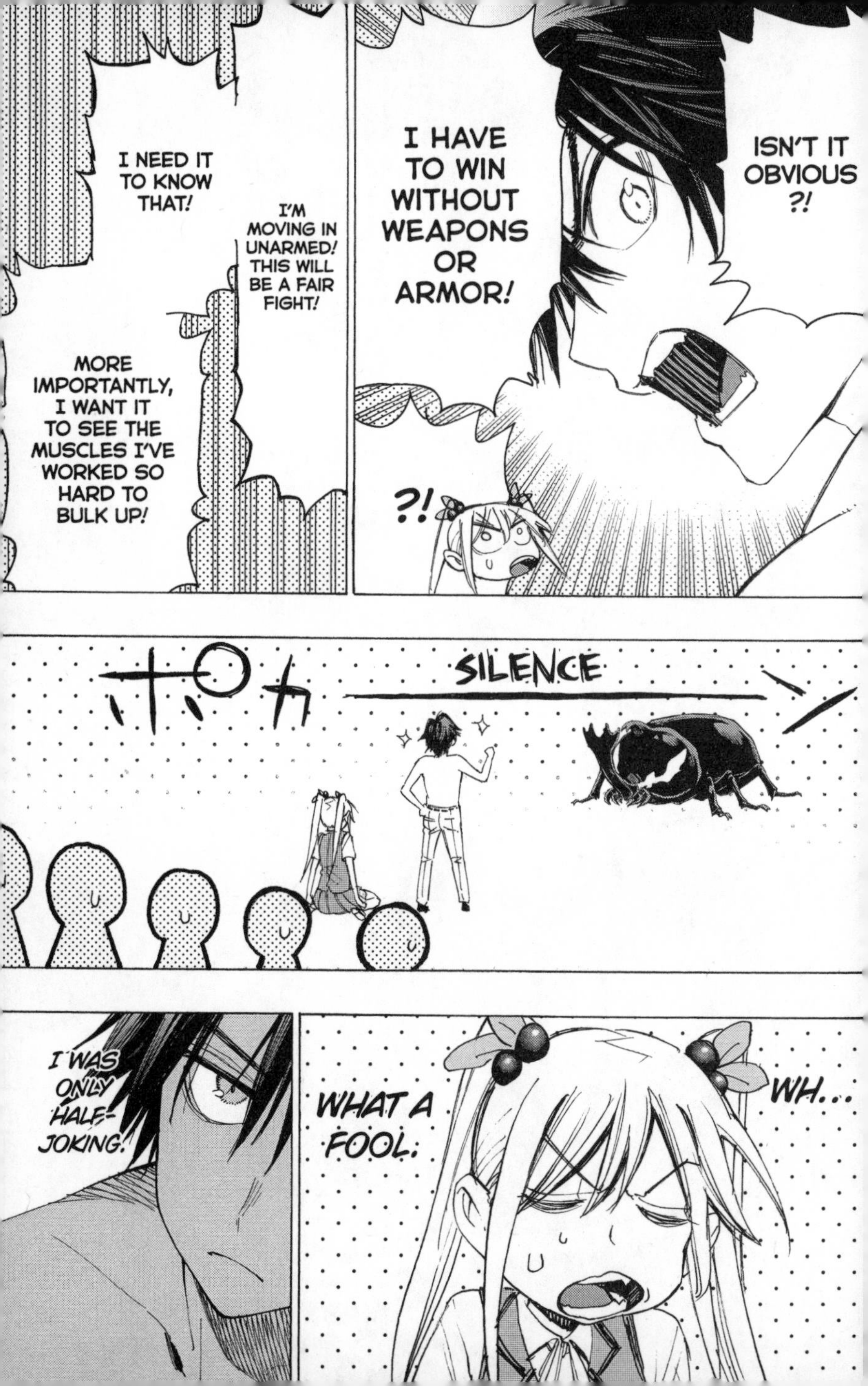
ISN'T IT OBVIOUS?!
I HAVE TO WIN WITHOUT WEAPONS OR ARMOR!
?!
I'M MOVING IN UNARMED! THIS WILL BE A FAIR FIGHT!
I NEED IT TO KNOW THAT!
MORE IMPORTANTLY, I WANT IT TO SEE THE MUSCLES I'VE WORKED SO HARD TO BULK UP!
SILENCE
WH...
WHAT A FOOL.
I WAS ONLY HALF-JOKING.

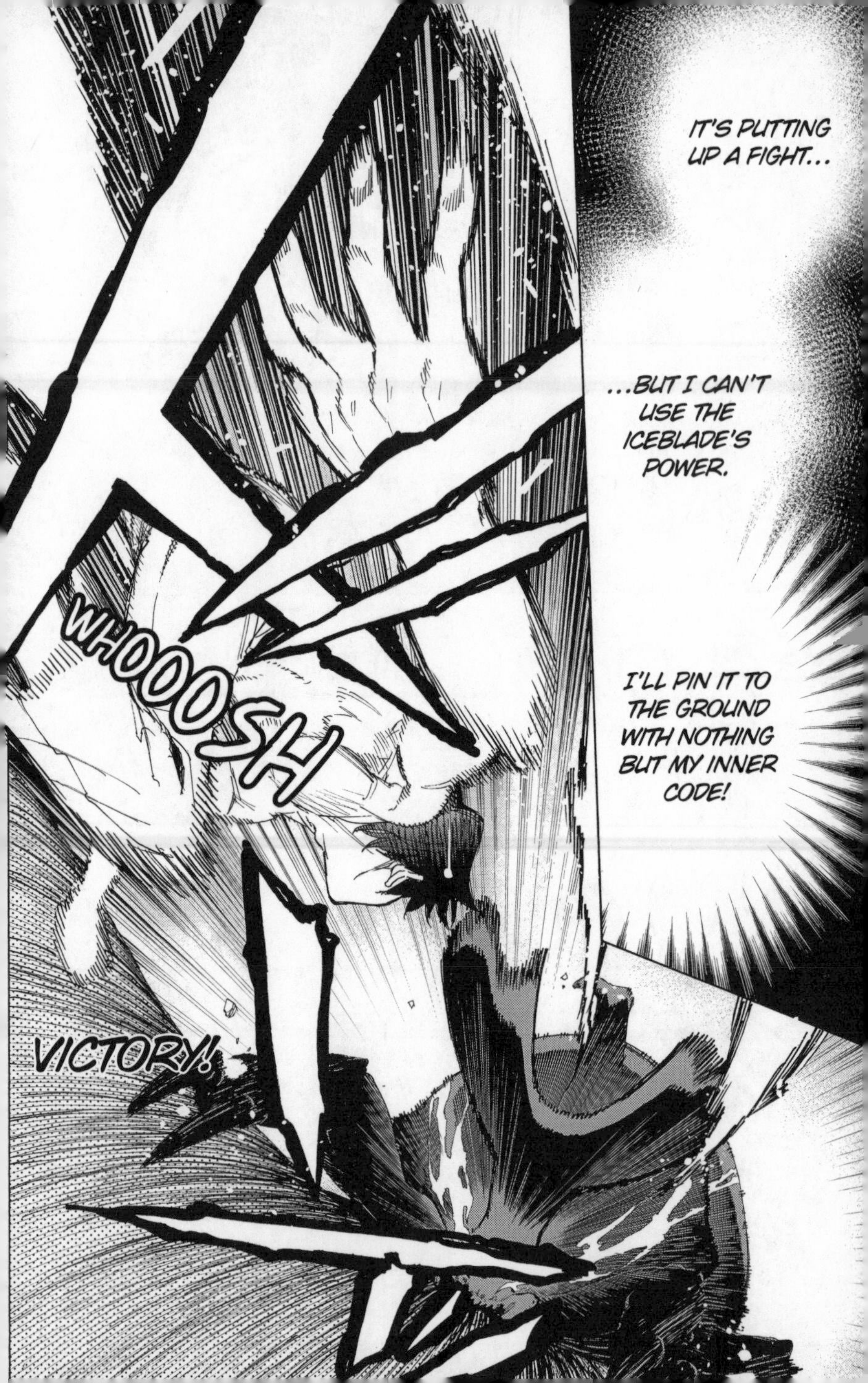
IT'S PUTTING UP A FIGHT...
...BUT I CAN'T USE THE ICEBLADE'S POWER.
I'LL PIN IT TO THE GROUND WITH NOTHING BUT MY INNER CODE!
WHOOOSH
VICTORY!

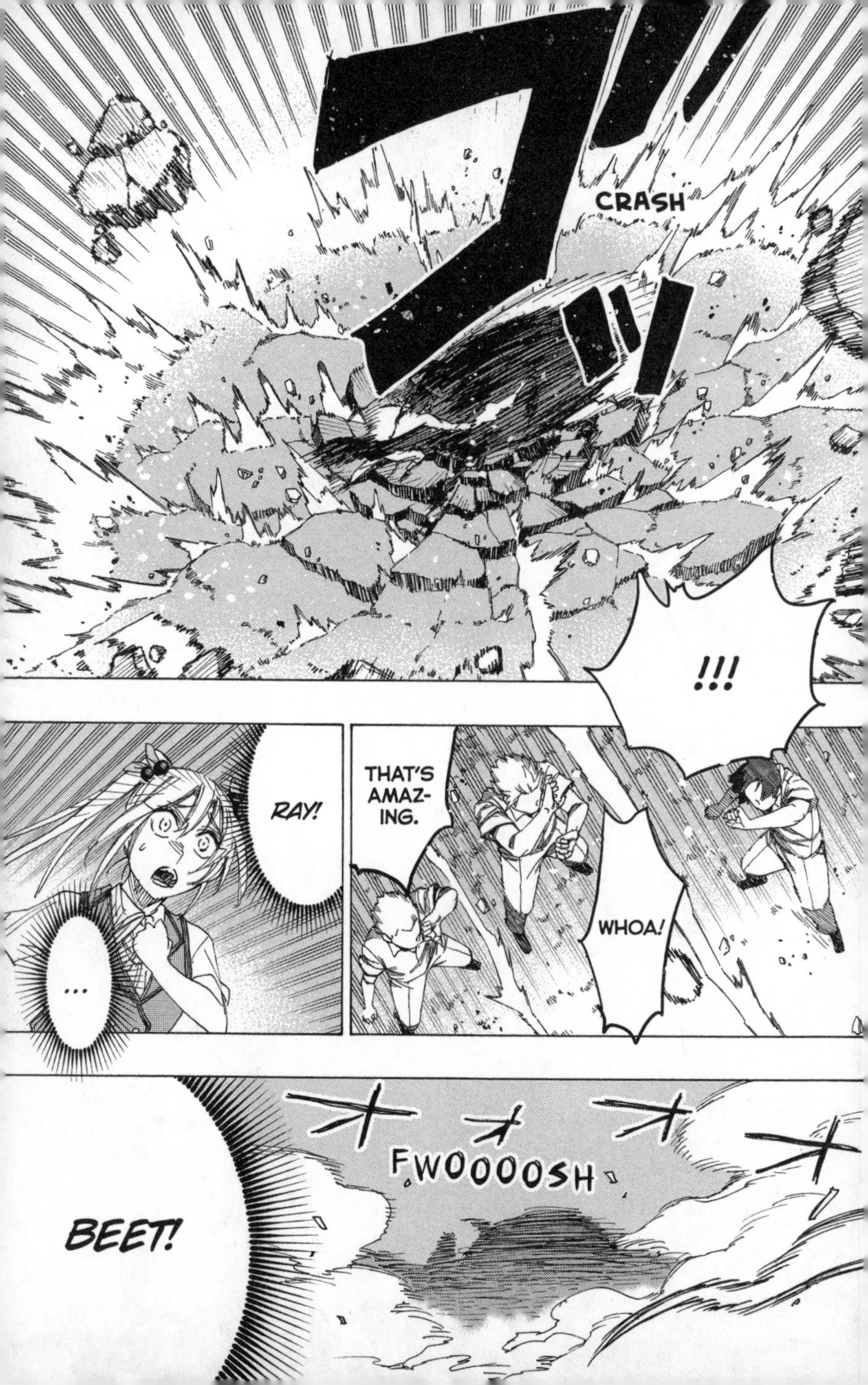
CRASH
!!!
THAT'S AMAZ-ING.
WHOA!
RAY!
...
FWOOOOSH
BEET!

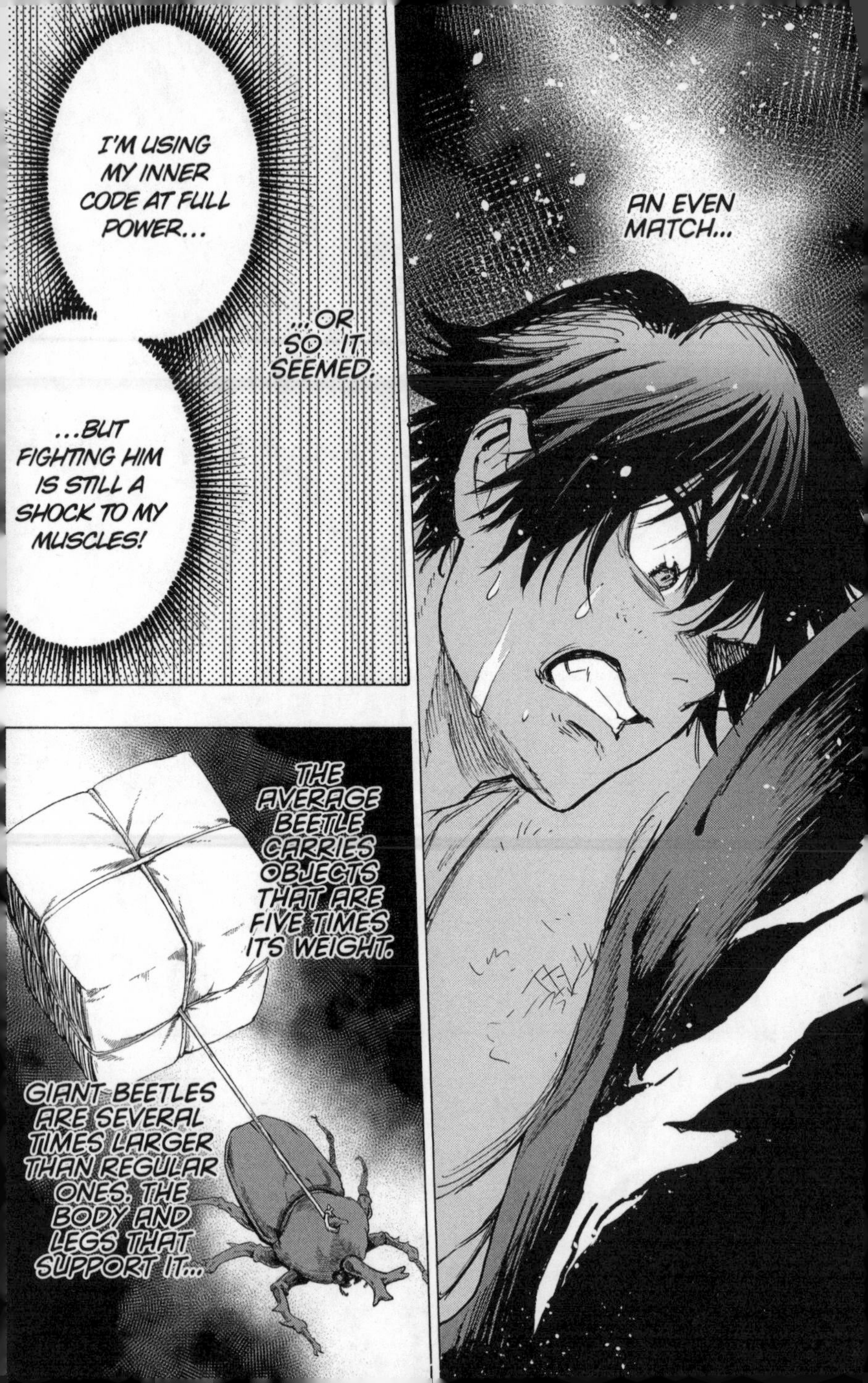
AN EVEN MATCH...
...OR SO IT SEEMED.
I'M USING MY INNER CODE AT FULL POWER...
...BUT FIGHTING HIM IS STILL A SHOCK TO MY MUSCLES!
THE AVERAGE BEETLE CARRIES OBJECTS THAT ARE FIVE TIMES ITS WEIGHT.
GIANT BEETLES ARE SEVERAL TIMES LARGER THAN REGULAR ONES. THE BODY AND LEGS THAT SUPPORT IT...

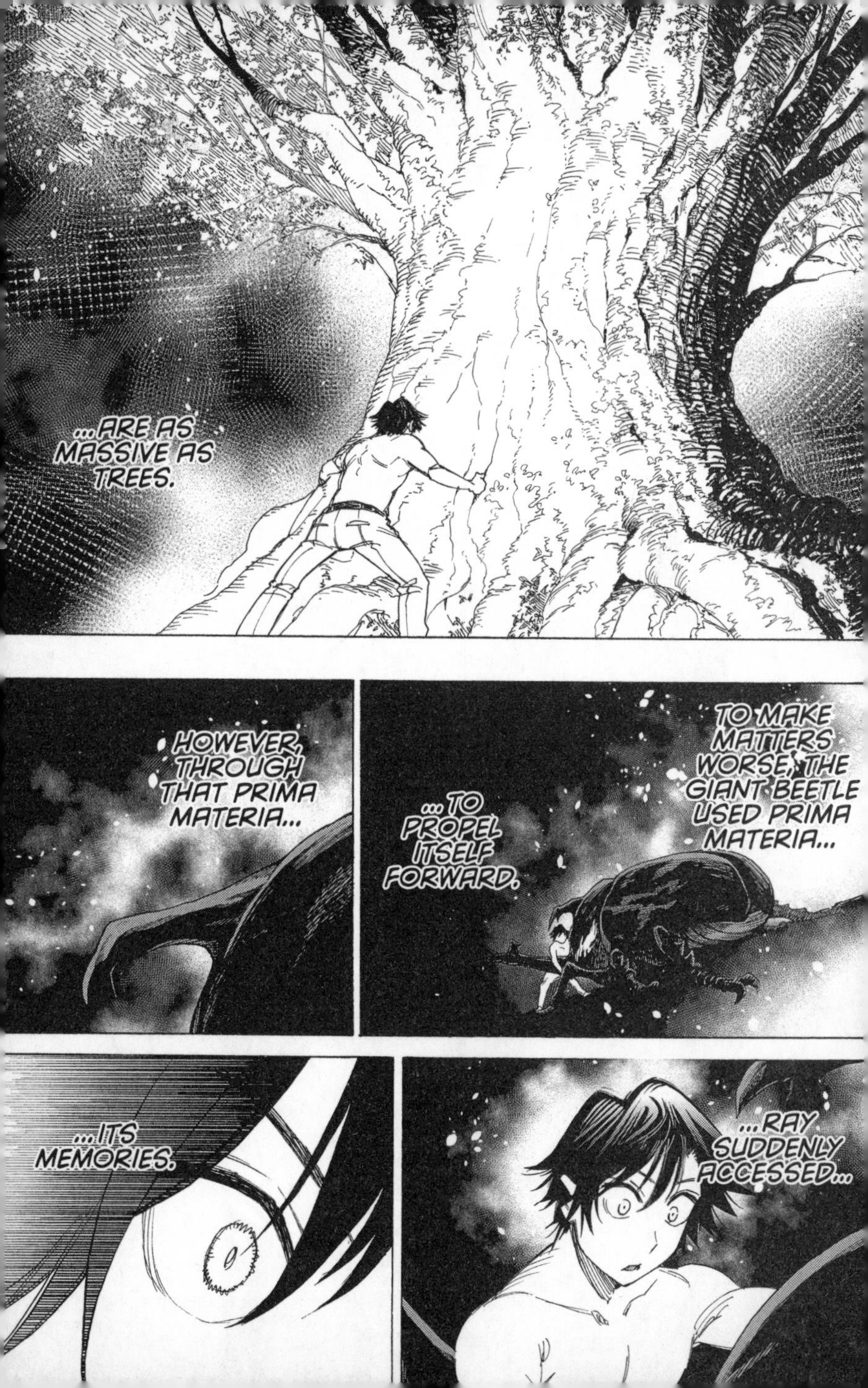
...ARE AS MASSIVE AS TREES.
TO MAKE MATTERS WORSE, THE GIANT BEETLE USED PRIMA MATERIA...
...TO PROPEL ITSELF FORWARD.
HOWEVER, THROUGH THAT PRIMA MATERIA...
...RAY SUDDENLY ACCESSED...
...ITS MEMORIES.

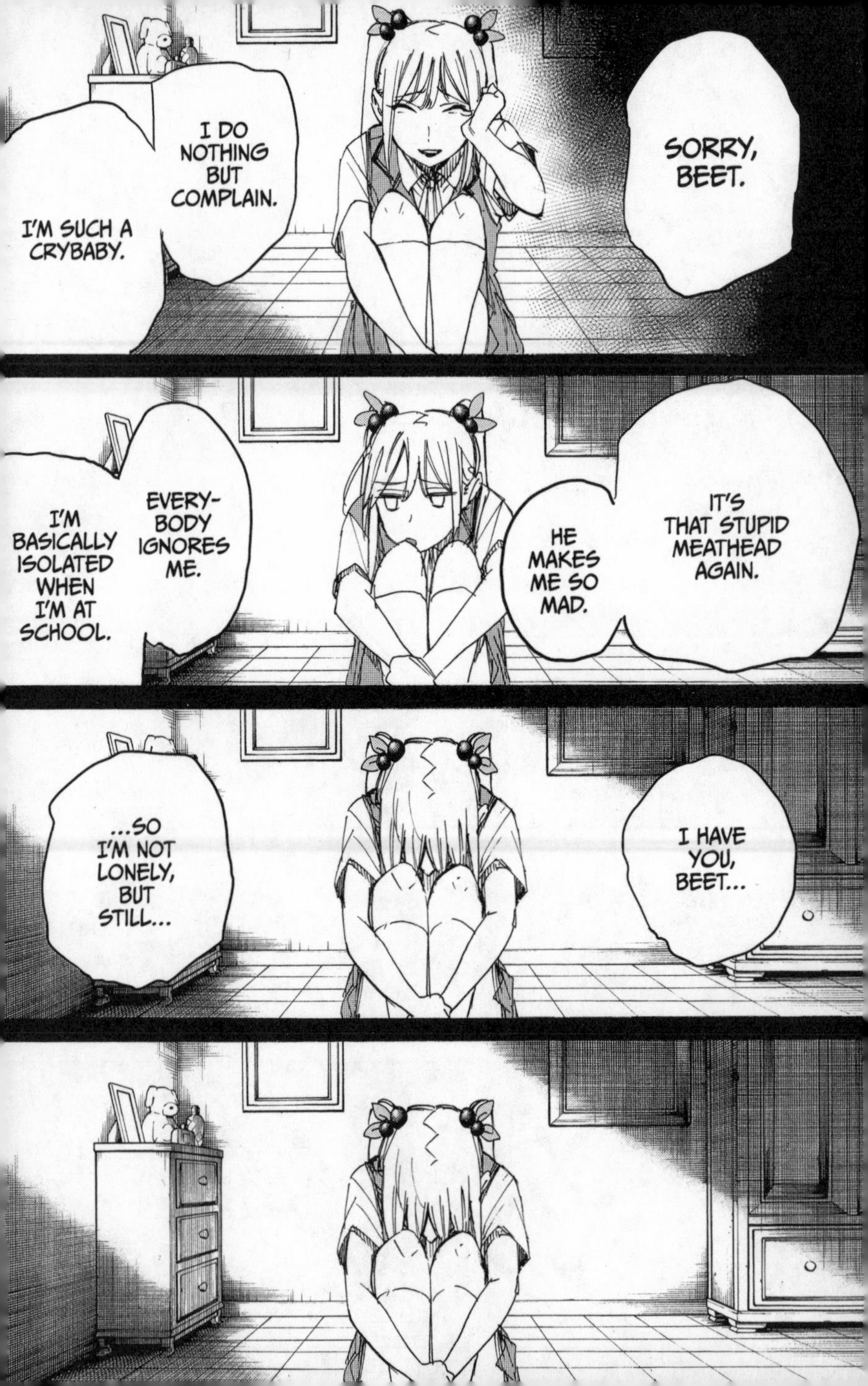
SORRY, BEET.
I DO NOTHING BUT COMPLAIN.
I'M SUCH A CRYBABY.
IT'S THAT STUPID MEATHEAD AGAIN.
HE MAKES ME SO MAD.
EVERY-BODY IGNORES ME.
I'M BASICALLY ISOLATED WHEN I'M AT SCHOOL.
I HAVE YOU, BEET...
...SO I'M NOT LONELY, BUT STILL...

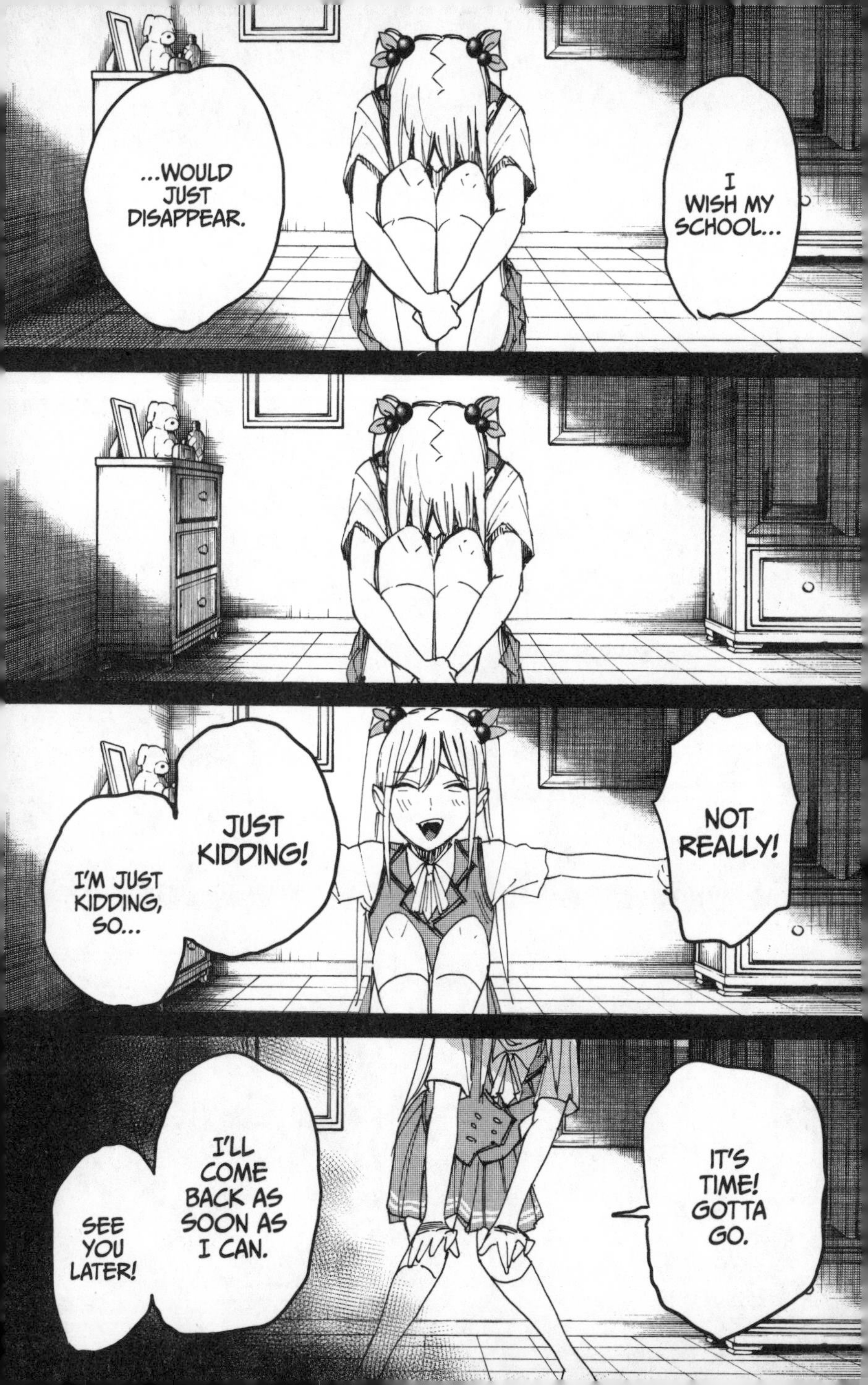
I WISH MY SCHOOL...
...WOULD JUST DISAPPEAR.
NOT REALLY!
JUST KIDDING!
I'M JUST KIDDING, SO...
IT'S TIME! GOTTA GO.
I'LL COME BACK AS SOON AS I CAN.
SEE YOU LATER!

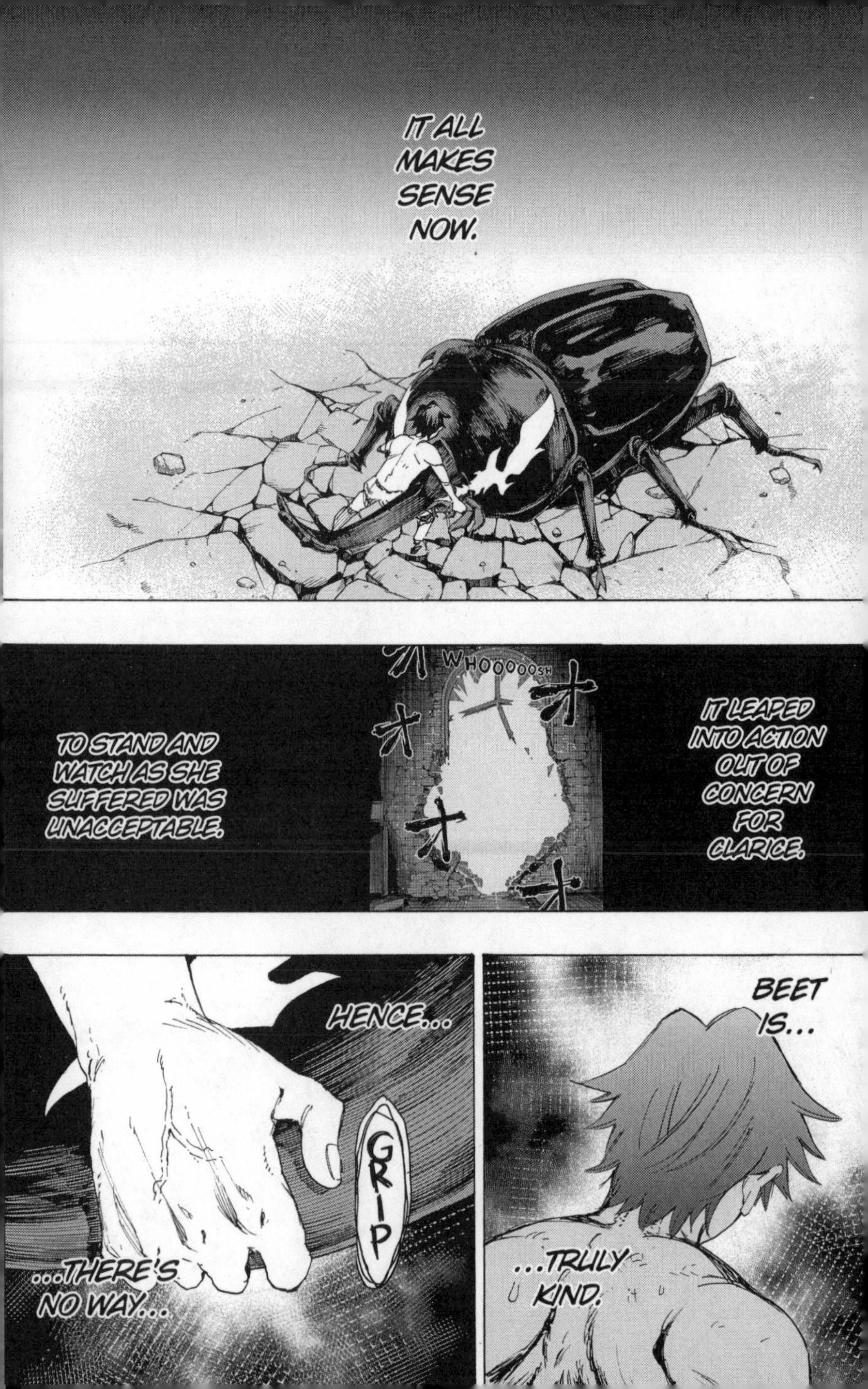
IT ALL MAKES SENSE NOW.
IT LEAPED INTO ACTION OUT OF CONCERN FOR CLARICE.
WHOOOOOSH
TO STAND AND WATCH AS SHE SUFFERED WAS UNACCEPTABLE.
BEET IS...
...TRULY KIND.
HENCE...
GRIP
...THERE'S NO WAY...

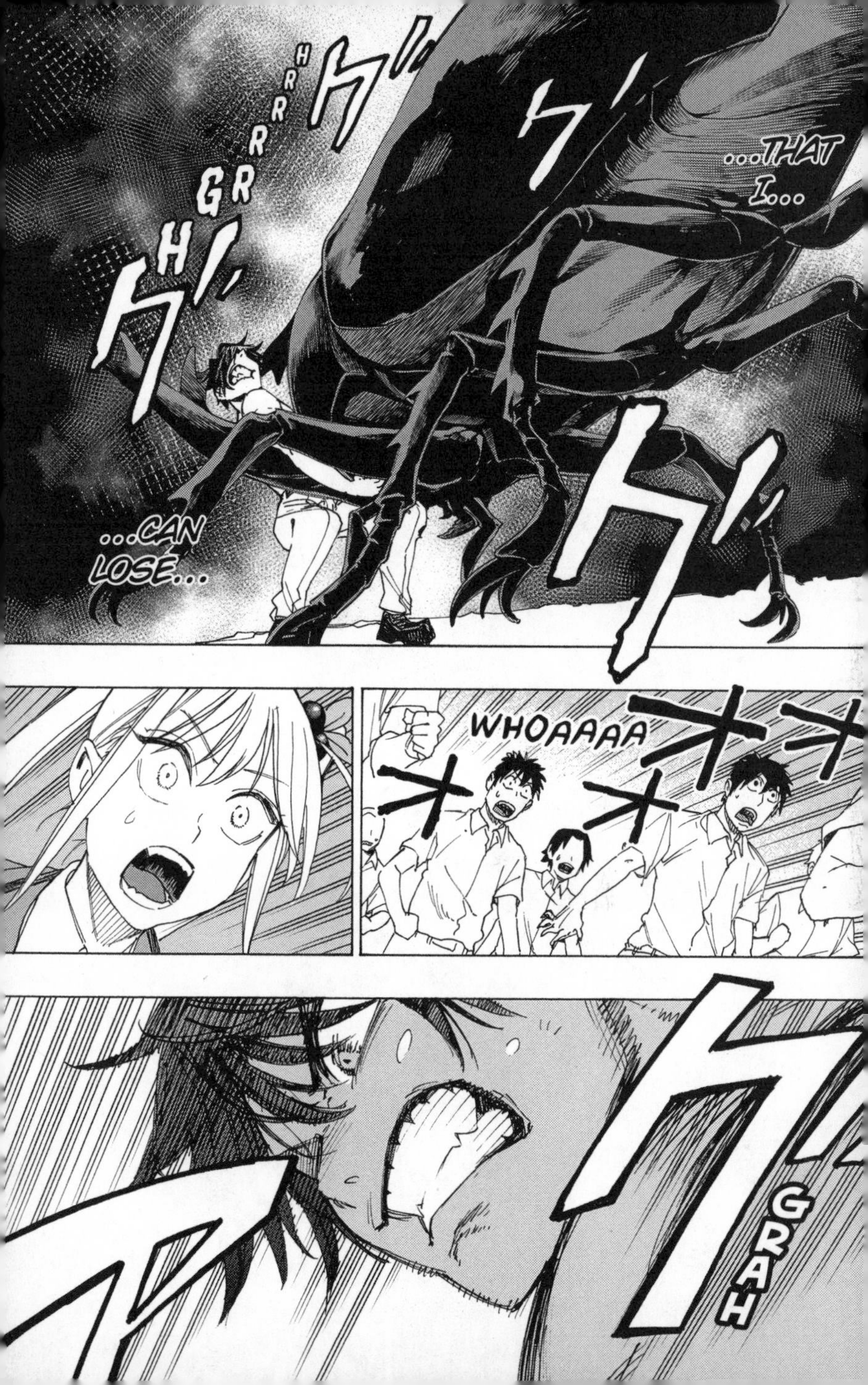
...THAT I...
H
GRRRRH
...CAN LOSE...
WHOAAAA
GRAH

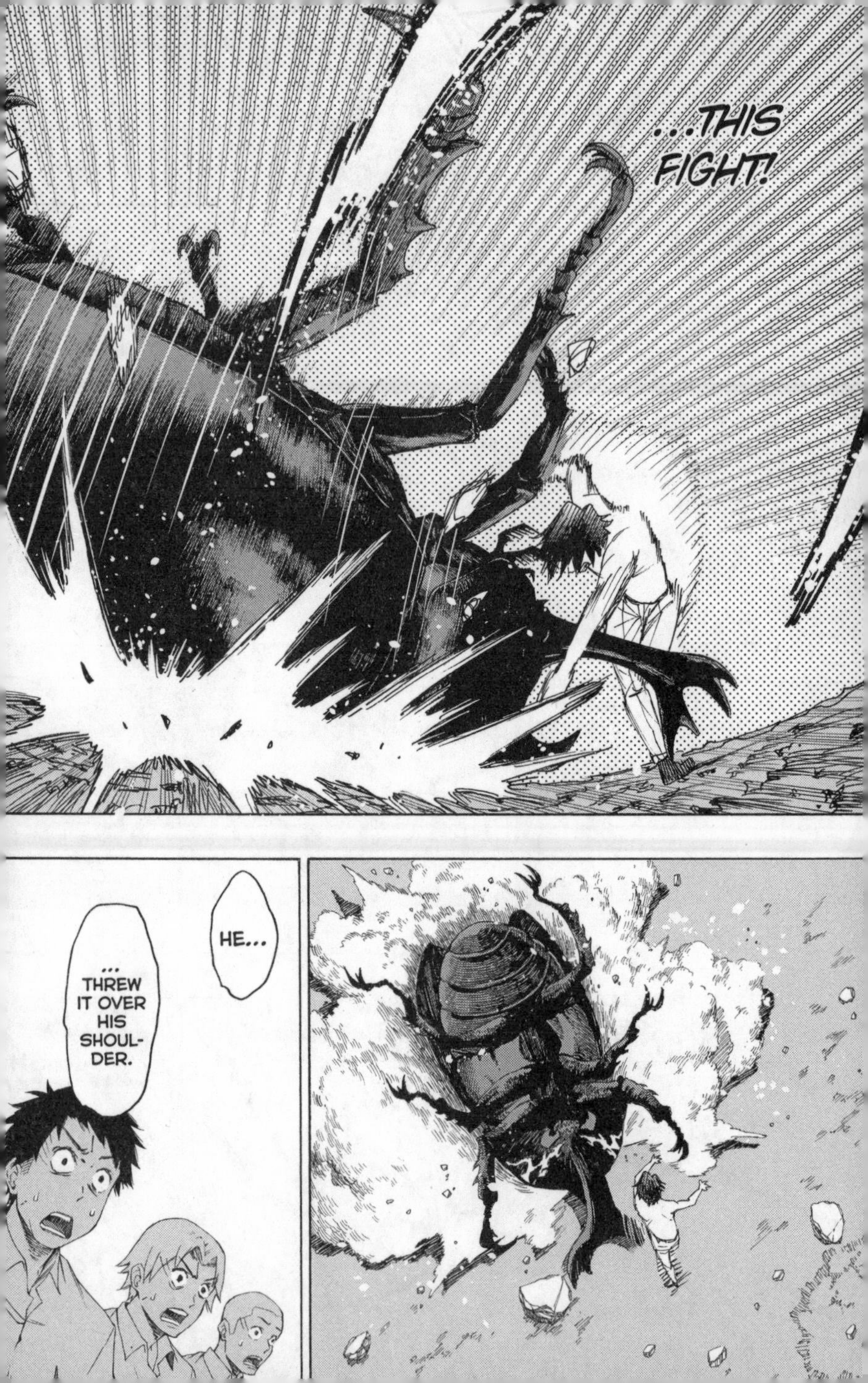
...THIS FIGHT!
HE...
... THREW IT OVER HIS SHOUL-DER.

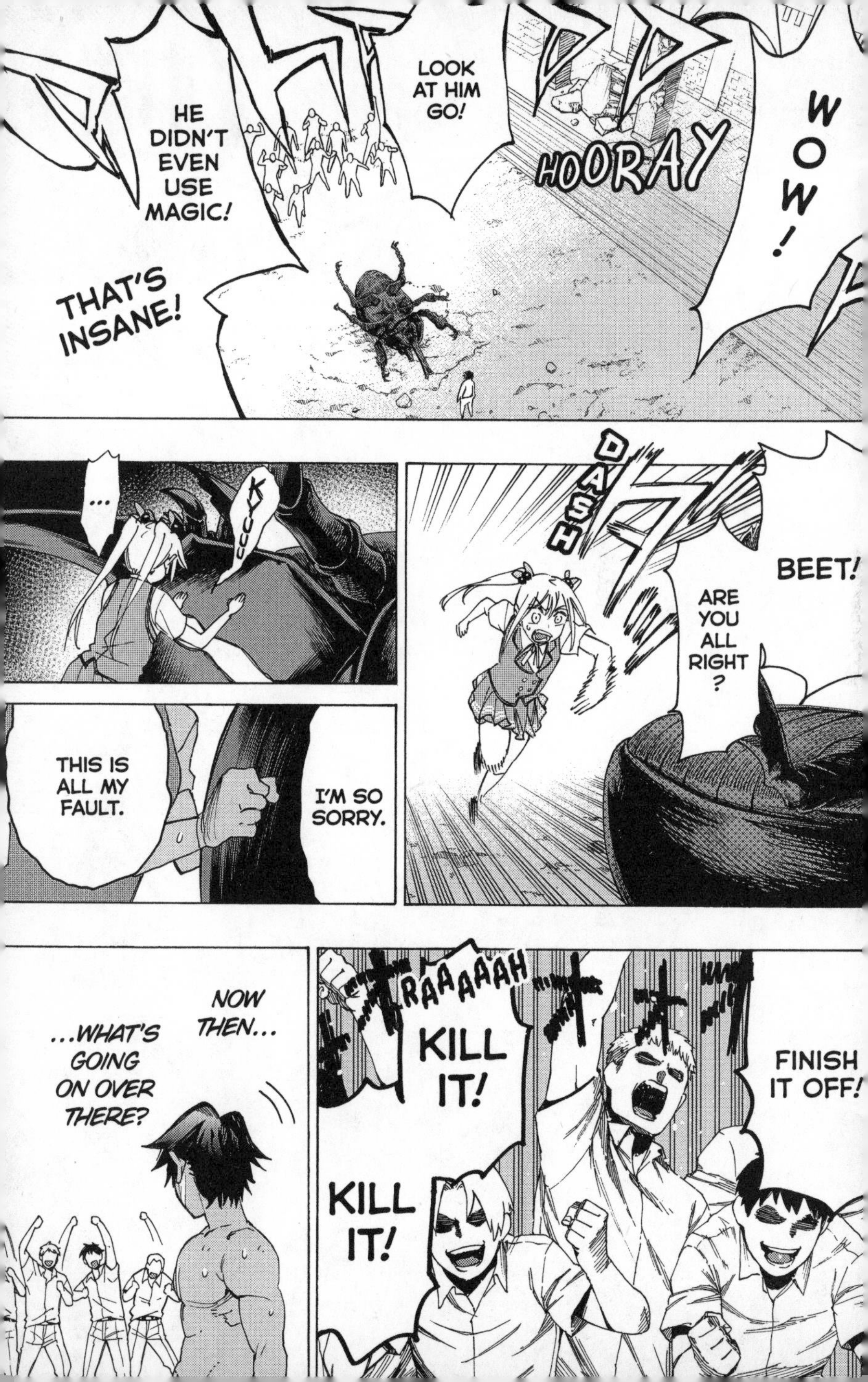
WOW!
HOORAY
LOOK AT HIM GO!
HE DIDN'T EVEN USE MAGIC!
THAT'S INSANE!
DASH
BEET!
ARE YOU ALL RIGHT?
...
KYUUUUU
I'M SO SORRY.
THIS IS ALL MY FAULT.
FINISH IT OFF!
RAAAAAH
KILL IT!
KILL IT!
NOW THEN...
...WHAT'S GOING ON OVER THERE?

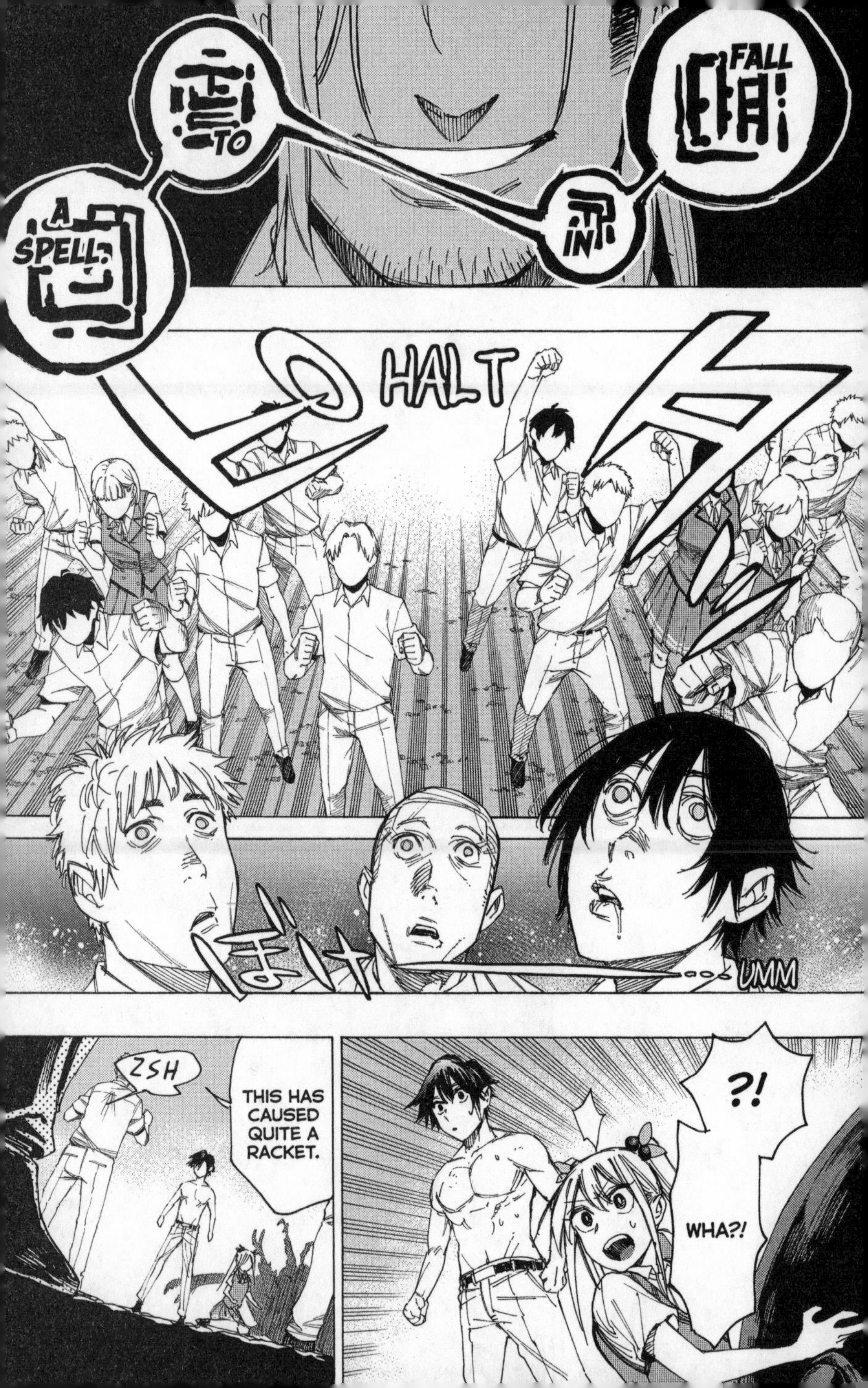
FALL
IN
TO
A SPELL
HALT
UMM
?!
WHA?!
ZSH
THIS HAS CAUSED QUITE A RACKET.

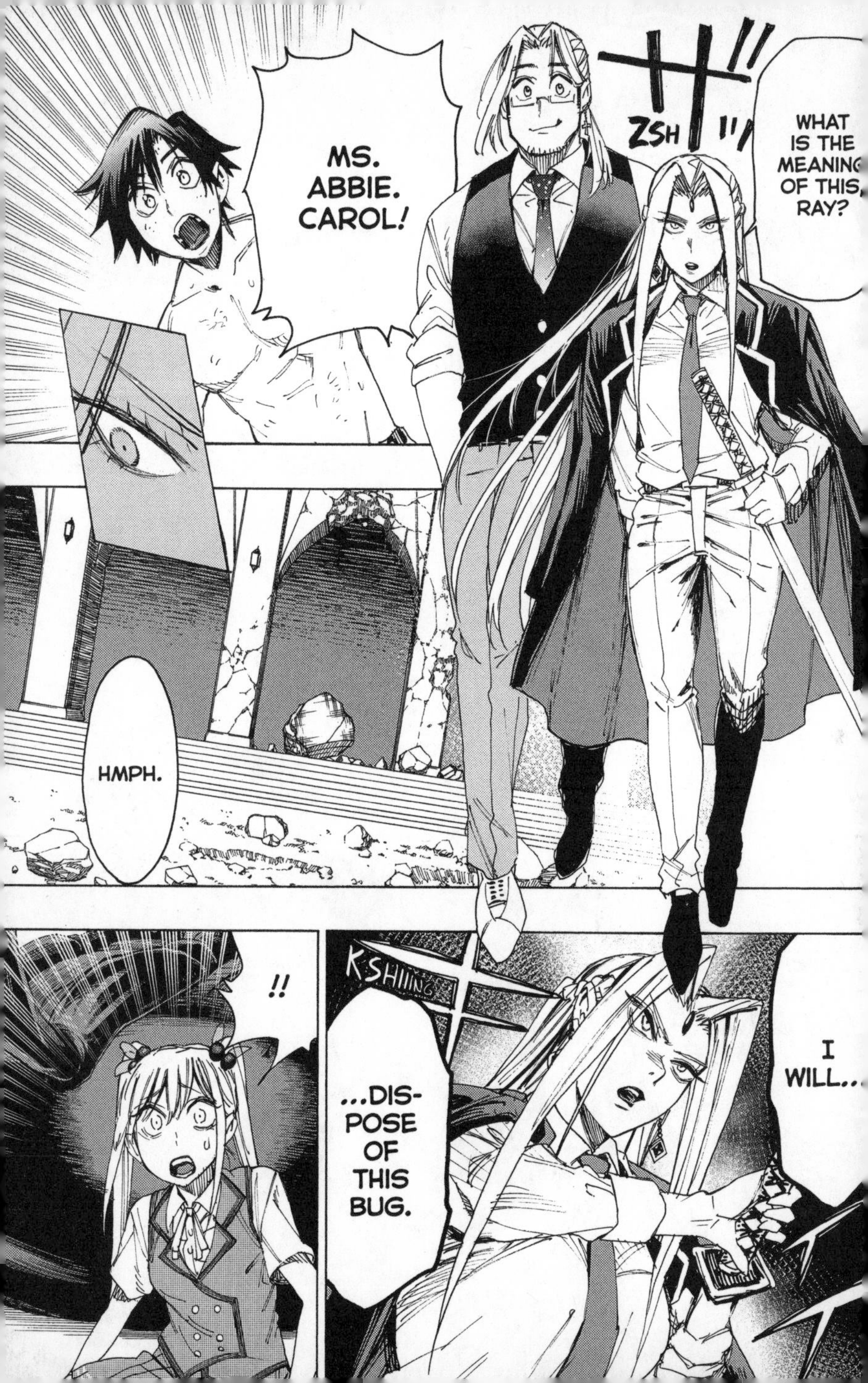
ZSH
WHAT IS THE MEANING OF THIS, RAY?
MS. ABBIE. CAROL!
HMPH.
KSHIIING
I WILL...
...DIS-POSE OF THIS BUG.
!!

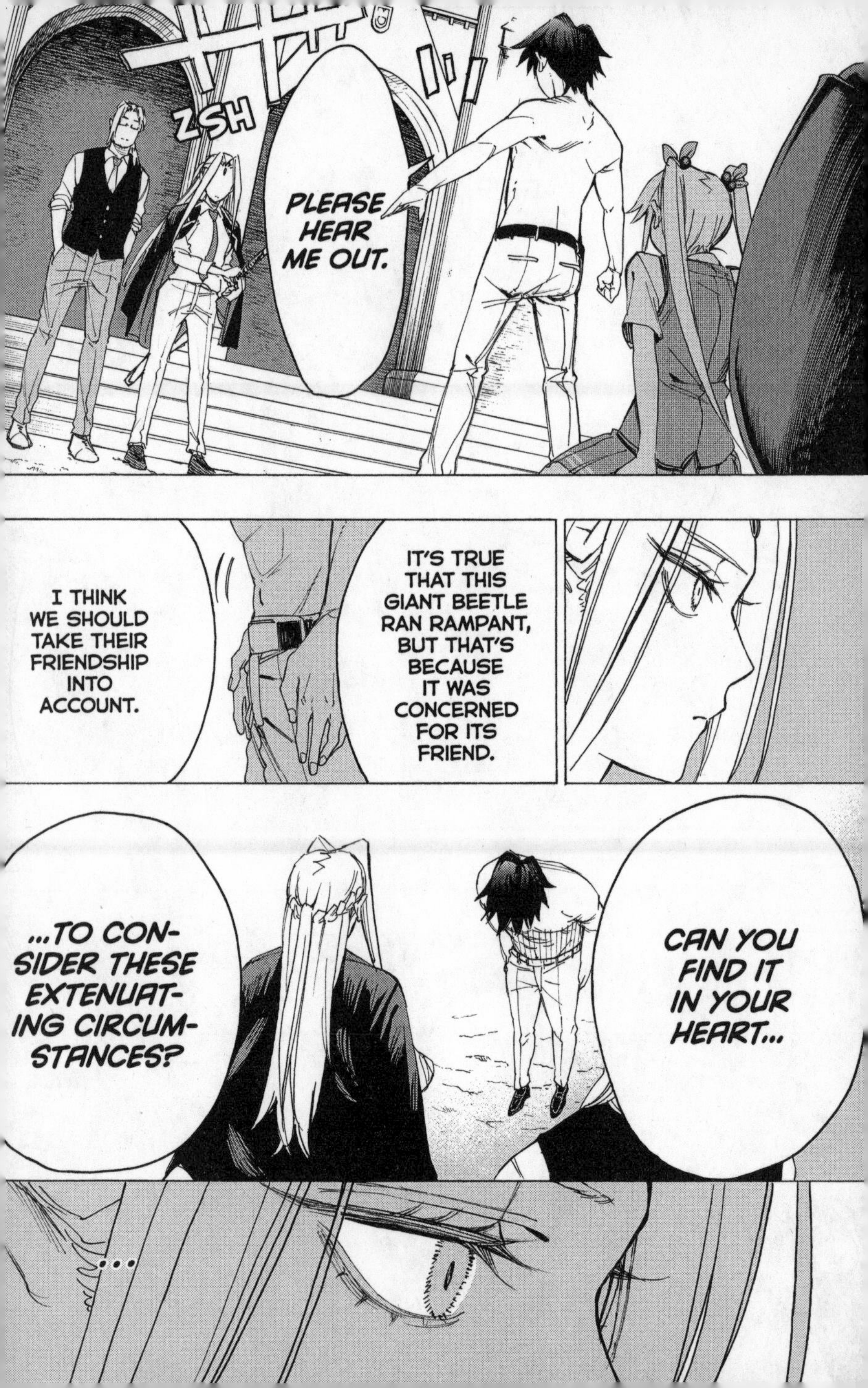
ZSH
PLEASE HEAR ME OUT.
IT'S TRUE THAT THIS GIANT BEETLE RAN RAMPANT, BUT THAT'S BECAUSE IT WAS CONCERNED FOR ITS FRIEND.
I THINK WE SHOULD TAKE THEIR FRIENDSHIP INTO ACCOUNT.
CAN YOU FIND IT IN YOUR HEART...
...TO CONSIDER THESE EXTENUATING CIRCUMSTANCES?
...

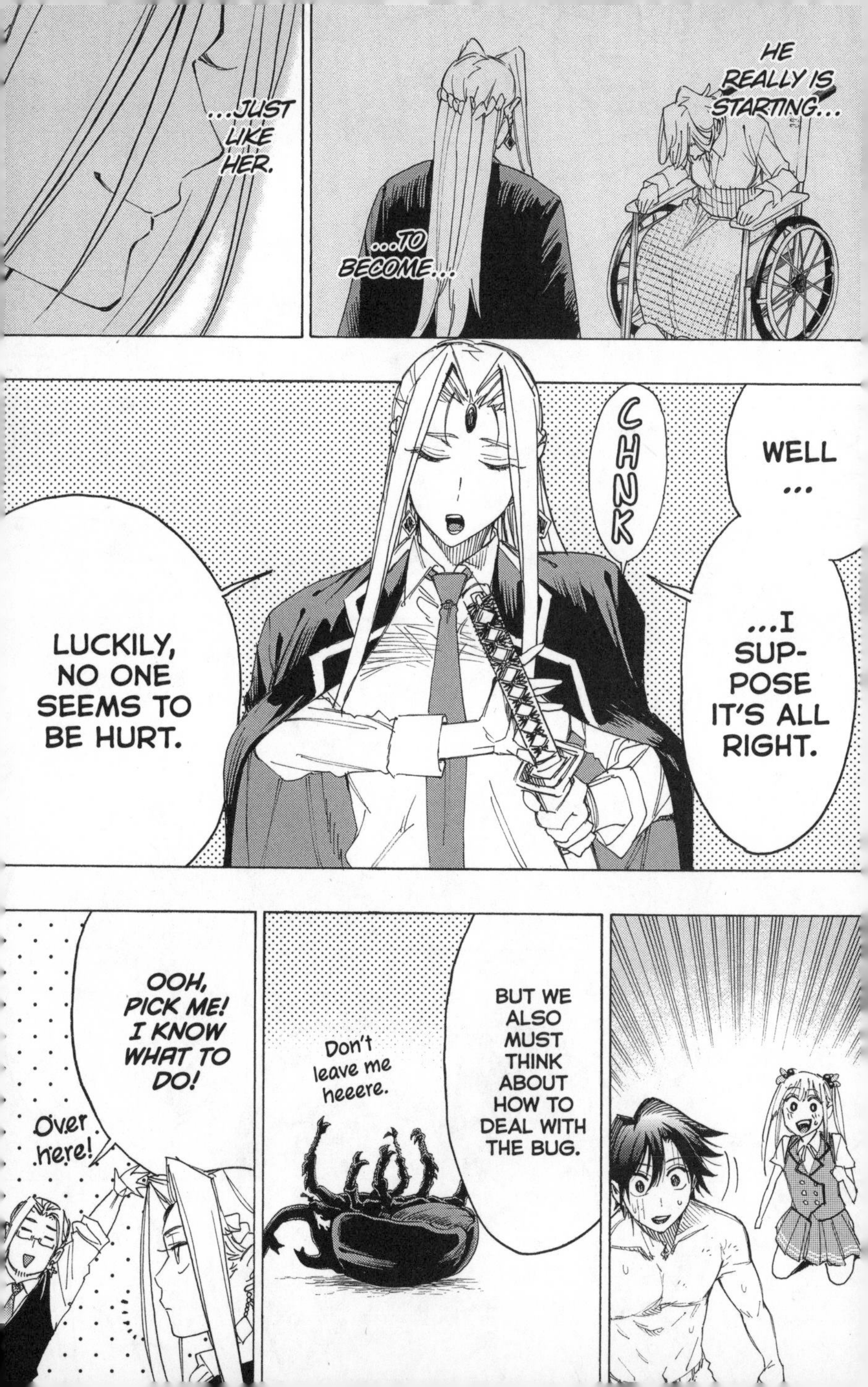
HE REALLY IS STARTING...
...TO BECOME...
...JUST LIKE HER.
WELL...
CHNK
...I SUPPOSE IT'S ALL RIGHT.
LUCKILY, NO ONE SEEMS TO BE HURT.
BUT WE ALSO MUST THINK ABOUT HOW TO DEAL WITH THE BUG.
Don't leave me heeere.
OOH, PICK ME! I KNOW WHAT TO DO!
Over here!

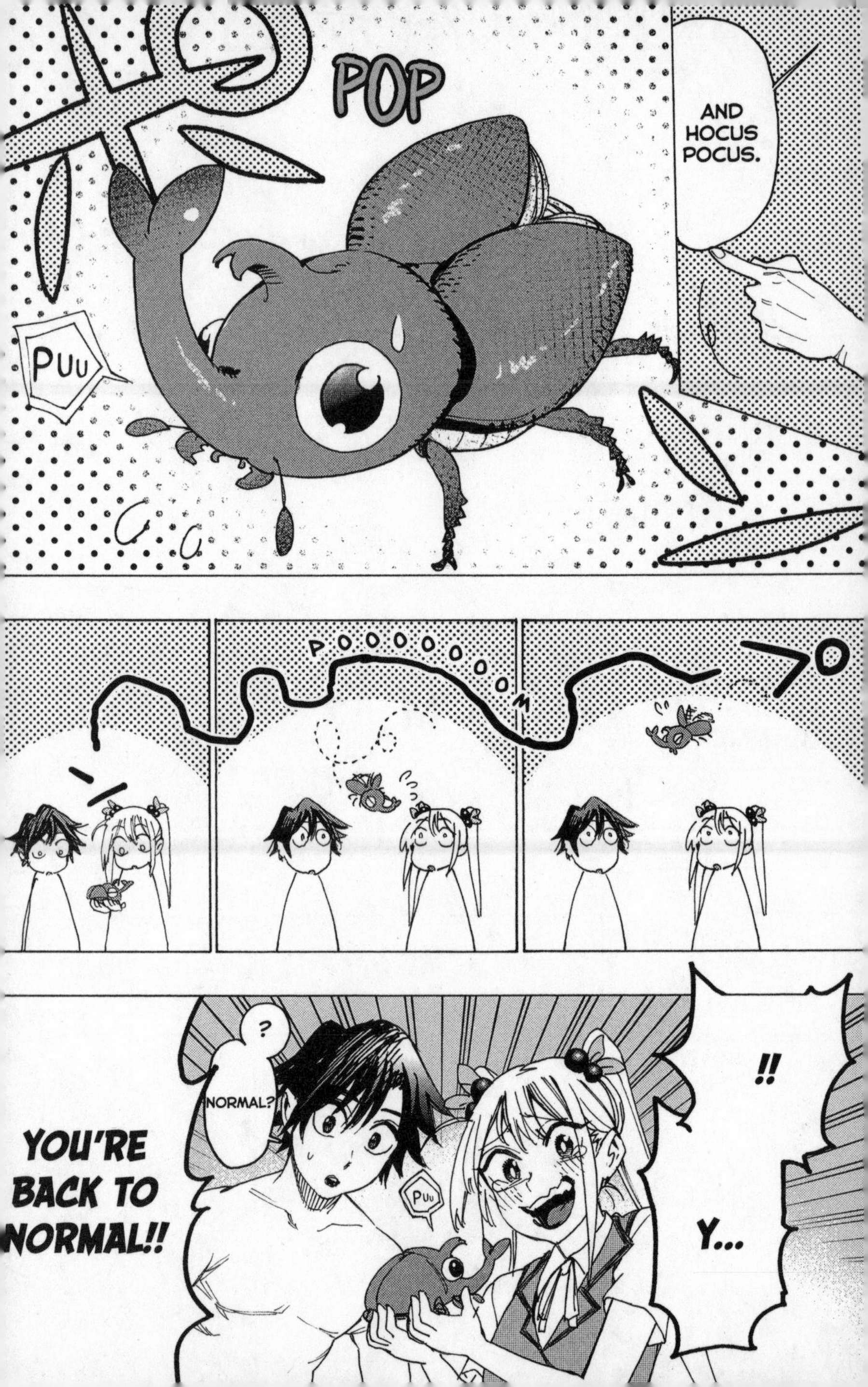
AND HOCUS POCUS.
POP
PUU
POOOOOOOOM
!! Y...
YOU'RE BACK TO NORMAL!!
?
NORMAL?
PUU

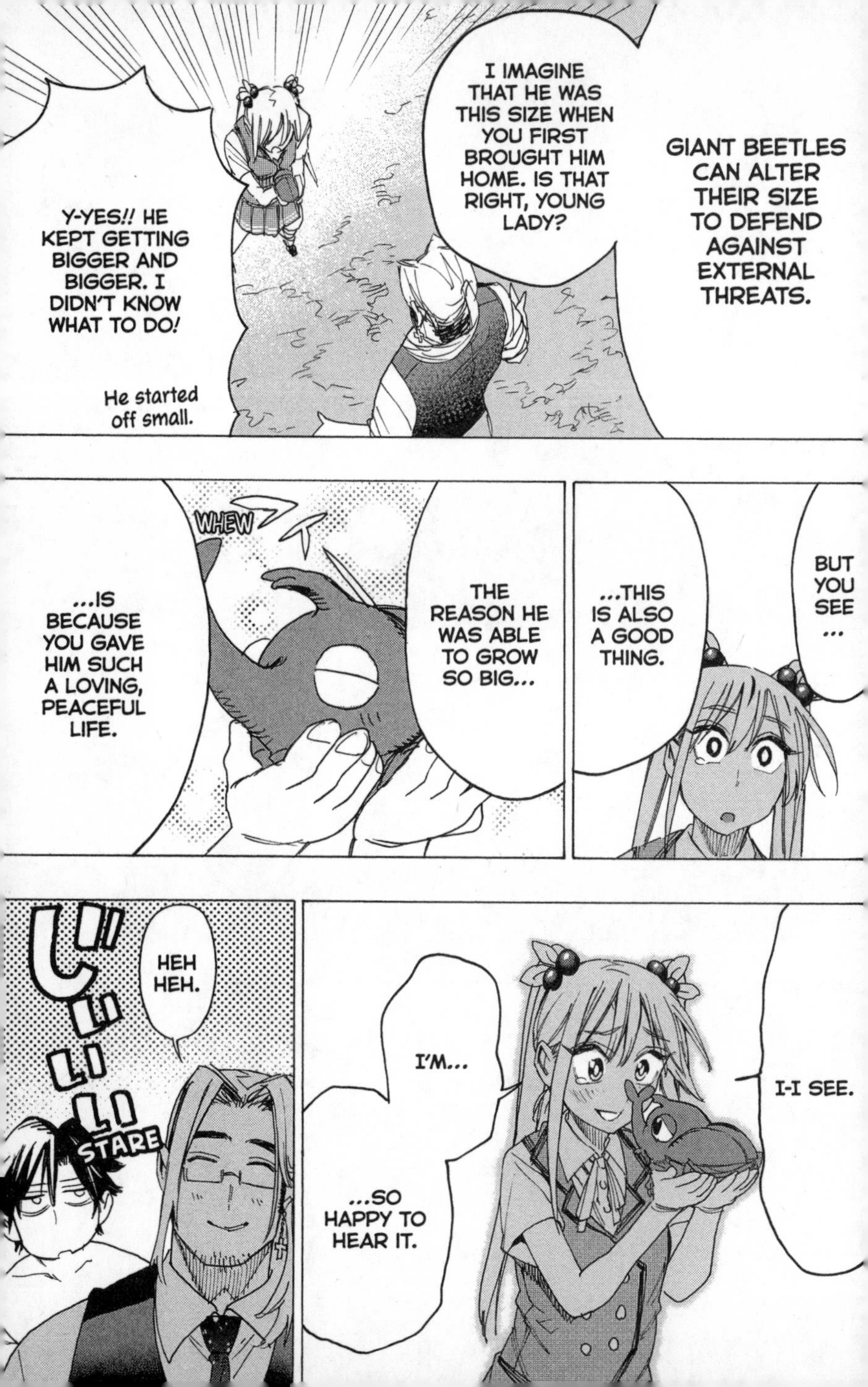
GIANT BEETLES CAN ALTER THEIR SIZE TO DEFEND AGAINST EXTERNAL THREATS.
I IMAGINE THAT HE WAS THIS SIZE WHEN YOU FIRST BROUGHT HIM HOME. IS THAT RIGHT, YOUNG LADY?
Y-YES!! HE KEPT GETTING BIGGER AND BIGGER. I DIDN'T KNOW WHAT TO DO!
He started off small.
BUT YOU SEE...
...THIS IS ALSO A GOOD THING.
THE REASON HE WAS ABLE TO GROW SO BIG...
WHEW
...IS BECAUSE YOU GAVE HIM SUCH A LOVING, PEACEFUL LIFE.
I-I SEE.
I'M...
...SO HAPPY TO HEAR IT.
HEH HEH.
STARE

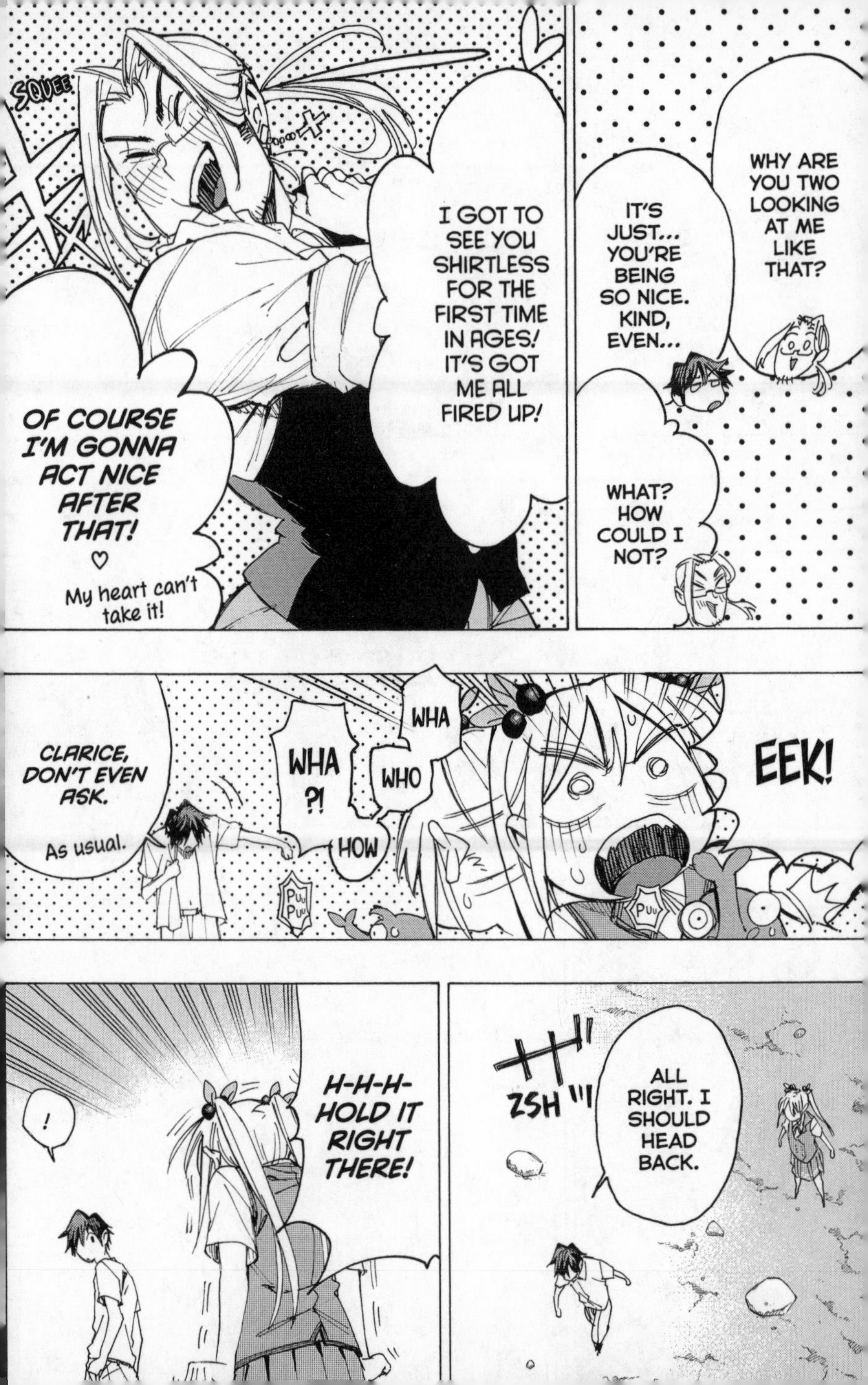

WHY ARE YOU TWO LOOKING AT ME LIKE THAT?
IT'S JUST... YOU'RE BEING SO NICE. KIND, EVEN...
WHAT? HOW COULD I NOT?
I GOT TO SEE YOU SHIRTLESS FOR THE FIRST TIME IN AGES! IT'S GOT ME ALL FIRED UP!
SQUEE
OF COURSE I'M GONNA ACT NICE AFTER THAT! ♡
My heart can't take it!
EEK!
WHA
WHO
WHA ?!
HOW
PUU
PUU PUU
CLARICE, DON'T EVEN ASK.
As usual.
ZSH
ALL RIGHT. I SHOULD HEAD BACK.
H-H-H-HOLD IT RIGHT THERE!
!

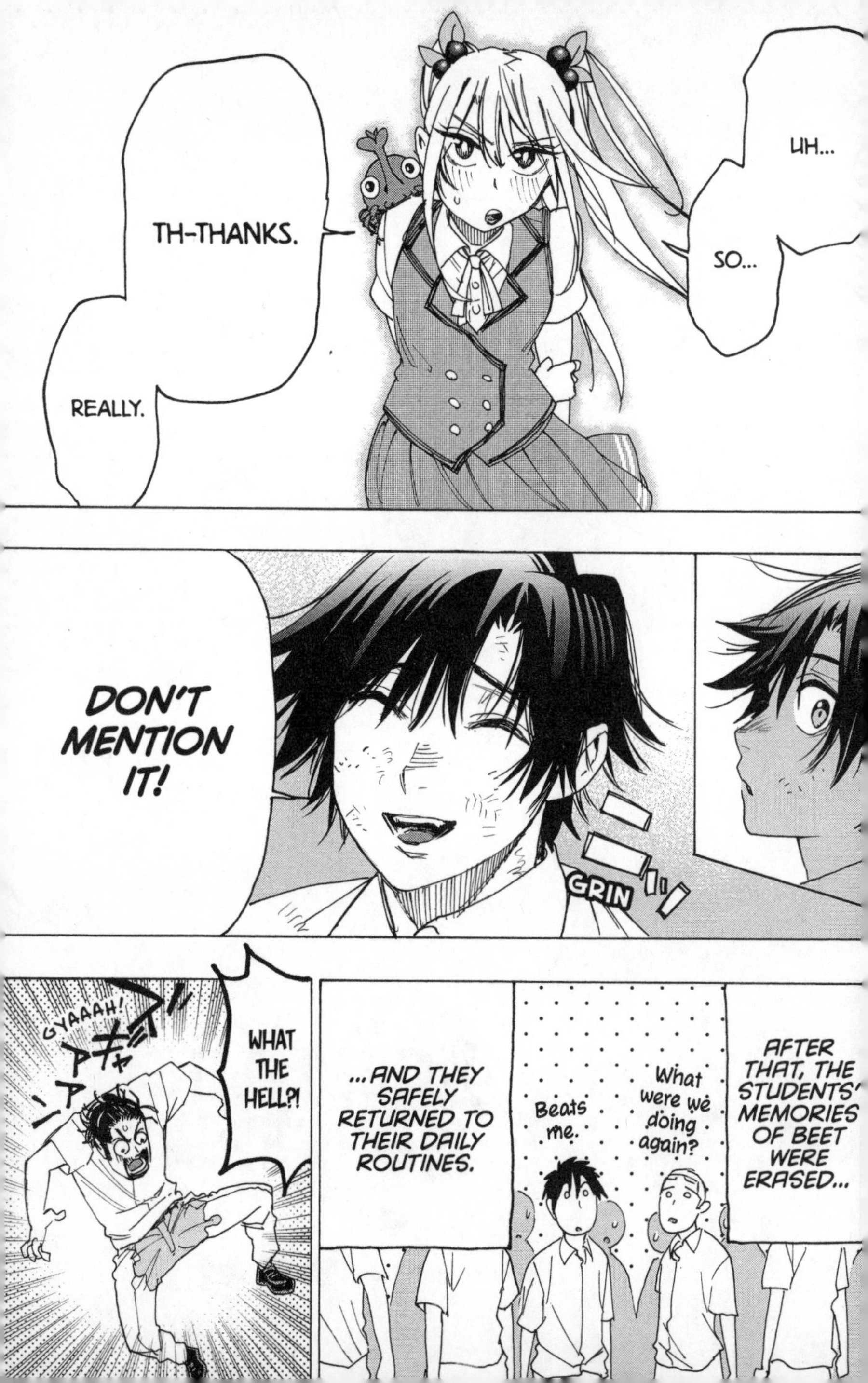
UH... SO...
TH-THANKS. REALLY.
DON'T MENTION IT!
GRIN
AFTER THAT, THE STUDENTS' MEMORIES OF BEET WERE ERASED...
What were we doing again?
Beats me.
...AND THEY SAFELY RETURNED TO THEIR DAILY ROUTINES.
WHAT THE HELL?!
GYAAAH!

The
ICEBLADE
SORCERER
Shall **RULE**
the
WORLD

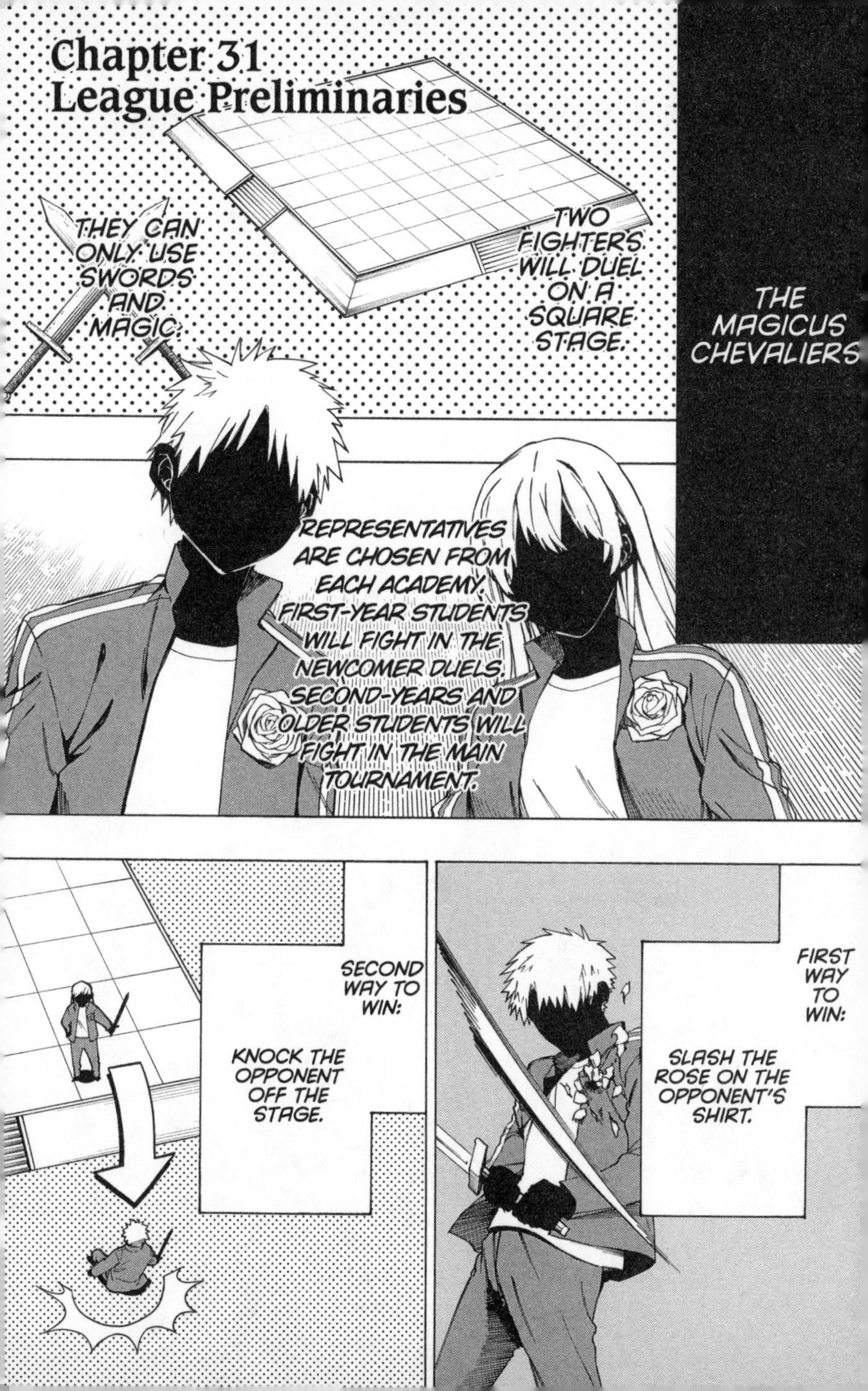
THE MAGICUS CHEVALIERS
Chapter 31 League Preliminaries
TWO FIGHTERS WILL DUEL ON A SQUARE STAGE.
THEY CAN ONLY USE SWORDS AND MAGIC.
REPRESENTATIVES ARE CHOSEN FROM EACH ACADEMY. FIRST-YEAR STUDENTS WILL FIGHT IN THE NEWCOMER DUELS. SECOND-YEARS AND OLDER STUDENTS WILL FIGHT IN THE MAIN TOURNAMENT.
FIRST WAY TO WIN:
SLASH THE ROSE ON THE OPPONENT'S SHIRT.
SECOND WAY TO WIN:
KNOCK THE OPPONENT OFF THE STAGE.

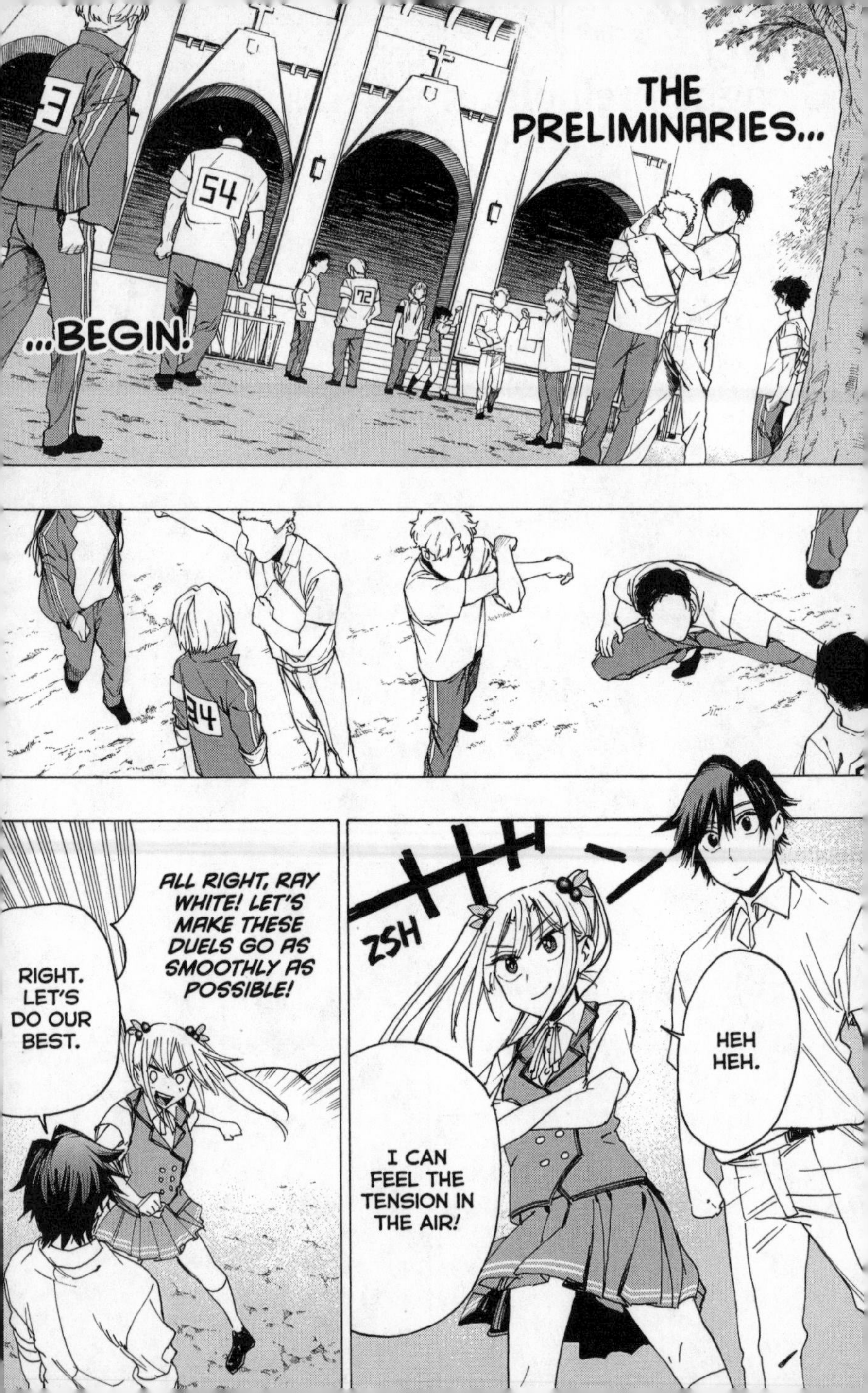
THE PRELIMINARIES...
...BEGIN!
ZSH
I CAN FEEL THE TENSION IN THE AIR!
HEH HEH.
ALL RIGHT, RAY WHITE! LET'S MAKE THESE DUELS GO AS SMOOTHLY AS POSSIBLE!
RIGHT. LET'S DO OUR BEST.

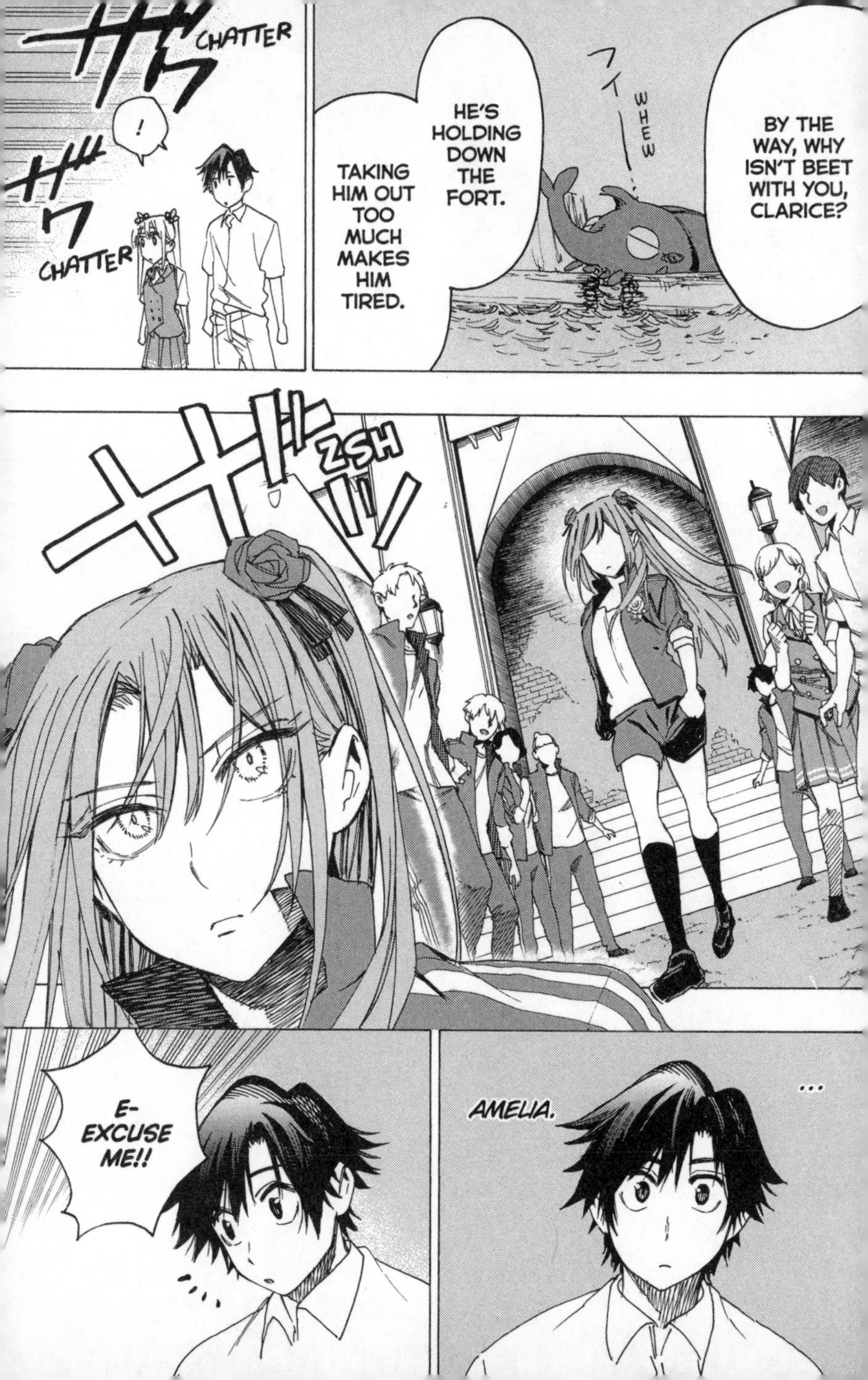
BY THE WAY, WHY ISN'T BEET WITH YOU, CLARICE?
WHEW
HE'S HOLDING DOWN THE FORT.
TAKING HIM OUT TOO MUCH MAKES HIM TIRED.
CHATTER
!
CHATTER
ZSH
...
AMELIA.
E-EXCUSE ME!!

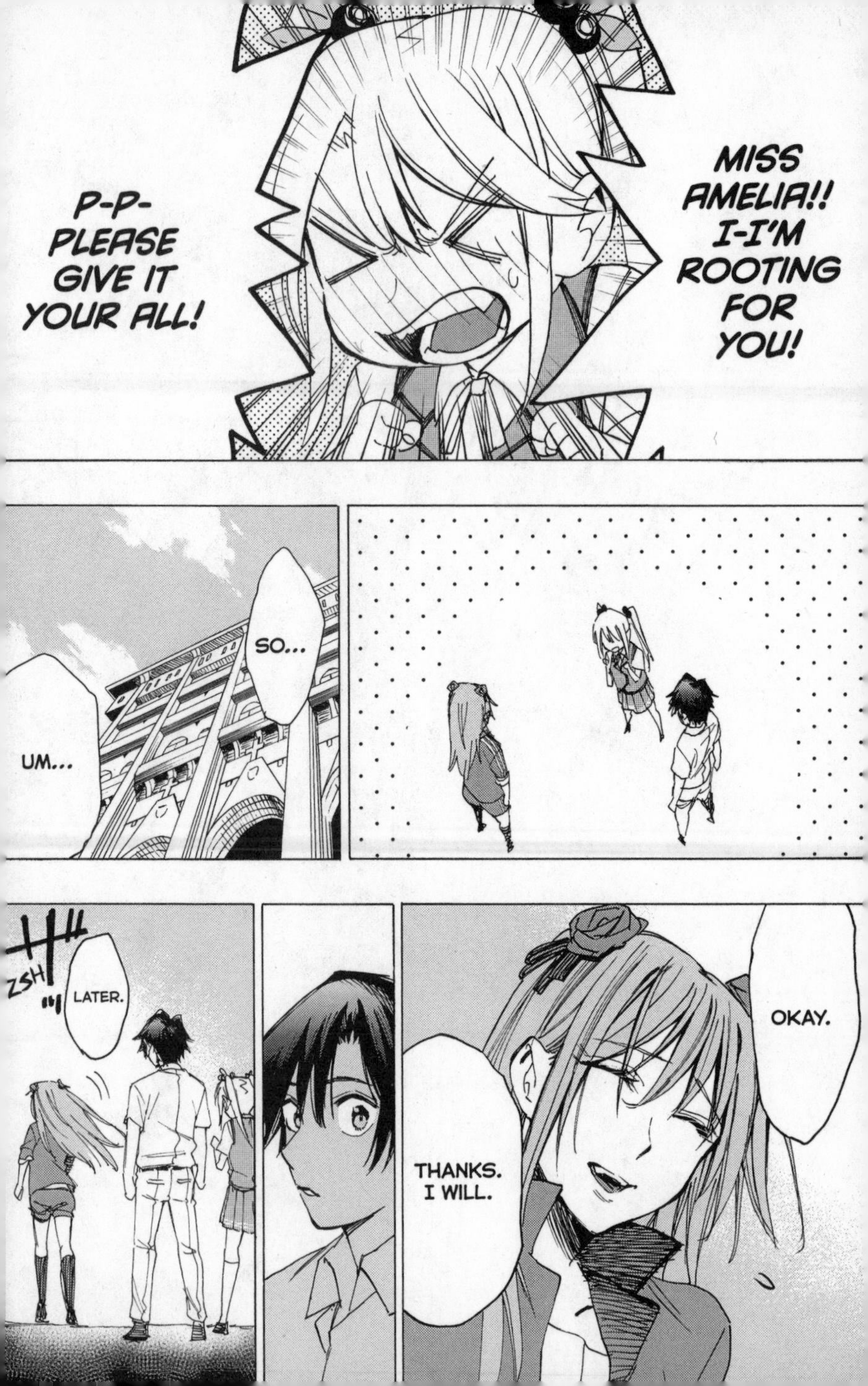
MISS AMELIA!! I-I'M ROOTING FOR YOU!
P-P-PLEASE GIVE IT YOUR ALL!
SO...
UM...
OKAY.
THANKS. I WILL.
LATER.
ZSH

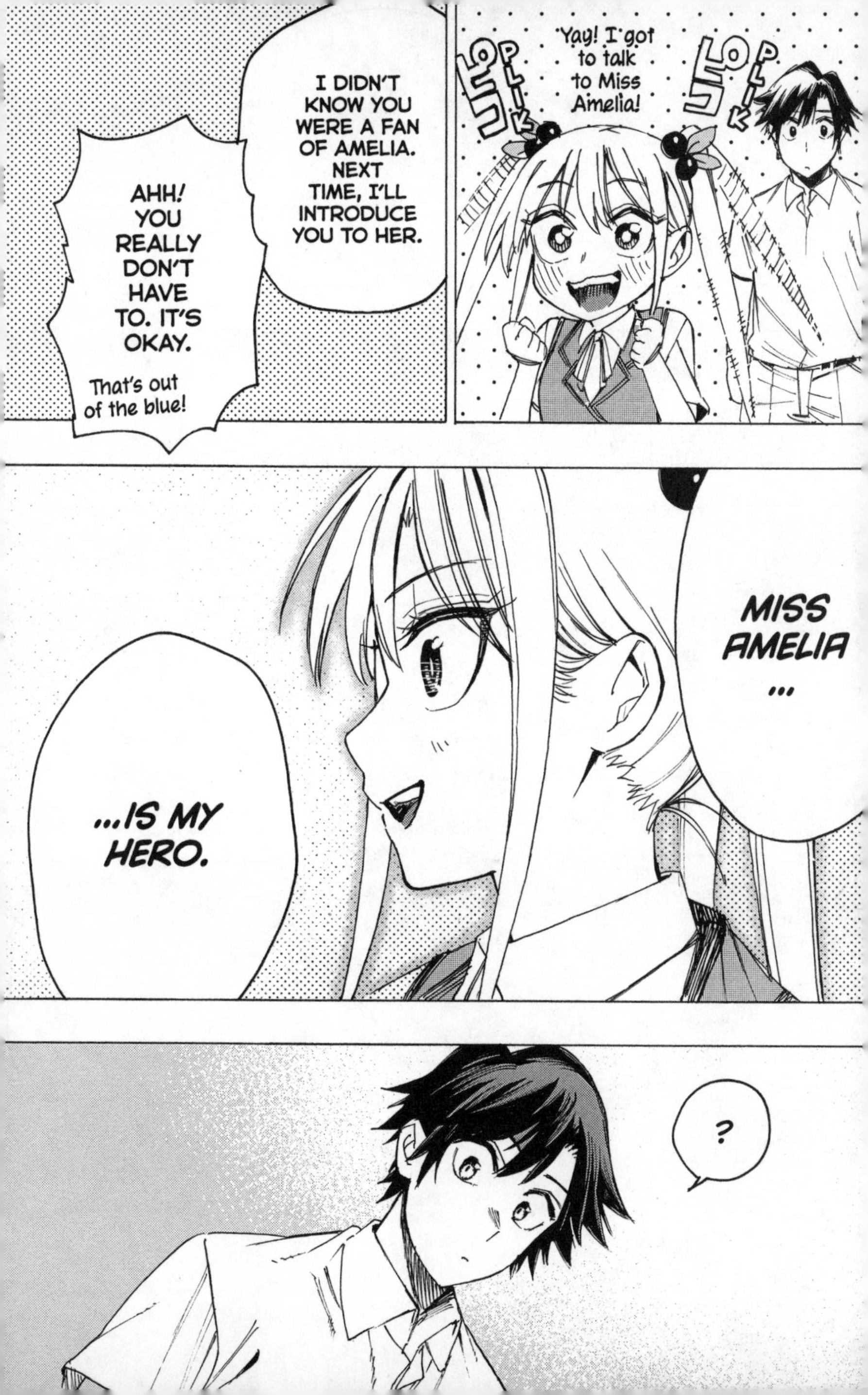
Yay! I got to talk to Miss Amelia!
I DIDN'T KNOW YOU WERE A FAN OF AMELIA. NEXT TIME, I'LL INTRODUCE YOU TO HER.
AHH! YOU REALLY DON'T HAVE TO. IT'S OKAY.
That's out of the blue!
MISS AMELIA ...
...IS MY HERO.
?

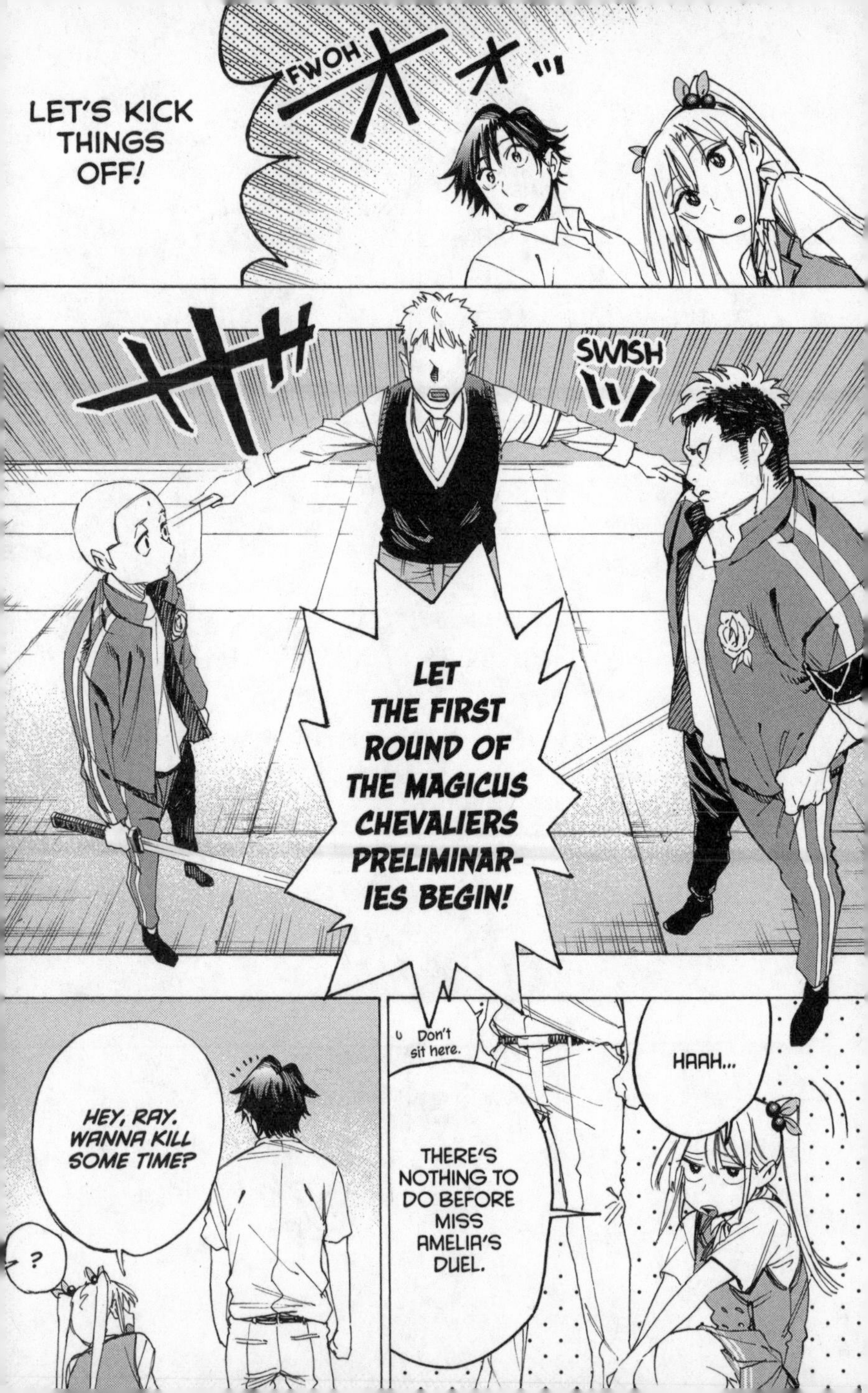
FWOH
LET'S KICK THINGS OFF!
SWISH
LET THE FIRST ROUND OF THE MAGICUS CHEVALIERS PRELIMINAR-IES BEGIN!
HAAH...
Don't sit here.
THERE'S NOTHING TO DO BEFORE MISS AMELIA'S DUEL.
HEY, RAY. WANNA KILL SOME TIME?
?

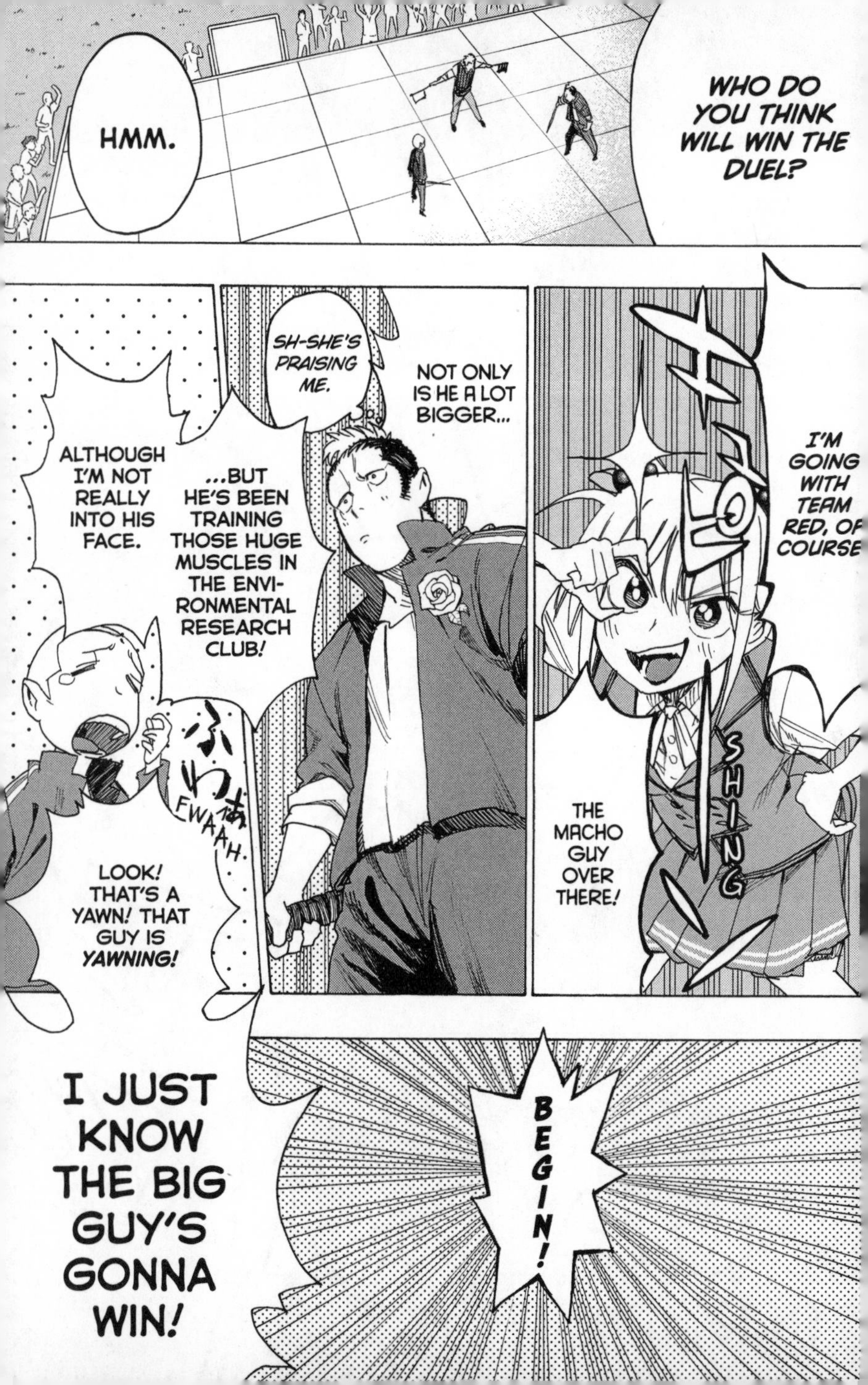
WHO DO YOU THINK WILL WIN THE DUEL?
HMM.
I'M GOING WITH TEAM RED, OF COURSE
SHING
THE MACHO GUY OVER THERE!
NOT ONLY IS HE A LOT BIGGER...
SH-SHE'S PRAISING ME.
...BUT HE'S BEEN TRAINING THOSE HUGE MUSCLES IN THE ENVIRONMENTAL RESEARCH CLUB!
ALTHOUGH I'M NOT REALLY INTO HIS FACE.
ふわあ
FWAAAH.
LOOK! THAT'S A YAWN! THAT GUY IS *YAWNING!*
BEGIN!
I JUST KNOW THE BIG GUY'S GONNA WIN!

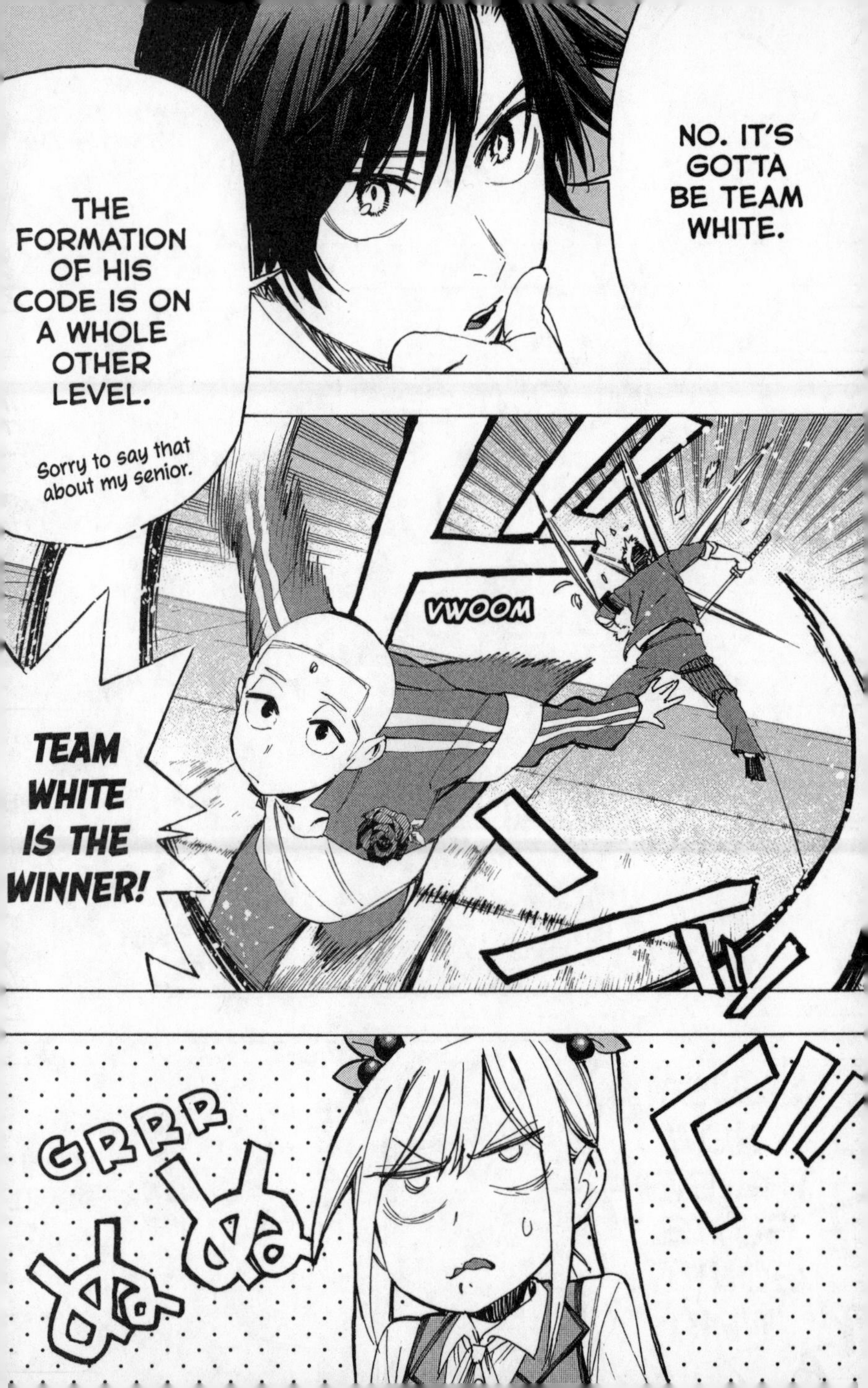
NO. IT'S GOTTA BE TEAM WHITE.
THE FORMATION OF HIS CODE IS ON A WHOLE OTHER LEVEL.
Sorry to say that about my senior.
VWOOM
TEAM WHITE IS THE WINNER!
GRRR

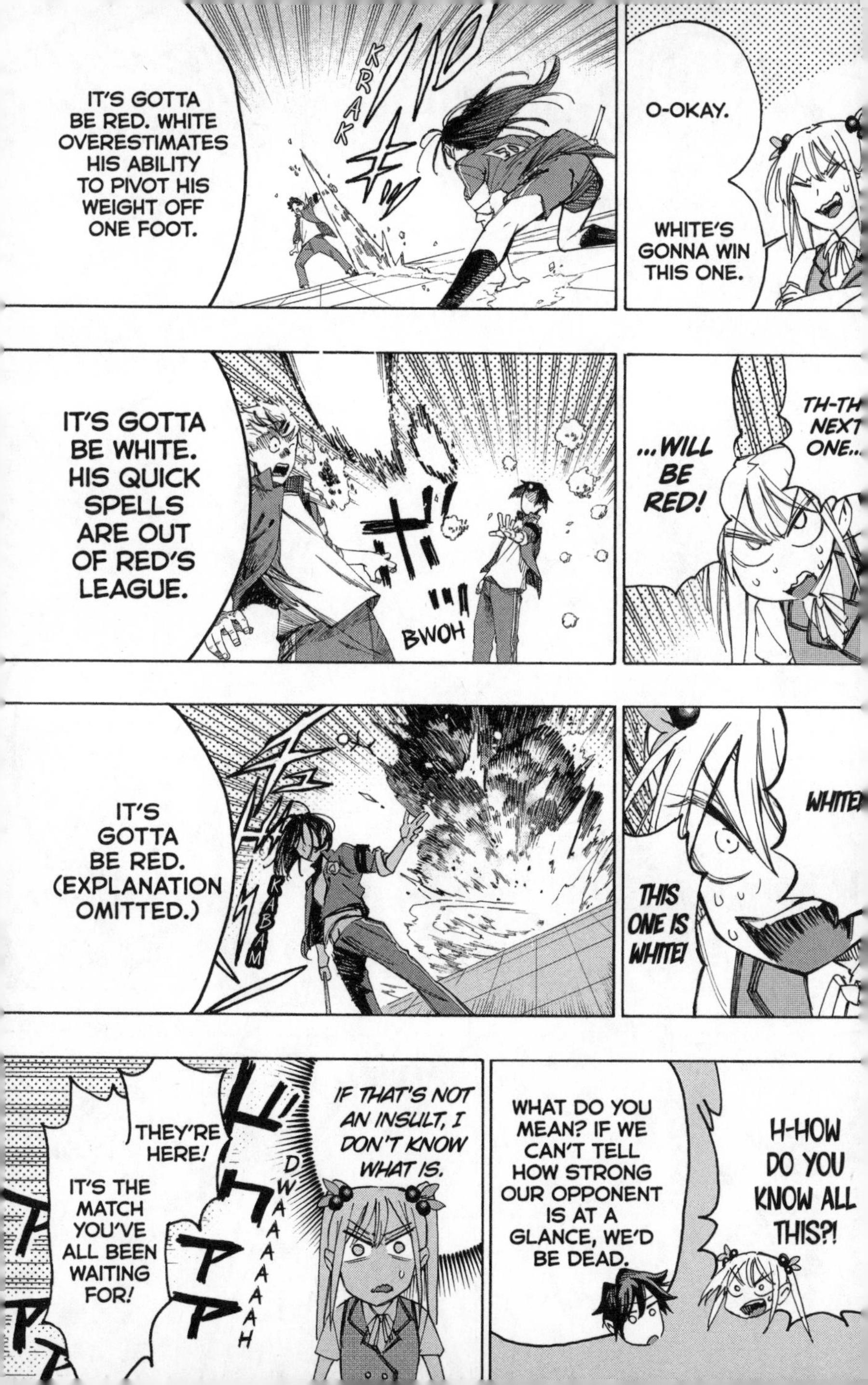
O-OKAY.
WHITE'S GONNA WIN THIS ONE.
IT'S GOTTA BE RED. WHITE OVERESTIMATES HIS ABILITY TO PIVOT HIS WEIGHT OFF ONE FOOT.
KRAK
TH-TH NEXT ONE...
...WILL BE RED!
IT'S GOTTA BE WHITE. HIS QUICK SPELLS ARE OUT OF RED'S LEAGUE.
BWOH
WHITE
THIS ONE IS WHITE!
IT'S GOTTA BE RED. (EXPLANATION OMITTED.)
KABAM
H-HOW DO YOU KNOW ALL THIS?!
WHAT DO YOU MEAN? IF WE CAN'T TELL HOW STRONG OUR OPPONENT IS AT A GLANCE, WE'D BE DEAD.
IF THAT'S NOT AN INSULT, I DON'T KNOW WHAT IS.
DWAAAAAAH
THEY'RE HERE!
IT'S THE MATCH YOU'VE ALL BEEN WAITING FOR!

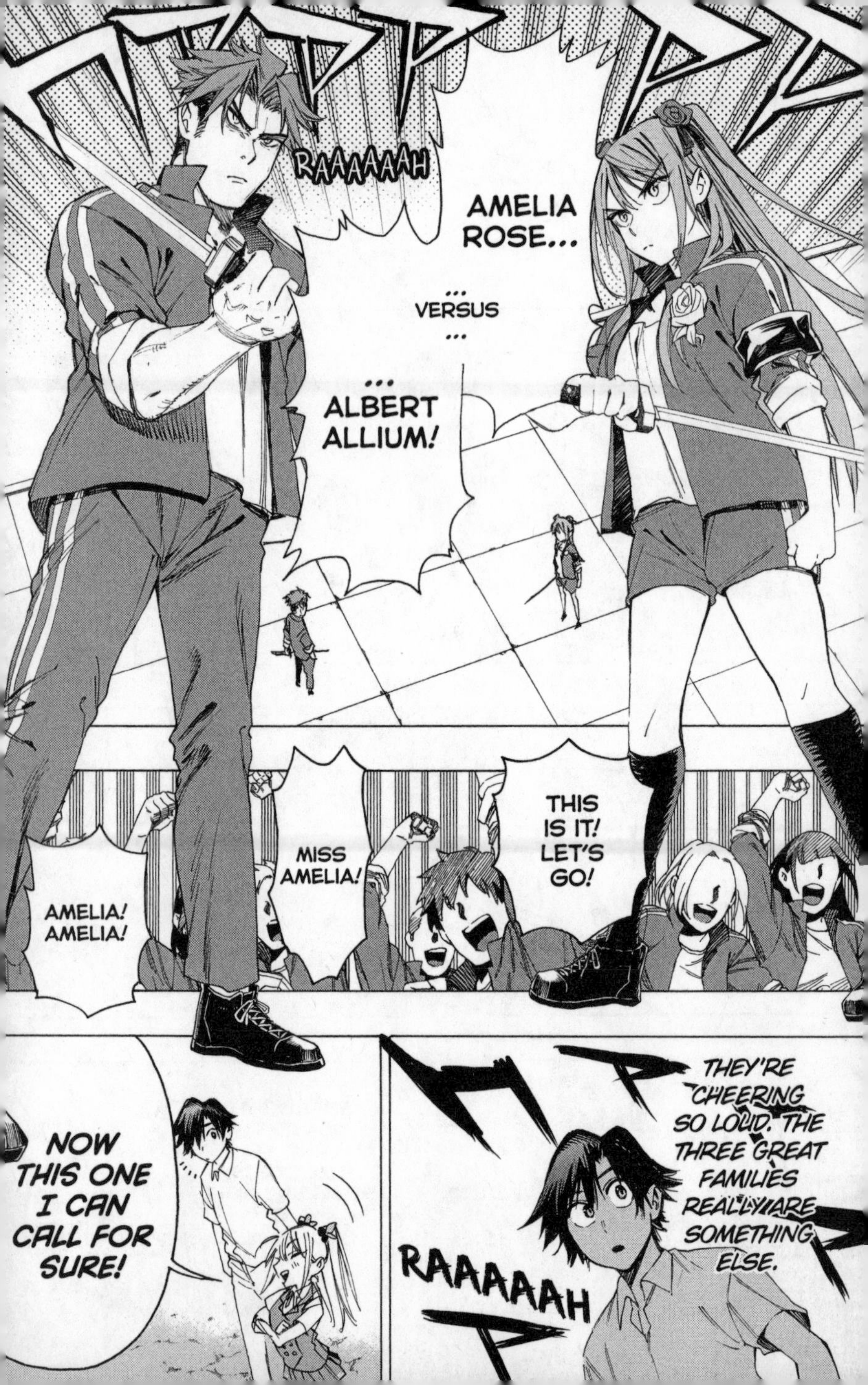
RAAAAAAH
AMELIA ROSE...
... VERSUS ...
... ALBERT ALLIUM!
THIS IS IT! LET'S GO!
MISS AMELIA!
AMELIA! AMELIA!
THEY'RE CHEERING SO LOUD. THE THREE GREAT FAMILIES REALLY ARE SOMETHING ELSE.
RAAAAAAH
NOW THIS ONE I CAN CALL FOR SURE!

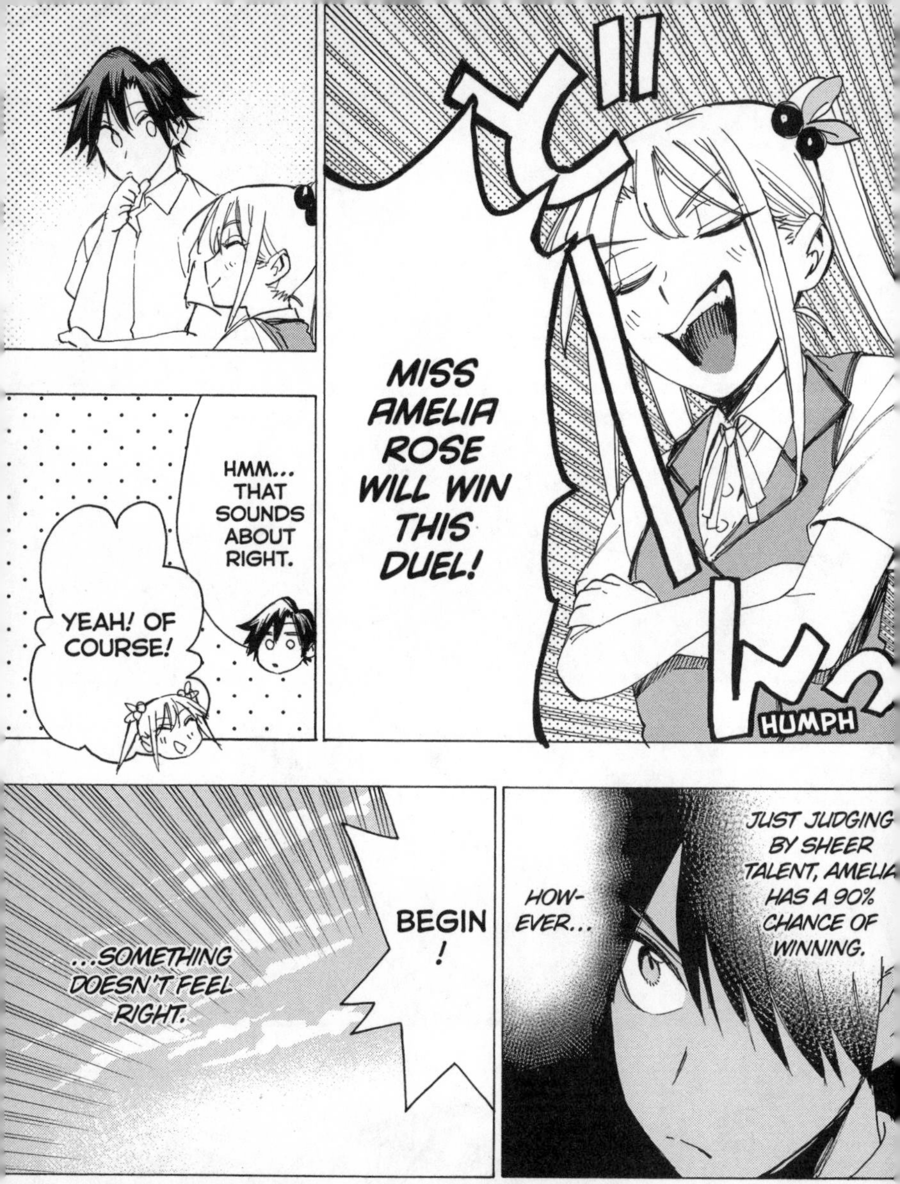
MISS AMELIA ROSE WILL WIN THIS DUEL!
HUMPH
HMM... THAT SOUNDS ABOUT RIGHT.
YEAH! OF COURSE!
JUST JUDGING BY SHEER TALENT, AMELIA HAS A 90% CHANCE OF WINNING.
HOW-EVER...
BEGIN!
...SOMETHING DOESN'T FEEL RIGHT.

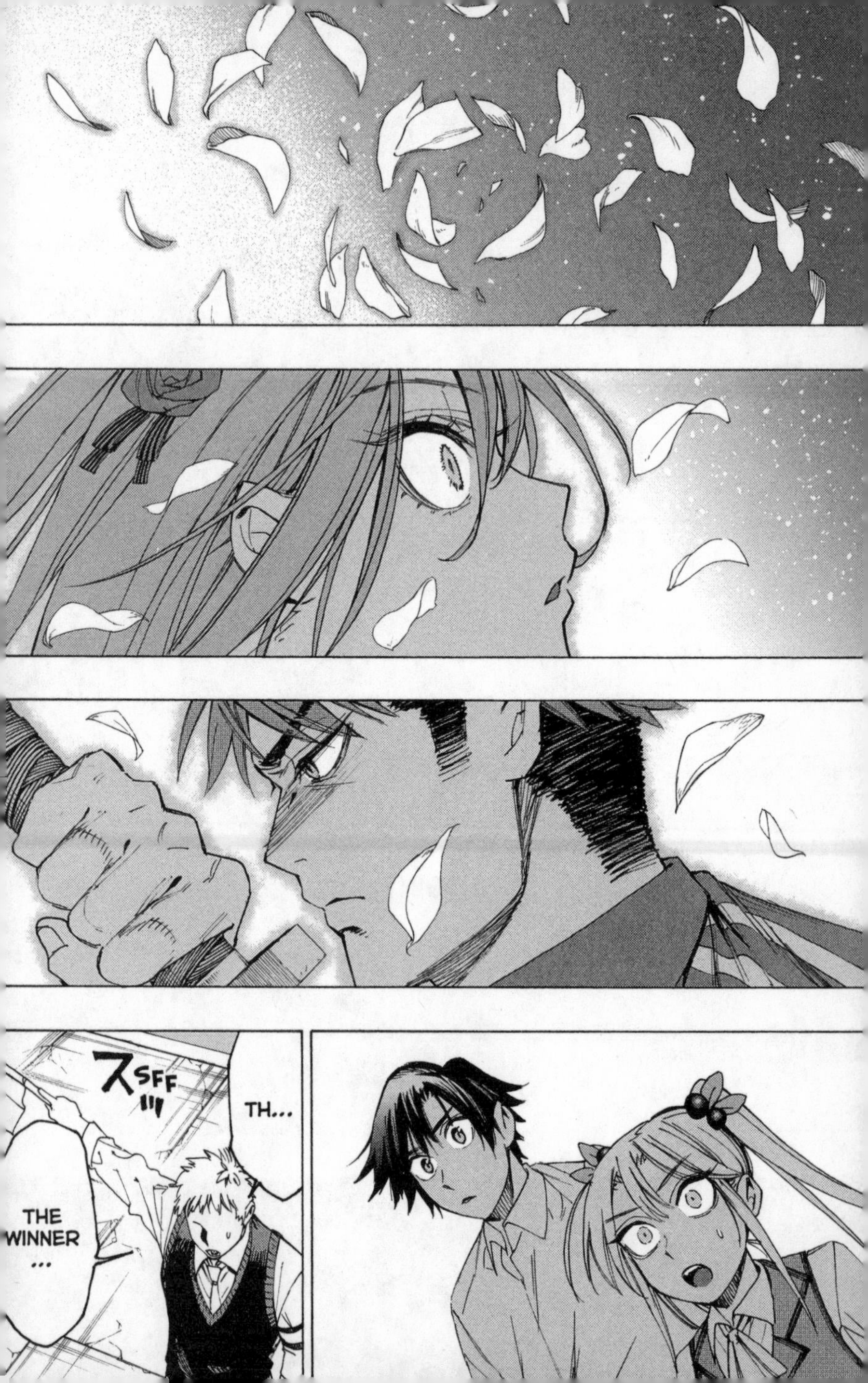
TH...
THE WINNER ...
スSFF
ッ

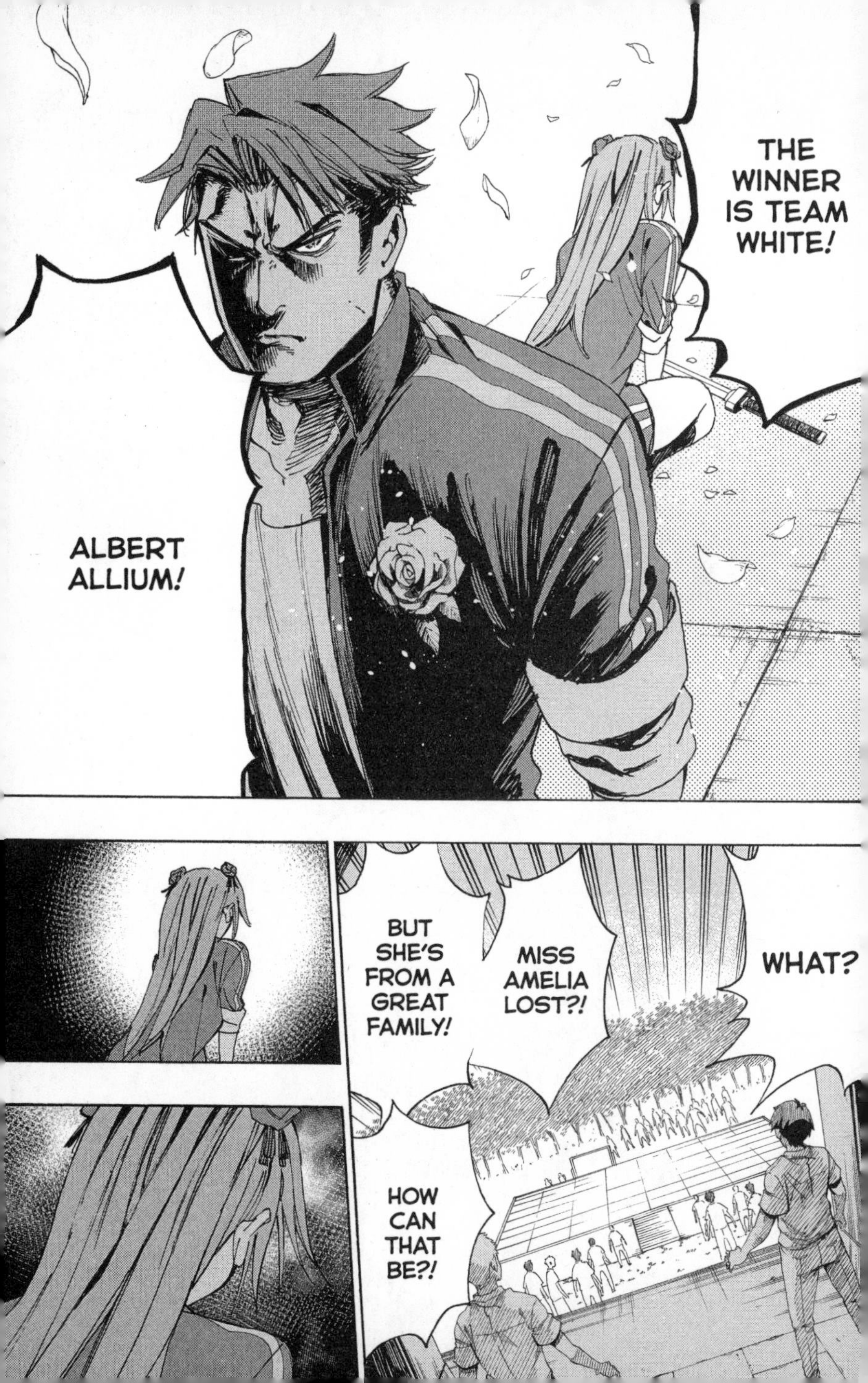
THE WINNER IS TEAM WHITE!
ALBERT ALLIUM!
WHAT?
MISS AMELIA LOST?!
BUT SHE'S FROM A GREAT FAMILY!
HOW CAN THAT BE?!

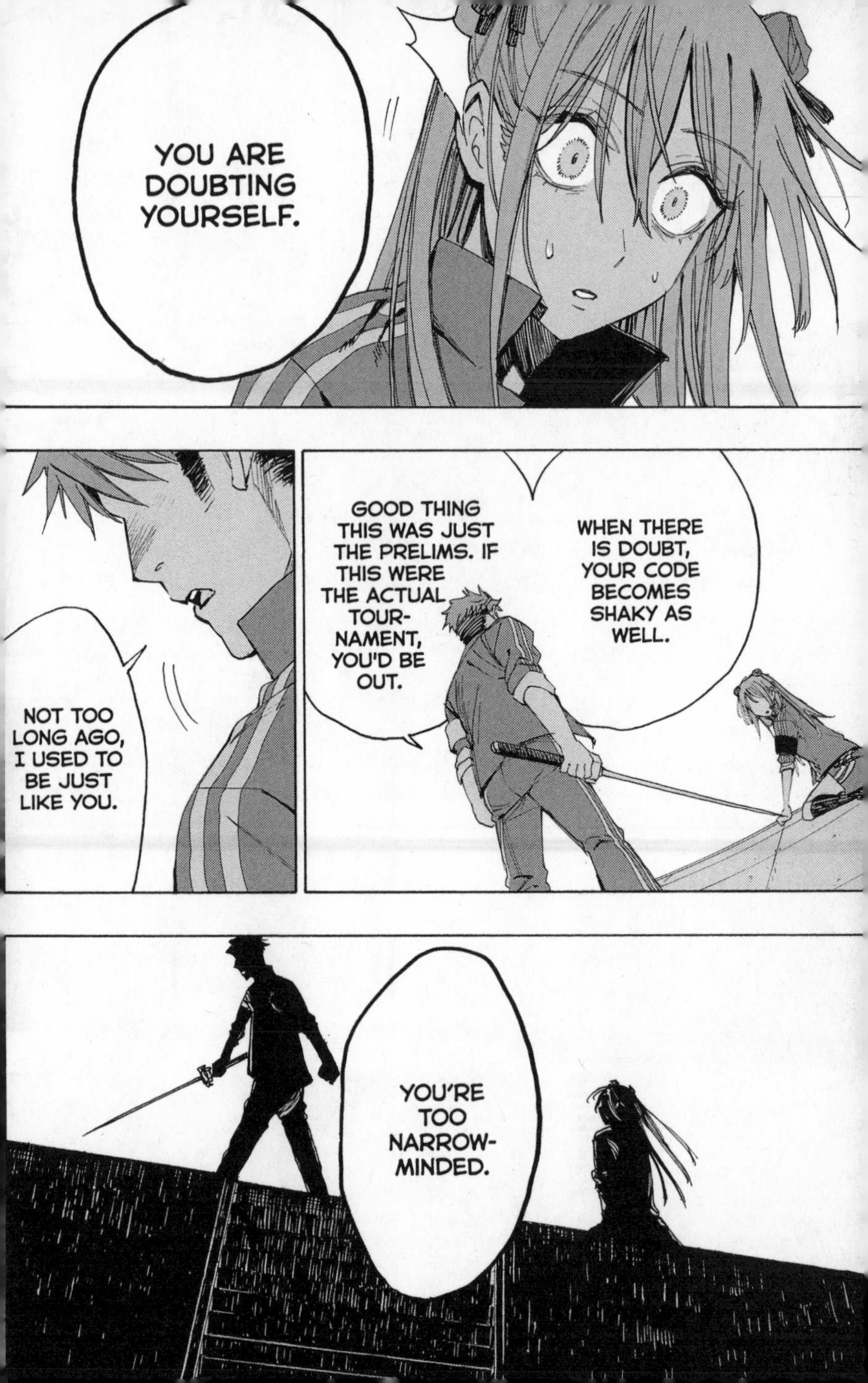
YOU ARE DOUBTING YOURSELF.
WHEN THERE IS DOUBT, YOUR CODE BECOMES SHAKY AS WELL.
GOOD THING THIS WAS JUST THE PRELIMS. IF THIS WERE THE ACTUAL TOURNAMENT, YOU'D BE OUT.
NOT TOO LONG AGO, I USED TO BE JUST LIKE YOU.
YOU'RE TOO NARROW-MINDED.

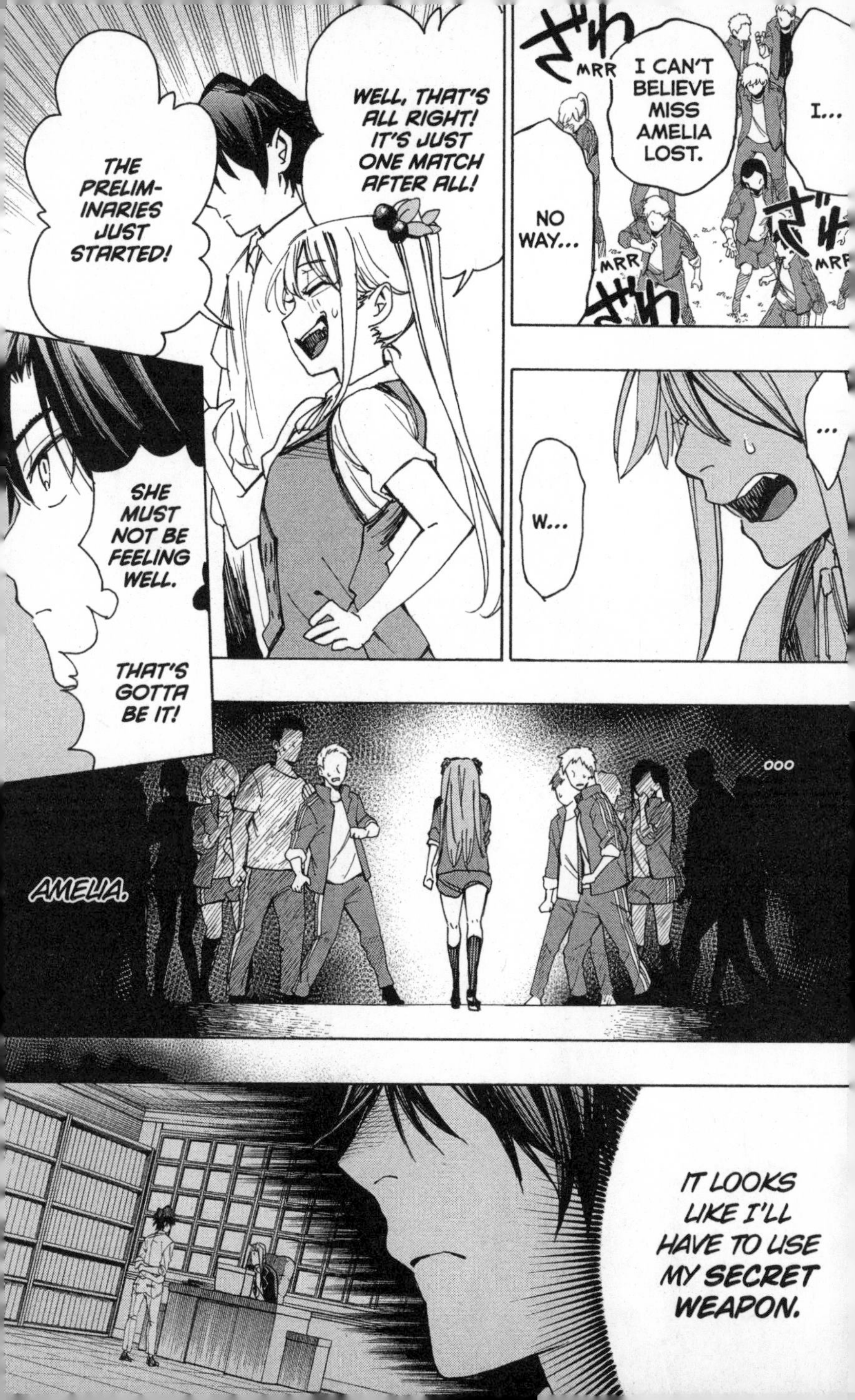
ざわ
MRR
I CAN'T BELIEVE MISS AMELIA LOST.
I...
ざわ
MRR
NO WAY...
MRR
ざわ
WELL, THAT'S ALL RIGHT! IT'S JUST ONE MATCH AFTER ALL!
THE PRELIM-INARIES JUST STARTED!
...
W...
SHE MUST NOT BE FEELING WELL.
THAT'S GOTTA BE IT!
ooo
AMELIA.
IT LOOKS LIKE I'LL HAVE TO USE MY SECRET WEAPON.

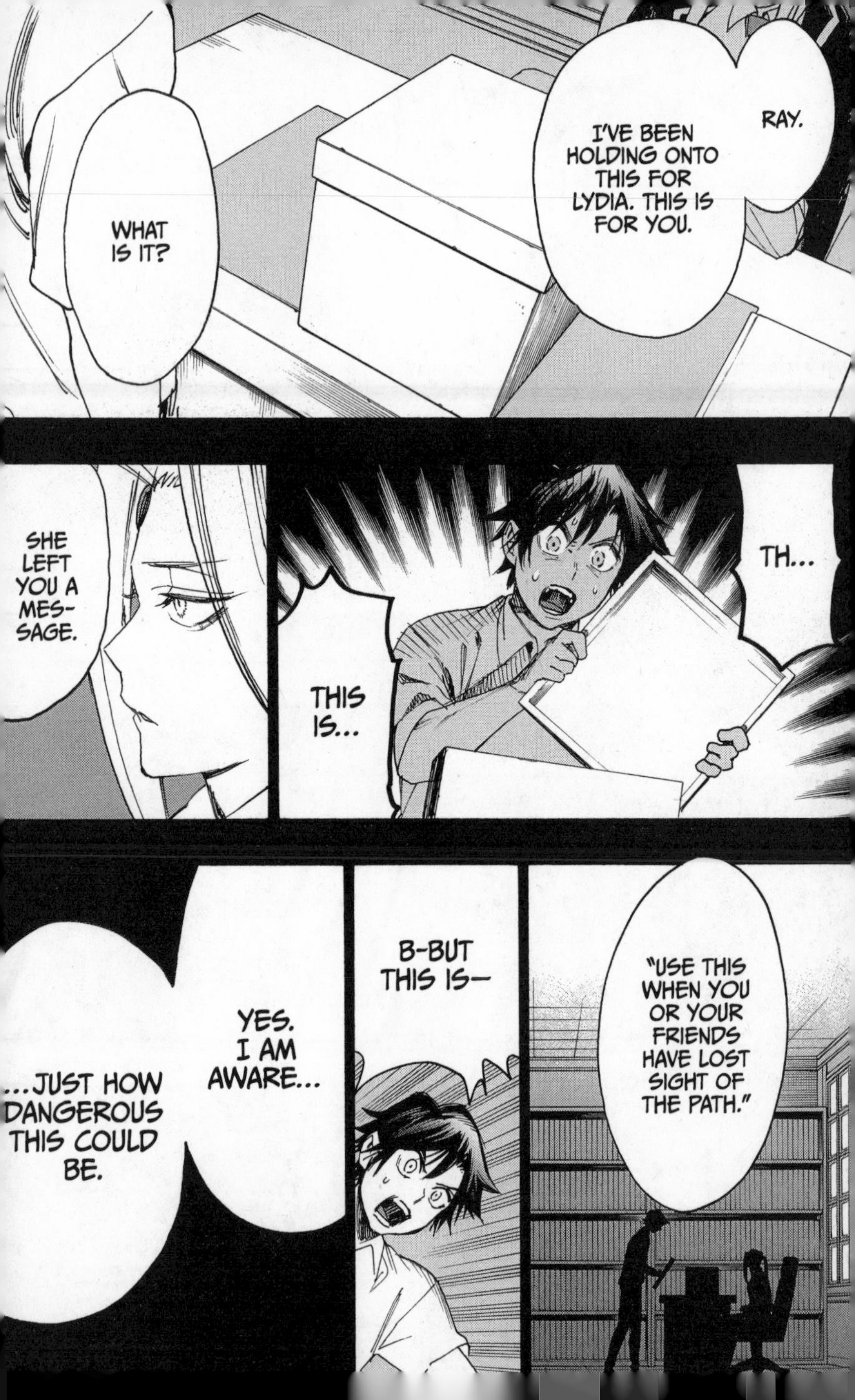
RAY.
I'VE BEEN HOLDING ONTO THIS FOR LYDIA. THIS IS FOR YOU.
WHAT IS IT?
TH...
THIS IS...
SHE LEFT YOU A MES-SAGE.
"USE THIS WHEN YOU OR YOUR FRIENDS HAVE LOST SIGHT OF THE PATH."
B-BUT THIS IS—
YES. I AM AWARE...
...JUST HOW DANGEROUS THIS COULD BE.

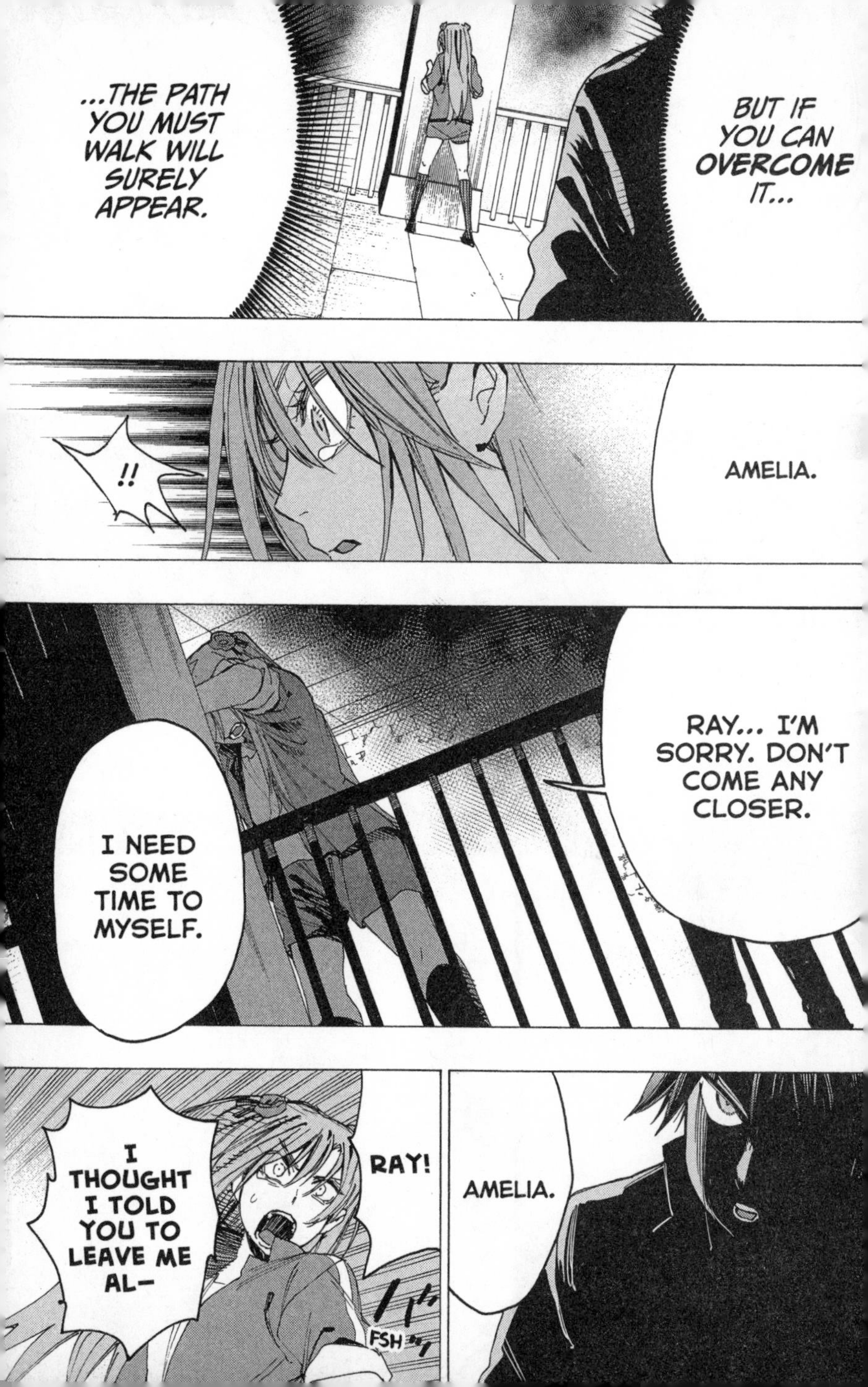
BUT IF YOU CAN OVERCOME IT...
...THE PATH YOU MUST WALK WILL SURELY APPEAR.
AMELIA.
!!
RAY... I'M SORRY. DON'T COME ANY CLOSER.
I NEED SOME TIME TO MYSELF.
AMELIA.
RAY!
I THOUGHT I TOLD YOU TO LEAVE ME AL—
FSH

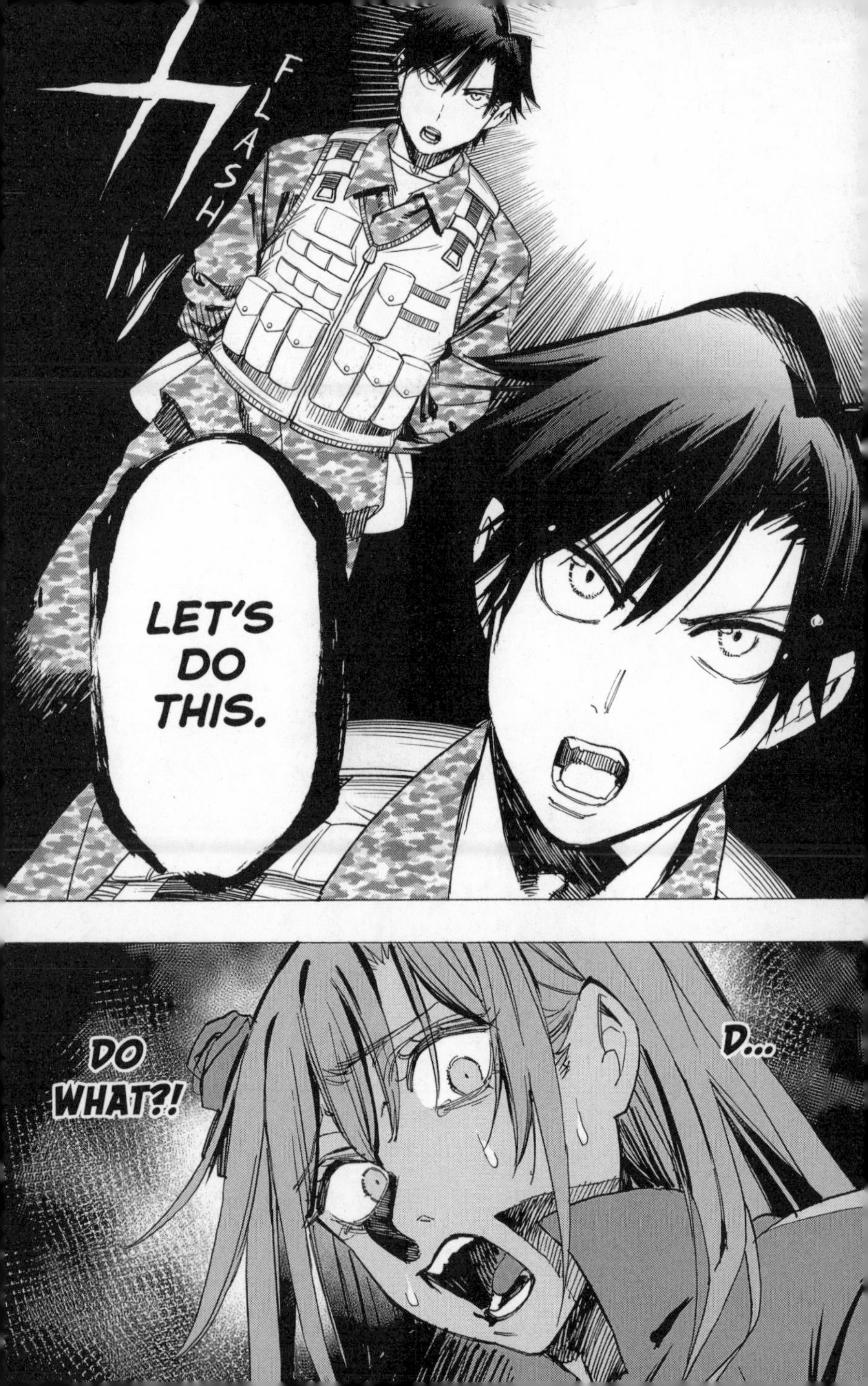
FLASH
LET'S DO THIS.
D...
DO WHAT?!

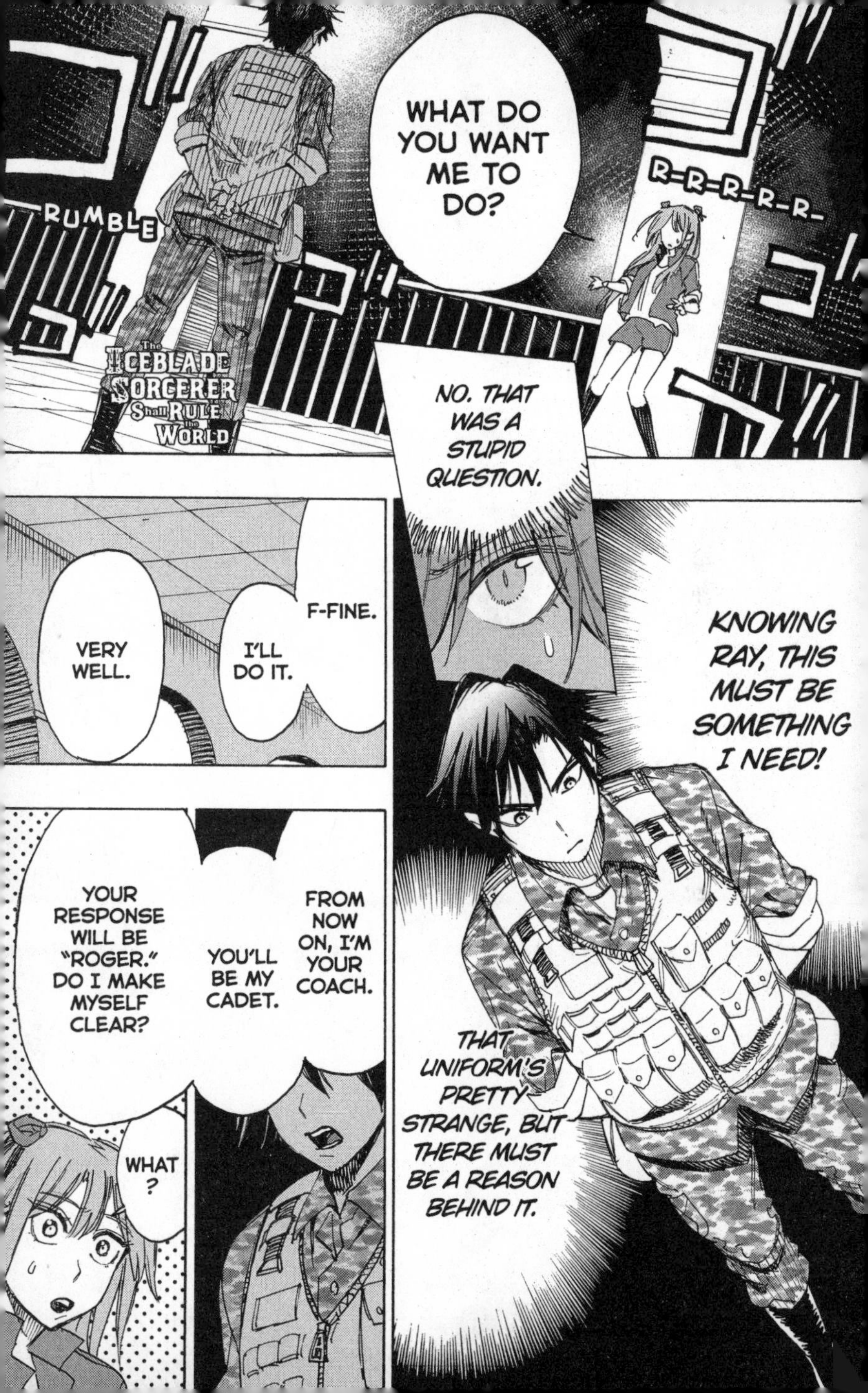
R-R-R-R-R-
WHAT DO YOU WANT ME TO DO?
RUMBLE
The ICEBLADE SORCERER Shall RULE the WORLD
NO. THAT WAS A STUPID QUESTION.
KNOWING RAY, THIS MUST BE SOMETHING I NEED!
THAT UNIFORM'S PRETTY STRANGE, BUT THERE MUST BE A REASON BEHIND IT.
F-FINE.
I'LL DO IT.
VERY WELL.
FROM NOW ON, I'M YOUR COACH.
YOU'LL BE MY CADET.
YOUR RESPONSE WILL BE "ROGER." DO I MAKE MYSELF CLEAR?
WHAT?

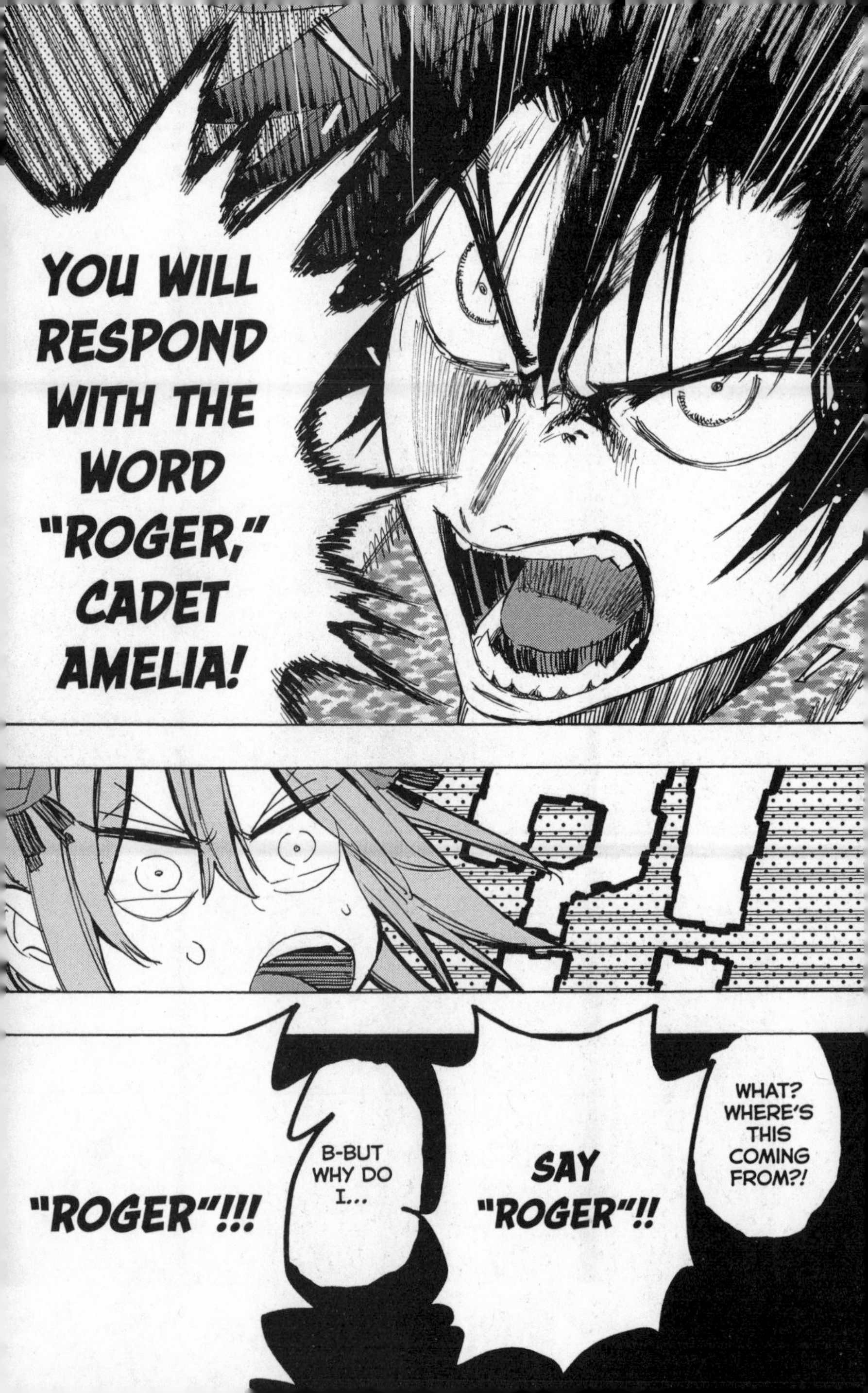
YOU WILL RESPOND WITH THE WORD "ROGER," CADET AMELIA!
WHAT? WHERE'S THIS COMING FROM?!
SAY "ROGER"!!
B-BUT WHY DO I...
"ROGER"!!!

GET MOVING! IT'S TIME FOR AINSWORTH BOOTCAMP!

Chapter 32 Roger

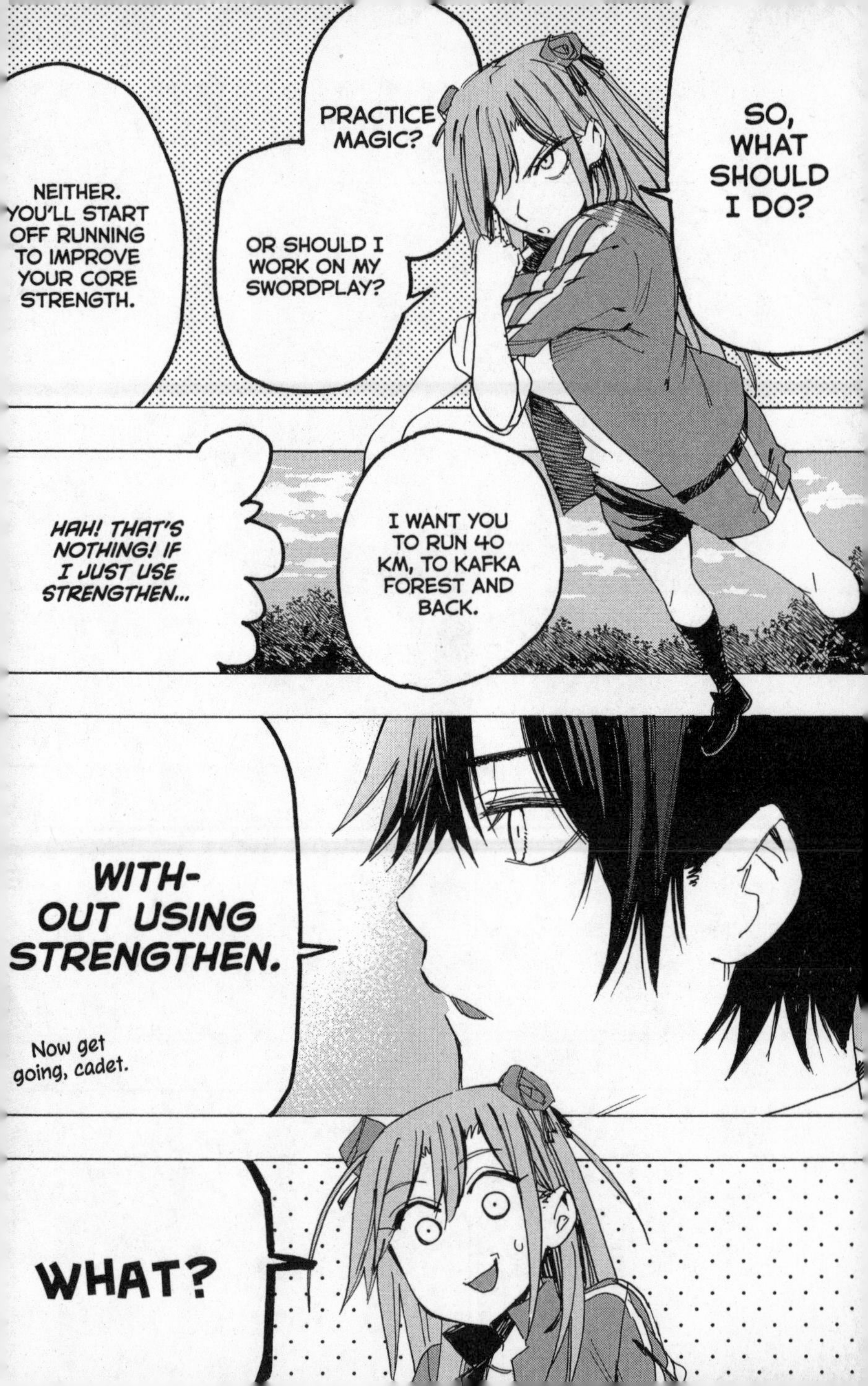
SO, WHAT SHOULD I DO?
PRACTICE MAGIC?
OR SHOULD I WORK ON MY SWORDPLAY?
NEITHER. YOU'LL START OFF RUNNING TO IMPROVE YOUR CORE STRENGTH.
I WANT YOU TO RUN 40 KM, TO KAFKA FOREST AND BACK.
HAH! THAT'S NOTHING! IF I JUST USE STRENGTHEN...
WITH-OUT USING STRENGTHEN.
Now get going, cadet.
WHAT?

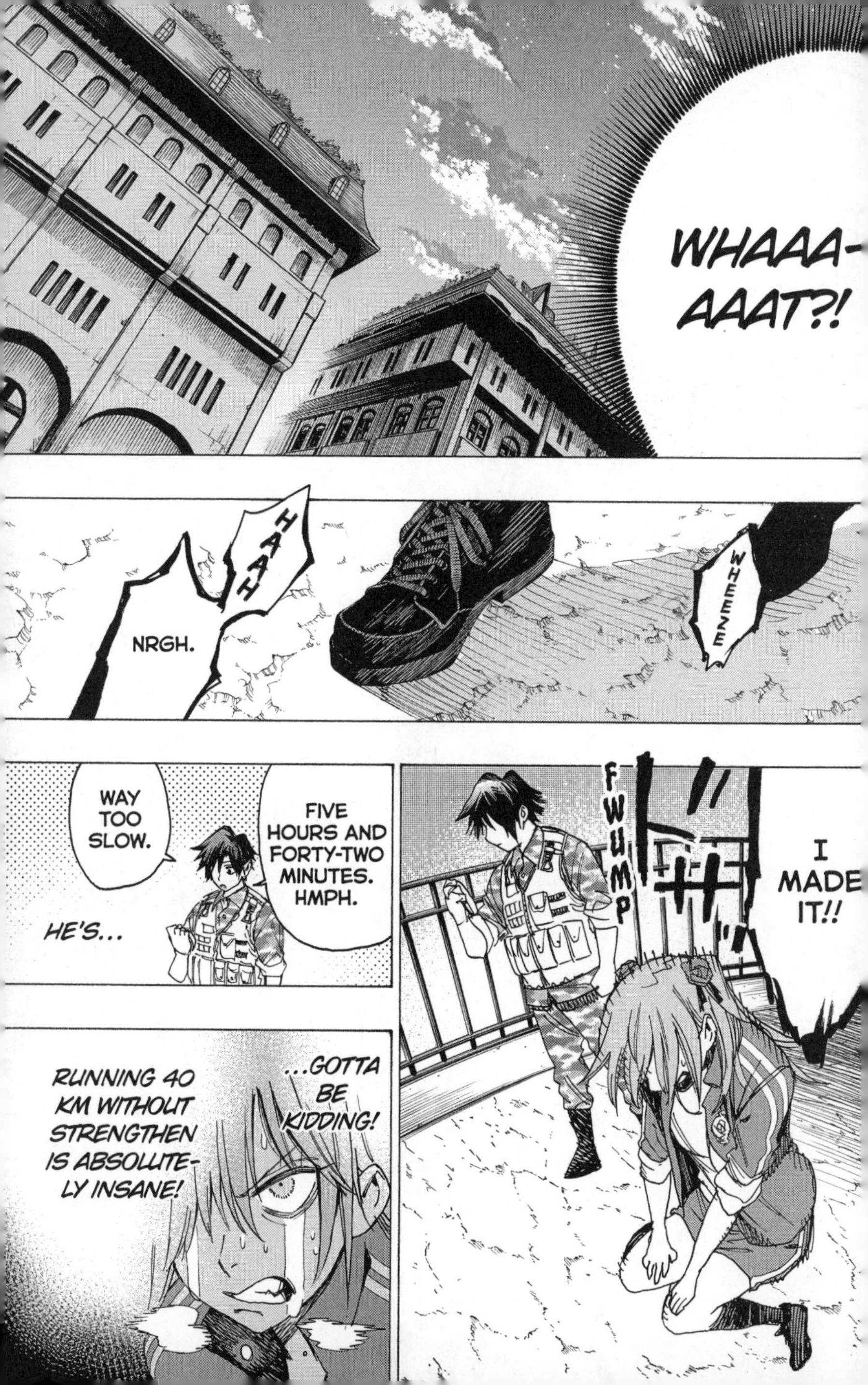
WHAAAA-AAAT?!
WHEEZE
HAAAH
NRGH.
I MADE IT!!
FWUMP
FIVE HOURS AND FORTY-TWO MINUTES. HMPH.
WAY TOO SLOW.
HE'S…
…GOTTA BE KIDDING!
RUNNING 40 KM WITHOUT STRENGTHEN IS ABSOLUTE-LY INSANE!

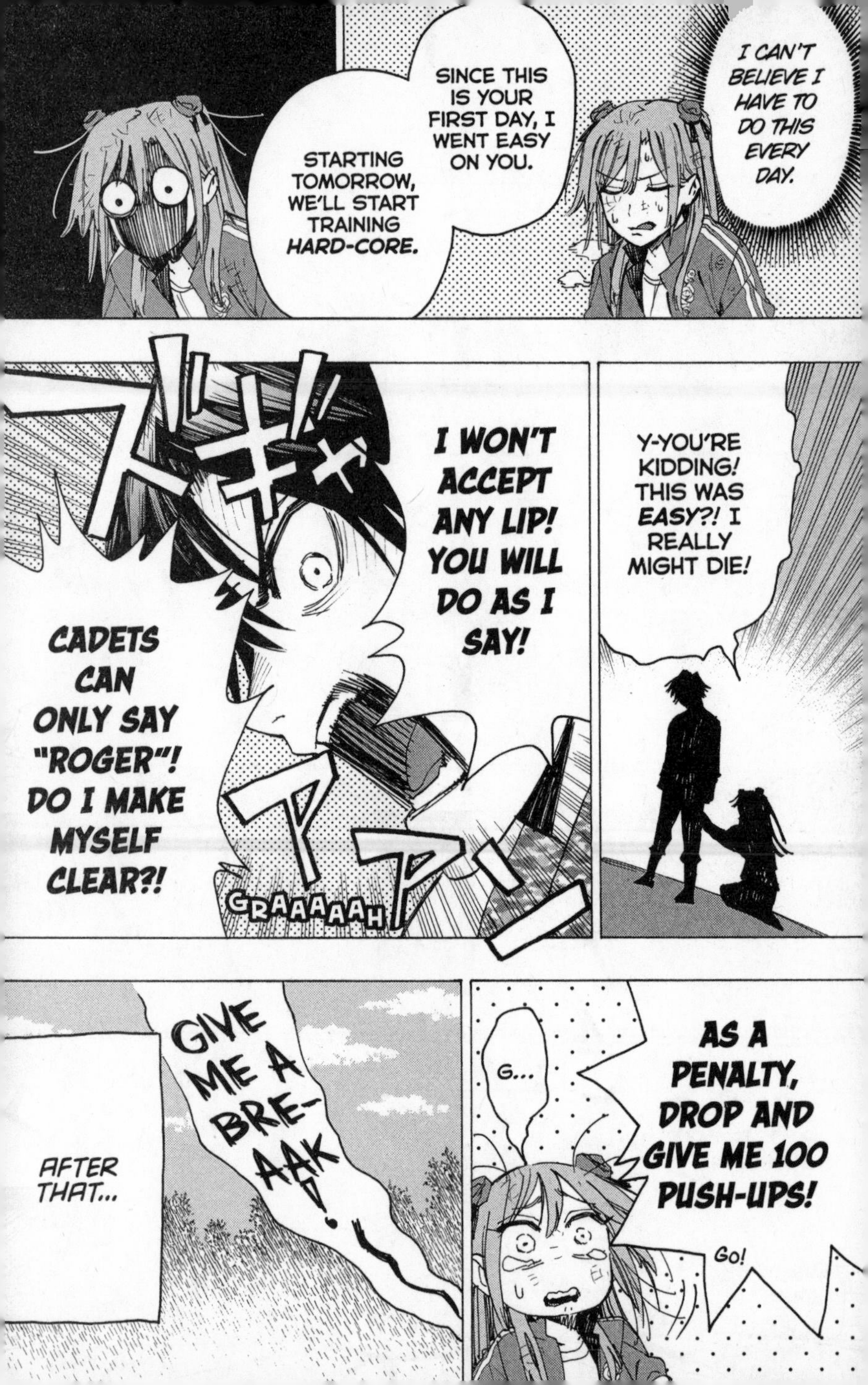
I CAN'T BELIEVE I HAVE TO DO THIS EVERY DAY.
SINCE THIS IS YOUR FIRST DAY, I WENT EASY ON YOU.
STARTING TOMORROW, WE'LL START TRAINING HARD-CORE.
Y-YOU'RE KIDDING! THIS WAS EASY?! I REALLY MIGHT DIE!
I WON'T ACCEPT ANY LIP! YOU WILL DO AS I SAY!
CADETS CAN ONLY SAY "ROGER"! DO I MAKE MYSELF CLEAR?!
GRAAAAAH
AS A PENALTY, DROP AND GIVE ME 100 PUSH-UPS!
GO!
G...
GIVE ME A BRE-AAK!
AFTER THAT...

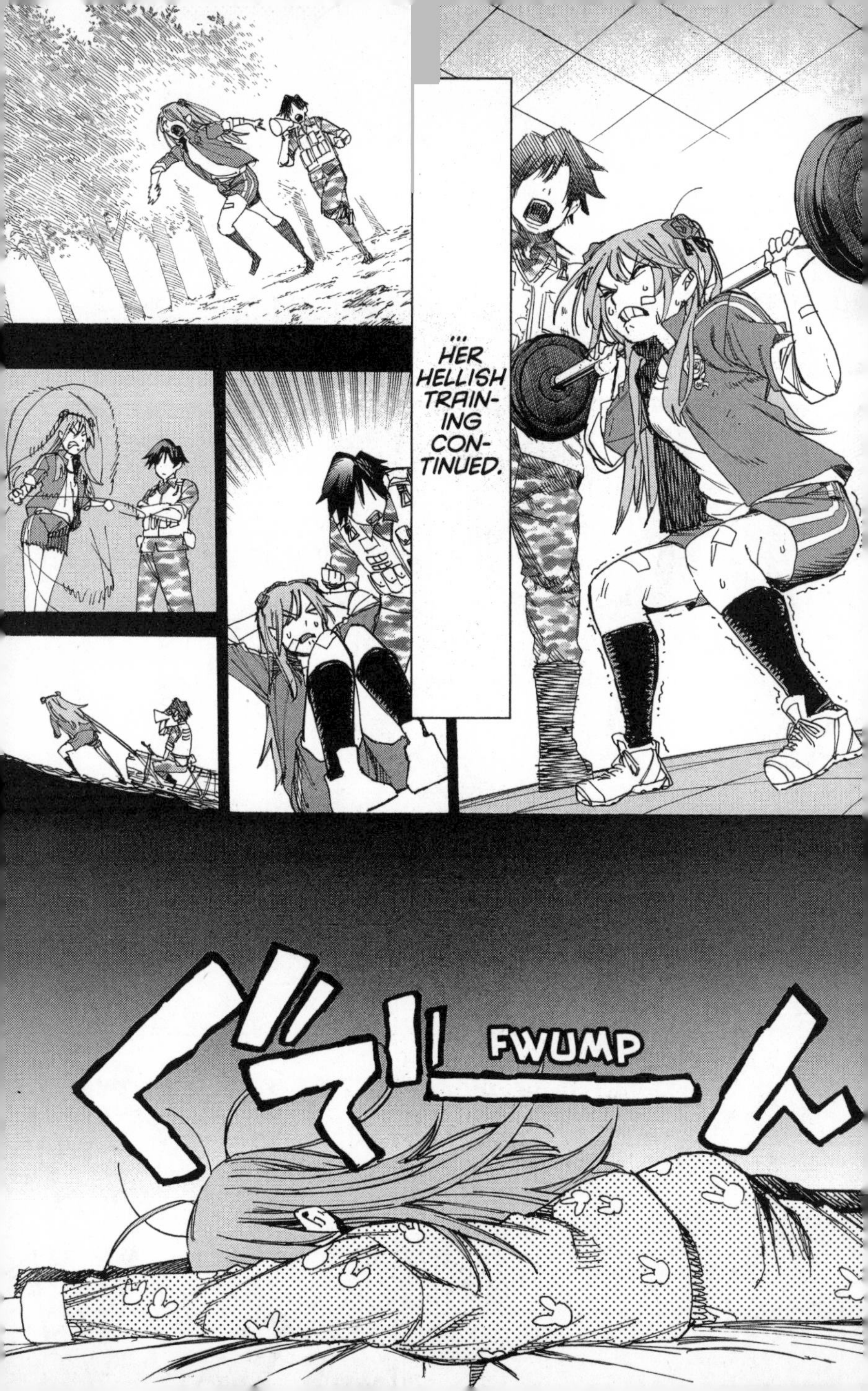
...HER HELLISH TRAIN-ING CON-TINUED.
グデーん
FWUMP

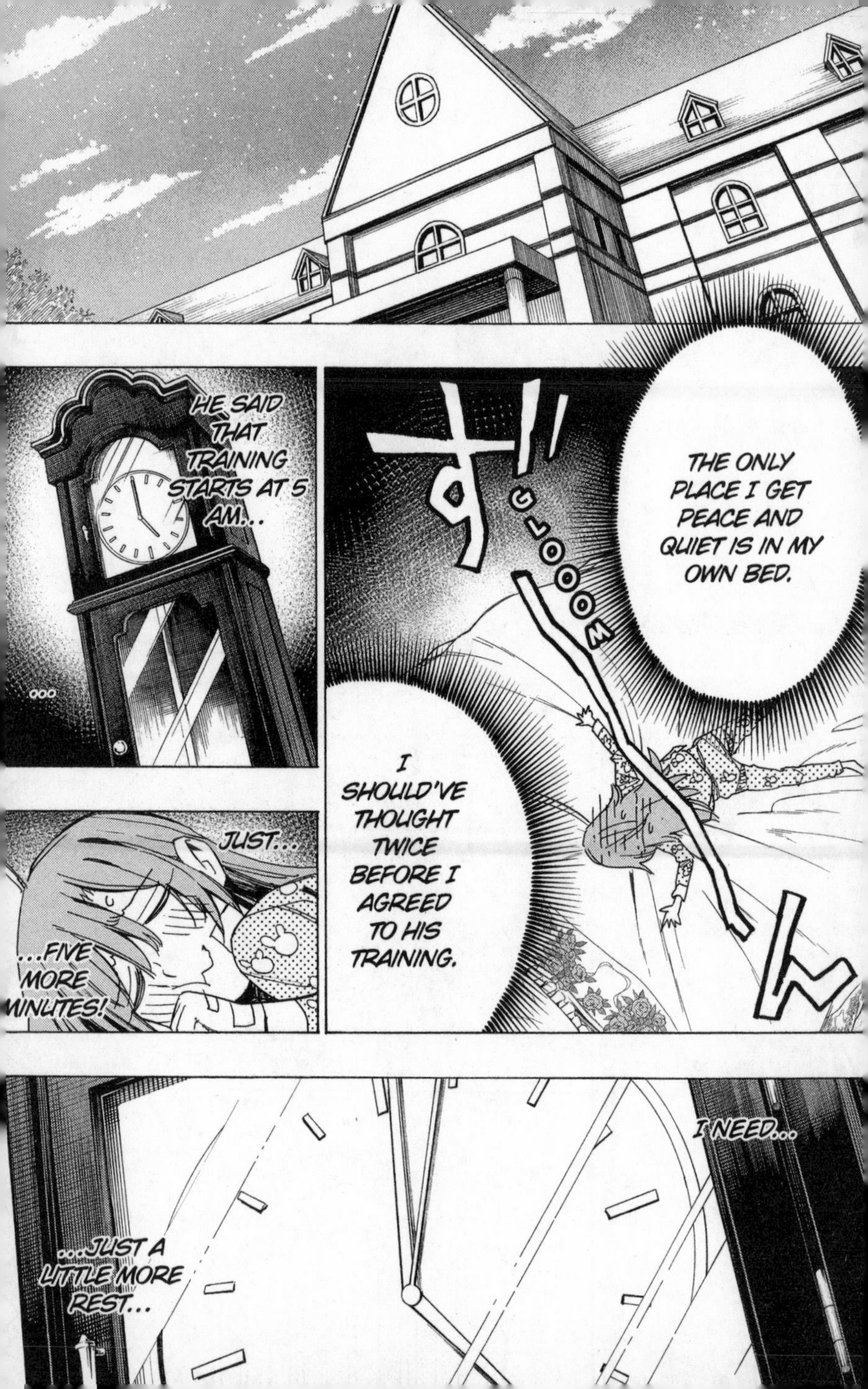
THE ONLY PLACE I GET PEACE AND QUIET IS IN MY OWN BED.
GLOOOOM
I SHOULD'VE THOUGHT TWICE BEFORE I AGREED TO HIS TRAINING.
HE SAID THAT TRAINING STARTS AT 5 AM...
...
JUST...
...FIVE MORE MINUTES!
I NEED...
...JUST A LITTLE MORE REST...

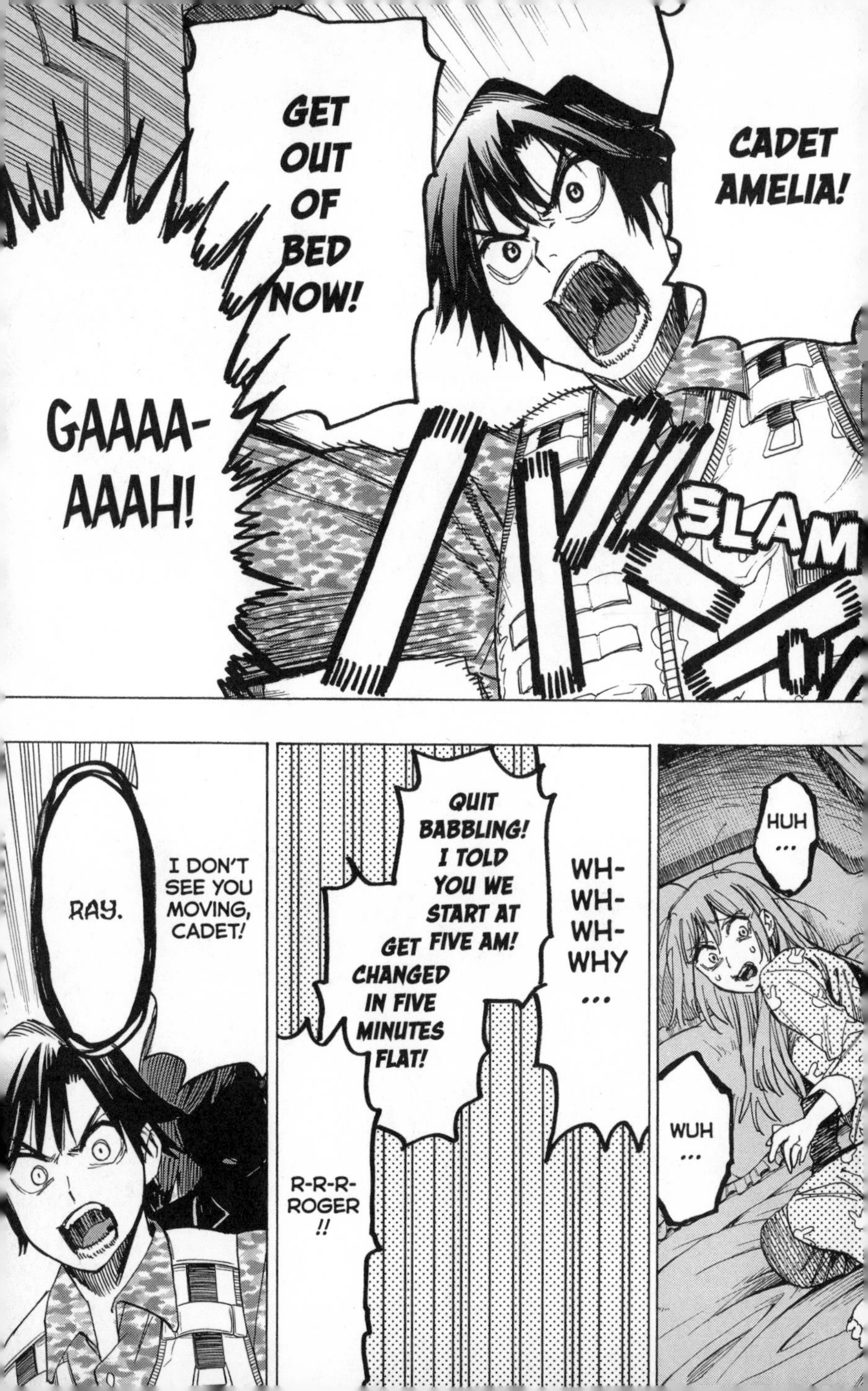
CADET AMELIA!
GET OUT OF BED NOW!
SLAM
GAAAA-AAAH!
HUH ...
WUH ...
WH-WH-WH-WHY ...
QUIT BABBLING! I TOLD YOU WE START AT FIVE AM!
GET CHANGED IN FIVE MINUTES FLAT!
R-R-R-ROGER !!
I DON'T SEE YOU MOVING, CADET!
RAY.

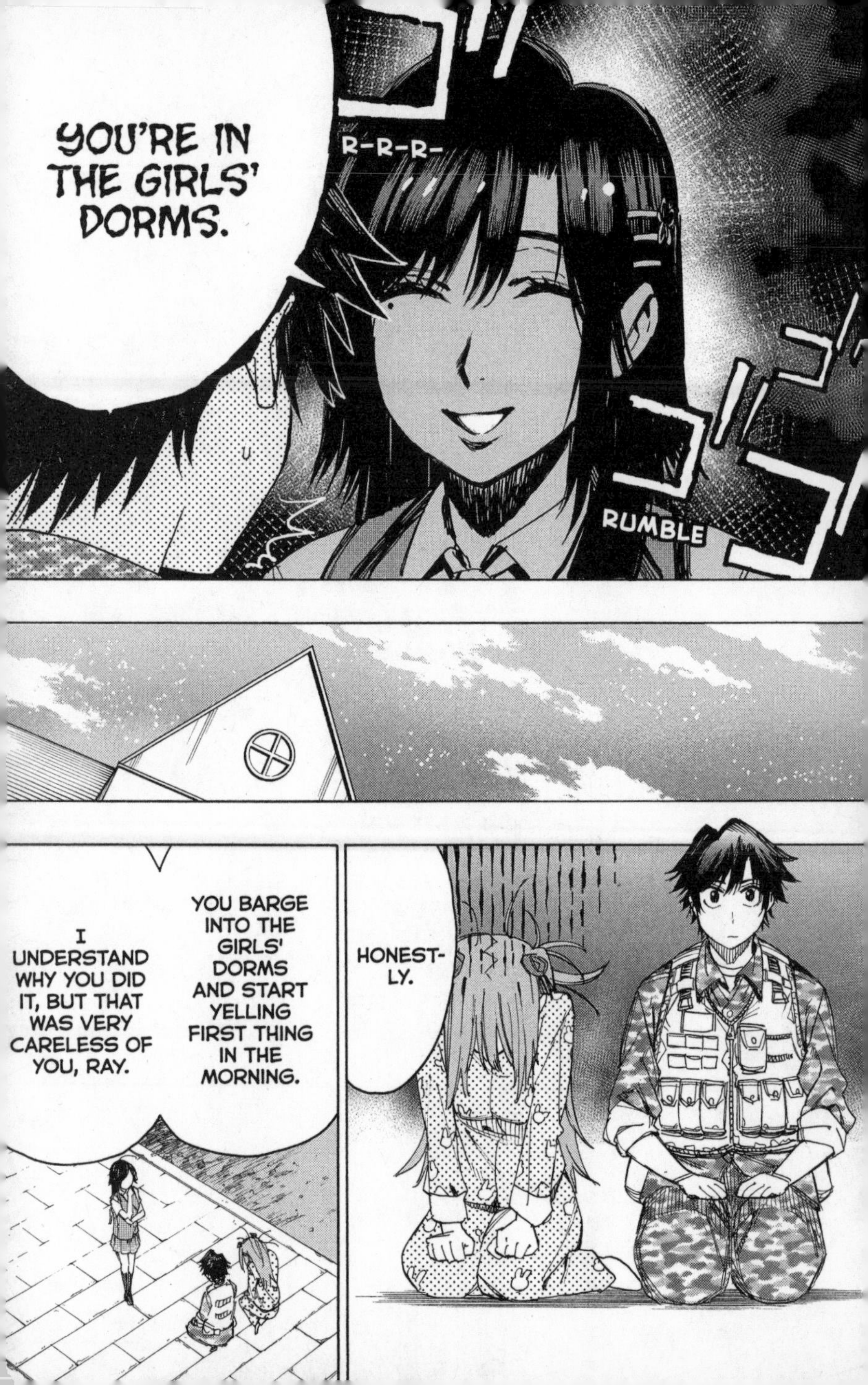
YOU'RE IN THE GIRLS' DORMS.
R-R-R-
RUMBLE
HONEST-LY.
YOU BARGE INTO THE GIRLS' DORMS AND START YELLING FIRST THING IN THE MORNING.
I UNDERSTAND WHY YOU DID IT, BUT THAT WAS VERY CARELESS OF YOU, RAY.

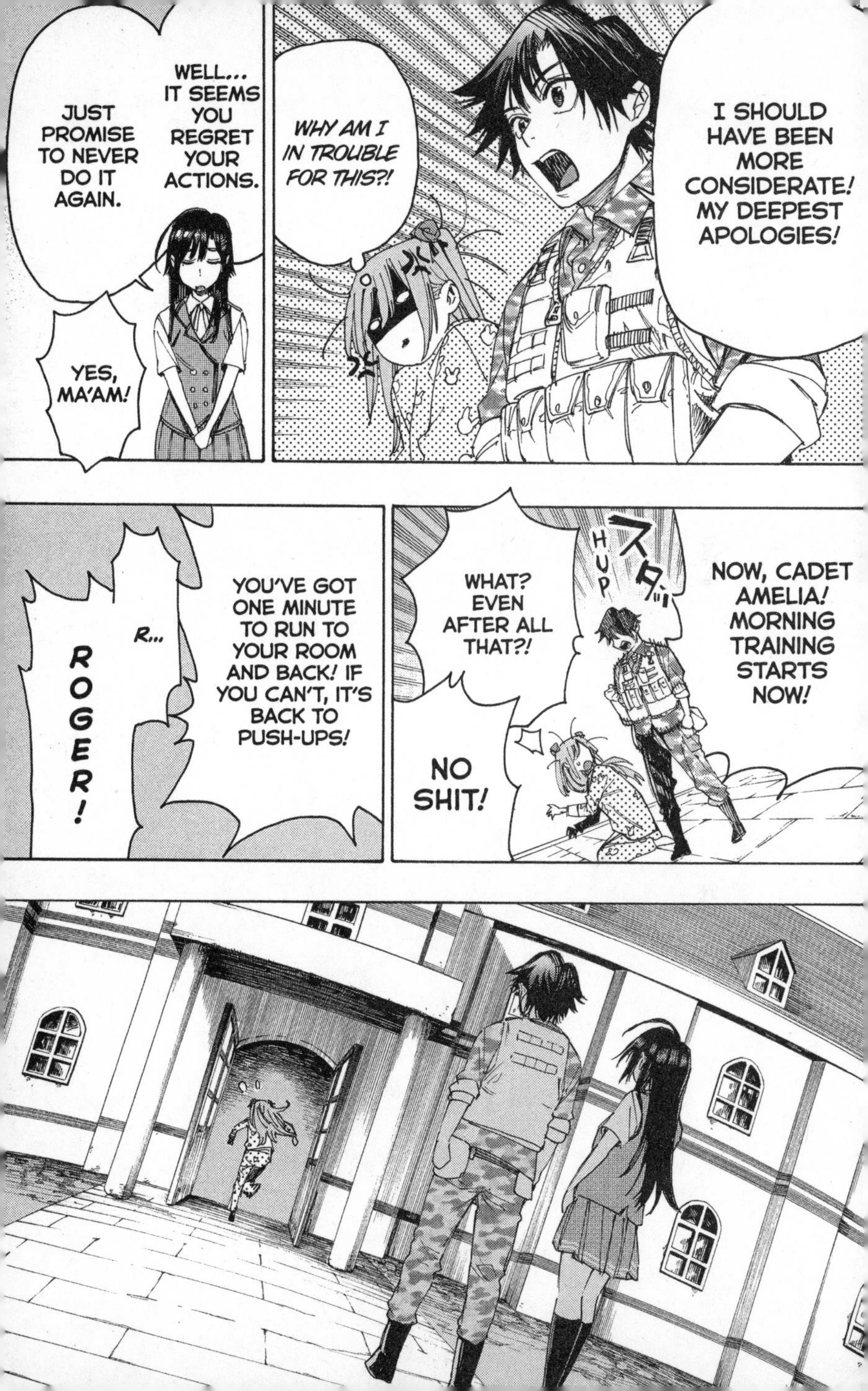
I SHOULD HAVE BEEN MORE CONSIDERATE! MY DEEPEST APOLOGIES!
WHY AM I IN TROUBLE FOR THIS?!
WELL... IT SEEMS YOU REGRET YOUR ACTIONS.
JUST PROMISE TO NEVER DO IT AGAIN.
YES, MA'AM!
NOW, CADET AMELIA! MORNING TRAINING STARTS NOW!
スタッ
HUP
WHAT? EVEN AFTER ALL THAT?!
NO SHIT!
YOU'VE GOT ONE MINUTE TO RUN TO YOUR ROOM AND BACK! IF YOU CAN'T, IT'S BACK TO PUSH-UPS!
R...
ROGER!

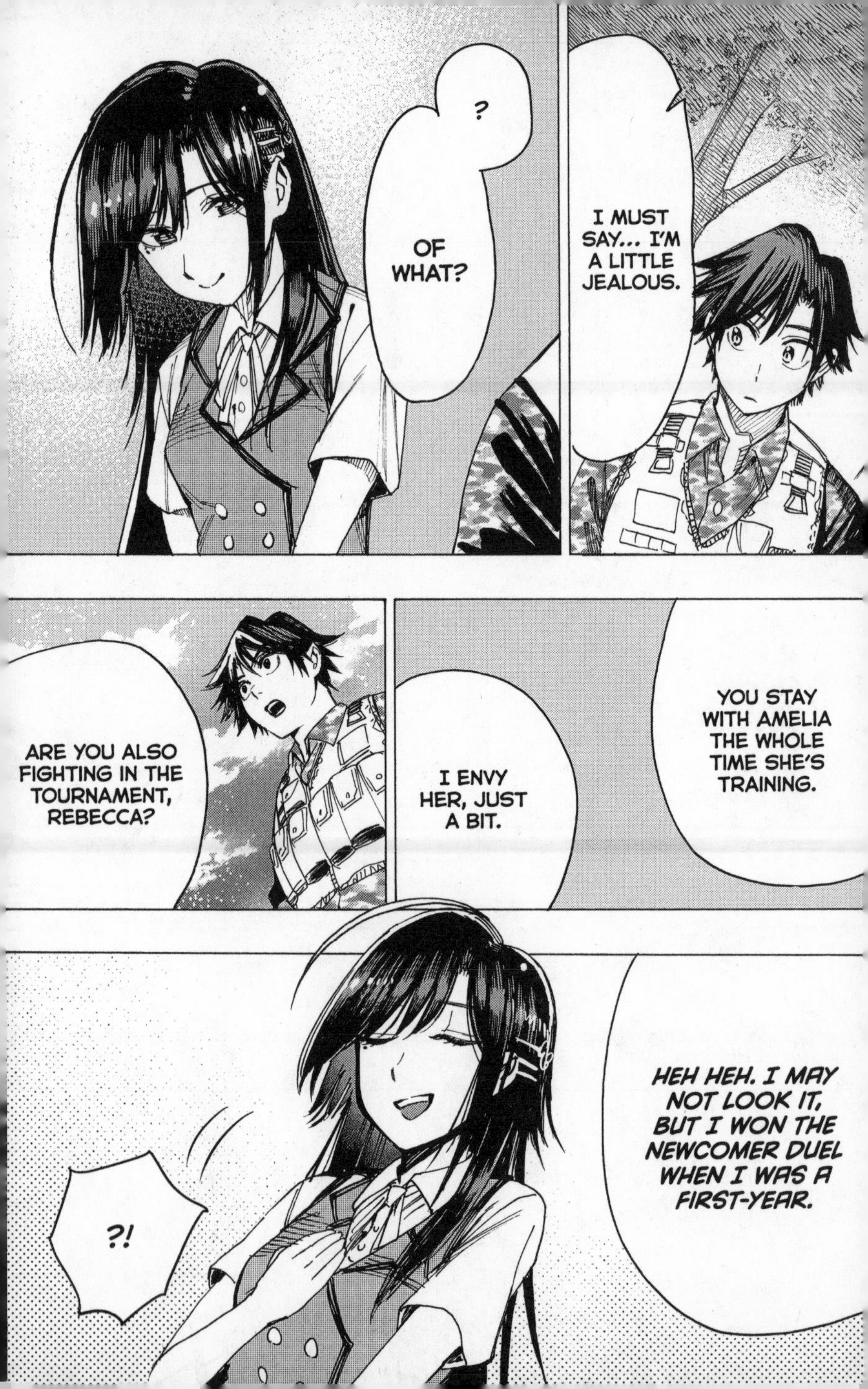
I MUST SAY... I'M A LITTLE JEALOUS.
?
OF WHAT?
YOU STAY WITH AMELIA THE WHOLE TIME SHE'S TRAINING.
I ENVY HER, JUST A BIT.
ARE YOU ALSO FIGHTING IN THE TOURNAMENT, REBECCA?
HEH HEH. I MAY NOT LOOK IT, BUT I WON THE NEWCOMER DUEL WHEN I WAS A FIRST-YEAR.
?!

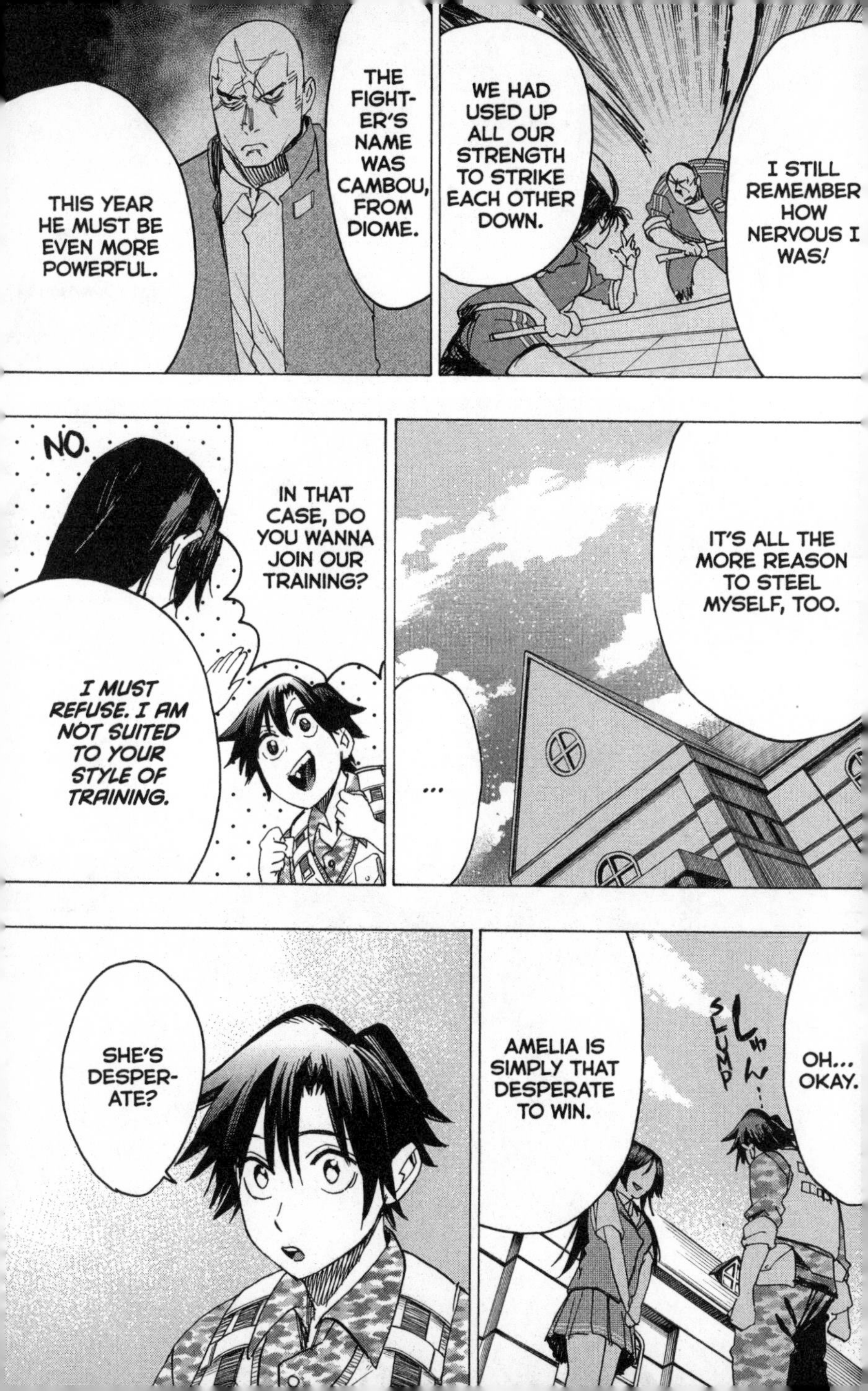
I STILL REMEMBER HOW NERVOUS I WAS!
WE HAD USED UP ALL OUR STRENGTH TO STRIKE EACH OTHER DOWN.
THE FIGHTER'S NAME WAS CAMBOU, FROM DIOME.
THIS YEAR HE MUST BE EVEN MORE POWERFUL.
IT'S ALL THE MORE REASON TO STEEL MYSELF, TOO.
...
IN THAT CASE, DO YOU WANNA JOIN OUR TRAINING?
NO.
I MUST REFUSE. I AM NOT SUITED TO YOUR STYLE OF TRAINING.
OH... OKAY.
SLUMP
AMELIA IS SIMPLY THAT DESPERATE TO WIN.
SHE'S DESPERATE?

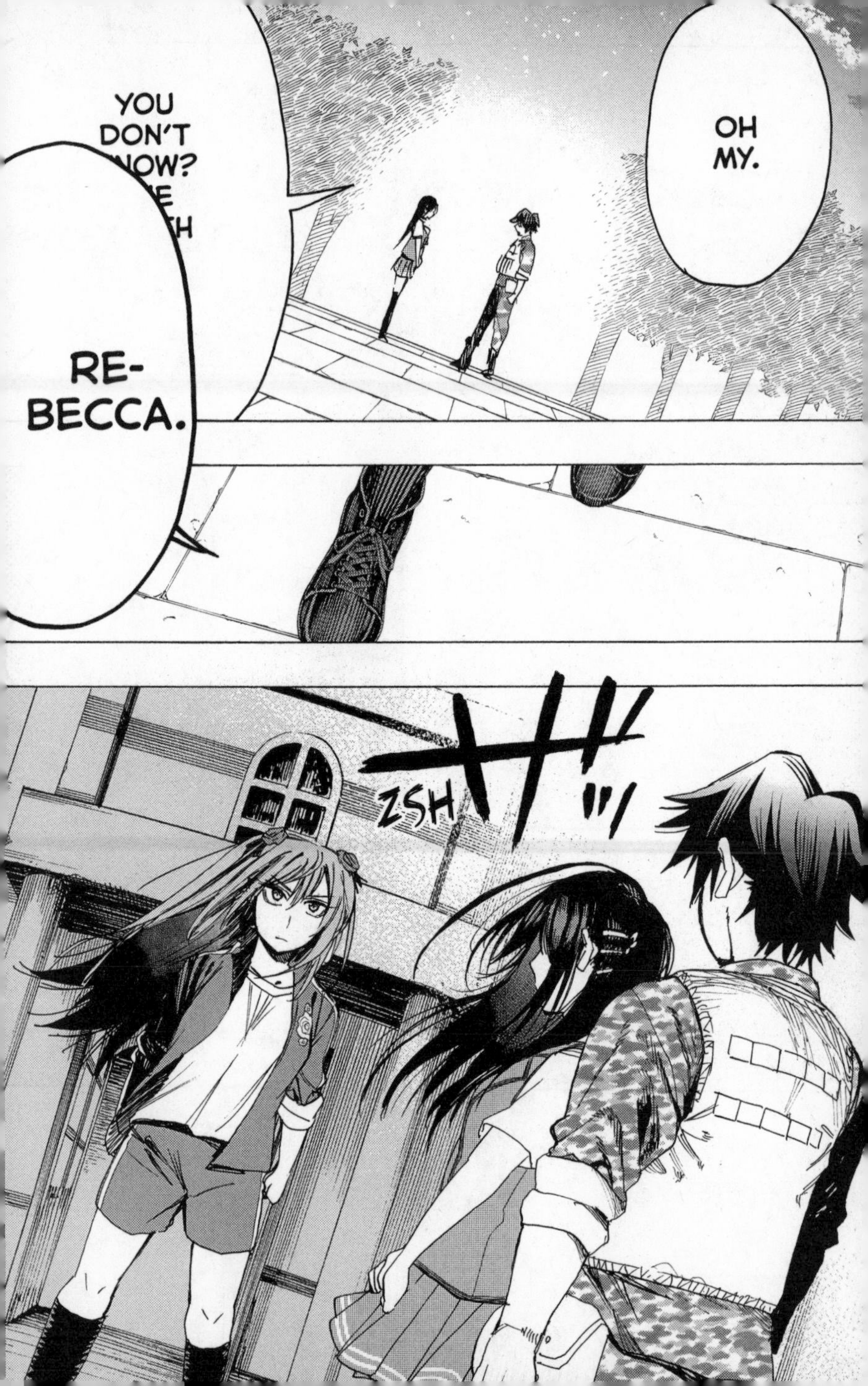
OH MY.
YOU DON'T
RE-BECCA.
ZSH

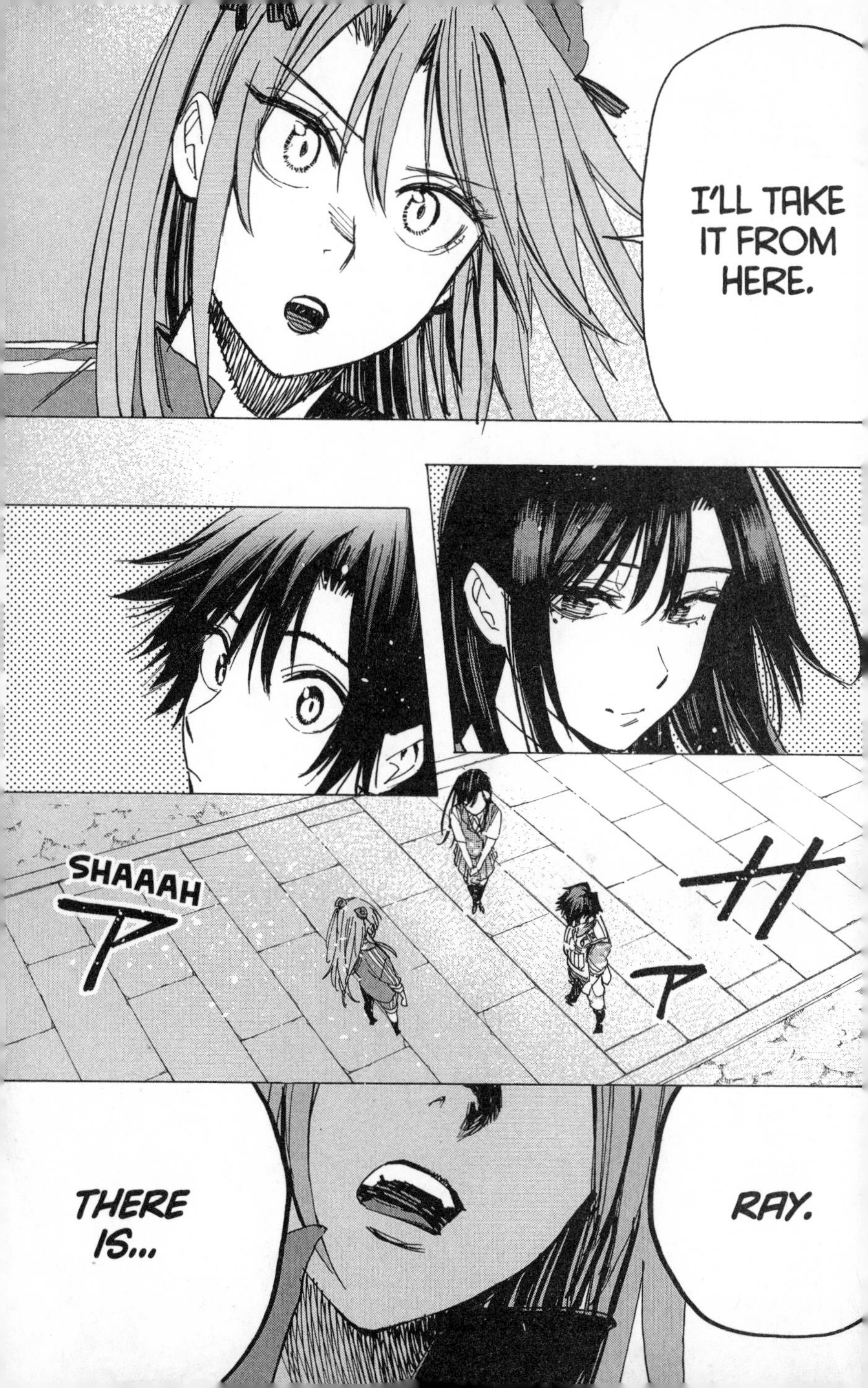
I'LL TAKE IT FROM HERE.
SHAAAH
RAY.
THERE IS...

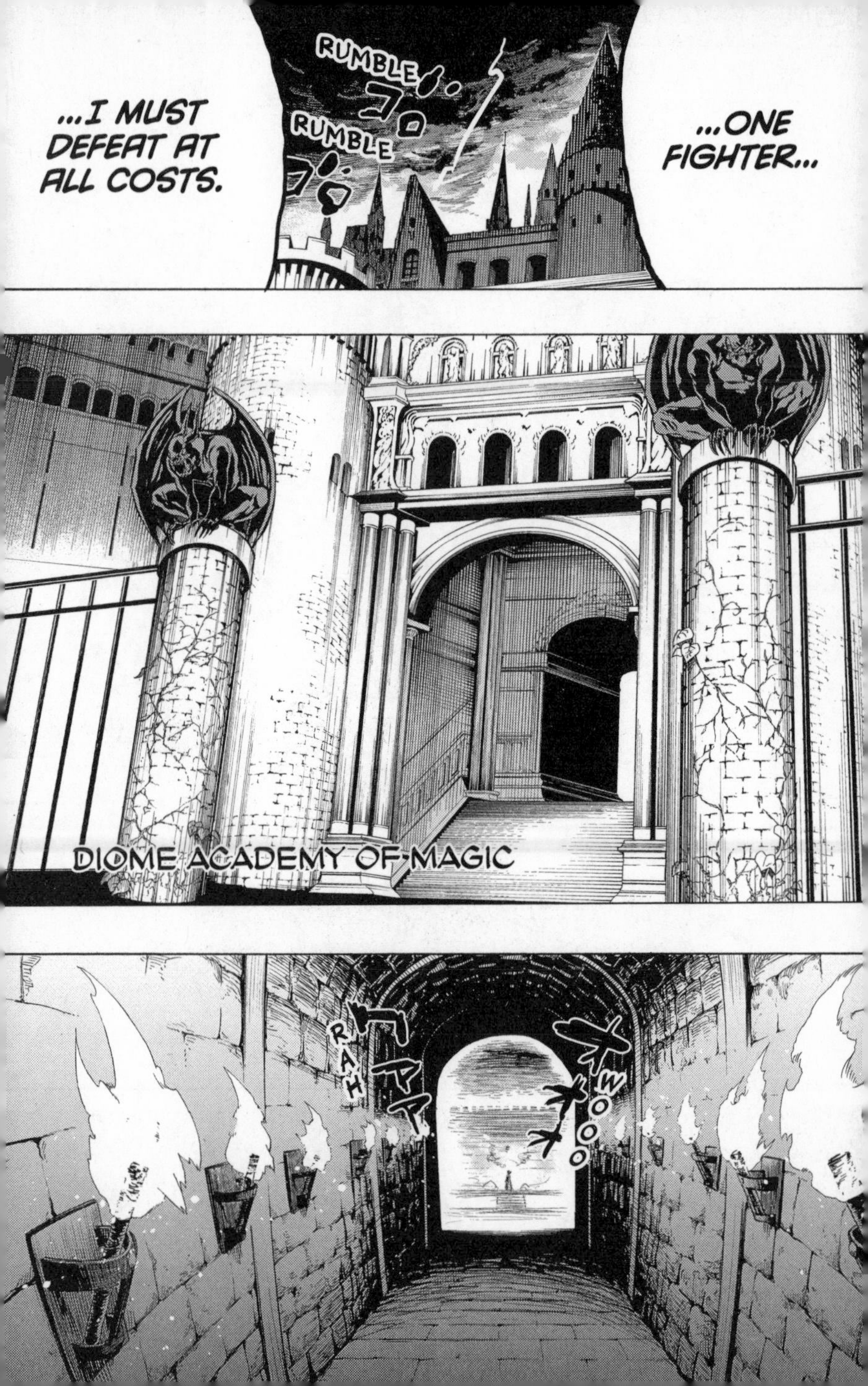
...ONE FIGHTER...
RUMBLE
RUMBLE
...I MUST DEFEAT AT ALL COSTS.
DIOME ACADEMY OF MAGIC
WOOOO
RAH

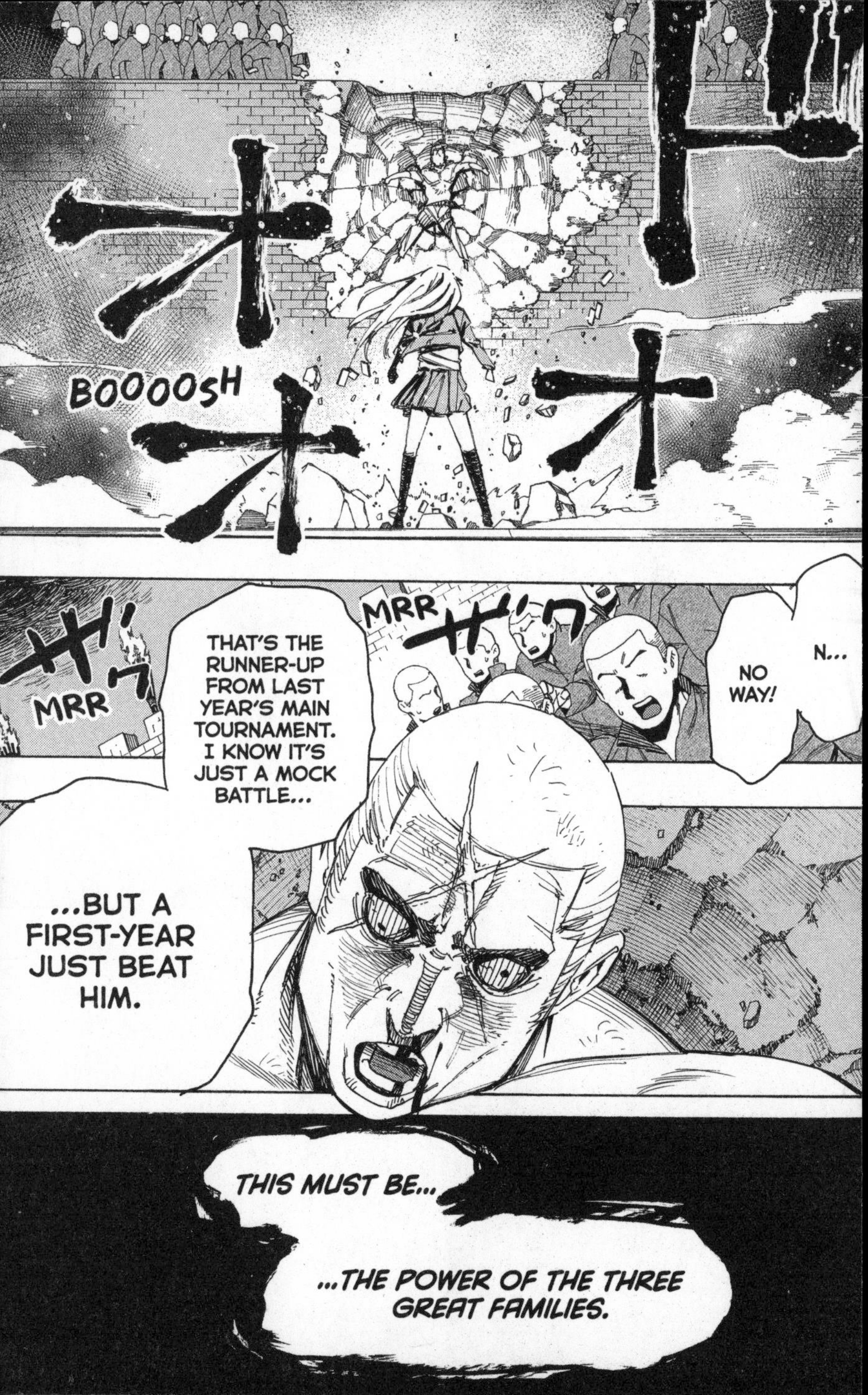
BOOOOSH
N...
NO WAY!
MRR
MRR
THAT'S THE RUNNER-UP FROM LAST YEAR'S MAIN TOURNAMENT. I KNOW IT'S JUST A MOCK BATTLE...
...BUT A FIRST-YEAR JUST BEAT HIM.
THIS MUST BE...
...THE POWER OF THE THREE GREAT FAMILIES.

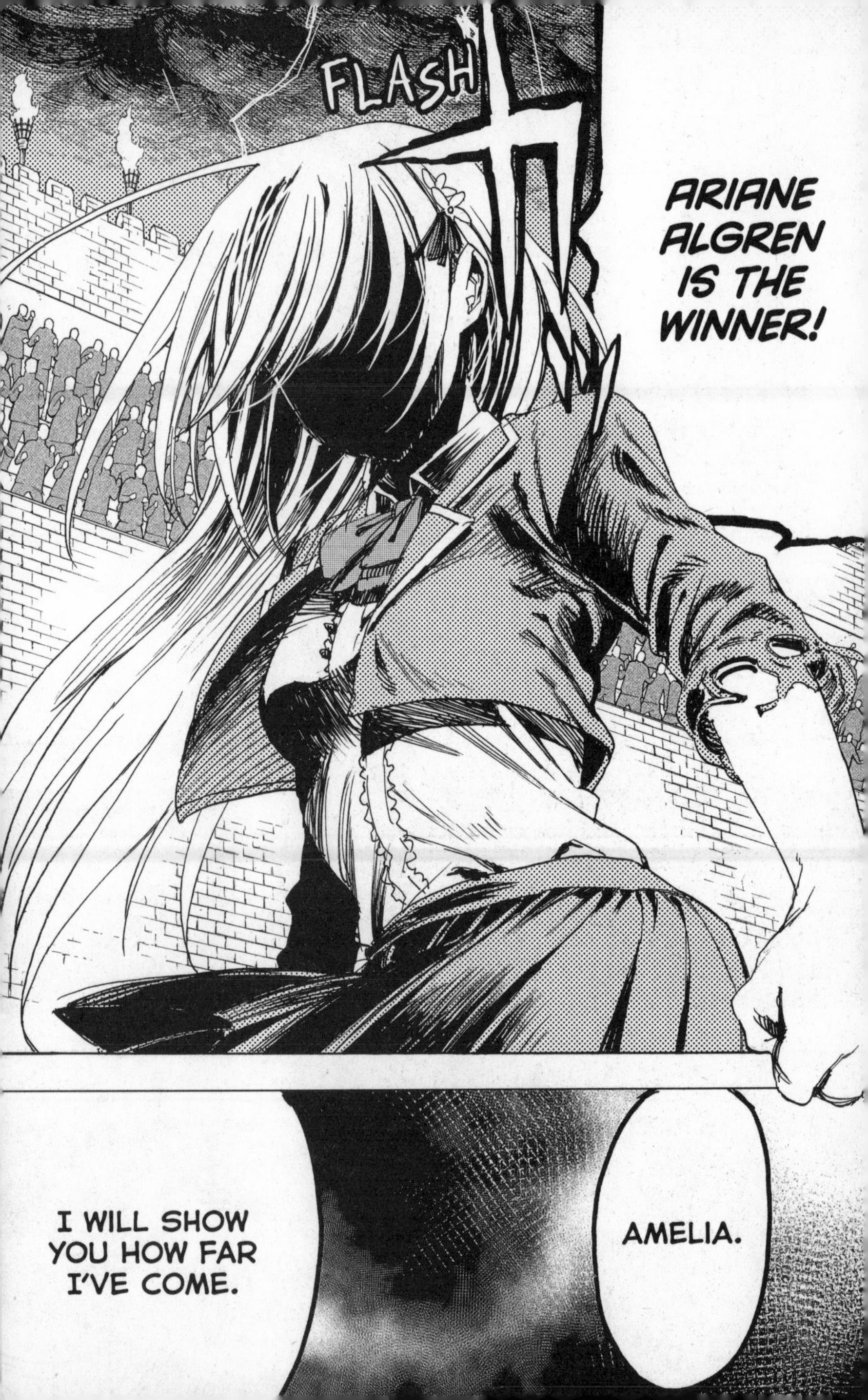
FLASH
ARIANE ALGREN IS THE WINNER!
AMELIA.
I WILL SHOW YOU HOW FAR I'VE COME.

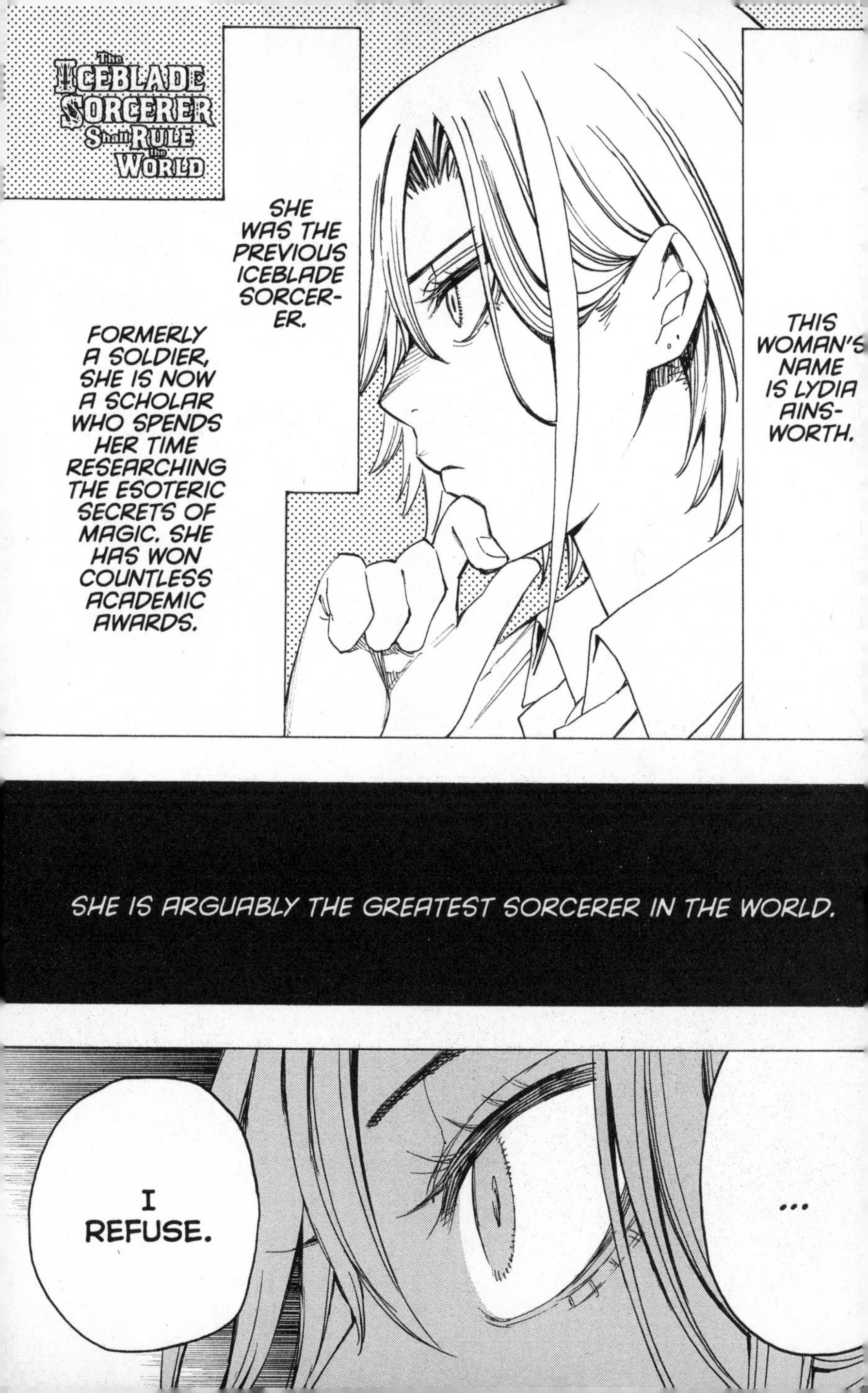
THIS WOMAN'S NAME IS LYDIA AINSWORTH.
SHE WAS THE PREVIOUS ICEBLADE SORCERER.
FORMERLY A SOLDIER, SHE IS NOW A SCHOLAR WHO SPENDS HER TIME RESEARCHING THE ESOTERIC SECRETS OF MAGIC. SHE HAS WON COUNTLESS ACADEMIC AWARDS.
SHE IS ARGUABLY THE GREATEST SORCERER IN THE WORLD.
...
I REFUSE.

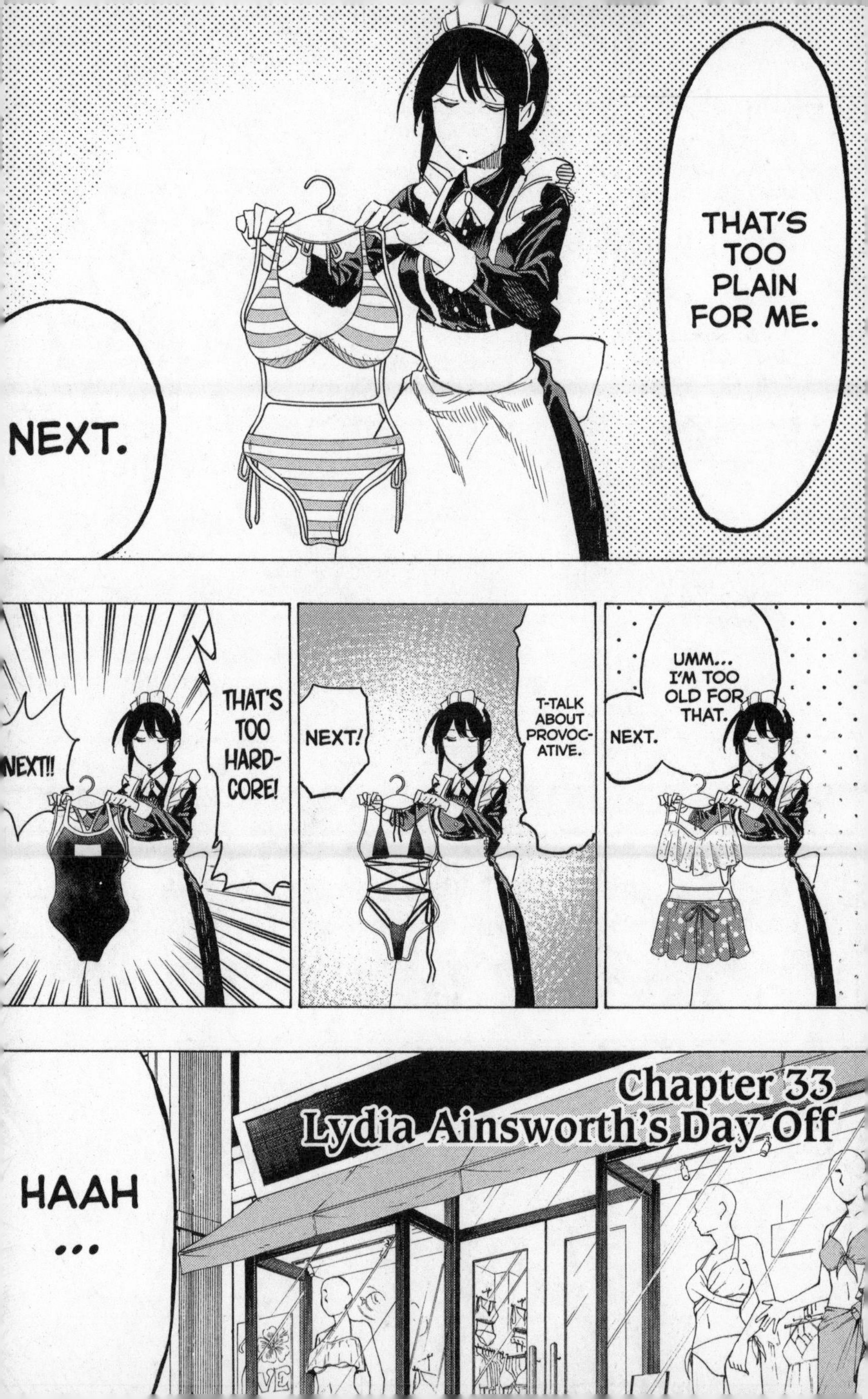
THAT'S TOO PLAIN FOR ME.
NEXT.
UMM... I'M TOO OLD FOR THAT.
NEXT.
T-TALK ABOUT PROVOC-ATIVE.
NEXT!
THAT'S TOO HARD-CORE!
NEXT!!
Chapter 33
Lydia Ainsworth's Day Off
HAAH
...

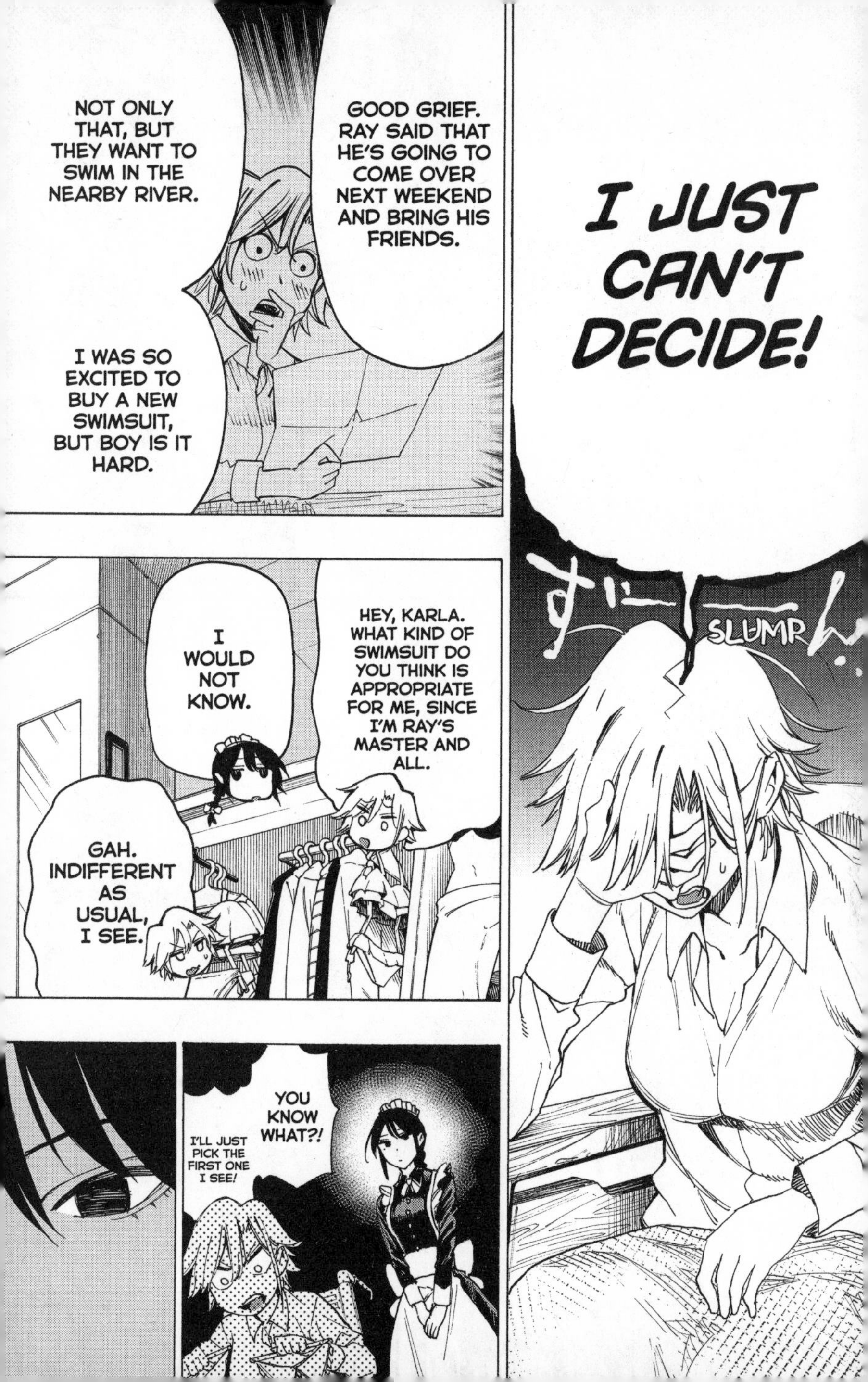
I JUST CAN'T DECIDE!
SLUMP
GOOD GRIEF. RAY SAID THAT HE'S GOING TO COME OVER NEXT WEEKEND AND BRING HIS FRIENDS.
NOT ONLY THAT, BUT THEY WANT TO SWIM IN THE NEARBY RIVER.
I WAS SO EXCITED TO BUY A NEW SWIMSUIT, BUT BOY IS IT HARD.
HEY, KARLA. WHAT KIND OF SWIMSUIT DO YOU THINK IS APPROPRIATE FOR ME, SINCE I'M RAY'S MASTER AND ALL.
I WOULD NOT KNOW.
GAH. INDIFFERENT AS USUAL, I SEE.
YOU KNOW WHAT?!
I'LL JUST PICK THE FIRST ONE I SEE!

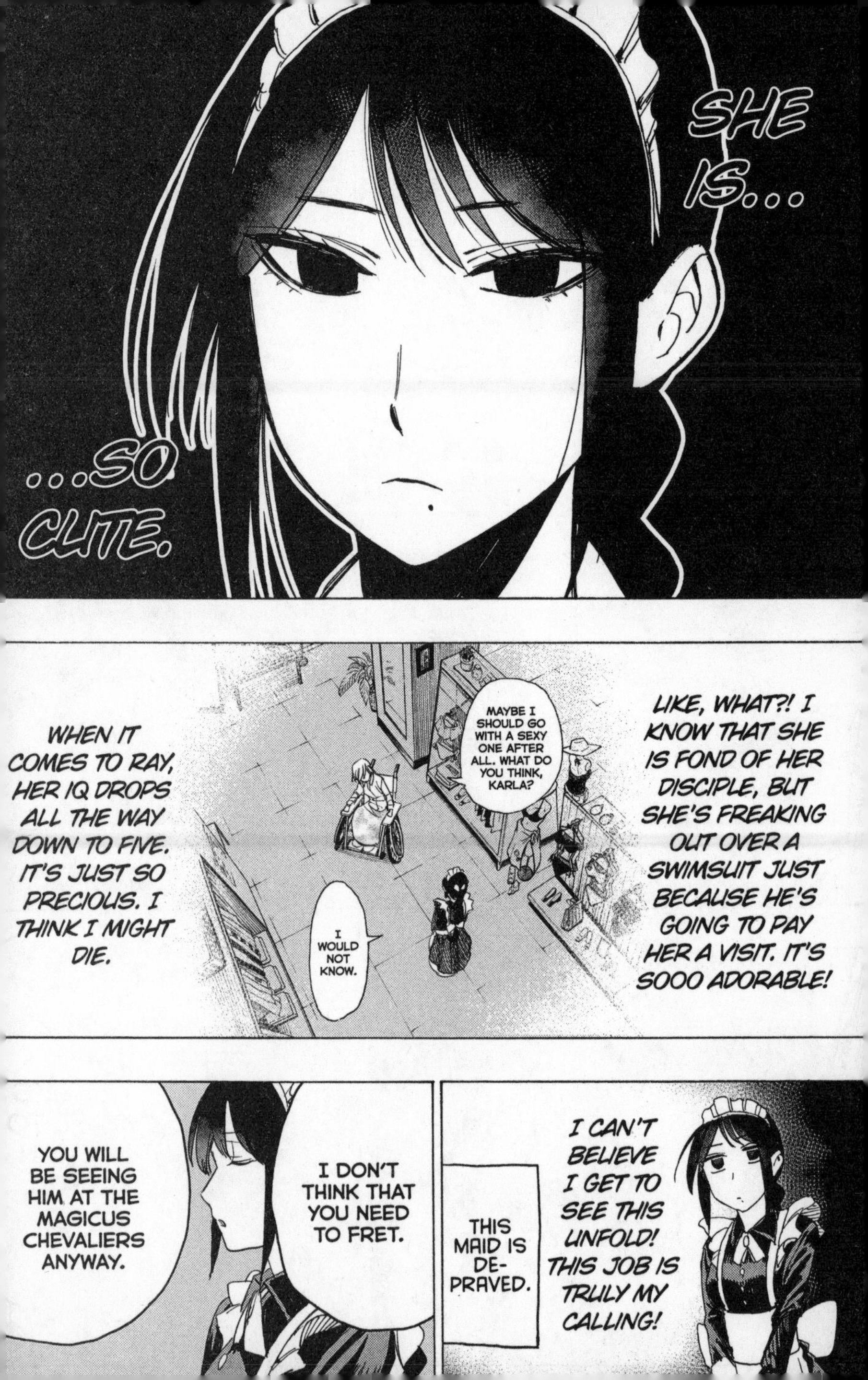
SHE IS...
...SO CUTE.
LIKE, WHAT?! I KNOW THAT SHE IS FOND OF HER DISCIPLE, BUT SHE'S FREAKING OUT OVER A SWIMSUIT JUST BECAUSE HE'S GOING TO PAY HER A VISIT. IT'S SOOO ADORABLE!
MAYBE I SHOULD GO WITH A SEXY ONE AFTER ALL. WHAT DO YOU THINK, KARLA?
I WOULD NOT KNOW.
WHEN IT COMES TO RAY, HER IQ DROPS ALL THE WAY DOWN TO FIVE. IT'S JUST SO PRECIOUS. I THINK I MIGHT DIE.
I CAN'T BELIEVE I GET TO SEE THIS UNFOLD! THIS JOB IS TRULY MY CALLING!
THIS MAID IS DE-PRAVED.
I DON'T THINK THAT YOU NEED TO FRET.
YOU WILL BE SEEING HIM AT THE MAGICUS CHEVALIERS ANYWAY.

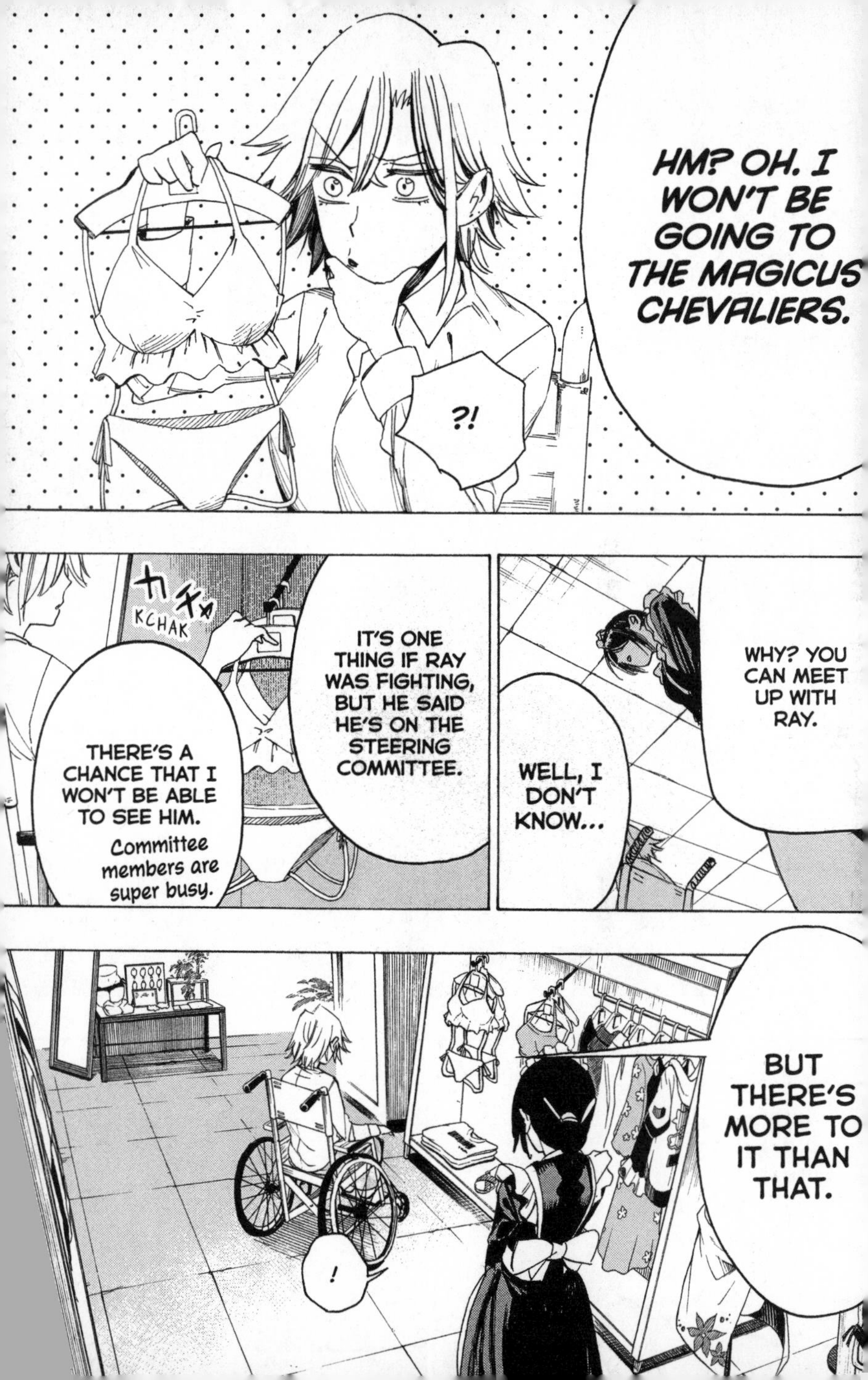
HM? OH. I WON'T BE GOING TO THE MAGICUS CHEVALIERS.
?!
WHY? YOU CAN MEET UP WITH RAY.
WELL, I DON'T KNOW...
IT'S ONE THING IF RAY WAS FIGHTING, BUT HE SAID HE'S ON THE STEERING COMMITTEE.
カチャ
KCHAK
THERE'S A CHANCE THAT I WON'T BE ABLE TO SEE HIM.
Committee members are super busy.
BUT THERE'S MORE TO IT THAN THAT.
!

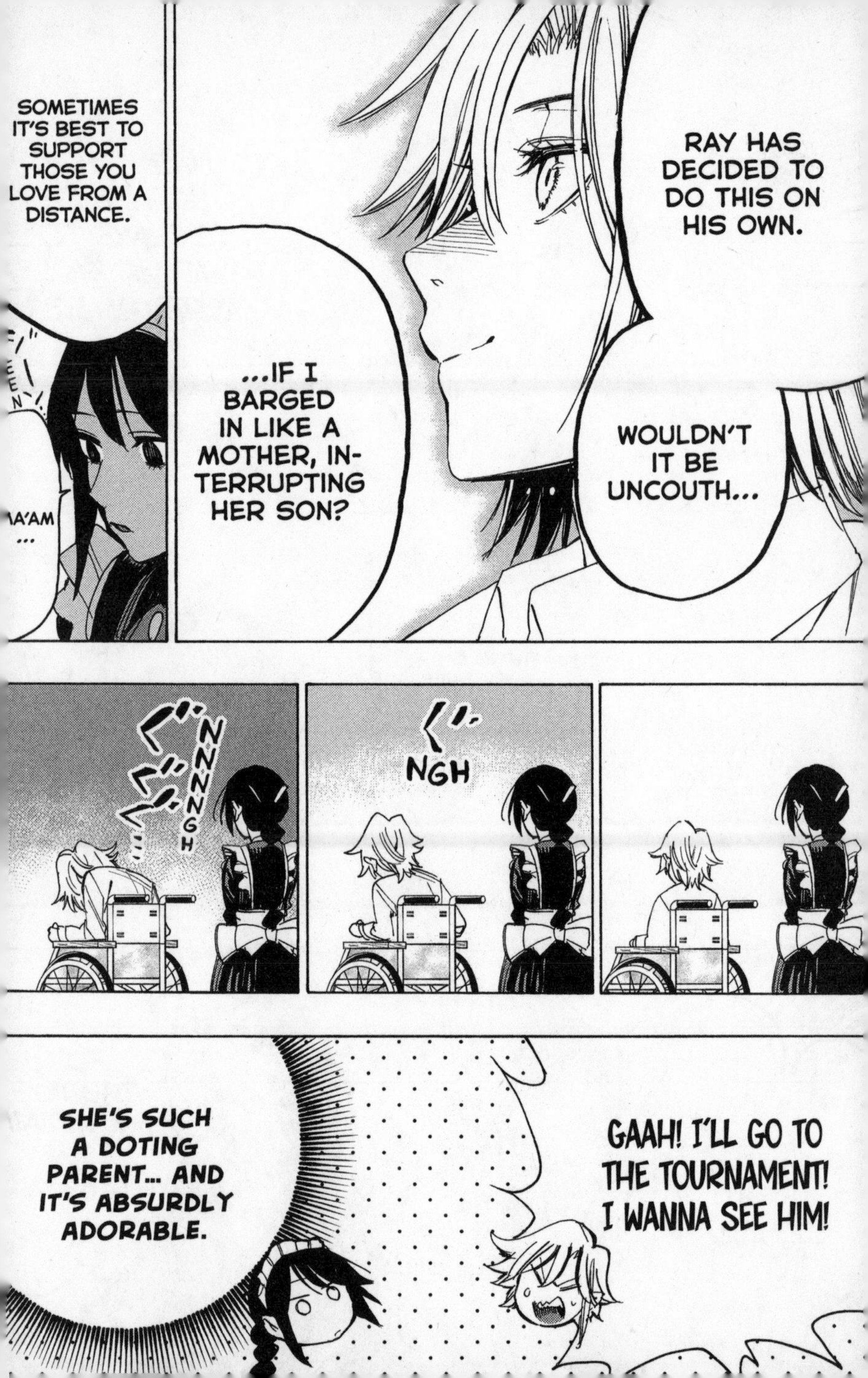
RAY HAS DECIDED TO DO THIS ON HIS OWN.
WOULDN'T IT BE UNCOUTH...
...IF I BARGED IN LIKE A MOTHER, IN-TERRUPTING HER SON?
SOMETIMES IT'S BEST TO SUPPORT THOSE YOU LOVE FROM A DISTANCE.
A'AM ...
NGH
NNNNNGH
GAAH! I'LL GO TO THE TOURNAMENT! I WANNA SEE HIM!
SHE'S SUCH A DOTING PARENT... AND IT'S ABSURDLY ADORABLE.

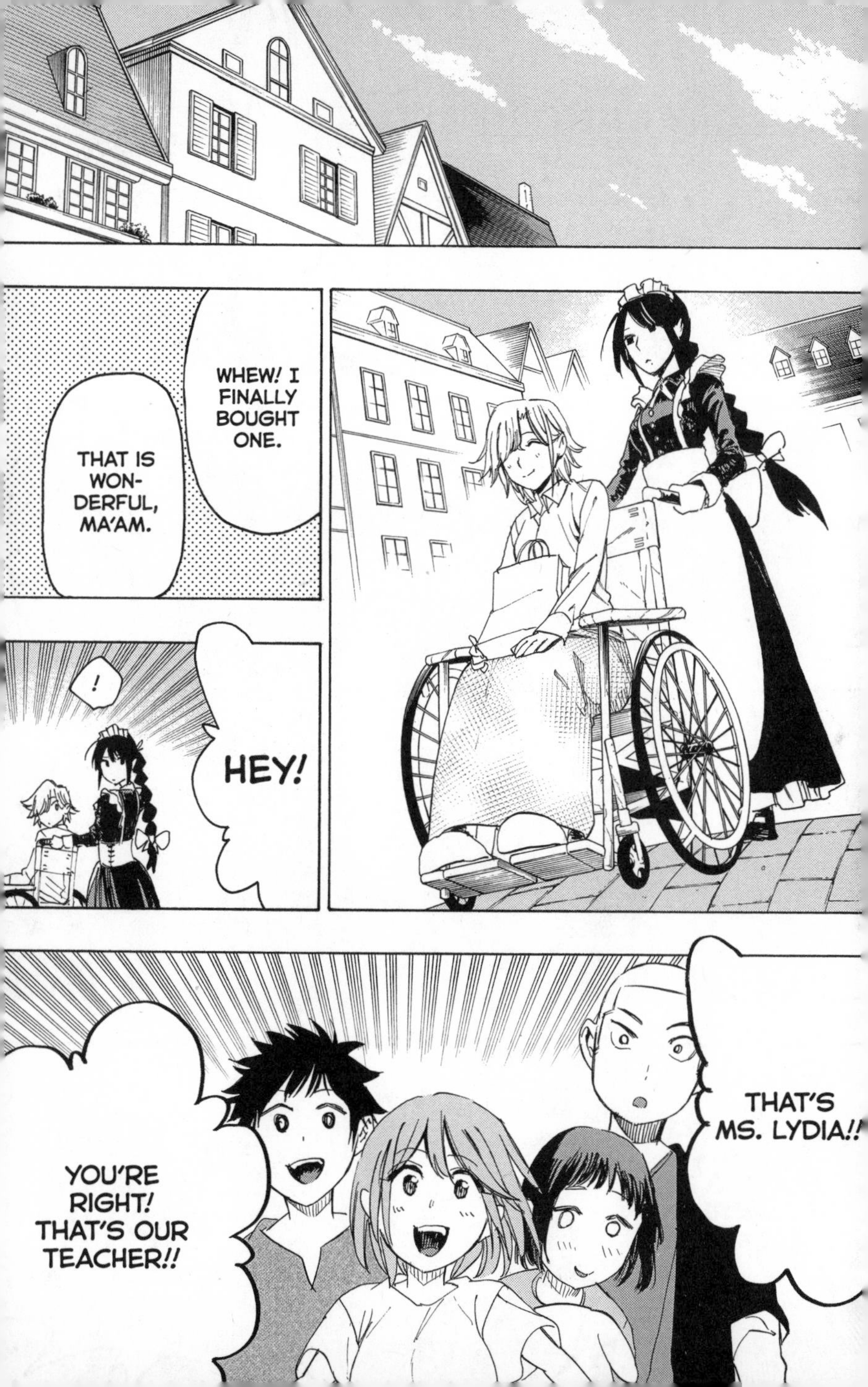
WHEW! I FINALLY BOUGHT ONE.
THAT IS WON-DERFUL, MA'AM.
HEY!
!
THAT'S MS. LYDIA!!
YOU'RE RIGHT! THAT'S OUR TEACHER!!

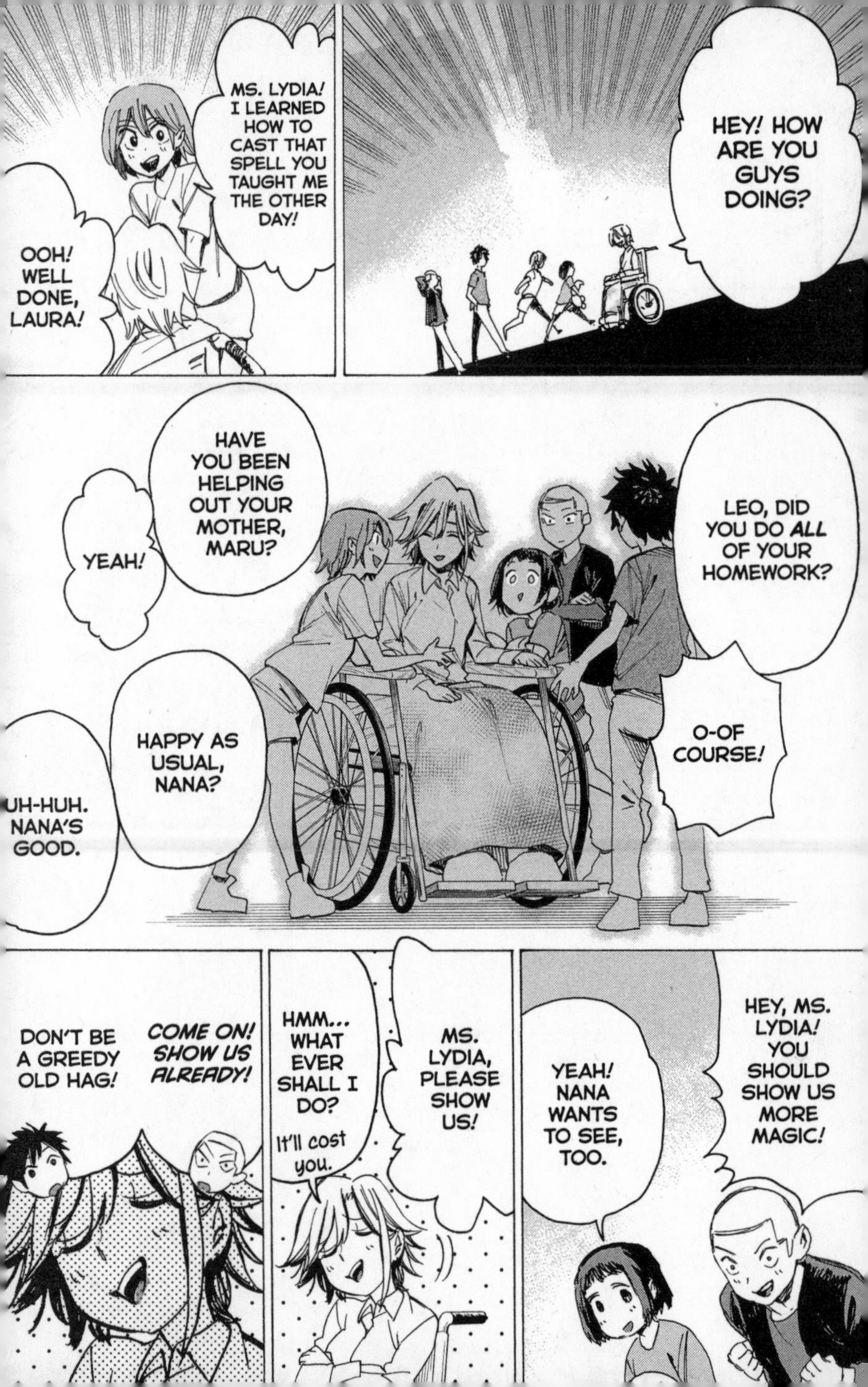
HEY! HOW ARE YOU GUYS DOING?
MS. LYDIA! I LEARNED HOW TO CAST THAT SPELL YOU TAUGHT ME THE OTHER DAY!
OOH! WELL DONE, LAURA!
LEO, DID YOU DO *ALL* OF YOUR HOMEWORK?
O-OF COURSE!
HAVE YOU BEEN HELPING OUT YOUR MOTHER, MARU?
YEAH!
HAPPY AS USUAL, NANA?
UH-HUH. NANA'S GOOD.
HEY, MS. LYDIA! YOU SHOULD SHOW US MORE MAGIC!
YEAH! NANA WANTS TO SEE, TOO.
MS. LYDIA, PLEASE SHOW US!
HMM... WHAT EVER SHALL I DO?
It'll cost you.
COME ON! SHOW US ALREADY!
DON'T BE A GREEDY OLD HAG!

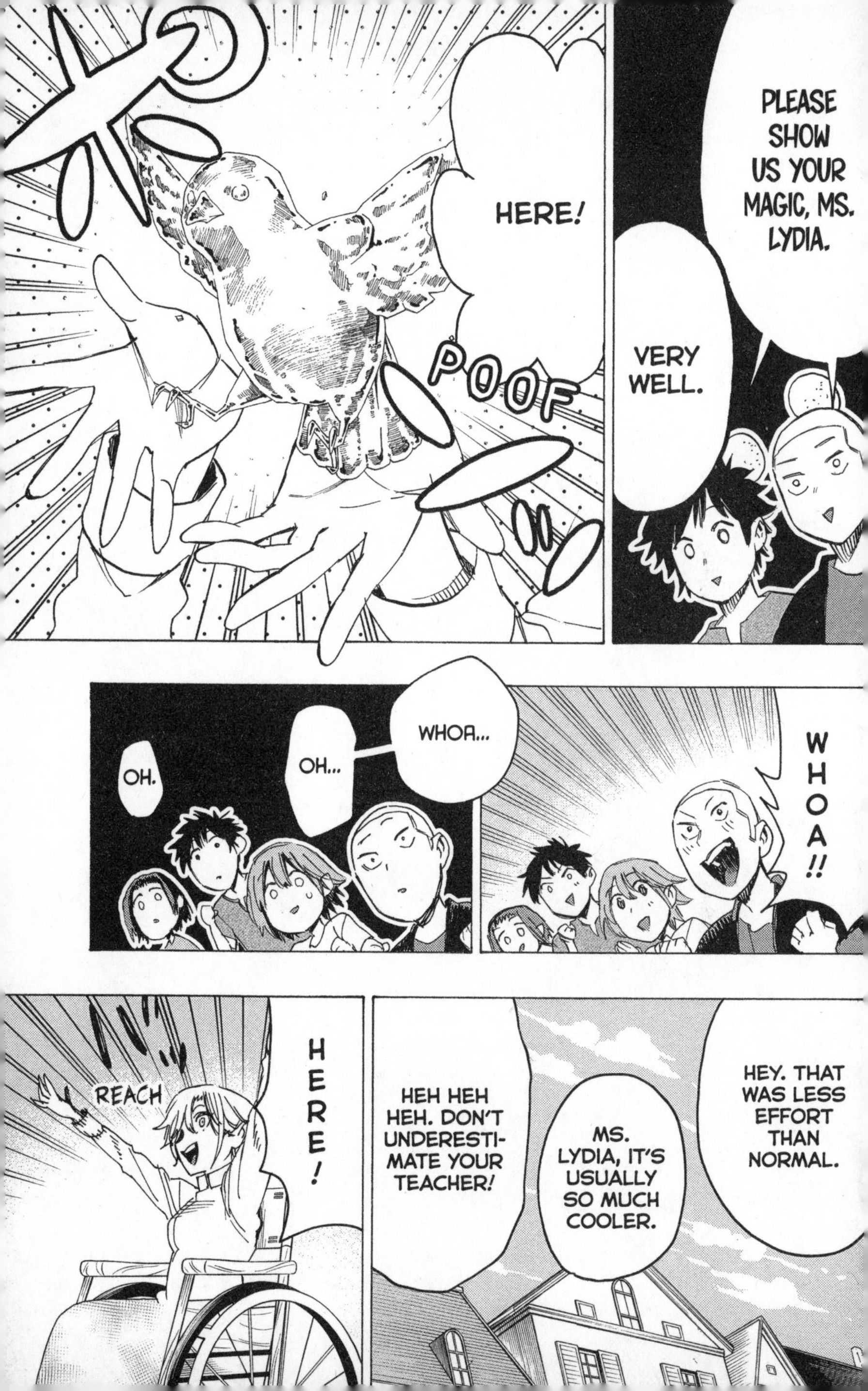
PLEASE SHOW US YOUR MAGIC, MS. LYDIA.
VERY WELL.
HERE!
POOF
WHOA!!
WHOA...
OH...
OH.
HEY. THAT WAS LESS EFFORT THAN NORMAL.
MS. LYDIA, IT'S USUALLY SO MUCH COOLER.
HEH HEH HEH. DON'T UNDERESTI-MATE YOUR TEACHER!
HERE!
REACH

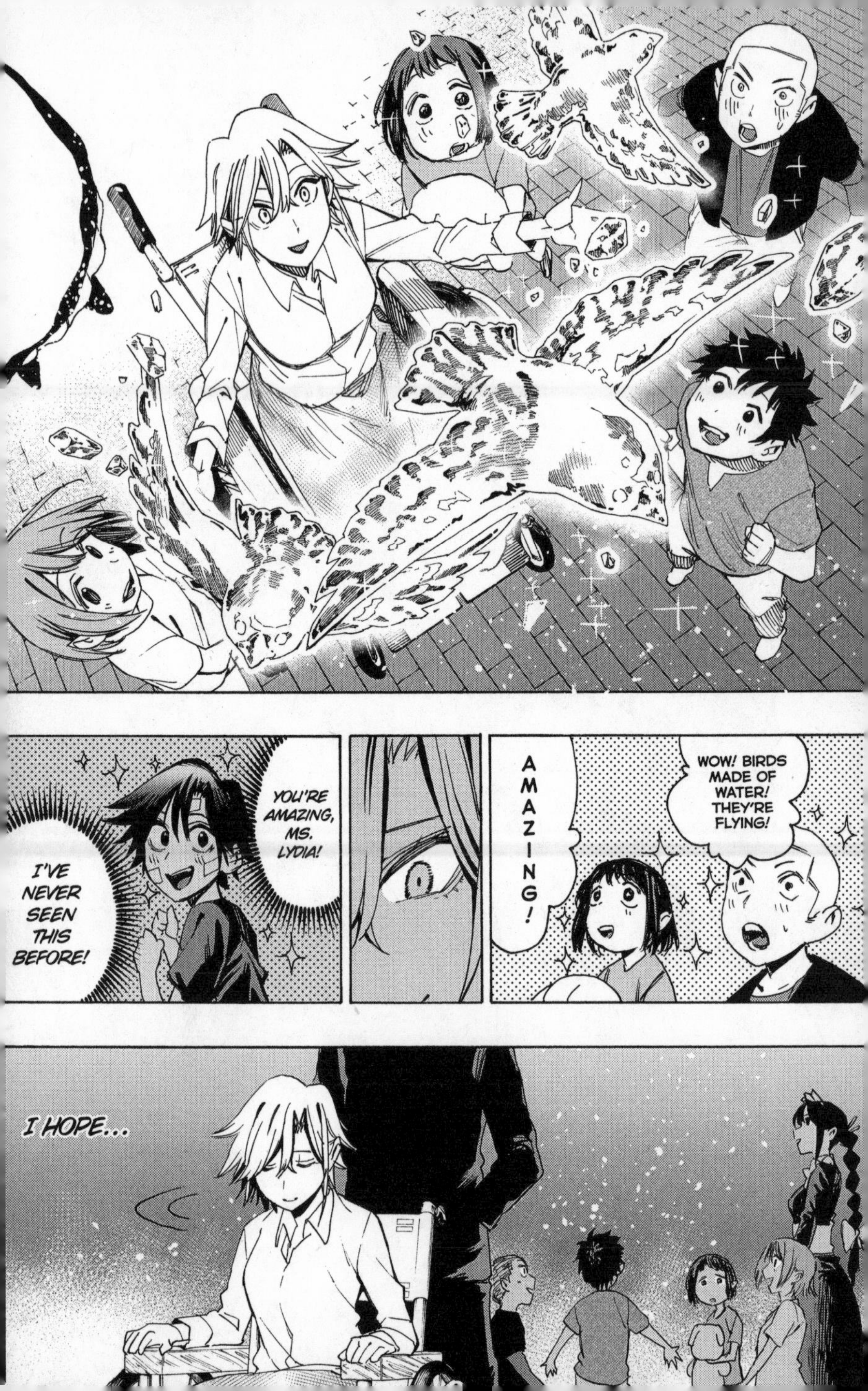
WOW! BIRDS MADE OF WATER! THEY'RE FLYING!
AMAZING!
YOU'RE AMAZING, MS. LYDIA!
I'VE NEVER SEEN THIS BEFORE!
I HOPE...

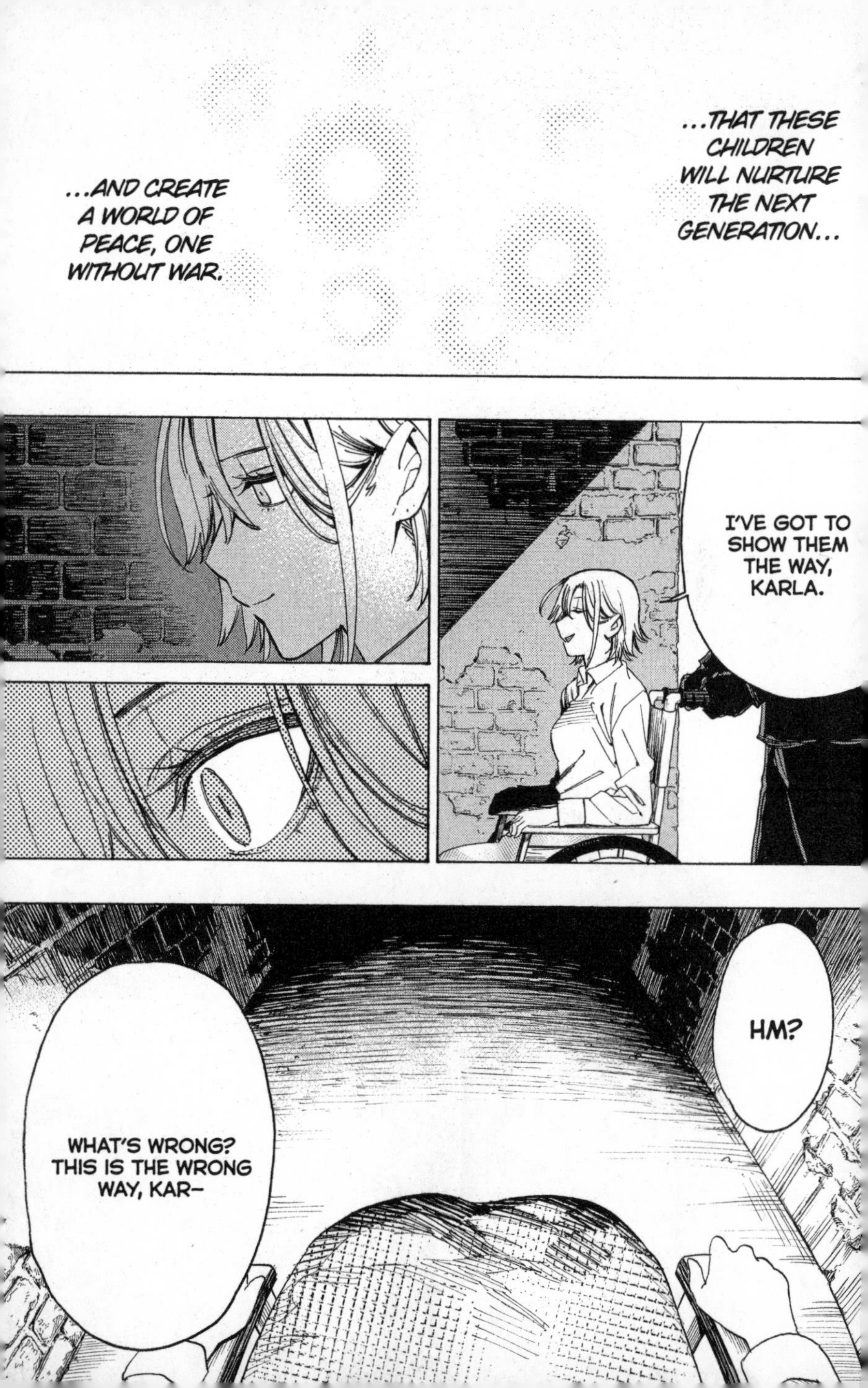
...THAT THESE CHILDREN WILL NURTURE THE NEXT GENERATION...
...AND CREATE A WORLD OF PEACE, ONE WITHOUT WAR.
I'VE GOT TO SHOW THEM THE WAY, KARLA.
HM?
WHAT'S WRONG? THIS IS THE WRONG WAY, KAR–

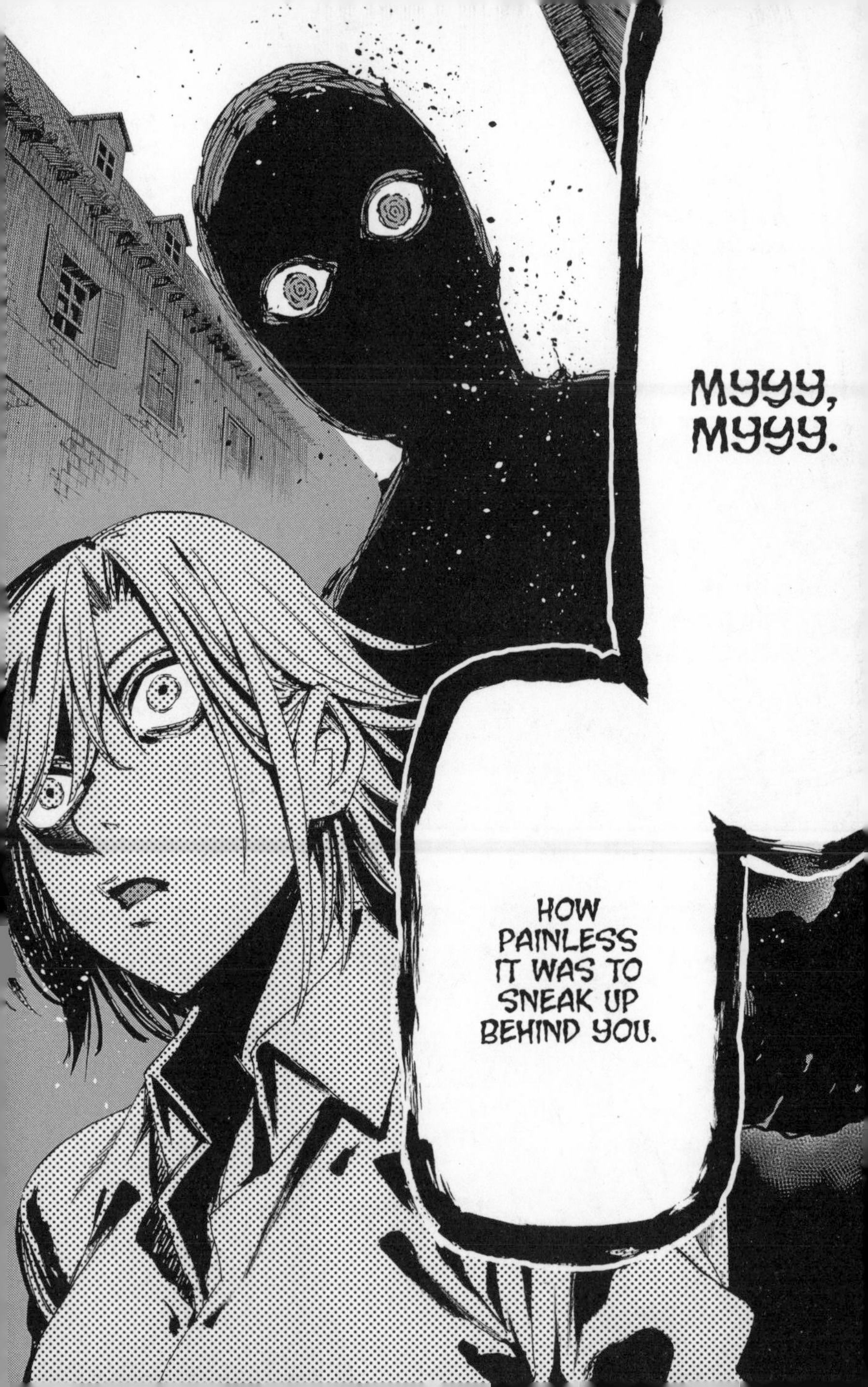
MYYY, MYYY.
HOW PAINLESS IT WAS TO SNEAK UP BEHIND YOU.

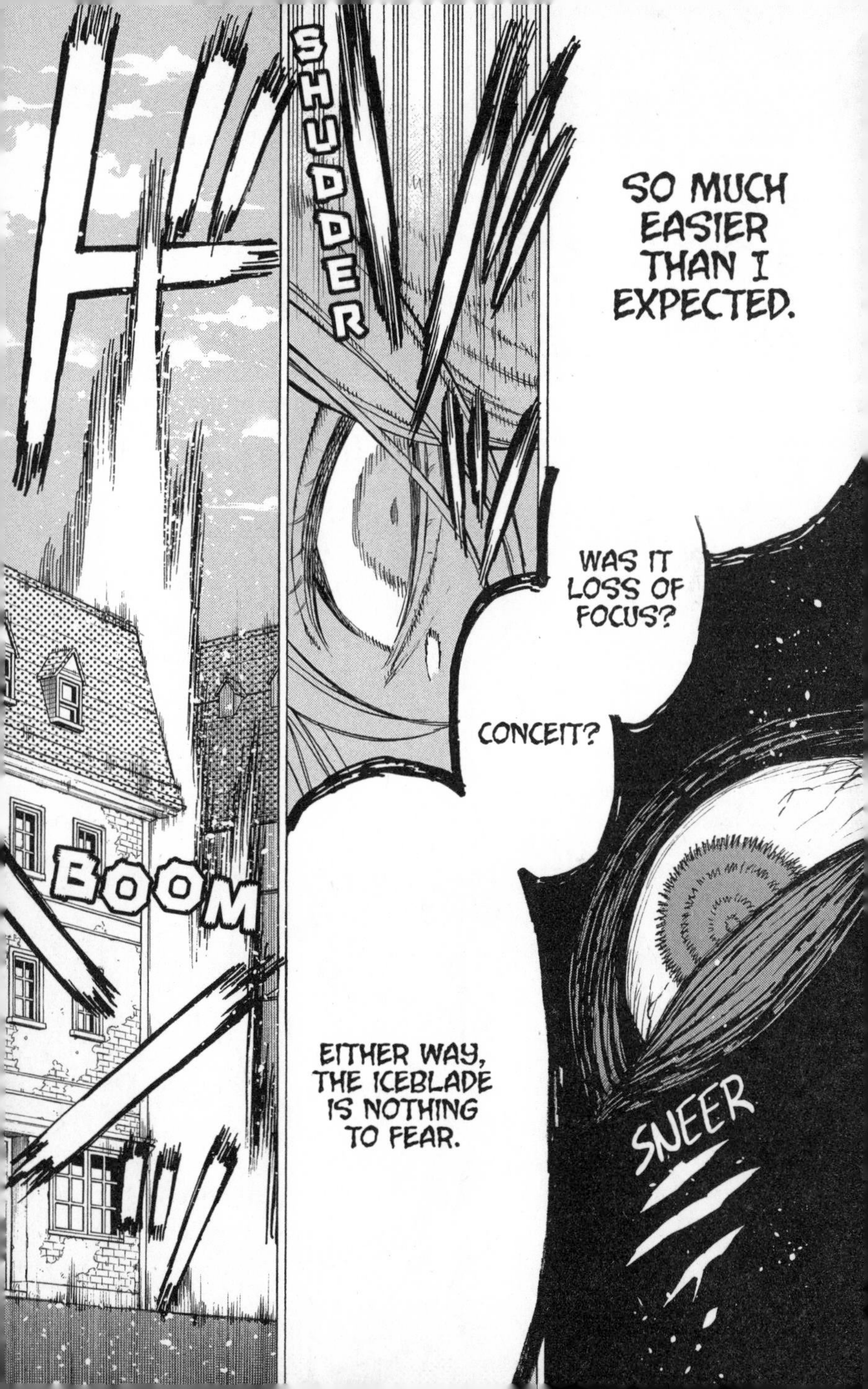
SO MUCH EASIER THAN I EXPECTED.
WAS IT LOSS OF FOCUS?
CONCEIT?
EITHER WAY, THE ICEBLADE IS NOTHING TO FEAR.
SNEER
SHUDDER
BOOM

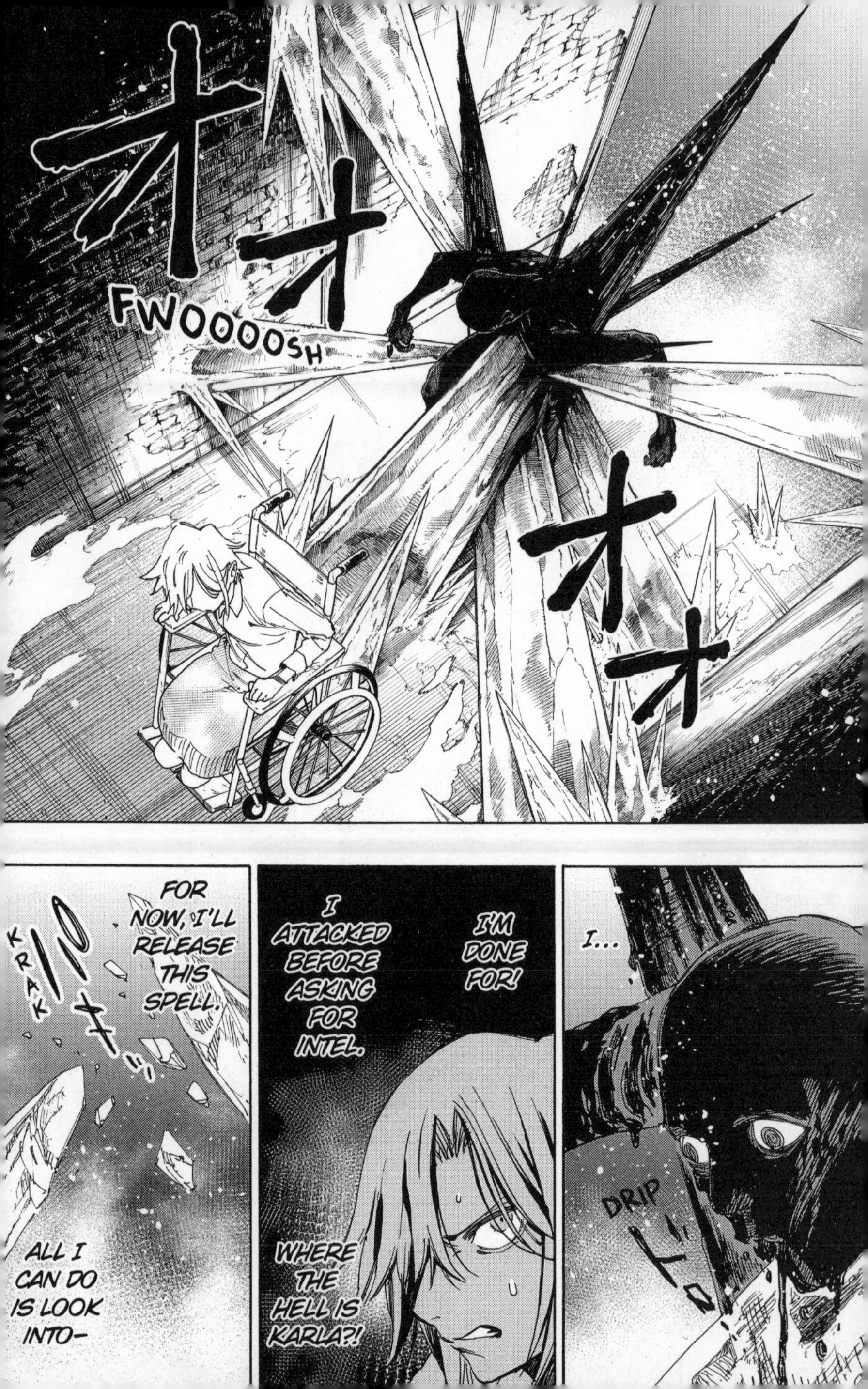
オオ
FWOOOOSH
オオ
I...
DRIP
I'M DONE FOR!
I ATTACKED BEFORE ASKING FOR INTEL.
WHERE THE HELL IS KARLA?!
FOR NOW, I'LL RELEASE THIS SPELL.
KRAK
ALL I CAN DO IS LOOK INTO-

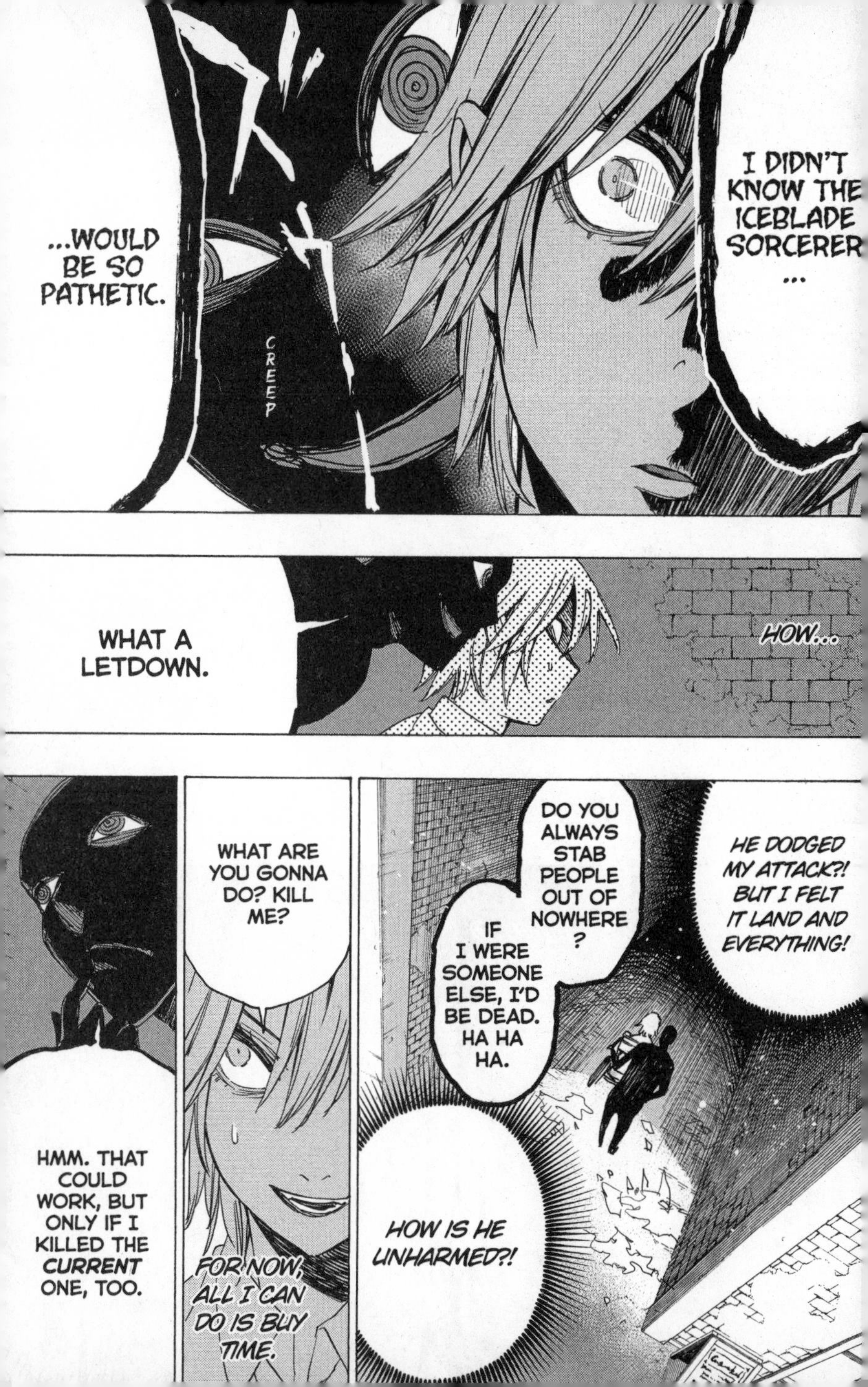
I DIDN'T KNOW THE ICEBLADE SORCERER...
CREEP
...WOULD BE SO PATHETIC.
HOW...
WHAT A LETDOWN.
HE DODGED MY ATTACK?! BUT I FELT IT LAND AND EVERYTHING!
DO YOU ALWAYS STAB PEOPLE OUT OF NOWHERE?
IF I WERE SOMEONE ELSE, I'D BE DEAD. HA HA HA.
HOW IS HE UNHARMED?!
WHAT ARE YOU GONNA DO? KILL ME?
FOR NOW, ALL I CAN DO IS BUY TIME.
HMM. THAT COULD WORK, BUT ONLY IF I KILLED THE CURRENT ONE, TOO.

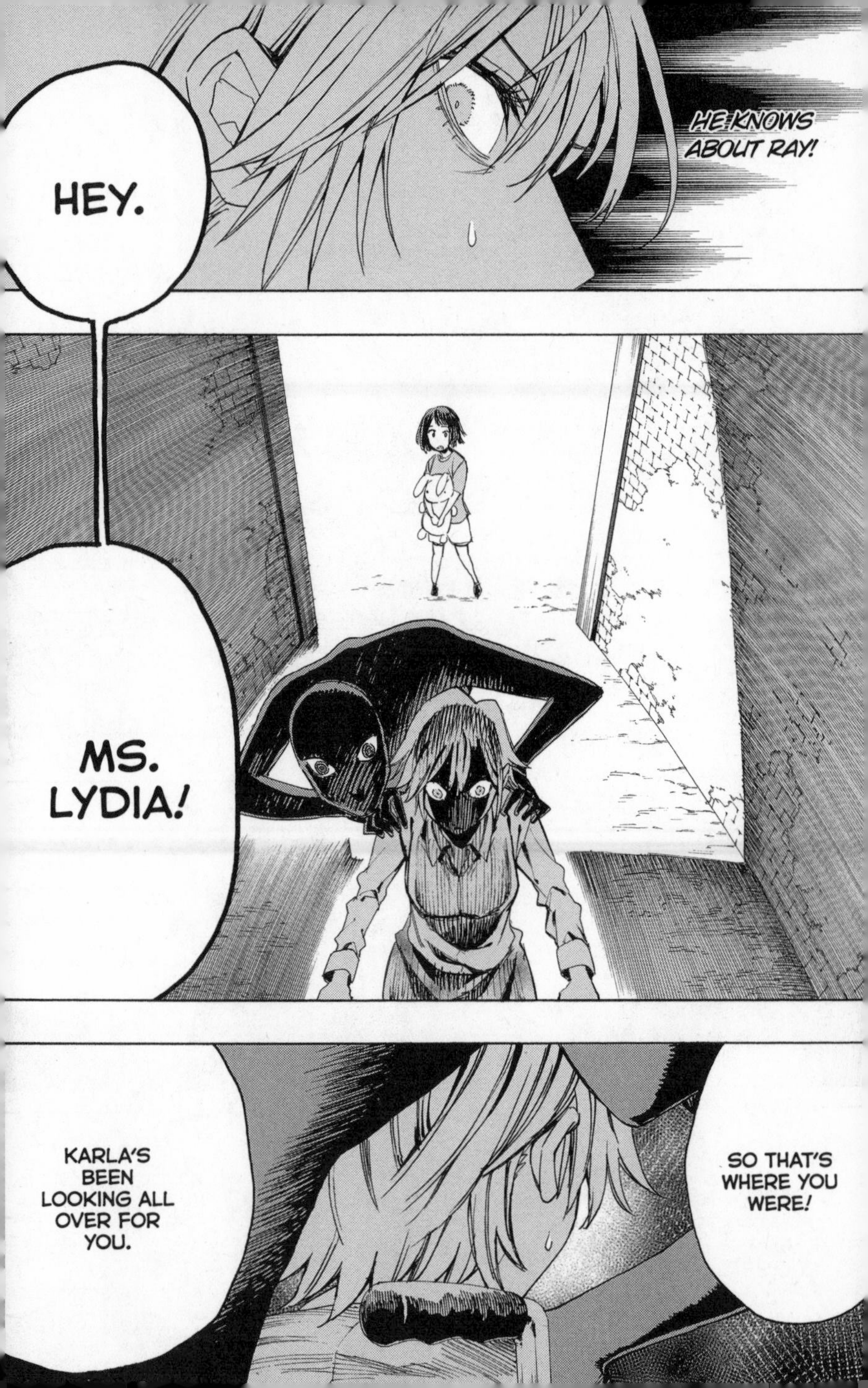
HE KNOWS ABOUT RAY!
HEY.
MS. LYDIA!
SO THAT'S WHERE YOU WERE!
KARLA'S BEEN LOOKING ALL OVER FOR YOU.

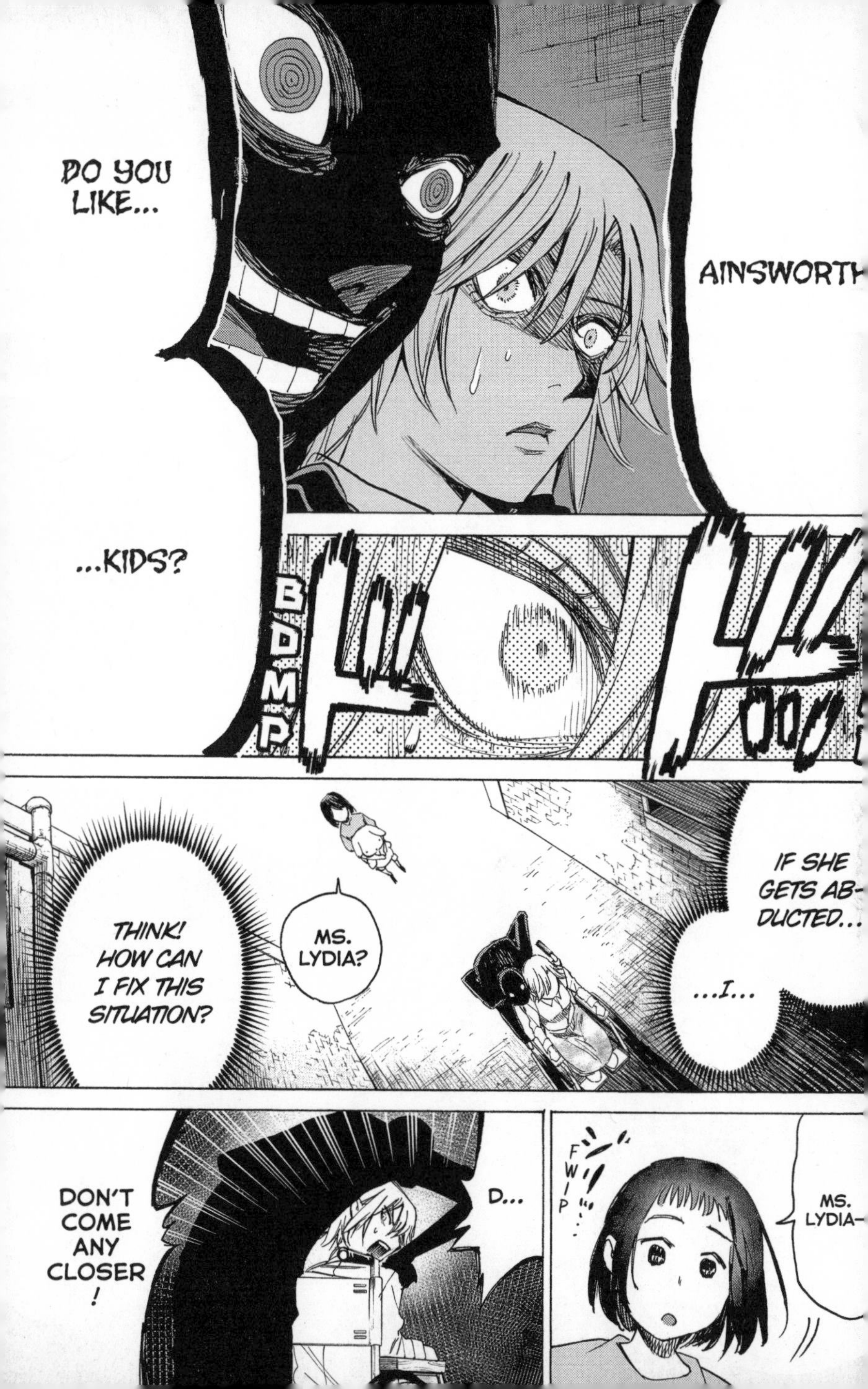
AINSWORTH
DO YOU LIKE...
...KIDS?
BDMP
IF SHE GETS AB-DUCTED...
...I...
MS. LYDIA?
THINK! HOW CAN I FIX THIS SITUATION?
MS. LYDIA–
FWIP
D...
DON'T COME ANY CLOSER!

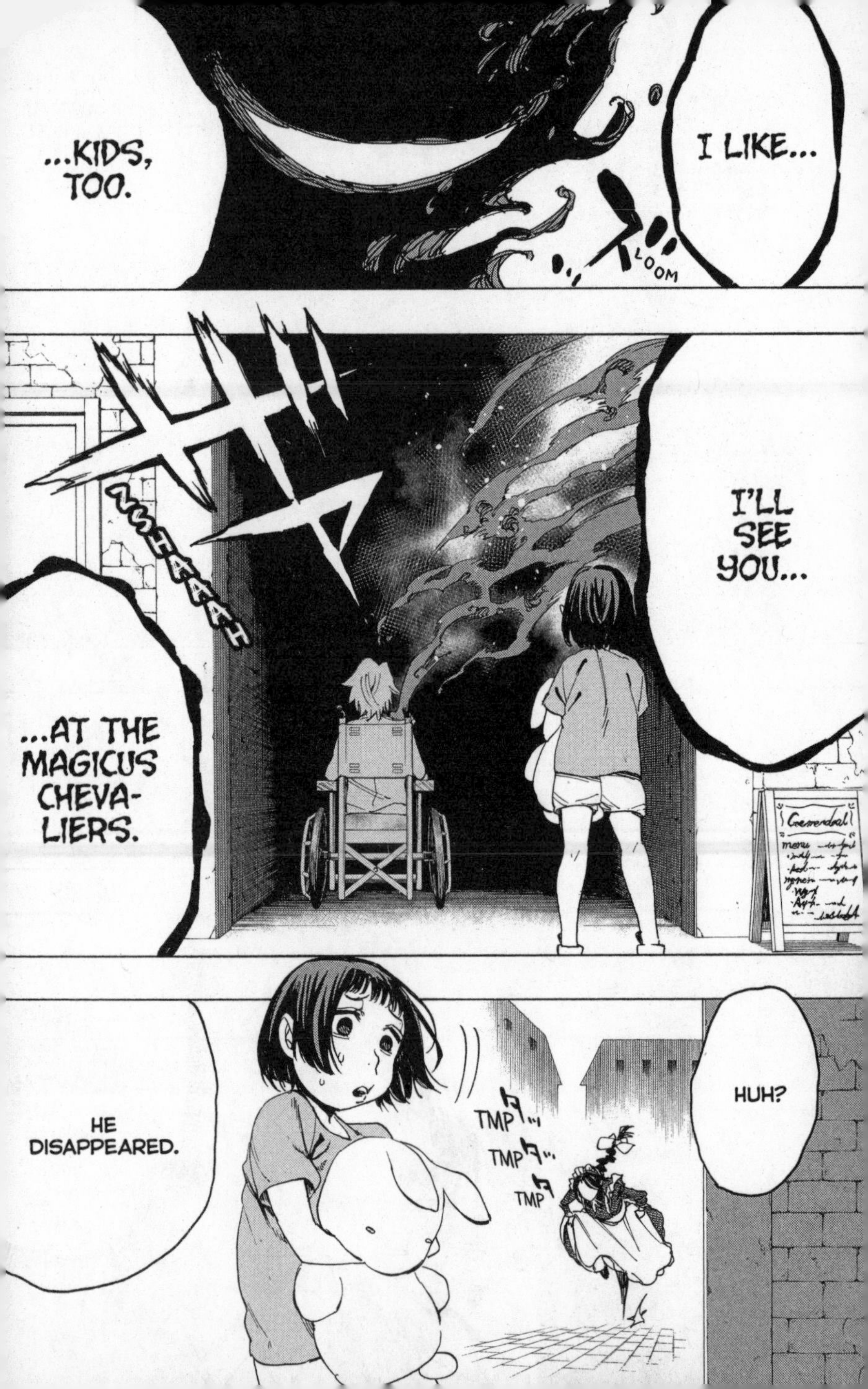
I LIKE...
FLOOM
...KIDS, TOO.
I'LL SEE YOU...
ZSHAAAAH
...AT THE MAGICUS CHEVALIERS.
HUH?
TMP
TMP
TMP
HE DISAPPEARED.

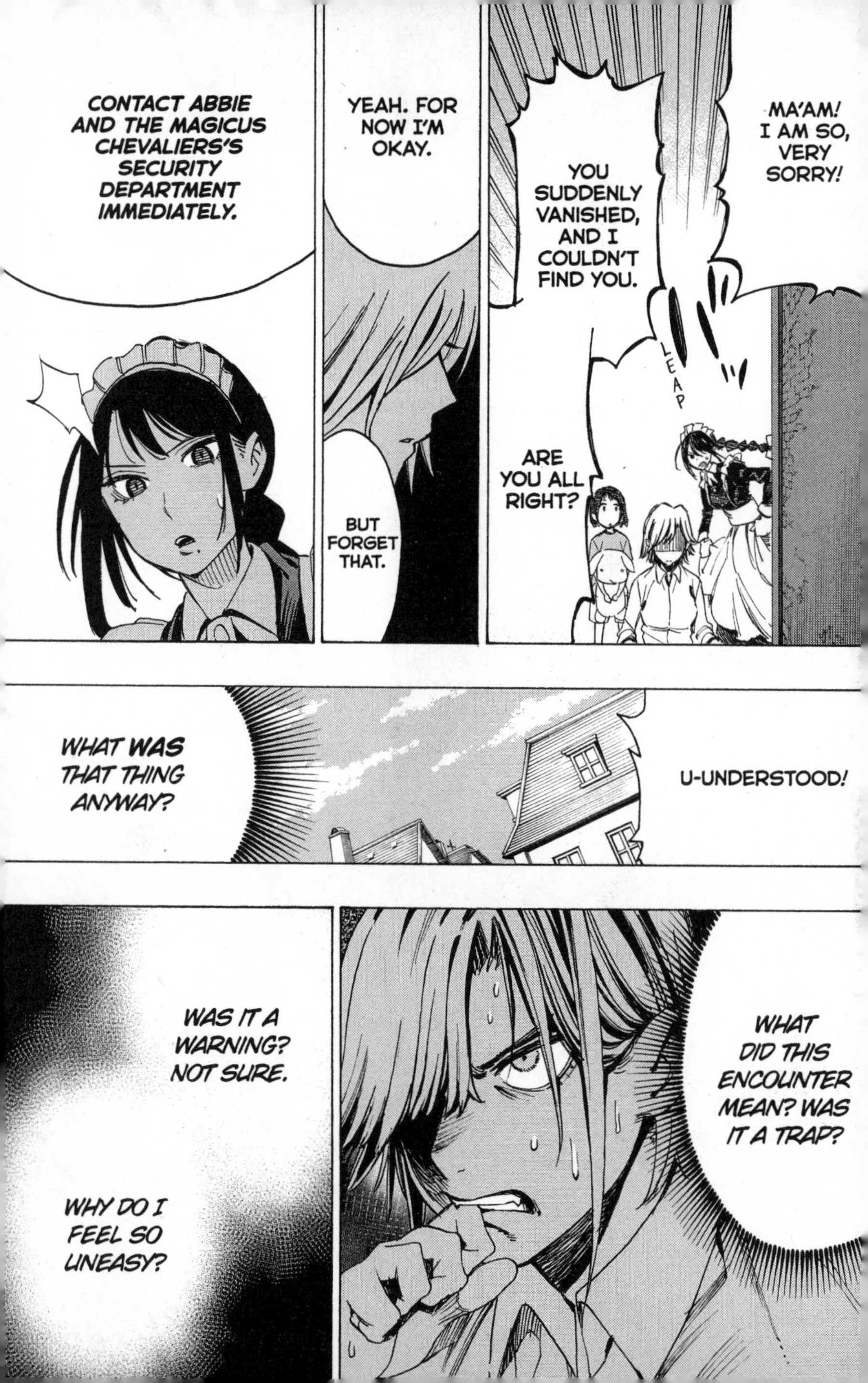
MA'AM! I AM SO, VERY SORRY!
YOU SUDDENLY VANISHED, AND I COULDN'T FIND YOU.
LEAP
ARE YOU ALL RIGHT?
YEAH. FOR NOW I'M OKAY.
BUT FORGET THAT.
CONTACT ABBIE AND THE MAGICUS CHEVALIERS'S SECURITY DEPARTMENT IMMEDIATELY.
U-UNDERSTOOD!
WHAT WAS THAT THING ANYWAY?
WHAT DID THIS ENCOUNTER MEAN? WAS IT A TRAP?
WAS IT A WARNING? NOT SURE.
WHY DO I FEEL SO UNEASY?

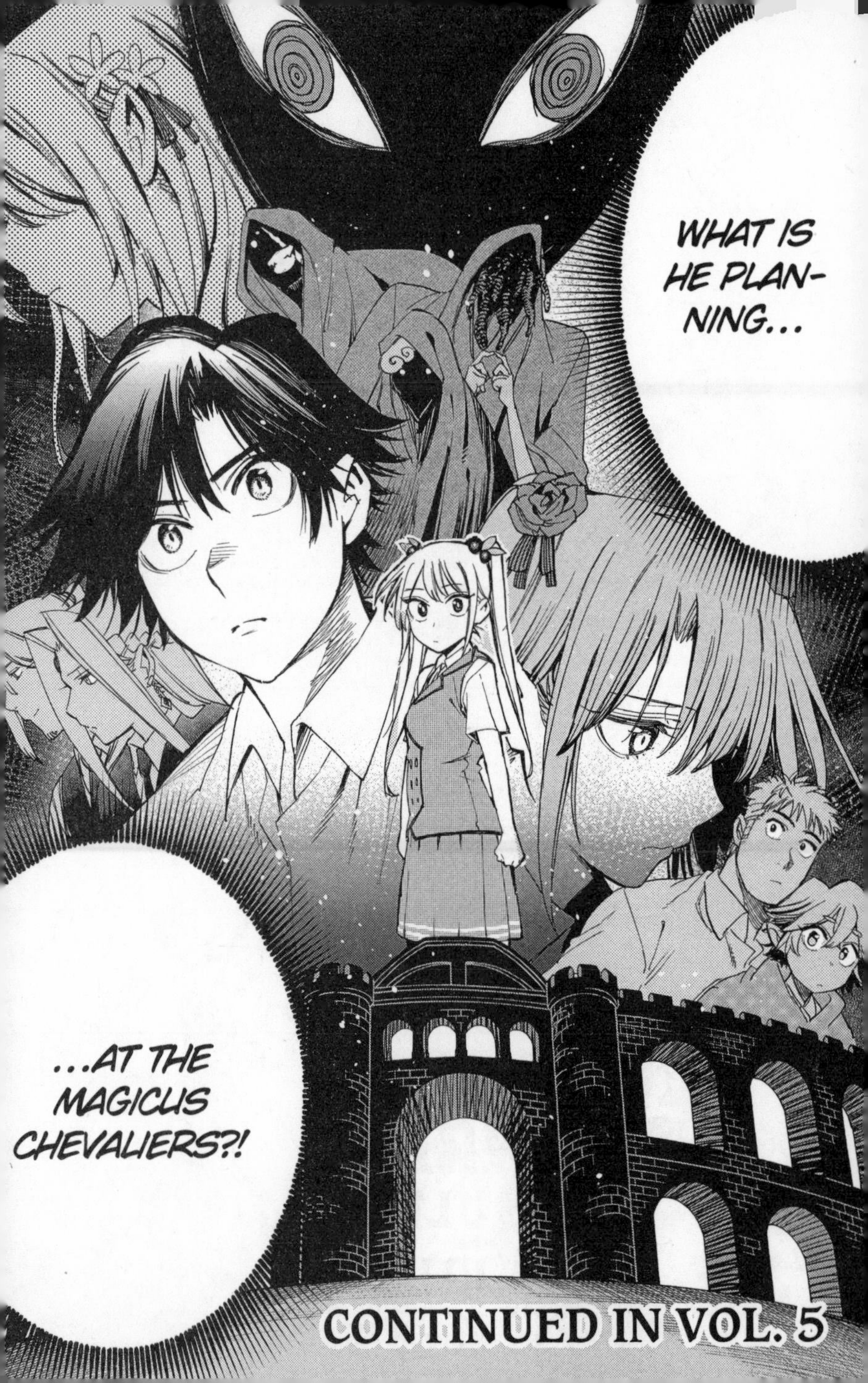
WHAT IS HE PLAN-NING...
...AT THE MAGICUS CHEVALIERS?!
CONTINUED IN VOL. 5

The ICEBLADE SORCERER Shall RULE the WORLD

THE ICEBLADE SORCERER SHALL RULE THE WORLD
Glossary

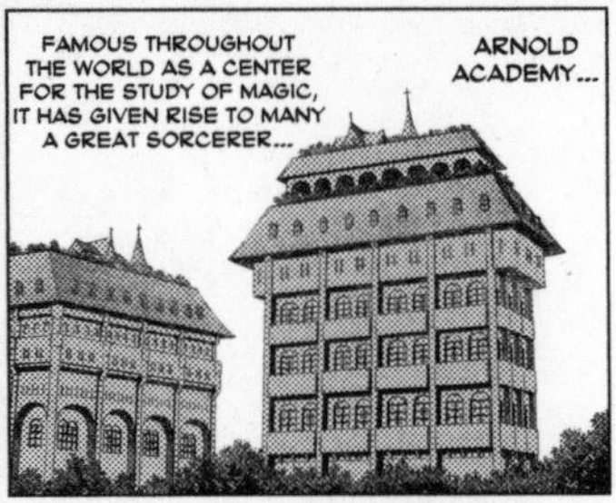
ARNOLD ACADEMY...
FAMOUS THROUGHOUT THE WORLD AS A CENTER FOR THE STUDY OF MAGIC, IT HAS GIVEN RISE TO MANY A GREAT SORCERER...

Arnold Academy of Magic

Widely known as the birthplace of magic, this academy is the leading institution among the three most historic and elite schools in the kingdom. It is also home to the world's greatest sorcerers. The protagonist, Ray White, is the first Ordinary in history to attend the academy.

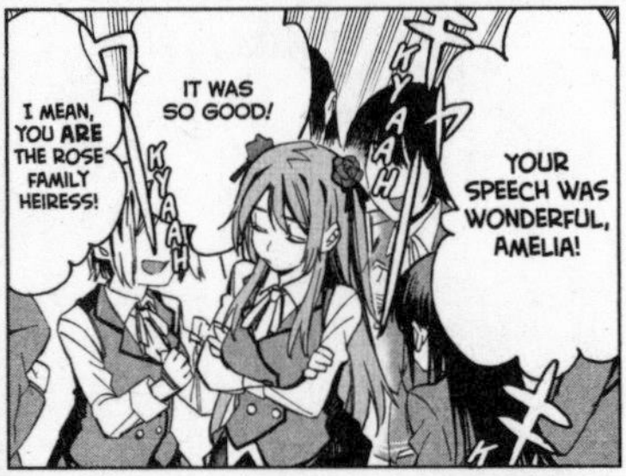
KYAAAH
YOUR SPEECH WAS WONDERFUL, AMELIA!
IT WAS SO GOOD!
I MEAN, YOU ARE THE ROSE FAMILY HEIRESS!
KYAAH

The Three Great Families

A name that refers to the three most prestigious families of sorcerers—the Rose, Bradley, and Algren families. Amelia is a member of the Rose family, which is seen as head and shoulders above the rest.

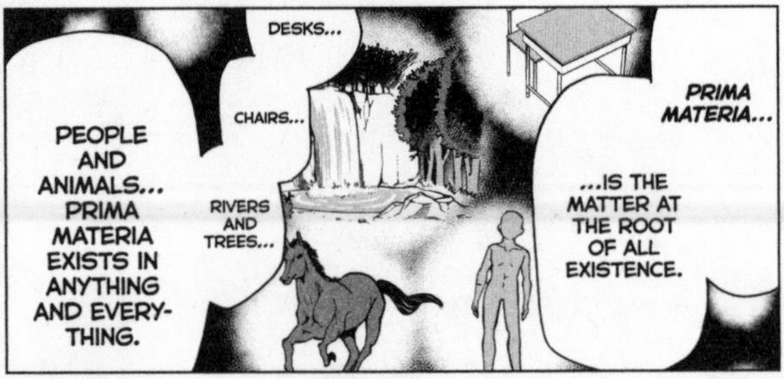
PRIMA MATERIA...
...IS THE MATTER AT THE ROOT OF ALL EXISTENCE.
DESKS...
CHAIRS...
RIVERS AND TREES...
PEOPLE AND ANIMALS... PRIMA MATERIA EXISTS IN ANYTHING AND EVERYTHING.

Prima Materia

Known as the matter at the root of all existence. Prima Materia is converted into a state of information known as "code," which then materializes into a material or phenomena known as "magic."

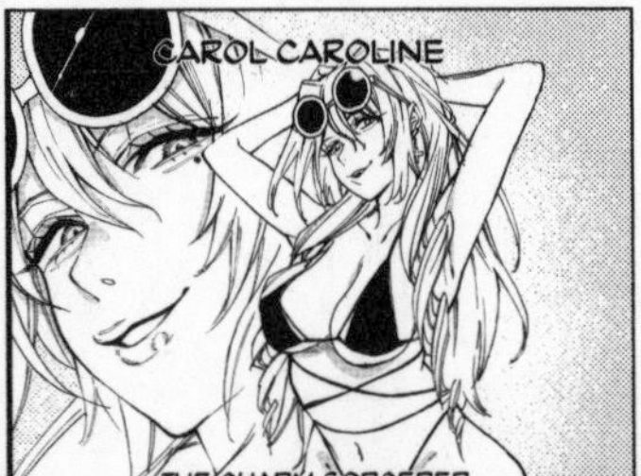
CAROL CAROLINE
THE CHARM SORCERER

The Seven Great Sorcerers

Sorcerers are separated by rank from lowest to highest; there is bronze, silver, gold, platinum, and divine. The seven most powerful sorcerers in the divine rank inspire awe and astonishment with their powers. They are known collectively as the Seven Great Sorcerers. The most famous of the seven sorcerers are Iceblade, Blaze, and Charm. However, only Blaze and Charm have revealed their true identities to the public. Very little is known about the other great sorcerers.

Eugenics

A mysterious organization that values ideals of eugenic supremacy. They are known for conducting inhumane experiments and using human lives as mere tools in the pursuit of magic. They are currently recruiting talented sorcerers and scholars worldwide to broaden their influence. While the nations of the world aim to destroy them, no one knows the size of their organization.

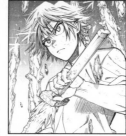

The Iceblade Sorcerer

The best close-combat fighter of the Seven Great Sorcerers. The current Iceblade Sorcerer—Ray White—possesses three main abilities: Deceleration, Lock, and Restoration. Deceleration lowers speed, Lock freezes objects in place, and Restoration reverts code formation and phenomena to its original state.

Engram

Also known as "magic memory." These neurons were discovered in the brain and found to be responsible for remembering magic. Engrams can be used to transplant magic into another sorcerer's mind.

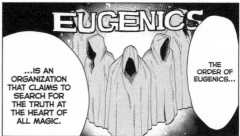

EUGENICS
THE ORDER OF EUGENICS...
...IS AN ORGANIZATION THAT CLAIMS TO SEARCH FOR THE TRUTH AT THE HEART OF ALL MAGIC.

Overheat

Magical matter exists in every sorcerer's brain; it is responsible for executing code theory in the frontal cortex. When a sorcerer feels extreme emotions or overuses their magic, their magical matter becomes uncontrollable—a state that is known as "Overheat." In this state, a sorcerer cannot cast normal magic, and casting in Overheat results in major side effects on the sorcerer. Currently, there is no cure for Overheat.

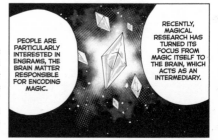

RECENTLY, MAGICAL RESEARCH HAS TURNED ITS FOCUS FROM MAGIC ITSELF TO THE BRAIN, WHICH ACTS AS AN INTERMEDIARY.
PEOPLE ARE PARTICULARLY INTERESTED IN ENGRAMS, THE BRAIN MATTER RESPONSIBLE FOR ENCODING MAGIC.

THERE ARE THREE MAJOR ACADEMIES OF MAGIC: ARNOLD, DIOME, AND MERCROSS.
DIOME
ARNOLD
THIS TOURNAMENT WILL DETERMINE WHICH ONE OF THEM HOUSES THE WORLD'S STRONGEST SORCERER.
MERCROSS

Magicus Chevaliers

A tournament that takes place once a year. It determines who the strongest sorcerer is among the three great academies—Arnold, Diome, and Mercross. First-year students participate in the newcomer duels, whereas second-years and older students participate in the main tournament.

FWOOOOO

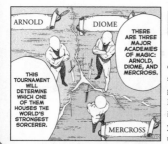

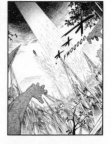

The ICEBLADE SORCERER Shall RULE the WORLD

Adventuring with Clarice

by Nana Mikoshiba

I had promised to meet Clarice in front of the school gates after class. We had planned on exploring a small forest in the kingdom.

"Ray, you're late!" she exclaimed.

"Sorry. Prep took me longer than expected," I replied.

"You prepared for this? For real?"

"Since we're going to the forest, I thought I'd prepare."

Her name was Clarice Cleveland. She was an upper noble and my most recent friend. She had a sharp tongue and wasn't very straightforward, but I think that was her way of showing affection. After all, she once told me that she didn't know how to get close to her peers.

Clarice and I had both volunteered to work on the Steering Committee for the Magicus Chevaliers, so naturally we ended up spending many hours together. While we were working, I asked her to teach me about insects, and she happily obliged.

We had planned to walk to a nearby forest that she used to frequent when she was young. It was close enough that we'd be able to walk there and back before curfew.

When we finally met up at the school gates, it felt like perfect timing.

"You don't need to bring such a big backpack," she criticized.

"I don't?" I asked.

"I doubt it. It's not like we're going to catch any bugs."

"Oh, okay. I thought I needed to pack more. If that's the case, no problem."

I walked back to my dorm and dropped off my backpack, returning with as little equipment as possible. When I came back, I showed Clarice the small satchel that hung from my waist. It had contained many small tools that I had thought might come in handy.

"You're bringing that instead?" she asked.

"Yeah," I answered.

"Whatever. Anyway, that will do. You really are a weirdo, you know that?"

"I am?"

"Uh-huh. No one's ever called you weird?"

I put my hand to my chin and mulled it over.

Come to think of it, people call me weird all the time.

"People call me weird all the time," I replied.

"Of course they do. But that's just who you are... Not that I mind."

Clarice mumbled the last part of her sentence, so I couldn't make out what she'd said.

"Huh? What did you say?"

"Nothing!" she yelped. "Anyway, let's get going!"

Clarice started running, and I quickly followed behind. I suddenly felt like I was being watched, but I chose to ignore it...for now.

Before I knew it, we had reached the small forest that was close to her childhood home.

"All right. This is it," she announced, standing proudly while crossing her arms.

"Nice," I replied. "Isn't this where you used to hang out when you were young?"

"Yeah! But my family always told me not to play in the forest," she said, her pigtails drooping.

Recently I'd noticed that Clarice's pigtails often reflected her mood. They made it abundantly clear how she was feeling, but she didn't seem to notice.

"Oh, your family. I remember you saying they didn't approve."

"Uh-huh. Since I'm a girl from a noble family, they wanted me to do something more ladylike, like playing with dolls. My father was the only one who understood me."

"Oh, really?"

"I was his pride and joy after all. Ah ha ha."

She lightly scratched her cheek, perhaps because she was feeling embarrassed. Her pigtails seemed to have perked up.

"My mother and my family were pretty strict. My father was the only one who let me play in the forest. But I was always alone, so... um! I've never brought a friend here before!"

It was clear that this place was very special to Clarice. I knew what I should say in response.

"I see. Thank you for taking me to such a special place, Clarice."

"Wh-Whatever! Hmph!" she pouted.

She swiftly turned the other way, but there was a hint of happiness in her face.

"Could you show me around the forest?" I asked.

"Of course! Leave it to me!" chirped Clarice.

I was following behind Clarice as she happily skipped through the forest, when a shadowy figure suddenly jumped out in front of us.

"Eeek!"

"Ngh!"

I leaped in front of Clarice to protect her from the shadow. As swift as it was, I managed to grab it with ease.

"Is this… a beetle?" I asked.

A fairly large beetle sat in my hand. That was when Clarice, who stood behind me, curiously poked her head out to see it. The beetle looked jittery as it clung to my shirt sleeve.

"Oh! Is that you Zeke?" she asked excitedly.

The beetle responded with a "Poom!"

In the blink of an eye, the beetle had run out of my hand and toward Clarice. Its antennae shook excitedly, as if waving hello.

"Do you two know each other?" I asked.

"Yeah! We always used to hang out! Seriously, I can't believe you've gotten so big!"

"Pooom!" Zeke beamed, making his way to the top of her head.

"Heh heh. This was our hang-out spot when we were young."

"Wow. I guess this is what they call a fateful reunion."

"Mhm! I haven't been back here since middle school. Would you mind if Zeke joined us?"

"Yeah, no problem."

"Thanks! Let's get back to our adventure!"

"Poom!"

With our new team assembled, we headed deeper into the forest.

The campus was abuzz with excitement as students trained for the preliminaries in the Magicus Chevaliers. With the tournament starting, many students stayed after school for individual training. And this afternoon was no different.

One bystander quietly watched as Ray and Clarice met at the front gates. It was none other than…Amelia.

"That's Ray, but who is that with him?" she whispered.

Coincidentally, Amelia had noticed them when she was passing the gates.

"I think that's Clarice Cleveland," she mumbled, trying to figure out who she was.

Amelia was the eldest daughter of one of the Three Great Families. As such, she attended many parties that were hosted by nobles.

Amelia had met the higher noble Clarice at these parties, but the two of them had only exchanged pleasantries—nothing more. This was mainly because Clarice would often stand in a corner alone. This had left an impression on Amelia, which was why she'd remembered her name.

"What's wrong, Amelia? Why'd you stop walking?" asked a familiar voice.

"Shh! Elisa! Over here!" Amelia said, waving Elisa over.

"Huh? Okay," Elisa replied.

They were now standing covertly behind a pillar.

"Ray is talking to a girl."

"Really?" Elisa said, quickly glancing at Ray and Clarice. "Oh, yeah, she's a Cleveland. A higher noble who's known for her pigtails."

Unlike Amelia, Elisa had never met Clarice. She simply had a good memory and remembered many faces and names. Elisa knew Clarice, because she was a famous higher noble. Plus, her pigtails stood out…in a good way, of course.

"Yeah, exactly. For some reason, she's talking to Ray," Amelia said.

"I think they're on the Steering Committee together," answered Elisa.

"The Steering Committee?"

"Uh-huh. For the Magicus Chevaliers."

"I see… That makes sense."

As Amelia listened to her friend, she continued to hide as she glared at the duo.

"Amelia, why are you watching them in secret?"

"What?! Don't you want to see what they're doing?!"

"Come to think of it, Ray usually only talks to his friends. Oh, right. I forgot that he talks to girls in other classes."

"Wait. He does?" Amelia said, taken aback.

"But that's because Ray's so nice," Elisa continued. "When he sees someone in trouble, he helps them. If a student drops their books, he's the first one to pick them up. I hear that he's especially popular with the older girls in the Gardening Club."

"Since when did that happen…"

Amelia had been so busy preparing for the preliminaries that she didn't notice it happening.

"Hey, it looks like they're leaving."

Before they knew it, Ray had come jogging back to Clarice. Together, they had passed through the school gates.

"Elisa, let's go!"

"Whaaat?! Amelia!!"

After signing out of school, the two girls started trailing Ray and Clarice.

Clarice was teaching me all sorts of facts about bugs.

"You can find a lot of pill bugs right here!" Clarice announced.

"Ooh! You're right!" I said.

We had just turned over a big rock. She was telling me about the pill bugs that hid underneath.

"Heh heh! You could call this my garden!"

"Wow. You know so much, Clarice."

"You can praise me more, you know," she said.

Her pigtails were taut—they were in a great mood. Just by looking at her stunning, straight hair, it was easy to see that she was elated.

But I wasn't just pulling her leg. I was impressed—she knew everything there was to know about bugs. I could tell that she loved them by the way she smiled and by how much she mentioned them.

"Heh heh. Now, let's move on to talk about beetles!" she said.

Zeke replied with a "Poom!" He sat on her head as he raised his antennae.

"You see, Zeke is incredible!"

Before I knew it, Zeke had climbed down from her head to the palm of her hand.

Zeke replied with a "Pui!" He raised his horns high, his wings buzzing with joy. This expression on his face brimmed with confidence.

"In this forest, Zeke is the king of the beetles!"

"He's a king?"

"That's right. He's the ruler of this forest—the thread that connects all the beetles. Zeke is incredibly strong."

"I see. I didn't know that type of ecosystem exists."

"He has tons of things to show us, so let's follow his lead."

"Sure thing."

With that, Clarice and I followed Zeke deeper into the forest.

Summer was fast approaching and daylight eventually started lasting longer.

However, since we had gone to the forest after school, it was already evening. I followed Zeke's lead, reassuring myself that it would be all right, as long as we made curfew.

But suddenly, we were faced with a large group of beetles.

Zeke lead us toward the group of twenty beetles with a triumphant "Poom!" All of them seemed to know each other quite well.

"Uh-huh. It looks like he wants to introduce us to his friends," Clarice said.

"I see," I replied.

Zeke headed toward the group and started talking to them. A few of them seemed hostile at first, but they quickly calmed down.

When things settled, one beetle came before us and started waving his antennae. It seemed that he was coming to greet us.

After that, Clarice, Zeke, and I continued to walk through the forest.

"Heh heh! His friends are so big!" she exclaimed.

"Yeah," I said.

"They used to be so small. Time really does fly."

"Poom!" replied Zeke.

She was a lot happier than usual; I would have even said she was beaming.

I guess nothing beats talking about your favorite things.

Clarice looked so happy, which made me happy, too.

"All right! On to the next... gwahhhh!"

It looked like she had tripped. She was falling straight to the ground. It would have been a cinch for me to catch myself, but that was not the case for Clarice.

"Clarice!" I shouted.

I then caught her in my arms.

"Wahhh!"

"Are you hurt?"

"I'm okay... because you were there to help me. So... thank you."

"Don't mention it. I'm just glad you're okay."

That was when I noticed that I was still holding Clarice. I helped her to her feet, then quickly let go.

"Sorry. I shouldn't have held you like that, even if you were falling."

"Whatever... it's not like I minded."

She muttered the last part so quietly that I couldn't hear what she'd said.

"Sorry, I didn't catch that. What did you say?"

"Nothing! Thanks for helping me!"

Her face turned beet red, and she started running away for some reason.

"Poom poom!"

Zeke chased after her and I followed suit.

"Whew. Let's take a break," Clarice said.

"Okay. Take this," I replied, taking a canteen out of my bag.

I lightly put my lips against it, drank from it, and then handed it to Clarice.

"Huh?"

"You don't need it?"

"No, it's just… I am thirsty. But it's almost like we're…"

She was staring so intently at the flask that I figured I must have done something wrong.

She always said that I was weird, so I was trying to be normal. I guess that didn't work.

"Here goes!" Clarice said.

With much determination, she started gulping from the flask. In fact, she drank every last sip.

"Aaaah. Y-Yes. Thanks."

"No need to thank me. Sorry… I only brought one. I guess that just one wasn't enough."

"Y-You realize that now?!" Clarice exclaimed, looking flustered.

Her pigtails were pointing straight-up. They seemed to be caught off guard.

"This should've been enough for two people. It looks like we needed more."

Clarice turned away once again. Her face was redder than ever.

"That's right! You should plan better next time!"

"Will do."

"Hmph!"

There was something cheerful about her beautiful, golden hair as the ends swayed.

"Okay. Let's head back."

"Yeah. Thanks for taking me here today. It was a really good experience. And thank you, too, Zeke."

"Poom!"

"I'll come back on summer break, Zeke. See you then!"

"Poom, poom!"

We bid farewell to Zeke at the entrance to the forest. He wouldn't leave Clarice's side—he seemed to adore her.

"I'm so glad I met you Clarice."

"Heh heh! Yeah, right!"

She went to turn away, but ended up tripping and almost falling to the ground.

"Got you. Are you all right?"

"Um… I'm sorry. This seems to keep happening."

She was once again in my arms. Our faces were so close they were practically touching. She was acting unusually meek, which was a breath of fresh air.

Just then I heard Amelia and Elisa calling out from behind me.

"Ray… Ray?"

I knew they'd been following us, but I chose to ignore them.

I thought they had a particular reason for following us, but it turned out that they were just curious. However, I didn't think they'd come out at a time like this.

"Oh! Um…"

Clarice immediately backed away and straightened herself up in an attempt to appear modest.

"Ray, what were you two doing out there?" Amelia asked.

"I should be asking you the same thing, Amelia."

"But I asked you first."

"Um, um…"

There was a sense of tension rising, and Amelia seemed kind of angry. Clarice was taking cover behind me.

"Ray!" Clarice said. "I'm gonna head home!"

She then started running into the distance.

"Clarice!" I called out.

As I stood there dumbfounded, Amelia and Elisa grabbed onto my shoulders.

"Ray…you've got a lot of explaining to do," Amelia said.

"Y-Yeah! I wanna know, too," Elisa chimed in.

"F-Fine…"

With that, I explained what had happened that day.

For some reason, Amelia put her hand to her chest. She seemed relieved. Elisa said, "Oh, I see," and giggled.

I hoped to one day have the opportunity to introduce the two of them to Clarice.

Today reminded me of something important: There is nothing more precious than spending time with my friends.

Young characters and steampunk setting, like *Howl's Moving Castle* and *Battle Angel Alita*

Beyond the Clouds © 2018 Nicke / Ki-oon

A boy with a talent for machines and a mysterious girl whose wings he's fixed will take you beyond the clouds! In the tradition of the high-flying, resonant adventure stories of Studio Ghibli comes a gorgeous tale about the longing of young hearts for adventure and friendship!

The adorable new odd-couple cat comedy manga from the creator of the beloved *Chi's Sweet Home*, in full color!

Praise for *Chi's Sweet Home*

"Nearly impossible to turn away... a true all-ages title that anyone, young or old, cat lover or not, will enjoy. The stories will bring a smile to your face and warm your heart."

—School Library Journal

Sue & Tai-chan
Konami Kanata

Sue is an aging housecat who's looking forward to living out her life in peace... but her plans change when the mischievous black tomcat Tai-chan enters the picture! Hey! Sue never signed up to be a catsitter! *Sue & Tai-chan* is the latest from the reigning meow-narch of cute kitty comics, Konami Kanata.

The boys are back, in 400-page hardcovers that are as pretty and badass as they are!

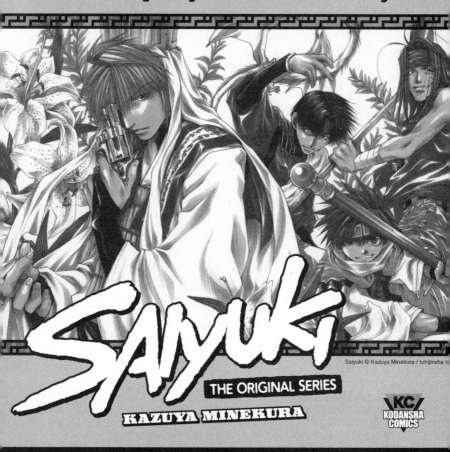

Saiyuki © Kazuya Minakura / Ichijinsha I

SAIYUKI

THE ORIGINAL SERIES

KAZUYA MINEKURA

KC/ KODANSHA COMICS

"AN EDGY COMIC LOOK AT AN ANCIENT CHINESE TALE." —YALSA

Genjo Sanzo is a Buddhist priest in the city of Togenkyo, which is being ravaged by yokai spirits that have fallen out of balance with the natural order. His superiors send him on a journey far to the west to discover why this is happening and how to stop it. His companions are three yokai with human souls. But this is no day trip — the four will encounter many discoveries and horrors on the way.

FEATURES NEW TRANSLATION, COLOR PAGES, AND BEAUTIFUL WRAPAROUND COVER ART!

A Kodansha Trade Paperback Original

The Iceblade Sorcerer Shall Rule the World 4 copyright © 2021 Norihito Sasaki/
Nana Mikoshiba/Riko Korie
English translation copyright © 2023 Norihito Sasaki/Nana Mikoshiba/Riko Korie

Published in the United States by
Kodansha USA Publishing, LLC, New York.

Publication rights for this English edition arranged through
Kodansha Ltd., Tokyo.

First published in Japan in 2021 by Kodansha Ltd., Tokyo
as *Hyouken no majutsushi ga sekai wo suberu*, volume 4.

ISBN 978-1-64651-627-8

Printed in the United States of America.

9 8 7 6 5 4 3 2 1

Translation: Kristi Fernandez
Lettering: AndWorld Design
Editing: Tomoko Nagano
Kodansha USA Publishing edition cover design by Matt Akuginow

Publisher: Kiichiro Sugawara

Director of Publishing Services: Ben Applegate
Director of Publishing Operations: Dave Barrett
Associate Director of Publishing Operations: Stephen Pakula
Publishing Services Managing Editors: Alanna Ruse, Madison Salters,
with Grace Chen
Production Manager: Jocelyn O'Dowd

KODANSHA.US

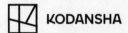 KODANSHA